The Letters of
GIACOMO LEOPARDI
1817–1837

ITALIAN PERSPECTIVES

SERIES EDITORS

Z. G. Barański & A. L. Lepschy

In the light of growing academic interest in Italy and the re-organization of many university courses in Italian along interdisciplinary lines, this book series aims to bring together different scholarly perspectives on Italy and its culture.

Italian Perspectives publishes books and collections of essays on any aspect and period of Italian literature, language, history, culture, politics, art, and media, as well as studies which take an interdisciplinary approach and are methodologically innovative. The series welcomes books written in English and in Italian.

The Letters of
GIACOMO LEOPARDI
1817–1837

Selected and translated by

Prue Shaw

Routledge
Taylor & Francis Group
LONDON AND NEW YORK
1998

For Claerwen and Lucinda

ITALIAN PERSPECTIVES 1

First published in 1998 by Northern Universities Press

Published 2017 by Routledge
2 Park Square, Milton Park, Abingdon, Oxon OX14 4RN
711 Third Avenue, New York, NY 10017, USA

Routledge is an imprint of the Taylor & Francis Group, an informa business

ISBN 13: 978-0-901286-97-0 (pbk)
ISSN: 1464-1879

Designed by The Design Works, Reading

Contents

List of figures

Acknowledgements

Like all Leopardi scholars, I am indebted to the labours of Francesco Moroncini, the editor of the monumental seven-volume Le Monnier edition of the letters (the final volumes brought to completion with the help of Giovanni Ferretti).[1] This edition, which contains not only the poet's letters but also those of his many correspondents, remains a fundamental research tool. Francesco Flora's edition of the *Lettere*, the fifth volume in his Mondadori edition of the complete works, *Tutte le Opere di* Giacomo Leopardi, contains only the poet's letters.[2] Based on renewed examination and checking of the original manuscripts, Flora's text very occasionally presents a minor variant on the Moroncini reading, and in one case restores a few lines of text omitted by Moroncini. My translation is based on the Flora text: when there is a discrepancy between this and Moroncini, attention is drawn to it in the footnotes. (I do not, however, note separately the many occasions on which Moroncini omits the signature at the end of a letter.)[3] Table II at the end of this book lists the letters in this volume and the corresponding numbers in Moroncini and Flora – thus letter 3, for example, is M48 and F32. References to the *Zibaldone* and to the *Poesie e Prose* in the Introduction and the notes are to Flora's Mondadori edition.[4] A more recent and very useful selection of Leopardi's letters is the one by Sergio and Raffaella Solmi in the Classici Ricciardi series *La letteratura italiana. Storia e testi*,[5] subsequently republished as two small paperback volumes by Einaudi.[6] A new edition of the letters by Franco Brioschi and Patrizia Landi will appear shortly.

My indebtedness to Leopardi's biographers will also be everywhere apparent. I must single out especially Rolando Damiani's *Vita di Leopardi*, a lucid and intelligent account of complex material, woven into an always readable and often gripping narrative.[7] That Damiani quotes very extensively from the letters, and when he does not quote is often para-

1 G. Leopardi, *Epistolario*, edited by F. Moroncini, 7 vols (Florence, Le Monnier, 1934-41).

2 G. Leopardi, *Lettere*, edited by F. Flora, fourth edition (Verona, Mondadori, 1963).

3 As in letters 1, 2, 3, 6, 31, 33, 36, 38, 45, 51, 53, 55, 60, 74, 75, 77, 78, 80, 84, 91, 92, 96, 97, 98, 101, 105, 109, 112, 115, 117, 119, 120, 123, 124, 128, 131, 140, 143, 148, 151, 152, 158, 159, 162, 167, 168, 171, 176, 177, 179, 181, 182, 186, 187, 188, 189, 192, 204, 209, 210, 211, 213, 215, 216, 218, 219. In letters 41, 42, and 44 the final brief phrase which accompanies the signature is also omitted.

4 G. Leopardi, *Zibaldone*, edited by F. Flora, sixth edition, 2 vols (Verona, Mondadori, 1961); *Poesie e Prose*, edited by F. Flora, eighth edition, 2 vols (Verona, Mondadori, 1965).

5 *La letteratura italiana. Storia e testi*, 52: G. Leopardi, *Opere, tomo* II, edited by S. and R. Solmi, (Milan-Naples, Ricciardi, 1966).

6 G. Leopardi, *Lettere. Scelta e commento a cura di* S. and R. Solmi (Turin, Einaudi, 1977).

7 R. Damiani, *Vita di Leopardi* (Milan, Mondadori, 1992).

phrasing them, is inevitable, for the letters themselves are a primary source for reconstructing not just many of the events of Giacomo's life, but, perhaps more importantly, his attitude to and feelings about those events. Giovanni Ferretti's *Vita di Giacomo Leopardi* is still helpful, its more old-fashioned, common-sense approach to the intricacies of family interactions and conflicts a useful corrective to any tendency (perhaps inevitable in the late-twentieth century) to over-psychologize the family situation.[8] Iris Origo's *Leopardi. A Study in Solitude* remains a sympathetic account in English of his life and character.[9] Ezio Gioanola's *Leopardi, la malinconia*, which draws directly on psychoanalytic thinking to confront the issue of Leopardi's depression and its connection with his creativity, is another important recent contribution to our understanding of the poet's psychology and history.[10] All four scholars provide ample documentation and extensive bibliographies.

My own particular 'take' on the Leopardi family perhaps requires a word of elucidation. Within the brief compass of an introduction, to give some sense of the dynamics of a family situation at once very remote from us and yet powerfully present in and evoked through the many letters addressed to family members (and often alluded to directly or indirectly in the letters to other people), I have drawn on some of the concepts and vocabulary of family therapy. My reason for doing this is a simple one: my own reading of a few key texts in this discipline helped me to reach a better understanding of relationships within the family. Although in one sense the story that emerges from the letters is linear and sequential, moving through time and constituting a narrative, in another sense an apter paradigm, one that fits the material better (or at least that large part of the material that bears directly on the family), would be a circular or systemic one. One gets a powerful sense that this family is locked into patterns of interaction which will never change, a web or a network from which no single individual can fight free.

I am well aware of the dangers – both linguistic (obfuscating jargon, psychobabble) and conceptual (over-simplification, glibness) – of appropriating terminology from a discipline not my own. It might in any case be thought anachronistic to use terminology and thinking which has evolved in a therapeutic context only in the last half century, and which is often dealing with acute manifestations like schizophrenia and anorexia, in relation to a family in the past where no member presented clinical symptoms. On the other hand, a great deal of the material here bears very directly on (and much of it is an enacting of) Leopardi's relationships with his parents and siblings – relationships which were very close, and at times painful and conflicted. Leopardi himself is an acute and subtle analyst of his own feelings and states of mind, and on occasion seems uncannily to prefigure modern perspectives. To think of his unresolved and unresolvable difficulties with his father in terms of ambivalent attachment and generational boundaries seems to me helpful, just as it is helpful to think of the family as being in certain crucial ways dysfunctional; but if it is objected that I am saying no more than that Leopardi did not get on with his father, and that conflict of this kind between the generations is not uncommon, and the family was in consequence unhappy, so

[8] G. Ferretti, *Vita di Giacomo Leopardi* (Bologna, Zanichelli, 1945).

[9] I. Origo, *Leopardi. A Study in Solitude*, second edition (London, Hamish Hamilton, 1953).

[10] E. Gioanola, *Leopardi, la malinconia* (Milan, Jaca Book, 1995).

be it. Tolstoy famously remarked that every unhappy family is unhappy in its own way. The Leopardi way can at least in part be characterised in terms of boundaries, attachment and ambivalence.

My own starting-point for thinking about these questions was my reading of John Bowlby's epoch-making study *Attachment and Loss*, with its key notion of ambivalent attachment and the quality of child-parent relationships which exhibit it.[11] A useful overview of the whole subject is provided in the handbook by Fritz B. Simon, Helm Stierlin and Lyman C. Wynne, *The Language of Family Therapy: A Systemic Vocabulary and Sourcebook*, where the sections on Autonomy, Binding, Boundaries, Closeness/Distance, Communication Theory, Double Bind, Enmeshment, Generational Boundaries, and Healthy/Functional Families cover the key issues, with suggestions for further reading.[12] Merely to run through the check-list of communication rules cited on p. 181 which correlate with family functionality is a sobering experience: none of them operated in the Leopardi household. Indeed Giacomo's initial quarrel with his father could be seen as a (doomed) attempt to bring some of these rules into play, and his adult life as an accommodation to his realization of the hopelessness of the case. Letters are first and foremost acts of communication between two individuals; many of those presented here are between members of a family; to try to place them in a broader conceptual framework of family communication or failure to communicate seems a legitimate undertaking.

Translation itself is another kind of communication. My last task is to thank those friends and colleagues who have taken an interest in discussing nuances of meaning in Leopardi's Italian and in helping me to resolve difficulties of interpretation; in particular, Rita Guerricchio, Lia Buono Hodgart, Fiorenza Ceragioli, Franco D'Intino, Judy Davies, and Laura and Giulio Lepschy; for equally thoughtful and patient reflection and comment on the English text, my husband Clive James; for their unfailing supportiveness at all times, my daughters Claerwen and Lucinda, to whom this book is dedicated *con tutto l'affetto.*

[11] J. Bowlby, *Attachment and Loss*, second edition, 3 vols (London, Penguin Books, 1991).

[12] F. B. Simon, H. Stierlin and L. C. Wynne, *The Language of Family Therapy: A Systemic Vocabulary and Sourcebook* (New York, Family Process Press, 1985).

Fig. 2 Leopardi's writing desk in the family library
Courtesy of Casa Leopardi

Introduction

The one thing that the reader of these letters will have to take on trust is that the man who wrote them, Giacomo Leopardi, is a great poet – *the* great poet of the Romantic age in Italy, a figure comparable in stature to Keats, Shelley, Wordsworth or Coleridge in England. Sadly, none of the many attempts to translate his poetry into English has established his name as one recognized even by enthusiasts for early nineteenth-century literature. (Readers who take Pushkin, Hölderlin, Lamartine in their stride are liable to look baffled at the mention of Leopardi, or volunteer hopefully that they loved the book but were not so keen on the film – Tomasi di Lampedusa's novel *Il gattopardo* is *The Leopard* in English). So 'absent' is Leopardi from Anglo-Saxon literary consciousness that, before attempting to explain why his letters seemed worth translating to mark this bicentenary of his birth, a few words to place him chronologically and geographically will be in order. And as is so often the case, his own words, taken from one of his letters [111],[1] do the deed more economically and resonantly than any commentator could hope to. Here, almost in note form, is his own account of the essential biographical facts, sent when he was twenty-eight years old to a friend in Bologna who was evidently planning to publish some of his works. (We do not know the details of the project, which like so many others in his life came to nothing.)

> Born of Count Monaldo Leopardi of Recanati, a city in the March of Ancona, and Marchioness Adelaide Antici of the same city, on the 29th of June 1798, in Recanati.
>
> Lived always in his birthplace until 24 years of age.
>
> He had no teachers except for the first rudiments, which he learned from tutors retained for the purpose by his father in the house. But he did have the use of a rich library collected by his father, a man with a great love of literature.
>
> In this library he passed the greater part of his life, for as long as and to the extent that his health, destroyed by his studies, allowed; these studies he began independently of his teachers at 10 years of age, and continued subsequently without any respite, making them his sole occupation.
>
> Having learnt Greek, without a teacher, he gave himself in earnest to philological studies, and persevered with them for seven years; until, his eyesight ruined, obliged to spend a whole year (1819) without reading, he turned to thinking, and formed a natural affection for philosophy; to it, and the fine literature associated with it, he has devoted himself almost exclusively until the present time.

[1] Numbers in square brackets refer to letters in this volume.

> At 24 years of age he went to Rome, where he refused holy orders and the hopes of rapid advancement offered him by Cardinal Consalvi as a result of pressing solicitations made on his behalf by Counsellor Niebuhr, at that time Envoy extraordinary from the Prussian court in Rome.
>
> Having returned to his birthplace, from there he went to Bologna, etc.
>
> In the course of 1816 and 1817 he published various translations and original articles in the *Spettatore*, a Milanese journal, and some philological articles in the Roman *Effemeridi* in 1822 [...]

The list of publications continues for half a page; it includes the literary as well as the erudite, poetry as well as prose, independent works as well as contributions to periodicals.

Here then are all the important points: noble birth; extraordinary intellectual precocity and a fierce determination to make something of it; frail health, the damaged eyesight especially troublesome; dedication to the classical languages and literatures; the scope and range of the early publications – scholarly, creative, or a combination of the two (translations from Greek and Latin, annotations on classical texts, original poems and essays, supposed translations of newly discovered ancient works – a Mediterranean equivalent in minor key of MacPherson's *Ossian*). One theme is missing, or implicit only: the geographical isolation of Recanati, a small provincial city set high along the top of a ridge of hills close to the Adriatic coast in the papal state (by universal acknowledgement the most backward part of central and northern Italy in the early nineteenth century); the intellectual and cultural isolation consequent on its marginal location; and Leopardi's desire to leave his birthplace in order to live in an environment more suited to his temperament and talents.

Noble birth is a crucial factor in the equation. The Leopardis were one of several dozen aristocratic families in Recanati, whose population numbered 15,000 people. The family palazzo, situated on the main street where it opens out and becomes a small square at one end of the town, is an impressive edifice; and there were land holdings in the surrounding countryside. But aristocratic rank was no guarantee of wealth, or even of a comfortable sufficiency. The many letters which touch on his financial predicament range from anger at his father's perceived unwillingness to help, to weary acceptance that perhaps it was not possible for him to do so:

> If I want to live away from home, I must provide for myself; I mean, not live off my father; because my father does not want to support me away from home, and perhaps he cannot, given the great shortage of ready cash we suffer from in this province, where owning property produces no income, and gentlemen live on what their land produces, not being able to convert it into money; and bearing in mind as well that my family's estate, though one of the largest in these parts, is sunk in debts. [149]

The general situation – that being a landowner does not generate an income – is exacerbated in the case of the Leopardis by the family's particular circumstances and by the household arrangements put in place to deal with them, which date from Giacomo's early childhood. His father had been financially feckless (indeed reckless) as a young man; as a consequence the family holdings were heavily mortgaged, and the whole estate and its management had been put into the hands of his wife, a ferociously able administrator. She kept up appearances to the outside world (the coachman, horses and servants were retained), but instituted a regime of iron frugality within the domestic walls; in the space of forty years, corresponding almost exactly to the life-span of her oldest son, she paid off the debts and restored the family's fortunes. The tension between a sense of aristocratic distinction and the impotence resulting from impecuniousness was to be the hallmark of Giacomo's existence.

But in reality the psychological constraints were more compelling than the financial ones: his father's unwillingness to support him away from home was, as they both well knew, more significant than his inability to do so. Both parents were very religious, in a rigid and controlling way which owed much to the Jesuits, with whom the family had long-standing ties. They were politically extremely conservative, at a moment in Italian history when the possibility of radical change seemed real and exhilarating to those of a more open and independent cast of mind. A single incident illustrates both aspects of their beliefs: when Napoleon's troops had first invaded the papal state in 1796, Count Monaldo had led a procession through the town, headed by an effigy of the Madonna which belonged to the family, praying for deliverance. His religious and political principles, stubbornly held and actively championed, were even reflected in the way he chose to dress: always in black, and wearing a sword – a living icon of reactionary attitudes.[2] If we add to this that Count Monaldo had literary ambitions, then the potential arena for conflict and competitiveness between father and son covers everything they cared about.

Giacomo was the firstborn, and therefore a particular focus for his father's ambitions, but soon had a brother (Carlo) and a sister (Paolina), very close to him in age and temperament, his fellow victims and natural allies in dealing with the inflexible and stifling domestic regime; later there were other children, of whom the two brothers who survived were much younger. The three oldest, all highly intelligent, were educated and brought up together at home, with private tutors and by their father. One room in the family library, which occupies a series of interconnecting rooms on the first floor of the palazzo overlooking the square, still has the table at which the three children sat in the centre of the room, and the raised desk to one side from which their father supervised their studies. Their cleverness was a source of great pride to him; both his pride and their cleverness were openly displayed in the exams he had them sit in public every year in the presence of an invited audience, during which they were interrogated (and replied) in Latin on an extensive syllabus, covering grammar, syntax, rhetoric, history, science, arithmetic, geometry and religion.[3] For all his many faults – the least appealing of which must be his readiness to justify whatever he decided to do as being what 'reason' required – it is difficult not to feel some sympathy with his genuine pleasure in his children's ability, however misguided his handling of it may seem.

2 Count Monaldo famously defined himself as probably *l'ultimo spadifero d'Italia* ('the last person in Italy to carry a sword'); his always wearing black was equally eccentric, and may have signified a voluntary identification with the Jesuits. The oddity of both parents' way of dressing was remarked on by their fellow townsmen.

3 The exams took place for five consecutive years (1808-1812); the programmes for them, drawn up by their father, are still kept in the library in the family palazzo. Members of the audience were allowed to ask their questions in Italian, but the children had to reply in Latin.

Their mother was a much more difficult case. Her narrow-minded and perhaps even obsessional piety made her devote herself to her children's practical needs (that was her duty), but, as her oldest son unforgettably described in a prose passage in his common-place book, the *Zibaldone*, she was secretly pleased if they died in infancy or as a result of childhood illness because then their future as saved souls in heaven was guaranteed.[4] (Of her twelve pregnancies, only five children survived to adulthood, and only two – Carlo and Paolina – outlived her.) The domestic regime was one of extreme watchfulness and control, endorsed by their mother in the interests of their spiritual well-being, and by their father in the interests of their rank, their education, and their future. Every moment of their time, every aspect of their existence, was programmed as part of his 'piano di famiglia' or family plan [30], the project which envisaged restoration of the family's fortunes and the continued residence in Recanati, as one of its leading families, of his heirs, and especially of his firstborn. The oppressiveness of this regime, brilliantly and chillingly evoked in a recent full-length study of the poet,[5] marked the gifted and sensitive child for life, determining both his temperament and his distinctive voice as a writer. It was a regime of unremitting surveillance and no warmth – 'our mother's gaze followed us everywhere: it was her only caress', Carlo is on record as saying in a memoir written many years later.[6] The oppressiveness, in conjunction with the reiterated claims that everything was done out of loving concern for the children's welfare, exactly embodies the situation Bowlby identified as being one of the most disturbing a child can experience, where constant verbal reassurance that everything is done in the child's own best interests is belied by its direct experience of its own sense of self and its inner world, and the impact on that world of its parents' behaviour. Father could sometimes be the children's ally against their mother (he was after all subject to the same stringent economies as they were), and so he became a figure of extreme ambivalence to them; but in reality his apparently greater emotional availability and affection was itself a mechanism of control and manipulation, as became all too clear when crisis point was reached and his oldest son attempted to leave home.[7] The extended household included elderly relatives of Monaldo's, and various tutors and prelates.[8] The children were never unobserved; and in a small provincial town where there were no obvious dangers, Giacomo had never left the house unaccompanied by an adult until Pietro Giordani came to visit him in 1818, when he

4 *Zibaldone* 25 November 1820. The passage does not explicitly identify the woman as their mother, but is generally acknowledged as being a description of her. It speaks of her 'marble coldness' (and secret joy) in the face of even the most harrowing death of an infant or young person; it also describes her methodical undermining of her children's self-esteem for their own supposed spiritual benefit.

5 E. Gioanola, *Leopardi, la malinconia* (Milan, Jaca Book, 1995). Gioanola uses psychoanalytic concepts as a key to understanding the poet's psychology and history; my own view of the family dynamics owes more to John Bowlby's classic study of child-parent relationships *Attachment and Loss* (second edition, London, Penguin Books, 1991), as will become apparent.

6 T. Teja-Leopardi, *Note biografiche sopra Leopardi e la sua famiglia* (Milan, Fratelli Dumolard, 1882), p. 29.

7 In Bowlbian terms father is the children's primary attachment figure, a role their mother, whose coldness and detachment seem pathological, was psychologically unable to fulfil. The damaging effects of extreme maternal detachment are a commonplace of therapeutic thinking. Count Monaldo's collusiveness with his children against his wife continued even when they were adults; see [97] n. 1 and [110] n. 1.

was already twenty years old, and when for the first time he went out alone to welcome his guest who was to stay at the inn down the road. This first act of rebelliousness – leaving the house unaccompanied, without asking permission, to welcome someone from outside the town and the state – can be invested with powerful symbolic force; Count Monaldo's misgivings about it were (in his own eyes at any rate) to prove only too well-founded.[9]

It would be difficult to overstate Leopardi's intellectual precocity. Already in his mid and late teens he had written, and was trying to publish, ambitious works on a wide range of subjects: to mention only some of the weightiest, two lengthy learned treatises;[10] a strikingly original and thoughtful contribution to the Romantic debate in Italy, first in the form of a letter sent to a Milanese literary journal (but not published) in 1816, the year the debate exploded in response to Madame de Staël's open invitation to Italian intellectuals to renew their stagnant literature by reading and translating the best works from abroad, and then in a long essay written in 1818 elaborating on these same ideas;[11] and a translation of book II of the *Aeneid*, which was published in a modest edition in February 1817. It is his attempt to arouse interest in this last work which serves as a starting-point for the letters in this volume.

Leopardi wrote to the poet Vincenzo Monti, the scholar Angelo Mai, and the intellectual and writer Pietro Giordani, telling each of them that the publisher would be sending a copy of the *Aeneid* translation, and asking for their comments and advice. The first two wrote conventionally polite, rather dull answers; Giordani's much more personal and engaged response aroused his young correspondent's passionate gratitude, and initiated an extraordinary epistolary exchange, in which it would be hard to say if human interest or literary interest is greater – if indeed in the case of Leopardi it is ever possible to separate the two. Giordani's sympathetic ear enabled Leopardi to express difficult feelings in the certainty of being given a hearing. In these early letters we witness, first, the sense of isolation and frustration of the gifted young man living in an alienating provincial environment where he feels patronized and belittled by those around him; then his painful coming to terms with the permanent physical damage (a curved spine, debilitating digestive disorders, failing eyesight) caused by the 'seven years of mad and most desperate study' [14] during his adolescence; and then, a year or two later, following the doomed attempt to escape from home and

8 Among the resident tutors at different times were Don Giuseppe Torres (an ex-Jesuit – the Jesuits had been suppressed in 1773 by Clement XIV, and ex-Jesuits were therefore a ready source of supply for tutors in aristocratic households, as Count Monaldo relates in his *Autobiography*); Don Sebastiano Sanchini; and Don Vincenzo Diotallevi.

9 In a letter written 18 months later to Pietro Brighenti he says: 'His [i.e. Giordani's] coming was the time at which my sons changed their thinking and their behaviour and I perhaps lost them then forever. Until that day they had never, *literally never*, been out of my sight and their mother's for an hour' [*mai, letteralmente mai, erano stati un'ora fuori dell'occhio mio, e della madre…*] (cited by R. Damiani, *Vita di Leopardi* (Milan, Mondadori, 1992), p. 138). It can be hard to get the measure of how unusual such domestic surveillance was in aristocratic households, but the letters make it clear that experience of other families of similar rank in the town confirmed the children's sense that it was extremely abnormal.

10 On the *History of Astronomy* and on *Popular Errors of the Ancients*.

11 The journal was the *Biblioteca Italiana*; the essay, entitled *Discourse by an Italian on Romantic Poetry*, was published posthumously.

Fig. 3 Portrait of Count Monaldo Leopardi
Courtesy of Casa Leopardi

Fig. 4 Portrait of Pietro Giordani
Courtesy of the Centro Nazionale di Studi Leopardiani

Recanati, the depression and despair to which it led, and out of which it can plausibly be argued his creative life as a poet was born. (*L'Infinito*, his first undisputed masterpiece, dates from these months.)

These moving letters show both a remarkable insight into and a capacity for analysis of his own inner world. We are immediately faced with one of the central paradoxes of reading Leopardi: the content of his letters may be depressing – indeed, it is at times the experience of depression itself – but the reading of them is not. The act of possessing and articulating his despair seems dauntingly intelligent and courageous; it is curiously energising for the reader. (A similar though more complex kind of thing happens with his greatest poems, which are about loss, desire, memory and disillusionment.) Giordani – himself a figure of considerable stature in Italian letters[12] and at 43 just two years older than Count Monaldo (so an ideal father figure to replace the flawed and problematical real one) – offered his young correspondent space, responsiveness, empathy: in a word, validation of his sense of self and his self esteem. From the outset he treated him as an intellectual and emotional equal. There is a tricky moment when Giacomo reproaches him for not being a careful enough reader, and Giordani disarmingly acknowledges: 'It's quite true that I foolishly mis-

[12] Byron, who had little time for literary men, and especially foreign ones, singled Giordani out as an exception: 'Except Giordani, and – and – and – (I really can't name any other) I do not remember a man amongst them, whom I ever wished to see twice [...]' (in *The Works of Lord Byron. Letters and Journals*, edited by R. E. Prothero, 6 vols (London, John Murray, 1901), V, 435).

understood your 'when'; and I replied very foolishly'.[13] The incident gives the exact measure of the distance between real and ideal father: such self-deprecation on the part of Count Monaldo is inconceivable. Less than six months after the first letter and in spite of the difference in age and status, the two are addressing each other as 'Voi', having already abandoned the deferential third-person 'Ella'; not much later they will switch to 'tu'. (By contrast, Giacomo addressed his father as 'Ella' throughout his life.) These grammatical markers, impossible to reproduce in English, exactly reflect the growing intimacy (in his father's case, the barrier to intimacy) between them. Giordani wrote to a friend in 1819: 'If you saw, if you only saw, the letters I'm getting. Only Dante could write them [...]'[14] The comment seems perfectly appropriate, not just because of the passionate engagement with life and literature and the relationship between the two, but because of the expressive energy and elegance with which these themes are elaborated.

The early letters to Giordani give an extraordinarily vivid sense of a process of self-discovery, of a young writer finding himself and speaking for the first time in his own voice. The contact with Giordani quickly becomes a lifeline, an indispensable condition for being able to face the world: 'in this cursed city I must get all my strength from my spirit and your letters' [9], 'as long as you write to me, I shall be happy' [13], 'you, the only person who can understand me' [38], 'as I cannot talk to anyone else, I talk to you about these feelings of mine' [40]. They form a first major block in the correspondence as it is here presented; they might be read as the opening section of an epistolary novel.

The task of choosing the 220 letters translated here from among the more than 900 extant letters could be viewed as the constructing of such a novel – the creating of a version, however tentative and imperfect, of that spiritual and psychological autobiography that Leopardi himself long intended to write but never did. A letter of 1829 lists among his as yet unrealized literary projects: 'The story of a soul, a Novel which would have little external action, and that very commonplace: but it would relate the inner experiences of a mind born noble and sensitive, from the time of its earliest memories until death' [153]. His own attempts to realize this project – repeated, fragmentary, never completed – have recently been edited in exemplary fashion by Franco D'Intino.[15] This selection of his letters could be regarded as a companion volume to that book: it offers a different take on the same material – his own story, told in his own words, in a discontinuous series of attempts to explain himself to the world.

Henry James remarked that there are two kinds of lives worth telling, lives of those who have done a lot, and lives of those who have thought a lot. Leopardi's is of the second kind: our epistolary novel has almost no plot. Almost nothing of note happened to him: unlike other poets who are his contemporaries, he did not die fighting for Greek independence, or

[13] M97, i.e. letter no. 97 in the monumental edition of the letters edited by F. Moroncini, *Epistolario di Giacomo Leopardi*, 7 vols (Florence, Le Monnier, 1934-1941), which includes not just Leopardi's own letters but those of his correspondents. Henceforth references in this form are to letters in the Moroncini edition. The letter is in answer to [12].

[14] Cited in Moroncini I, in the note on page 277.

[15] G. Leopardi, *Scritti e frammenti autobiografici*, edited by F. D'Intino (Rome, Salerno Editrice, 1995).

defending his honour in a duel, or sailing a small boat in stormy weather. He did not even go walking in the Lake district; or travel to another country for reasons of health, as he would have liked to do. The plot, such as it is, is a psychological one: the desire to leave Recanati, and the thwarting of that desire; the need to escape from father and from home, and the inevitability of his returning each time he does get away, until finally he would rather die than go back; the emergence against all the odds of a uniquely compelling and individual poetic voice.

Such incidents as there are tend to be connected with the mechanics of the correspondence: the unreliability of the post in the first instance and the frustrations it caused (inducing on occasion near despair); the inexplicable failure to receive acknowledgement of certain letters; then, sinisterly, the realization that a 'domestic censorship' was being exercised by his father, who had become worried by his son's liberal political sympathies, and, after Giordani's visit in 1818, laid the blame squarely at the feet of his new literary friends. Thus the marvellous letter to Giordani's friend Giuseppe Montani [24] analysing the relationship between literature and nationhood was never received by its intended recipient, for it never left *casa* Leopardi. The watchfulness and control which governed the children's lives – and the need to elude it – has become a defining condition of the correspondence.

The first real event, inevitably it seems, is a non-event, or a failed event: Leopardi's attempt to leave home on attaining his majority in 1819. He had no clear plan in mind other than an absolute imperative to escape from an oppressively restrictive environment. The passport he obtained was for Milan, the home of Giordani, Monti, Mai, the *Biblioteca Italiana*, and the romantics – a passport for literature and the life of the mind. His bid for freedom generated an extraordinary group of four letters: the disingenuous letter [28] to a family friend, Saverio Broglio D'Ajano, whose help he requested in obtaining the passport, which he needed to travel outside the papal state; the letter to his brother Carlo [29], whom he had not taken into his confidence about his plan (it was to be opened after his departure, so that Carlo would not be implicated in the guilt); the letter to his father [30], enclosed in the one to Carlo, and to be passed on by him after the escape (another letter never seen by its intended recipient, but – significantly – never destroyed); and finally, when the attempt failed because his father came by chance to learn of the request for a passport, a second letter [31] to Broglio D'Ajano explaining why he had been less than candid. The letter to his father, with its dignity, pain, bitterness, regret, rage and immense sadness, is the first uncompromising text in a series – the letters to his father written over the next eighteen years – which taken together provide us with text-book material for a case study of ambivalence.

The official who had issued the passport mentioned it to an uncle who in turn mentioned it to Count Monaldo, who asked that it be sent to him. The passport was then left in a drawer, where in theory Giacomo was free to take it and use it when he pleased. But he no longer felt able to do so: 'I was found out and prevented not by force, which could not do it, but by prayers' [33], he later explained, 'they used prayers and grief' [32]. The analysis in the letter to Broglio D'Ajano of his father's behaviour, the deviousness and manipulativeness of his *modus operandi*, is acute and merciless. His mother was never told about the escape attempt, which became another secret shared by some members of the family and not others; to those friends who knew of it his father dismissed it as mere youthful waywardness.

The letters to Giordani enable us to chart the slide into despair which followed. The continuing inability to read and hence to work was accompanied by a listlessness and lack of energy so profound as to suggest a nervous breakdown. There is an extraordinary letter which describes a state close to catatonia: 'If at this moment I were to go mad, I think my madness would be to sit forever with my eyes staring, my mouth open, my hands between my knees, without laughing or crying or moving except when forced to from the place where I happened to be. I no longer have the energy to conceive any desire, not even for death' [34]. *Noia* (tedium or ennui or life-weariness) is experienced as physical suffering: 'tedium not only weighs on me and wearies me, but it torments me and tears me like a terrible pain' [34]. Contact with Giordani is now more than ever a lifeline: 'I beg you to go on being fond of me, and to remember me, and to believe that I love you as best I can, and I'll always love you, and I want you to write to me' [34]. Paradoxically, it is when he begins to feel a little better that he finds he can weep, and his despair broadens into a generalized sense of the wretchedness of the human condition: 'if sometimes I find myself a little less disconsolate, then I have the strength to weep, and I weep because I am happier, and I weep for the wretchedness of men and the nothingness of things. There was a time when the wickedness of men and virtue's misfortunes moved me to contempt, and my grief sprang from contemplating iniquity. But now I weep for the unhappiness of slaves and tyrants, oppressed and oppressors, good and bad, and in my sadness there is no longer any spark of anger, and this life no longer seems to me worth the fighting' [35]. Coupled with this comes an acute sense of loss, an awareness that something is irretrievably gone. Mourning for the pastness of the past, and a longing for what cannot be recovered – childhood, now explicitly identified with the possibility of happiness, though it is a happiness by default – is at the heart of the experience: 'because the tenor and the habits and the events and the places of this life of mine are still those of my childhood, I cling with both hands to these last remnants and these shadows of that blessed and blissful time, when I hoped for and dreamed of happiness, and as I hoped and dreamed enjoyed it, and it has gone and will never come back, surely never again' [35]. For Leopardi, not allowed to be a child when he was a child, and yet, as we shall see, not allowed to be a fully autonomous adult either when he had grown up, childhood becomes a time, a place, a theme of extraordinary imaginative force.

Leopardi did not leave Recanati until late 1822, when he went to stay with relatives in Rome for six months. His uncle, Marquess Carlo Antici, had ecclesiastical ambitions for this gifted nephew (he managed to ensure that his own unremarkable son later became a cardinal). There was a family tradition of making a career in the church: an uncle of Giacomo's mother had been a cardinal; Giacomo himself had worn clerical dress and tonsure throughout adolescence, as though high church office were his natural destiny. (His parents seem to have encouraged this when it became clear that his frail health and deformity made it unlikely that he would marry and produce an heir. The rights of primogeniture were transferred to Carlo.) This visit to Rome, too little and too late, is documented in the wonderfully vivid and irreverent letters he sent home describing both the Antici household and the broader social scene. There are letters to his father – circumspect, reassuring, and critical of just those things his father would disapprove of, including the lack of order in the Antici household (the regimentation of home had been intolerable to Giacomo, and experienced by him as a prison, but with typical ambivalence he finds its opposite equally disturbing [63]); letters to his sister Paolina – gossipy, affectionate, and very concerned at her desolation when her projected marriage came to nothing; but above all letters to his brother Carlo, to whom alone he was able to confide his hopes and disappointments not just in the literary but in the erotic domain as well.

His need to speak openly to his brother, and his sure knowledge of the horror his parents would feel if these letters fell into their hands, led to subterfuges and intrigue. There was a conspiratorial arrangement to send letters under a false name (originally set up by Carlo, who was hoping to receive *billets doux* from his cousin Marietta in Rome, but used by the brothers for their own purposes when she declined to oblige);[16] there were repeated injunctions that under no circumstances are certain things to be mentioned at home (especially the attempts to secure some kind of employment that might enable him to be self-supporting and thus not return to Recanati); and panic when he thinks that a letter to Carlo may have been seen by his parents ('almost all I talked about was women and silly stories').[17] Carlo had already confided that he missed not just Giacomo's physical presence in the house, but the linguistic licence they allowed one another in the rare moments when they were alone together.[18] It would be easy to dismiss this as just two boys in a straight-laced household defiantly using scurrilous language behind their parents' backs; but it is surely also a telling indicator of the need to break free from the constraints under which they were obliged to function, if they were to achieve autonomy and a sense of self. The words they use in the letters are the usual anatomical ones (*coglione*, *cazzo*): they correlate with the denial of the bodily, the physical, the vital, the instinctual, the passionate ('nature', in Leopardian terminology, as distinct from Monaldo's 'reason') which was both the essence and the *raison d'être* of the domestic regime. (The habit continued: years later, when Giacomo is in Bologna, it is startling and touching to find Carlo writing to him in response to the news that he is once again suffering from acute constipation: 'se mi ami, caca!'[19]) The Roman letters have been described as a kind of Leopardian *Le rouge et le noir*;[20] the disenchanted picture they paint is counterbalanced by the single moving letter [69] which describes a visit to Tasso's tomb, whose simplicity, smallness and bareness become a touchstone for true values against the grandiosity, frivolity, licentiousness and idleness of the capital.[21]

At the end of April 1823 Leopardi returned to Recanati. The pattern of the correspondence now becomes an alternation of home and away-from-home: the letters fall into groups

[16] The name they had chosen was Sofia Ortis. Foscolo's novel *Le ultime lettere di Iacopo Ortis* made the name Ortis one of great literary resonance.

[17] M450.

[18] M441.

[19] M757: 'if you love me, shit!' Giacomo's earliest surviving letter, a jocular effort written at the age of 11 to a neighbour, Marchioness Roberti, in the person of the befana (the witch who brings sweets to good children at epiphany) uses the words *piscia* and *merda*. It was confiscated by his father and not given to its intended recipient: the pattern of censorship is already in operation.

[20] D'Intino (see note 15), p. lxii.

[21] Sadly, a much more ostentatious chapel, dating from later in the nineteenth century, now replaces the setting Leopardi described.

depending on where he is writing from, the sequence going roughly Recanati, Rome, Recanati, Bologna-Milan-Bologna, Recanati, Florence-Pisa-Florence, Recanati, Florence-Rome-Florence, and finally Naples. Rather than giving an account of this as a sequence approximating to a plot, it seems more useful to pick out threads in the narrative, themes which develop over the length of the correspondence. The background of the tapestry, the constants which never change, are the unreliability of the post, the state of his health, and his worries about money. We may consider each of these briefly before moving on to the incidental and local pleasures of the letters – his impressions of the different cities he stayed in, his broader intellectual concerns at any given point, his capacity for lasting friendships, especially with foreigners; and finally to the themes of major interest which unfold over the whole length of his life – family relationships and destinies, his own emergence as a writer and a poet.

The unreliability of the post never ceased to be a cause of concern. Just 19 months before Giacomo's first letter to Giordani, the Congress of Vienna, in June 1815, had decided on Europe's destiny in the aftermath of Napoleon's campaigns and his defeat. Italy was restored to something close to her pre-Napoleonic, pre-revolutionary state: a collection of politically independent units, with Austria in control of the Lombardo-Veneto, the papal State restored to the Pope, Tuscany a grand Duchy, Piedmont with Genoa annexed to it under the house of Savoy, Parma and Modena small independent Duchies, Lucca an independent republic, and Naples a part of the kingdom which included the Southern mainland and Sicily. This political fragmentation is reflected in the complexities of the practical arrangements for postal services,[22] the different systems of coinage in use, and in political censorship for letters between different parts of the country. It is difficult to know whether letters which fail to arrive have got lost in the post or been confiscated by the censors; getting letters to and from Giordani, known for his liberal and anti-clerical sympathies, is often a problem; a false name has to be used when writing about Ranieri, a friend in later years, to avoid his identification by the authorities [177].

Many of the letters give a brief report on their writer's health – always a matter of concern to his friends and family – and on the whole these are stoical and uncomplaining. Occasionally there is a sense of elation when he feels really well, but much more commonly the frustration at achieving less than what he knows he is capable of. The only note of real bitterness occurs when he writes to his mother wearily countering what seem to have been explicit accusations of hypochondria.[23] There are very few letters to her – just four, compared to the scores he wrote to his father – but one cannot attach too much significance to this, as she is very insistent in her letters that he not write to her separately, since she knows what it costs him in terms of eye-strain. (His letters to other members of the family are in any case normally shared, hence the need for vigilance in writing confidentially to Carlo.) Three of the letters to his mother are included here: the innocuous one from Rome, which assures her of his safe arrival there [58]; the one just mentioned where he denies that his

22 See B. Caizzi, *Dalla posta dei re alla posta di tutti. Territorio e comunicazioni in Italia dal XVI secolo all'Unità* (Milan, FrancoAngeli, 1993).

23 The letter from the family to which he is replying is not extant. The bibliography on Leopardi's medical condition and history is vast; the subject has most recently been reviewed in R. di Ferdinando's *L'Amarezza del lauro. Storia clinica di Giacomo Leopardi* (Bologna, Cappelli, 1987).

health problems are all in his imagination [164]; and the even more chilling one in which, living in Naples in a state of near destitution, he repeats to her the request that he had already made to his father for a small allowance like the one paid to Carlo [192].

Money worries are never far from his mind. Attempts to find gainful employment – which must be kept hidden from his father, for whom the need or desire to earn a living was regarded with aristocratic disdain – are a recurring theme. Early on, he hoped to find a position in the Vatican library. Mai ('the most disobliging librarian in Europe', according to Stendhal[24]) was not much help here [52]. Later there were various possibilities for academic appointments, abroad as well as in Italy [98, 102], including improbably at one point a university chair in Natural History, a subject about which he candidly admitted he knew nothing [151]. But these possibilities were for the most part not pursued enthusiastically, not just because of problems connected with his health, with travelling, with the weather – travelling in summer or winter was impossible because of the effect of extremes of heat and cold on his delicate constitution – but on account of the difficulty he would have in making his voice carry to a large audience, and the disrespectful attitude of students.[25] There was an extended period in the mid-1820's of doing editorial work for the Milanese publisher Antonio Fortunato Stella – first a commentary on Petrarch, then the preparation of a prose anthology, and finally a poetry one – which was in the long term debilitating and demoralising, because it felt like hack work. Stella drove a hard bargain financially,[26] and was not solicitous even in making the payments he had promised: Leopardi had on occasion to spell out the embarrassment he would be caused if the money owing did not arrive [120]. The final desperate determination, when he was already a writer and scholar of international repute, to do anything to get away from home produced a letter which makes almost unbearable reading:

> I am resolved, with the little money that remains from when I was able to work, to set out on a journey to seek health or to die, and never to return to Recanati again. I will not be particular about what I do; any situation compatible with my health will suit: I shall not mind humiliations; because there does not exist a humiliation or abasement greater than what I suffer living in this centre of European boorishness and ignorance. I no longer have anything to lose, and even putting my life at risk, all I risk is gaining something. Tell me *in all sincerity* if you think that in Florence I could manage to survive by giving lessons or talks on literature *at home*; and if I would find something quickly; because the money I have to live on won't last long. I mean literary lessons of any kind at all, even the most elementary: of language, grammar, and suchlike. [161]

He explains in a post-script: 'I'm asking you this question about giving lessons, because I cannot compose, write, read. I could give lessons, that is teach, having someone else do the reading.'

[24] Stendhal, *Rome, Naples and Florence*, translated by Richard N. Coe (London, John Calder, 1959), p. 259.

[25] See M730, M731. The respiratory problems caused by the curvature of his spine became worse with age. When he read his poem *Al Conte Carlo Pepoli* to the Accademia dei Felsinei in Bologna he was barely audible; see Moroncini IV, 82 n. 1.

[26] Initially the salary was ten *scudi* a month, later increased to twenty. Giordani had complained a few years earlier that he had trouble living on thirty.

Leopardi's evident desperation inspired his Tuscan friends to organise an income to support him for a year in Florence: it is to them – 'Agli amici suoi di Toscana' – that he would dedicate the *Canti.* His capacity for friendship, for inspiring affection and loyalty in those who knew him well, seems to have been great. It was not much in evidence in Recanati – there are eye-witness accounts of active hostility and taunting by local youths when he was an adolescent.[27] But elsewhere the story was different. The foreign contacts he made in Rome remained in some cases friends for life. Carlo Bunsen emerges with great credit as someone to whom he felt he could always turn in extremis [91, 92, 209, 210]. Some of his most thoughtful and revealing letters are to foreigners, for example to the Belgian Jacopssen [71]; and later to the Swiss De Sinner [176, 185, 187, 211, 218]. He made many friends in Bologna, where Antonietta Tommasini and Adelaide Maestri, and their respective husbands, came to seem like a second family to him [141], and where he took the trouble to track down a former family servant, Angelina, who was delighted to see him; he subsequently became godfather to her child [93, 95, 102]. In Florence he had a large circle of friends: in one letter he names eleven of them to whom he particularly asks to be remembered. His antipathy to Niccolò Tommaseo ('that crazy fool Tommaseo, who is despised in Italy and makes people think he's a great man in Paris' [218]) is quite exceptional, and is a response to Tommaseo's hostility towards him for his less-than-enthusiastic judgment on a piece of his work [80]. (Stella had asked for Leopardi's opinion without revealing its authorship.) Tommaseo was not above making a cheap crack about Leopardi's hunched back.[28]

Finally there is the friendship in his last years with Antonio Ranieri, the dashing young Neapolitan exile he met in Florence, whose success with the ladies he vicariously enjoyed. Ranieri was infatuated with and pursuing an actress, Maria Maddalena Pelzet, and was being pursued by Fanny Targioni Tozzetti, who ingratiated herself with Leopardi as a way of getting access to his friend, as Leopardi himself wryly notes [196]. Leopardi intervened on Ranieri's behalf to effect a reconciliation with Ranieri's estranged father [177, 179, 181], leading eventually to their moving together to Naples and setting up house, where Ranieri's sister Paolina was their housekeeper. The record is muddied by Ranieri's account of the friendship in his *Sette anni di sodalizio*, a distasteful book written decades after the events it describes by a rancorous old man trying to defend his reputation against charges of parasitism.[29] There are no love letters (in their stead we have *Alla sua donna*, a poem whose title its author glossed as 'la donna che non si trova', the woman who cannot be found); the few letters to women friends for whom he felt more than friendship, especially the flighty Fanny [175, 189], are touchingly dignified.[30] But he was obviously much loved by some people. Through all the many letters to friends we build up a sense of his

[27] See Damiani, p. 56.

[28] See Damiani, p. 501. Tommaseo, a fervent Catholic, was dismissive of Leopardi's philosophical views, which he attributed to his deformity and ill-health; Leopardi answered attacks of this kind in [185].

[29] A. Ranieri, *Sette anni di sodalizio* (Naples, Riccardo Ricciardi Editore, 1919).

[30] Fanny's contribution to our understanding of the poet is limited to her infamous remark – surely as revealing of her limitations as of his – in conversation with Matilde Serao, decades after his death: 'My dear, he stank' [*Mia cara, puzzava*].

social persona: the exquisite courtesy and unfailing *signorilità* is corroborated by the comments of outsiders on him, which always emphasise his dignity, his modesty, his gentleness of manner, and his apartness.

Leopardi's impressions of the different cities he stayed in constitute an incidental pleasure of the correspondence. He was pleased with Bologna ('a very quiet, very cheerful, very hospitable city' [81]; 'I am missing Bologna, though, where I was almost feted, where I made many more friends in nine days than I did in Rome in five months, where people think only of living cheerfully without calculation, where outsiders have no rest on account of the attentions lavished on them, where clever men are invited to lunch nine times a week' [82]); disappointed in Milan ('Milan materially and morally is all a garden of the Tuilleries' [82]); not impressed with Florence, in spite of his many friends there ('These alleyways they call streets suffocate me; this universal filth sickens me' [142]); and delighted with Pisa, whose appeal he describes in detail in a letter to Paolina:

> I like the look of Pisa much better than that of Florence. This Lungarno is a spectacle so fine, so spacious, so grand, so lively, so cheerful, that it's captivating: I've not seen anything like it in Florence, or Milan, or Rome; and truly I don't know if in the whole of Europe many views of this sort are to be found. Then in winter people walk about there with great pleasure, because there's almost always an air of spring: so that at certain times of day the street is full of people, full of carriages and pedestrians: you hear ten or twenty languages spoken, a splendid sun shines on the gildings of the cafés, the shops full of pretty wares, and onto the windows of the buildings and the houses, all of fine architecture. Apart from that, Pisa is a mixture of big city and small city, of urban and rustic, a mixture so romantic that I've never seen its like.' [122][31]

He is resigned to the chaos of Naples, where the arrival of cholera causes him to move to the countryside; but by this stage the letters are fewer and shorter, and only to his father and De Sinner does he write at any length.

The broader intellectual concerns which occupy him at certain points make fascinating reading. We have his thoughts on the value of translating [2, 3, 12], on the role of the ugly in art [4], on the relation between spoken and written language [4], on literature and nationhood [24, 56], on what needs to be done in Italian literature [40], on the cult of antiquarianism in Rome [63], on the function of periodicals in the cultural life of the nation [75], on the editing of classical texts and Italy's poor performance in this area compared with English and German scholarship [78, 80], on his lack of enthusiasm for Petrarch [109], on the need for Italians to have contact with foreign cultures [109], on the desolate prospects for literature in Europe in the early 1830s [188], and on many other topics

On the domestic front, we follow Paolina's and Carlo's attempts to escape from home. In her case, self-evidently, such an escape was only realistically possible through marriage, but in reality, as it turned out, this was true for him as well. We can track the repeated failure of plans to arrange a marriage for Paolina, leading to her real desperation at the prospect of

[31] Leopardi's sojourn in Pisa is richly documented in *Leopardi a Pisa*, edited by F. Ceragioli (Pisa, Electa, 1997), the catalogue of the exhibition *Leopardi a Pisa* which celebrates the bicentenary of the poet's birth.

ending her life in a convent or at home ('the place where I live is *casa* Leopardi; and you know better than me what life there is like..').[32] No fewer than three prospective husbands fail to measure up financially or to be sufficiently motivated by her modest dowry and plain looks [57, 66, 69, 72]; and in fact she never married, making *Nelle nozze della sorella Paolina* (On his Sister Paolina's Wedding) – written when her hopes seemed destined to be fulfilled – a poem of great poignancy. She remained a prisoner at home, with her mother as goaler ('she wanders all over the house, she's everywhere, at all hours..');[33] she devoured books, especially English and French novels, and said she had read more than 2000 volumes;[34] she was allowed no friends, and still had to resort to deviousness to receive letters from outsiders (correspondents were told to address their letters to Don Sanchini, who would signal their arrival by placing a flower-pot on his window-sill). She described her existence after her brothers had left home as a kind of death. (She was, as it happens, no mean letter writer herself.) In later life she became distinctly eccentric, spending extravagantly on clothes (by now the family fortune had been restored, after forty years of sacrifices), and – a thing Leopardi scholars find hard to forgive – acting the grande dame and giving away her brother's letters to all and sundry.

Carlo's escape took the form of marrying an unsuitable cousin against his parents' wishes (itself an uncanny echo of Count Monaldo's marriage against the wishes of his mother). He did this when his father was temporarily away from home – perhaps the only way he could do it. To his brother, who had unwisely given their father guarantees about his steadiness [144, 146, 152], it was a shocking move, and it caused a cooling in their relationship. As a result of the marriage, which removed him from the house but not the town, Carlo forfeited the primogeniture rights which had passed to him because of Giacomo's ill-health, and which now passed to Pierfrancesco; he failed to regain them in spite of a court case he mounted contesting his father's will. He too in middle age became eccentric and difficult, as parsimonious as his mother, much loathed by the local townspeople, whose needs he exploited as a money-lender, and who, it is reported, desecrated his corpse in its coffin at his funeral. All three children were marked and damaged for life by their upbringing. In the light of Carlo's failure to carve out his own destiny, Giacomo's doing so seems all the more remarkable.

What the letters reveal about Leopardi's development as a writer and poet can be considered under two heads: the writing itself, and the practicalities of publication. Some of the major themes of his poetry and thinking are touched on or explored in the letters: the role of illusions in human life; the relationship between nature, reason, and truth; the predicament of the gifted and sensitive spirit trapped in an ugly body (the 'velo indegno' of *Ultimo canto di Saffo*); the problem of virtue. There are occasional parallels between the content of individual letters and poems, but (disappointingly) nothing at all about the writing of those poems. There is a letter, responding to a request from his cousin for a poem to commemorate a friend's brother who had died, on his inability to write poems to order. In it he

[32] M469.

[33] Cited by Damiani, p. 59.

[34] Damiani, p. 62.

describes the process by which his poems come into being, insisting on the necessary lapse of time between first inspiration and final execution:[35]

> In my life I've written only a very small number of short poems. In writing them I've never followed anything but an inspiration (or frenzy); when it came on me, in two minutes I formed the outline and plan of the whole composition. When that's done, it is always my habit to wait for another moment to come, and when it does come (which normally happens only a few months later), then I set about composing, but so slowly, that it isn't possible for me to finish a poem, even a very short one, in less than two or three weeks. This is my method, and if inspiration does not come of its own accord, it would be easier for water to come from a tree trunk than a single line from my brain. [76]

This is comparable to the canonical Romantic texts on the role of inspiration in poetic composition – on its not being subject to an act of willing: Keats's 'if Poetry comes not as naturally as the Leaves to a tree it had better not come at all', and Shelley's 'Poetry is not like reasoning, a power to be exerted according to the determination of the will. A man cannot say "I will compose poetry." The greatest poet even cannot say it.'[36] The same point is made, a little more tartly, when he concludes: 'it is certain that asking a difficult and unproductive nature like mine for a poem is the same as asking me for a bishopric: the latter I cannot give, and the former I cannot write to order.'

The invisible thread – the story one could hardly guess from reading the letters – is Leopardi's emergence as a lyric poet, as distinct from a poet of commitment to public issues (to the state of the nation, and the need to do something about it). The two strands develop in parallel, and in intricate inter-relationship, but whereas he is able to talk about the patriotic poems, and actively promote their publication, there is nothing in the letters about the *piccoli idilli*. (*Idillio* or 'idyll' is the term he used for those poems which spoke most directly from and about his inner world, his subjectivity.) There is, for example, no mention of *L'Infinito* or of *La sera del dì di festa*. The silence is surely significant: whereas he can explain the poems which conform to a poetic of patriotic concern, the private poems are less easy to account for, and, as we know, were not published until years after they were written.[37] There is a gap of several years in the mid-1820s in which he hardly writes poetry at all. When he casually mentions at the end of a short letter to Paolina from Pisa that he has written 'poems just like the ones I used to write, and with the heart I once had' [135], it is a magical moment – one of the poems is *A Silvia*, which itself initiates the great flowering of his lyrical gift in the *grandi idilli*.

[35] Wordsworth's account in the Preface (1800) to *Lyrical Ballads* of 'emotion recollected in tranquillity' is not dissimilar.

[36] *The Letters of John Keats*, edited by M. B. Forman, fourth edition (London, Oxford University Press, 1952), p. 107; P. B. Shelley, *A Defence of Poetry* [1821], in *Shelley's Prose*, edited by D. L. Clark (Albuquerque, The University of New Mexico Press, 1954), p. 294.

[37] Both *L'Infinito* (The Infinite), written in 1819, and *La sera del dì di festa* (or *La sera del giorno festivo*, as it was originally called: The Evening of the Holiday), written in 1820, were first published in December 1825 in *Il nuovo ricoglitore*.

What can be tracked through the letters are the attempts to get his work published: the story makes fascinating, if dispiriting, reading. The carelessness of the printers is a persistent theme, his own fanatical attention to detail unrelenting. Lack of money was always a problem. Early on his father approved the scholarly publications, which might lead to an ecclesiastical position (there were, as we have seen, various attempts to get a job in the Vatican, or use Vatican influence to get a job elsewhere in the state). But the creative works were another story, and were often published in spite of his father's active obstructiveness. The two early patriotic canzoni[38] were finally published in Rome – the manuscript originally sent to Giordani in Piacenza either got lost in the post or was confiscated by the authorities – but Leopardi was desperately disappointed with the shoddy look of the finished product, the many misprints and the cost [21]. He next tried to have three new poems[39] printed in Bologna, asking Giordani's friend Pietro Brighenti to supervise their publication; Brighenti suggested he reprint the patriotic poems as well. His father got wind of this, and contacted Brighenti behind his back, urging him not to reprint the patriotic canzoni, and demanding to know what the new ones were about.[40] His son's sense of outrage at this typical deviousness and high-handedness is reflected in the letter he wrote to Brighenti when he found out – another extreme expression of filial hostility and anger:

> I thank my father [...] for the permission he grants me to print *my* canzoni. But he does not want the two Roman ones to be reprinted. He is quite right. He wanted you to tell him the titles of the unpublished ones. He did the right thing. He does not want the first one printed. Again, quite right: not to my mind, to be sure, but it is quite right that *in my writings* his opinion should prevail, because I am and always will be a child, and not capable of making decisions for myself. That leaves two canzoni. For these two (about which at last and by chance it is my turn to have a say) I say there is no need to put the printers to the trouble, and so let's put an end to the matter, and the bother I must have caused you. [44]

His father objected to the first two poems on the grounds of their supposed political subversiveness. The title alone of the third one, inspired by a recent local scandal (the death of a young woman following an abortion), was enough to arouse his apprehension: 'he immediately imagined a thousand filthy things in the execution of it, and a thousand improprieties in the subject, which can come into the mind of a person who, although very intelligent and quite well read, yet has no idea of the literary world.' Only *Ad Angelo Mai* met with his

[38] *All'Italia* (To Italy) and *Sopra il monumento di Dante* (On the Monument to Dante).

[39] *Nella morte di una donna fatta trucidare col suo portato* (On the Death of a Woman Killed with her Unborn Child); *Ad Angelo Mai quand'ebbe trovato i libri di Cicerone della Repubblica* (To Angelo Mai, on his Discovering the Books of Cicero's *De re publica*); *Per una donna inferma di malattia lunga e mortale* (For a Woman Suffering from a Long and Fatal Illness).

[40] The whole complicated episode is related by Damiani, pp. 176-183, with excerpts from Count Monaldo's and Brighenti's letters as well as Leopardi's. It is extraordinary to witness father and son, living under the same roof, unable to communicate except obliquely through a third party in Bologna. Carlo in later life described his father's reaction to the political canzoni as one of pure fright [*Nostro padre si pelò per la paura*]; cited in G. Leopardi, *Epistolario*, edited by P. Viani, 3 vols (sixth reprint, Florence, Successori Le Monnier, 1907), III, 431.

approval: 'The title of the second unpublished one was luckily found to be quite innocent. It's about a Monsignor', as Giacomo noted sarcastically. Then he rashly added: 'But my father cannot conceive of someone for whom all subjects provide an opportunity to speak of what matters most to him, and he has no inkling that under that title is hidden an Ode full of horrible fanaticism.' This outburst, even if intended ironically, was ill-advised: Brighenti, as we now know but Leopardi never did, was an undercover informer for the Austrian authorities, and in fact *Ad Angelo Mai* (the only one of the five poems actually printed on this occasion) was subsequently banned in the Lombardo-Veneto, a fact he tried to keep from his parents.[41] When he finally managed to publish the volume of ten *Canzoni* in Bologna in 1824, there were again problems with the censor, permission to print being twice refused [77]. At a certain point he simply started taking steps to ensure that his parents did not see what he published. He arranged for the proofs of the *Canzoni* to be sent to him in Recanati care of a fictitious name, Alberto Popoli.[42] Later, to let Carlo know that he was sending him a book, again care of a fictitious name, he inserted a sentence in English in one letter, setting it out on three short lines as though it were a quotation from a poem, in order to allay his parents' suspicions should the letter fall into their hands.[43] When the *Canti* at last appeared in 1831, he sent a copy to Carlo, but urged him to show it only to Paolina and Pierfrancesco, and then to keep it hidden and safe from their parents [178].

The publication history of the *Operette morali* – a collection of philosophical prose meditations, many of them in dialogue form – was no less troubled. Calling into question received ideas and comfortable assumptions as they do, and all the more effectively for their ironical lightness of touch, they are radically incompatible with Monaldo's principles. But first there were practical difficulties. Three of the dialogues were published separately in the *Antologia* without Leopardi's approval and to his great displeasure: the book had been planned as a unity, he had to explain to the editor, and lost its point if broken up into fragments [101].[44] He sent this number of the *Antologia* to Carlo and Paolina under a false name and urged them to hide it [104].[45] There were, as always, problems with the censor [106].[46] Then he was horrified to find that Stella was proposing to publish the book in an unsuitable

[41] M481.

[42] M592, M598, M599, M604, M605: the instruction is repeated to Brighenti in five separate letters, indicating a high degree of anxiety. When the book appeared it too was banned in Lombardy [M879].

[43] M976. The 'quotation' reads:

> You will find, at the same address at
> Which I sent you the moral performations, [*sic*]
> Another small book of mine.

The 'small book' is probably *Versi*, 1826.

[44] The three were *Dialogo di Timandro ed Eleandro*, *Dialogo di Cristoforo Colombo e Pietro Gutierrez*, and *Dialogo di Torquato Tasso e del suo Genio familiare*; they appeared in the January issue in 1826.

[45] And to Luca Mazzanti in Recanati, who had asked for a copy of the dialogues printed in the *Antologia*, he wrote: 'I shall be pleased to send you my Dialogues as soon as I get the copies. But first I ask you to promise me faithfully and inviolably not to show them to anyone at all in Recanati.' [M910]

[46] And on a practical level a real anxiety that if the manuscript were handed to the censor it might never be recovered [M885]. The censors had even insisted on vetting the commentary on Petrarch.

series (The Ladies' Library for light reading) [113]. He refused to allow the book to be sold in Recanati, in order to avoid having it come into his father's hands.[47] When finally his father did read it, he wanted changes made and brought pressure to bear to that end. Leopardi dealt as tactfully as possible with the unsolicited advice:

> God knows how grateful I am to you for your advice about my book. I swear to you that my intention was to write *poetry in prose*, as the custom is nowadays; and so to follow this or that mythology as I chose; as one does in poetry, without in consequence being thought a pagan, Moslem, Buddhist etc. [...] As for correcting the passages you indicate, and which at the moment I cannot call to mind, I promise I will think seriously about it; but God knows now whether it would be *physically* possible for me, I don't say to correct the book, but to reread it. You must trust the experience I have in these matters by now, that any declaration or protest I were to publish would only create a scandal, and whatever there might be in the book that was dangerous would only be more sought out, more remarked on, and more harmful. [171]

It is hardly surprising that he felt embattled.

The battle continued on another front with the publication in January 1832 of Count Monaldo's *Dialoghetti sulle materie correnti nell'anno 1831*, a work which seems to have been conceived in direct competition with the *Operette*, using the same dialogue form, and designed to champion sound reactionary principles in politics and religion. The book was published anonymously, but at some point the publisher let slip the information that the author's name was Leopardi. Giacomo's initial pleasure in his father's success [180, 182] turned to horror when he realized that the book was being attributed to him, and rumours were circulating that he was a convert to reactionary views. He felt forced to issue public denials of authorship. To Giampietro Vieusseux, the editor of the *Antologia*, he wrote:

> I declare that I am not the author of the book entitled *Dialoghetti sulle materie correnti nell'anno 1831*, which some people are attributing to me. Please publish this declaration in your worthy Journal the Antologia. [...]
>
> Please also arrange, if it is possible (as I hope it will be), for this declaration, *with my name*, to be included in the list of contents on the cover of the issue, and, if possible, on a separate line (a new paragraph), so that it cannot be missed. [183]

It is instructive to compare the letter written at the same time to his cousin Peppe, which asks him to place a similar disclaimer of authorship of 'those filthy, fanatical, awful dialogues' [184] in a Roman journal, with the letter to his father explaining why he has done so: 'I thought it unworthy to usurp in a way what is owing to someone else, and above all to you. I am not the man to tolerate taking the credit for another's merits' [186]. The contrast between them, too easily dismissed as hypocrisy, is better understood in terms of ambivalence; it forces us to reflect on the central question of his relationship with his father.

The ambivalence which informs Leopardi's attitude to so many aspects of his life – solitude, study, death, and even Recanati itself, are all at different times seen as very positive or very negative – is nowhere more apparent than in his attitude towards his father. For his

[47] Ferretti, p. 305.

father, as he says over and over again in the letters to him, he felt respect, concern, affection: genuine respect for a man of principle, though the principles are very different from his own, and not ones he can admire; genuine concern at his displeasure or distress, even when he himself is the cause of it; and even genuine affection. These feelings co-exist alongside barely concealed loathing for certain aspects of his father's behaviour – those aspects which do not acknowledge and respect his own autonomy.[48] We have the independent testimony of an acquaintance in Florence that Leopardi always spoke of his father with respect and even affection (his behaviour, that is, correlates with the expressions in his letters), but that he felt the difference in their principles was an irreconcilable barrier to co-existence in the same house or town. He can only cope with his father's behaviour and his own ambivalence when he is away from home; whenever he comes back, he goes into crisis mode, with despairing letters and strange behaviour.[49]

Giacomo's ambivalence is experienced by Monaldo as a lack of intimacy. An alert reader points out that no letter of Monaldo's to his son (and there are 135 of them) fails to speak of his love, as though soliciting reciprocity of devotion. On one occasion he complains in so many words that his son's letters are too dry, too lacking in any sense of closeness or confidence. Giacomo, with his usual courtesy, sensitivity and willingness to try to explain himself, attempts to account for the feeling of constraint. He describes the barrier to intimacy between them as depending on habits which date back to earliest childhood. There is no reason to suppose that what he says in this letter about his love and his gratitude is anything but true:

> You reproach me for the dryness of my letters [...] You would like me to see your heart for just one moment; and on this subject allow me to make a protest and a declaration, which from now on may always serve to shed light on the way I feel towards you. I tell you, then, and protest with all possible truthfulness, before God, that I love you as tenderly as it is or ever was possible for any son to love his father; that I recognize very clearly the love you feel for me, and that I feel a gratitude as heartfelt and as deep as human gratitude can ever be for what you have done for me and for your tenderness; that I would willingly give you all my blood, not just from a sense of duty, but from love [...] If then you sometimes desire in me more closeness and more displays of intimacy towards you, the lack of these things comes simply from the habit contracted in infancy, a habit that brooks no disobedience and cannot be conquered, because it goes back too far and began too early. [127]

The son has insight into the difficulties of the relationship, and their origin, but there is no corresponding insight from his father. Monaldo endlessly acts out the need for control,

[48] Ambivalence in Bowlbian terms is exactly this: an attachment to the person, but deep uneasiness about some of the things the person does. The behaviour of the attachment figure causes distress precisely because it is the attachment figure, the person who is loved. (The extreme case is sexual abuse of a child by a parent, but as counsellors have learnt in recent years, to remove the abused child from its attachment figure is often to compound the damage; what the child wants is usually not to lose its parent, but for the distressing behaviour – the abuse – to stop.)

[49] He is well aware of the strangeness of his *strani modi di vita* [192]; in modern terms we would describe his behaviour as neurotic or obsessional. There was a family history of relatives tormented by *scrupoli*, or obsessive-compulsive behaviour: Count Monaldo refers to two of them in his *Autobiography*.

the failure to acknowledge a boundary, the failure to respect the otherness of the other person: the publication history, with all the many attempts to interfere with, suppress, or change what his son has written, can be seen as a territorial dispute, the fight by Giacomo to establish a boundary around his own autonomy. (Monaldo's utter incomprehension of what is at stake is reflected in a mournful letter in 1828 complaining that he never gets to see what Giacomo publishes any more.)[50] The failure by a parent to acknowledge and respect a boundary can be experienced by the child as an attack on selfhood, an erosion of self-esteem: Leopardi himself repeatedly identified loss of self-esteem as the determining factor in the escape attempt and the breakdown which followed [27, 29, 40]. These family therapy notions of ambivalence and boundaries provide what is inevitably a rather simple psychological model for what in reality is an infinitely complex relationship and history, but they help explain how he can feel such extremes of emotion (tenderness and concern; contempt and anger) towards the same person and virtually at the same time.

Giacomo's self-esteem, undermined by his mother on principle from early childhood, was under attack more insidiously by his father, who had seemed to be his ally and to share his sense of who he was and what he might achieve, and yet had proved unable to understand and endorse the reality. In retrospect his father's co-responsibility for the ruin of his health must have been inescapably clear, even if never consciously articulated.[51] The letters from Carlo Antici to Count Monaldo during the 'seven years of mad and most desperate study' urging him to think of his son's health and to encourage him to take exercise and fresh air – and the wilful obtuseness of Monaldo's replies – make disturbing reading. Here Monaldo has failed to establish a boundary in a different, almost literal, sense: Giacomo's appetite for study was limitless, and no limit was placed on it. Carlo famously described Giacomo as an adolescent reading and writing late at night bent over the last guttering flame of the candle – a haunting image, as one sees the damage to spine and eyesight *in fieri*, as it is happening. Count Monaldo, the champion of reason and its self-elected spokesman (when he founded a periodical he called it, inevitably, *La voce della ragione*),[52] had been unable as a father to act even with ordinary common sense or reasonableness. Giacomo's loss of health and of a normal physique, and the loss of happiness consequent on it, cannot be separated from the boundless sense of possibility (hopes, dreams, desires) experienced precisely as he was depriving himself, with his father's active collusion, of the possibility of ever achieving them. Childhood for Leopardi is the place where everything is possible; adulthood is the place where almost nothing is.[53]

[50] M1282.

[51] Damiani, p. 384, cites the oral testimony (elicited in her old age) of a young girl, the sister of the landlady in the house where Leopardi lived in Pisa, to the effect that he had confided to her that his hunched back was a consequence of his father's having made him study too much as a boy.

[52] 'The Voice of Reason'. It was published from 1832 to 1835.

[53] An arresting (and even more concrete) instance of a lack of boundary is provided by family mealtimes in the Leopardi household, where Giacomo sat next to his father, who cut up the food on his son's plate well into adulthood; later Giacomo would insist on eating alone. The family therapy notion of 'enmeshed' families seems strikingly applicable.

Giordani gave what Leopardi's father would not or could not give, an unconditional endorsement of his autonomy and right to choose his own destiny, and express his genius in his own terms. Giordani immediately and intuitively had the measure of his young correspondent. With prescience and real generosity of spirit, and speaking (as it turns out) for posterity, he wrote in 1819 to a friend: 'he is boundlessly, frighteningly great. You cannot imagine how great he is'.[54] Many years after Leopardi's death, when his stature was no longer in doubt, a visitor called on his mother and, as a way of paying her a compliment for being by implication the mother of a genius, quoted Virgil's words to Dante in the *Divine Comedy*: 'Benedetta colei che di te s'incinse' (Blessed is she who bore you). All she was able to say in reply was: 'Che Dio gli perdoni' (May God forgive him).

All scholars who work on Leopardi try to identify the moment at which *nasce Leopardi*, the moment when the Leopardi who will become a great poet is born. For Rolando Damiani it is 1815, the year of his 'conversion to literature', when he is 16 or 17 years old, and discovers himself and an identity separate from his father's in the solitude of the family library. For Ezio Gioanola it is the breakdown and depressive crisis in 1819, the year of his 'conversion to philosophy', when his inability to read and study drives him deep into his own inner world. My own choice would be a simpler one, midway between these two. It is the moment when he picks up his pen to answer Giordani, when he starts to express – and to communicate to a wider world beyond the confines of the family and of Recanati – the sense of self, of who he is and what he is about, which his parents were unable to come to terms with for as long as he lived.

[54] Cited in Moroncini I, 275, n. 1.

A note on the translation

Some of the problems faced by a translator of Leopardi's letters should be mentioned briefly, not because I think I have solved them – they are insoluble – but to suggest areas in which the translation may not do justice to the original. This is apart from the generic difference between the two languages, familiar to anyone who works with them (and well illustrated by the typical ansaphone message which invites one to speak, in Italian, after the *segnale acustico* – seven syllables, Latinate, mellifluous, almost a line of verse, and in English after the *beep* – monosyllabic, Anglo-Saxon, direct, earthy). To make the English version sound like English, and not like translatorese, was a constant challenge; I am far from sure that I have always risen to it.

There is for a start the inevitable loss in gradations of intimacy in English, which has no way of marking the three possible forms of address offered by nineteenth-century Italian (*Ella, voi, tu*). Even when the chillingly formal *Mio Signor Padre* of the first letter to his father [30] becomes the slightly less chilly but still very formal *Carissimo Signor Padre*, and then, after the death of his brother Luigi, *Caro Papà*, Leopardi always addresses his father in the third person, an ineradicable marker of the distance between them. With Giordani, as we have seen, he quickly passes from *Ella* to *Voi* and then to *tu*; with other friends like Vieusseux the passage to *voi* usually happened quickly, as it did with all the people he was close to. Male friends of his own age (Papadopoli, Pepoli, Puccinotti, Ranieri, his cousin Peppe) and of course his brother and sister are normally addressed as *tu*. Some indicators of intimacy should register, for example the affectionate nicknames used by and with his siblings, whereby Giacomo becomes Giacomuccio, which is then shortened to Muccio, which in its turn becomes Mucciaccio or Buccio (the equivalent series in English might be James, Jamie, Jimmy, Jimbo, Jim); for Giordani he quickly stops being *signor Contino*, and becomes Giacomino. Carlo is often affectionately Carluccio or Carlino, Paolina is Pilla, and Pierfrancesco is Pietruccio.

The effortlessly *signorile* tone of many of the letters, which ought perhaps to sit oddly with the intensity of emotion so often being expressed, but never does, is another challenge. Forms of leave-taking, or signing off, were particularly difficult. *Mi comandi, se son buono*, and the many elegant variations on the same idea, become in English banal or laboured. Beginnings were difficult too: often, though not always, emphatic forms in *-issimo* correlate with deference and formality rather than intensity of feeling. (*Carissimo Signor Padre* loses something however one translates it.) A more general difficulty is that the language of affection and friendship in the early nineteenth century can sound to modern ears like the language of passion. Shelley wrote to his Oxford friend Hogg quite unselfconsciously as *Best-beloved*, exactly equivalent to Leopardi's *Dilettissimo* to Giordani. The way Leopardi writes to Ranieri is no different from the way he writes to Giordani, even before meeting him, or indeed to his brother Carlo ('Who could tell you how much I love you, and how much I long to kiss you again!' [88]). I have for the most part left such effusions as they stand, even if they occasionally sound slightly fevered or over-ripe to modern ears ('My dear angel', 'My divine friend').

The twentieth-century equivalents of certain words seemed best avoided because, while they correspond exactly in meaning to the Italian, they feel anachronistic in an early nineteenth-century context. Thus I render *letterato* as *man of letters* and not as *intellectual*; *malinconia* for the most part as *dejection, desolation, despondency*, or even Byron's *depression of spirits*, but not simply as *depression*, which seems inescapably twentieth-century. *Melancholy* will rarely do, and is in any case impossible in the plural, as Leopardi so characteristically uses it (*le mie malinconie* – Keats's 'my glooms' seems too idiosyncratic). Where terminology is precise and complicated, as in the names of money and coins in the different parts of Italy, I have kept the original Italian terms (*scudi, baiocchi, paoli*, etc);[1] likewise the terms *canzoni, canti*, and *idilli* (roughly, 'odes', 'songs' and 'idylls') have a special resonance in Leopardi which usually seemed better served by preserving them.

The combination of powerful feeling and self-conscious stylistic elaboration was another challenge. Although these are primarily acts of communication between one individual and another at a given moment in time, they are also – in some cases strikingly so – literary compositions, letters to posterity.[2] They were in many cases drafted with care, and painstakingly copied out – often by Carlo or Paolina – and the draft retained by their author, who seems, for example, to slip naturally into alliteration at moments of strong feeling. Phrases like *sono un figlio di famiglia, la cui figliolanza non finisce mai*; or *la noia, madre per me di mortifere malinconie*; or *procacciandomi un poco di pane colla penna* are almost poetic in their intensity, and yet in context seem quite spontaneous and unstudied. Most of this is inevitably lost in the English version.

Some of Leopardi's letters, for example all those to his Aunt Ferdinanda, the only member of the older generation he seems to have been able to talk to as a young man, were almost certainly destroyed by the family. It seems a small miracle that so many others survive. My hope is that some sense of their brilliance and their interest survives in translation.

1 Rough equivalents in value can be calculated by reference to Bolton King's *A History of Italian Unity 1814-1871*, 2 vols (London, James Nisbet and Co. Ltd, 1899), II, 397.

2 As early as 1820, when he was barely 21 years old, Leopardi was asked by Brighenti whether he was thinking of publishing his letters, and his reply, though negative [M278], shows that it was a possibility he did not categorically rule out.

The Letters

1

Leopardi, eighteen years old and living in a provincial backwater where he was cut off from any contact with metropolitan cultural and literary life, on privately printing a translation of Book II of the 'Aeneid' wrote to a number of established men of letters, hoping to arouse their interest and initiate a correspondence. One of them was Pietro Giordani, a leading Milanese intellectual. This letter to him, though formal and rather stilted, is the beginning of what was quickly to become a remarkable exchange between the older established writer and the aspiring young poet twenty-five years his junior.

To Pietro Giordani • Milan

Recanati, 21st February 1817

Dear Sir. Hating mediocrity in literature fiercely as I do (which does not mean that I hate myself, for I am worthless), I am well aware that there are scarcely two or three others in Italy to whom I could turn if I did not turn to you. For a long time now I have desired to do so, but have never dared, and now I do it fearfully, taking the opportunity provided by the book you will be offered in my name by Mr. Stella.[1] And first of all I beg you most warmly to forgive me my boldness in writing to you first, and in adding to that boldness the burden of a book; and not to punish me by taking offence. The book itself, revealing my worthlessness to you, will punish me. God forbid that I should seek your judgment on it. I tell you as sincerely as possible what you already well know to be the case, for many others as it is for me: that knowing the opinion held of any literary work by even twenty men of letters, I reckon that I know nothing if I do not know your opinion. Nor am I so foolish that I do not know that a critical comment of yours is worth much more than the praise of a hundred others; but to criticize one must read, and the reading of a thousand bad lines of verse is an intolerable torture for a true man of letters. If it pleases you not to reject my poor offering, I shall be able, remembering it, to boast occasionally that the gift of a book of mine was accepted by you. If I may be allowed to ask another favour, I beg you not to disdain considering me always from now on, dear Sir, your most humble, most devoted servant,

Giacomo Leopardi.

[1] Antonio Fortunato Stella (1757-1833), the Milanese publisher who had printed the translation of *Aeneid* II, and with whom Leopardi was later to be closely involved on numerous literary projects; see [78, 80], etc.

2

Giordani's enthusiastic response[1] *aroused Leopardi's passionate gratitude.*

To Pietro Giordani • Milan

Recanati, 21st March 1817

Dearest Sir. That I should see and read the hand of Giordani, that he should write to me, that I can hope henceforth to have him as my teacher: these are things I can scarcely believe. You would not be amazed at it, if you knew how long and how passionately I have yearned for this, because things long desired seem impossible when they are present. I want you wholly to believe everything I write now and later, even the smallest phrases, because every one of them, and this I promise you, will come from the heart. This I insist on: all the rest I will ask for. My first letter was more a product of respect than of affection, because affection, welcome and honourable between equals, often gives offense to one's superiors. Now that you in your two precious letters give me permission to do so, be certain that I shall speak to you with all affection.[2] You are quite right to think that the cause of that affection was your distinction in the studies I love. Your writings alone have spoken to me about you, because here where I am there is not a living soul who speaks about Men of Letters. But I do not know how it is possible to admire someone's virtues, especially when those virtues are great and exceptional, without forming an affection for the person. When I read Virgil, I fall in love with him; and when I read the great living men, I do so even more ardently. You are quite right to say that there are very few of them, and so the affection shared between just three or four people is all the more intense. You who know how rare and how valuable a great man is, will not be amazed at what I write to Monti and to Mai,[3] and you will not think that I do not feel what I write, or that I would wish to abase myself and annihilate myself before them, if I did not firmly believe that I ought to do so: and certainly when I do so I feel the pleasure that man naturally feels when he does what he ought. Sickened and disheartened as I am by the mediocrity which assails us and suffocates us, almost believing (after reading the Journals and other wretched modern writings, for I do not read old ones, as their lack of reputation persuades me of their insignificance) that literature no longer offers anything beautiful, I cannot tell you how great is my need to turn to the Classics among the dead, and to you and your great friends among the living, from whom I principally take comfort and strength, seeing that true literature is still alive. When I write or reread things that I have in mind to publish, and I come upon some passage to my liking (and here I remind you of the promise I made to speak to you honestly), I ask myself as a quite natural thing, what will Monti and Giordani say about this? because I cannot be satisfied with the judgment of the

[1] M30 and M34: Giordani's second letter, sent before he received a reply to his first, seems to have been prompted by his learning in the interim of Leopardi's extreme youthfulness.

[2] The phrase 'with all affection' echoes Giordani's closing words in M30.

[3] Vincenzo Monti (1754-1828), the poet, and Angelo Mai (1782-1854), the scholar, the other two writers to whom he had sent his translation of *Aeneid* II.

less-than-great, and it would not matter to me if someone else were to praise what you disliked; on the contrary, I would think it bad. And when something that I like is not liked by the few people I give it to read, I appeal to your judgment and your friend's, and to tell the truth I am obstinate; and it has almost never happened that where writing is concerned someone has made me change my mind. I have often pitied Alfieri, whose tragic style, in those times of universal corruption, seemed intolerable; I do not know what that great Italian felt on seeing his style condemned by all, censured by the most famous men of letters, and Cesarotti (so highly praised then) begging him publicly to change it; or how he could remain firm in his resolve, and entrust himself to the judgment of posterity: a judgment now pronounced, which declares his tragedies immortal. Certainly finding oneself alone in a true opinion is frightening, and often to our own selves constancy seems cowardice; indifference to foolish judgments, pride; thinking one understands better than other people, presumption. Good for Alfieri for standing firm; had he not done so, he would now be in the same position as his judges.

I have a huge, perhaps immoderate and insolent, desire for glory, yet I cannot bear it when things of mine that I do not like are praised, and I do not know why they are reprinted, the damage done to me being greater than any benefit to those who republish them without my knowledge. Reading those things, you will have laughed, but your laughter was surely not malicious, and I am happy at that. And so that you forgive me the folly of having published them, I'll tell you that almost everything I have published will never appear again with my consent, and that I have condemned to the darkness two other really large (not great) works already prepared and sent to the printers.[4]

No other man of letters, apart from the three you know about, has had from me a copy of the second book of the *Aeneid*, on which I still have not pronounced judgment. I have written, and straight from the heart, to them alone, satisfying, although with some trepidation, a long-standing and deep desire. That my book had many faults I already believed; now I would swear to it, because Monti has told me it is so (a much appreciated and eagerly awaited comment). I am not writing to him, because I am afraid of being a nuisance, but please do thank him for it warmly in my name. But it is no great thing to tell a blind man: You're on the wrong track, if you do not add: Go in this direction. Nothing means as much to me as understanding the faults in something of mine, because I know the immense usefulness of it, and I think that having once seen and noted a defect, I may afterwards always be mindful of avoiding it. But I dare not ask anyone to show them to me, because I know that it is very tiresome to pick out the faults in a work, especially when there is more bad than good. In the meantime I want you to know that a copy of my book is already covered with corrections and changes. I would like at some point to have got it right, and to have cut what you and Monti do not like; but I have no hope of it. You say in your role as Teacher that translating is most useful at my age; this is certainly so, and something experience makes very clear to me. Because when I have read some Classic, my mind is in a frenzy and becomes confused. Then I set about translating the best, and those beauties, of necessity examined and passed in review one by one, take their place in my mind, and enrich it and leave me in

[4] The two works are an essay on Marcus Cornelius Fronto and the *Saggio sopra gli errori popolari degli antichi.*

peace. Your judgment gives me heart and encourages me to carry on.

Do not talk to me about Recanati. I am so fond of it that it would furnish fine ideas for a treatise on Hatred of one's birthplace, for which, if Codrus was not *timidus mori*, I would be *timidissimus vivere*.[5] But my birthplace is Italy, for which I burn with love, thanking heaven for having made me an Italian, because after all our literature, little cultivated though it may be, is the only legitimate offspring of the two true ancient literatures, and you certainly would not want fate to have forced you to become great in French or German, and as you go deeper into the mysteries of our language you will feel sorry for the others, and for the writers who have to use them; as has happened very often to me, who know my language so much less well than you do. If I were forbidden to use it, even if I were given complete mastery of a foreign language, I think I would put aside any hope of becoming something in true literature, and I would give up my studies.

What you say about the good that the nobility could do for literature is very true, and I fervently wish that for once the reality may show it to be so. Your words fire me and flatter me; but I do not think I will be able to conquer my own nature and other people's. Nonetheless you can be certain that if I live, I shall live for Literature; I do not want to (nor could I) live for anything else.

But your book gives me great hopes for literature:[6] it is a gift as welcome to me as a new work by Boccaccio or Della Casa would have been, and all the more so because you have always been ungenerous towards the public with your writings, to our great loss and no loss to you. I have already begun to read it, and I cannot believe that with these examples in front of them young Italians should choose to go on writing badly. In any event much has been gained, and no one now would wish to return to the middle or the end of the eighteenth century. From your other writings I had deduced the delicacy of your heart and the very rare refinement of your temperament: but in these, and in your precious letters, I see them delightfully depicted. I say nothing of the accomplishment of the writing, because these things seem sacred to me and not to be profaned by talking about them when it is not appropriate.

I have chattered so much that I will have made you feel sleepy. Your letters have given me heart. I have seen that you are a gentleman who can put up with me, and also take on the task of teaching me. And so that you can see how much I trust in your kindness, I have written to Stella asking him to send you a manuscript of mine.[7] I would like you to scrutinise it, and first of all tell me if you think it good for the flames, to which I would cheerfully consign it at once. It is very short, but I do not want you to wear yourself out by reading it, much less by replying to me. My heart will leap up every time I receive a letter from you, but the expectation and the knowledge that you have written in your own good time will increase my pleasure. With all my soul please believe me, and give me an opportunity of showing myself to be, your true and most affectionate servant,

Giacomo Leopardi.

[5] *afraid to die; very afraid to live.*

[6] Giordani had sent him a copy of his book *Alcune prose di* P. Giordani, Milano 1817.

[7] The manuscript contained the poem *Appressamento della morte* (The Approach of Death).

3

Moved by Giordani's continuing interest and concern, Leopardi unburdened himself in a long letter in which for the first time he talked directly about his frustration and his sense of isolation living in Recanati. Giordani was still unaware of the true state of his health and of his family's impoverished circumstances.

To Pietro Giordani • Milan

Recanati, 30th April 1817

Oh how many times, my dearest and eagerly-awaited Mr Giordani, have I entreated heaven that it should make me find a man outstanding in heart, in mind, in learning, so that, having found him, I might ask him to deign to concede me his friendship. And in truth I thought my wish would not be granted, because I scarcely thought it possible that these three things, each so seldom found on its own, could all exist together. Oh blessed be God (and I say it straight from the heart) who has granted me what I asked, and made me recognize my error. And so I beg you, let there henceforth be between us utter and complete intimacy, yet respectful on my side as is fitting in a younger person, and on your side entirely without constraint. You urge moderation in my studies with such warmth and as a matter of such concern to you, that I wish I could show you my heart, so that you might see the feelings roused in it by reading your words: words which, unless my heart changes form and substance, will never perish, no not ever. And to reply as best I can to such affection, I shall tell you that in truth my constitution is not weak, but very weak, and I will not deny that it has suffered a little from the labours I have subjected it to for six years. Now however I have greatly moderated them; I study no more than six hours a day, very often less, I write almost nothing, I do my limited reading of the Classics in all three languages in small format volumes which can comfortably be carried in the hand, so that I almost always study in the Peripatetic manner, and, *quod maximum dictu est*,[1] I often tolerate for many, many hours the horrible torture of remaining idle. O who would ever have thought that Giordani would take up the defence of Recanati? O my dearest Mr Giordani, this calls to mind the *si Pergama dextrâ*.[2] The cause is so desperate that a good advocate will not suffice, nor would a hundred. It is all very well to say: Plutarch and Alfieri loved Cheronea and Asti. They loved them and did not live in them. In this fashion I shall love my birthplace too when I am far away from it; now I say I hate it because I am in it, for after all this poor city is guilty of nothing except not having done me one good thing in the world, starting with my family. Remembering the place where one passed one's childhood is a very fine and sweet thing. It is a very fine thing to say, here you were born, providence wants you here; say to a sick man: if you try to get better, you are quarrelling with providence; say to a poor man: if you try to improve your lot, you are opposing providence; say to a Turk: do not take it into your head to get baptized, for providence made you a Turk. This axiom is

[1] *to cap it all.*

[2] *Aeneid* II, 291-2: '*if by one hand our towers* could be defended, by this hand, by my own, they would have been.'

a flesh-and-blood sister of Fatalism. But here you are in the first rank, in a bigger city you would be in the fourth or fifth. This seems to me basest arrogance, and quite unworthy of a great soul. With virtue and intelligence one wants to stand out, and who will deny that in big cities these qualities shine out infinitely more brightly than in small cities? To want to stand out on account of one's wealth, and to be content with foregoing countless pleasures (I do not say pleasures of the body, which do not concern me, but of the mind) out of love of being in charge and in order to be at centre stage, this seems to me something worthy of a barbaric age, and such as to make me howl and grow wild. But here you can be more useful than anywhere else. Firstly, I do not choose to give my life for these few people, nor to give up everything to live and die for their benefit in an animal's lair. I do not believe nature made me for this, nor that virtue wants from me such a terrifying sacrifice. In the second place, whatever are you thinking? That the March and the south of the Roman State is like Romagna and northern Italy? There, the word literature is heard very frequently: there, there are newspapers, academies, salons, booksellers in very great numbers. The Gentlemen read a little. The ignorance is in the common people; otherwise they would not be the common people any more; but very many people do their best to study, very many think of themselves as poets, philosophers, whatever. They are anything but, yet that is what they would like to be. Almost all of them think themselves well able to judge in literary matters. The mad judgments they pronounce arouse rivalry, make people argue, talk, and laugh about literary studies. A great mind makes its own way: there are those who admire and respect it, and those who envy it and would like to crush it, there is a crowd that makes room for it and knows what it is doing. There, promoting literature is a useful occupation, dominating with one's intelligence is the goal of a fine ambition. Here, my dear Sir, everything is senselessness and stupidity. Outsiders are amazed at this silence, this universal sleep. Literature is a word not heard. The names of Parini, Alfieri, Monti, Tasso and Ariosto and all the others need to be explained. There is not one person who cares about being something, not one to whom the name ignoramus seems strange. They say it about themselves in all sincerity and they know they are speaking the truth. Do you think that a great mind would be appreciated here? Like a jewel in a dung heap. You were quite right to say (and you know where) that the rarer literary studies are the less they are held in esteem, because the less their value is recognized. That is precisely what happens in Recanati and in these provinces where intelligence is not counted among nature's gifts. I am certainly no great thing: but yet I have a few friends in Milan, I subscribe to Journals, I order books, I have the odd thing of mine printed: no other citizen of Recanati has ever done any of this *a Recineto condito*.[3] You would think that many people must be around me, requesting journals, wanting to read my bits and pieces, asking me for information about the men of letters of our age. Not at all. When the Journals have been read in my family, they go to sleep on the bookshelves. Nobody has any interest in my things, and that is fine; but it is much less so with other books: indeed I shall tell you without conceit that our library has no equal in the province, and there are only two others which are less good. Over the door is written that it was created for the townsfolk too and in theory it is open

[3] *since the founding of the city.*

to everyone.[4] Now how many people do you think make use of it? Nobody, ever. Oh, just observe if this is terrain which can be cultivated. And as for studying, do you think it can be done properly here? I will not say that with the whole library I very often do not have books, not just books I would like to read, but books which are supposedly indispensable; and so do not be amazed if you sometimes become aware that I do not have some Classic. If one wants to read a book one does not have, if one wants to see it even just for a moment, one must obtain it at one's own expense, have it sent from far away, without being able to choose or know before buying, with a thousand difficulties along the way. Here no one else sends for books, it is impossible to borrow, you cannot go to a bookseller, pick up a book, see what you are after and put it back down: so there is no sharing of expense, it all falls on us. One is continually spending on books, but there is no end to the spending, getting hold of everything is a desperate business. But not having a man of letters to talk to, keeping all one's thoughts to oneself, not being able to air and discuss one's opinions, innocently show off one's studies, ask for help and advice, take heart in the many hours and days of exhaustion and listlessness – do you think all this is a fine diversion? To start with I had a head full of modern maxims, I scorned, or rather spurned, the study of our language, all my own original scribblings were translations from French, I scorned Homer, Dante, all the Classics, I would not read them, I wallowed in the reading I now detest: who caused me to change my tune? The grace of God, but certainly no man. Who guided me in learning the languages I needed? The grace of God. Who ensures that I do not make some blunder at every turn? No one. But suppose that all this is nothing. What is there in Recanati that is beautiful? that a man might care about seeing or learning? nothing. Now God made this world of ours so beautiful, men have made so many fine things, there are so many men that anyone who is not senseless yearns to see and to know, the world is full of wonders, and at eighteen years of age am I to say, I shall live and die in this den where I was born? Do you think that these desires can be curbed? that they are unfair, excessive, insatiable? that it is a folly not to be satisfied with seeing nothing, not to be satisfied with Recanati? You have been misinformed that the air of this city is salubrious. It is very changeable, damp, salty, hard on the nerves and no good at all for certain constitutions on account of its thinness. Add to all this the stubborn, black, horrendous, barbarous melancholy that eats into me and devours me, and feeds on studying, and increases if I do not study. I do know (and I have felt, but now no longer feel) what that sweet melancholy is that brings forth beautiful things, sweeter than cheerfulness; it is, if I may be permitted to put it this way, like twilight, whereas this is thickest horrible night, it is a poison, as you say, which destroys strength of body and of spirit. Now how am I to get free of it, if all I do is think and live on thoughts, without a distraction in the world? and how make the effects stop, if the cause continues? What is this talk of distractions? The only distraction in Recanati is study: the only distraction is the thing that is killing me: all the rest is tedium. I know that tedium can do me less harm than exhaustion, and so often I settle for tedium, but this increases my melancholy, as is natural, and when I have had the misfortune of talking to these people,

4 The inscription over the library door reads: *Filiis amicis civibus Monaldus de Leopardis Bibliothecam A. MDCCCXII.*

which seldom happens, I go back to my studies full of gloomiest thoughts, and I go brooding and ruminating on that blackest of subjects. It is not in my power to remedy this, nor to prevent my frail health from being destroyed, unless I leave the place which caused the illness and which foments it and increases it more every day, and which allows no recreation to someone who thinks. I see clearly that to be able to continue my studies I must break them off at once and give myself a little to those things they call worldly, but to do this I want a world that entices me and smiles at me, a world that shines, even if it is with a false light, a world strong enough to make me forget for a few moments what is above all close to my heart, not a world that makes me recoil at once, that turns my stomach, enrages me and saddens me and forces me to run back for comfort to the very thing from which I wanted to escape. But you know very well that I am right, and your second letter shows me that you do; in it you urged me of your own accord to make a tour of Italy, although later (and I know very well why), with admirable intentions for which I am very grateful, you chose to speak to me in a different manner.[5] And so I have chattered on at length to show you that what you hold to be quite certain I too hold to be quite certain.

I shall tell you honestly, since you ask me, how heaven (which I thank from my heart for it) led me to hear about you and to want you to know that I had. Poor Marquess Benedetto Mosca (whom I know you loved), a cousin of my father's, came one day to pay a brief visit to his relatives, and on that one occasion we two spoke together, I say spoke, because when I was little and he was a child we had romped together here in Recanati for a long time, and I must have prattled to him then. Afterwards I did not see him again, but I know that he liked me and wanted to see me again, and perhaps we would have seen each other again soon, been in touch by letter certainly, because I was writing one to him which would have been the first, when I learned of his death, and I cannot think of this death, which cut short so much, without anguish and turmoil of spirit. The only thing he told me about you was this: that he knew and, if I am not mistaken, had been taught by Giordani, who, he added (and I am repeating his very words, and your modesty must put up with it this once), is now *the leading writer in Italy*. Just imagine if the leading writers in Italy were known in Recanati. I was then 15 years old, and was engaged in ambitious studies, Grammars, Greek and Hebrew Dictionaries and suchlike, tedious but necessary. I paid no attention to it at all. But at the beginning of last year, seeing your name at the foot of the circular for the *Biblioteca Italiana*,[6] I remembered those words, and when I received the small volumes of the *Biblioteca* I knew which were your articles, first by guesswork and then with certainty as regards one or two of them, and that was enough for me then to recognize them all. Now what can I say? If I tell you that they gave stability and strength to my conversion which was just getting under way,[7] that once I had tasted that food the other modern things that earlier had seemed delicious to me now seemed disgusting, that I waited for the *Biblioteca* with infinite longing, and when I received it I read it as greedily as a starving man, that I must have read and reread your articles ten or so times, that now that there are no more of them I have an urge to throw away the issues of that journal,

[5] Giordani's letter had been phrased diplomatically in order not to alarm Count Monaldo.

[6] A Milanese periodical.

[7] The conversion from scholarship to literature, described in more detail at the beginning of the next letter.

every time I receive them and find nothing in them for me, your modesty will be provoked. I will confess frankly that I only know the titles, and of only two of your works, I mean the translation of Juvenal and the *Panegyric*, and with equal frankness I will tell you that I was thinking of getting hold of something of yours, when I received from you (and I am truly most grateful for them) your prose works which are pure gold; I have some things to say about them, but because those things are certainly of no great value and this letter is already very long and looks as if it is going to be very long indeed, I shall save them for another time.

I am delighted to see that in your very kind letter of the 15th of April you get down to talking about my studies. I shall answer whatever you write me, telling you honestly when your opinions have come into conflict in my mind with different opinions, so that you can see how much I need you really to act as my teacher, and, taking pity on the weakness and insignificance of my thoughts, set about making good the deficiences. Propriety of concepts and expression is exactly what distinguishes a Classical writer from a second-rate one (and the richer the language is, the more difficult it is to observe propriety in expression): this is a truth so obvious that it was the first one I became aware of when I began thinking seriously about literature; and after this I readily saw that the quickest and surest way of achieving this propriety was to translate good writers from one language into another. But that, when the intellect has reached a certain solidity and maturity, one must of necessity compose first in prose and then in verse, in order to know with some certainty in what direction nature is calling it – I tell you frankly that this did not seem to me to be the case. Speaking of myself I may be deceived, but I shall tell you, as I perceive it, what happened and is happening to me. Since I began to be a little acquainted with beauty, poets alone have given me that warmth and that burning desire to translate and to make what I read my own; and nature and passions alone have given me that most violent longing to compose, but in a strong and elevated manner, causing my soul as it were to grow huge in all its parts, and to say to myself: this is poetry, and to express what I feel verse is needed, not prose, and to set about writing verses. Won't you allow me to read Homer, Virgil, Dante and the other great poets now? I do not know if I could stop myself doing so, because reading them I feel a pleasure that cannot be expressed in words, and it very often happens that I am sitting quietly and thinking of something quite different and I hear some line of poetry by a classical author that some member of my family recites by chance, and instantly I am trembling and I find I am forced to attend to that poem. And yet it has happened to me that I have found myself alone in my study with my mind calm and free, at an hour very friendly to the muses, and picked up Cicero, and reading him felt my mind make such efforts to raise itself, and been tormented by the slowness and heaviness of that prose, so that even though I wanted to carry on reading I could not, and I started on Horace. And if you allow me to read them, how can you expect me to know those great poets and taste them and savour them and consider their beauties one by one, and then restrain myself from rushing after them? When I see nature in these places that really are lovely (the only good thing my birthplace has) and especially at this time of year, I feel myself so carried away, that I would think it a mortal sin to be indifferent to it, and to let this youthful ardour pass, and to want to become a good prose writer, and to wait twenty years or so to give myself to poetry, after which, firstly, I will not be alive, and second, these thoughts will have gone; and my mind will be colder or certainly less warm than it is now. I do not mean that in my view, if nature calls you to poetry, you have to follow without having any other interests, on the contrary I hold it to be quite certain and self-evident that poetry requires infinite study and labour, and that the art of poetry is so deep that the further ahead one gets the more one recognises that perfection is in a place one did not even think of in the beginning. Only I think that art should not stifle nature, and I think that advancing by degrees and wanting to be first a good prose writer and then a poet is against nature; on the contrary, nature first makes you a poet and then with the cooling of age grants the maturity and composure necessary for prose. Don't you allow anything at all to Horace's *mens divinior*?[8] If you do, how can you expect it to stay hidden and its owner not to be aware of it in the ardour of youth, when he sees nature, when he reads poets? and once he has become aware of it, how could he possibly hesitate and let time pass and want first to become a good prose writer, and then attempt poetry in the way you say, insecurely as it were and fearfully. Or do you think the 'divine soul' is a fairy tale or that the species has died out? and then which is the true poet? The person who has studied most? And why are all those who have studied, and who are highly intelligent, not poets? I do not think it is possible to cite a case of a true poet who did not begin to write poetry as a youth; or that many poets can be cited who achieved distinction in prose as well, and of these few I think it is true that they were poets first and prose writers later. And in fact it seemed to me that in words and language it was much more difficult in prose than in poetry to preserve that propriety without affectation and with complete fluency and naturalness, because in prose affectation and effort stick out like a buffalo in the snow, as the Florentines say, and in poetry they are less visible, firstly, because very many things which are affectations and seem forced in prose are not so in poetry, and very few that are not so in prose are so in poetry; secondly, because even those which really are affectations in poetry are easily hidden by the harmony and the poetic language, so that they are barely glimpsed. Certainly when I translate verse, I easily manage (even doing everything I can to preserve the force the expressions have in the text) to give an original air to the translation, and to disguise the effort; but when I translate into prose, to achieve this I work infinitely harder, and in the end I probably do not achieve it. So I had reached the conclusion that to translate poetry takes a great and poetic spirit and thousands of other things, but to translate into prose requires more practice and much more reading, and perhaps also (and I think this is absolutely necessary) a few years living where people speak correctly, a few years living in Florence. And similarly in writing poetry, if I want to follow Dante, perhaps I will manage to make his language my own and to clothe my thoughts in it and to write lines of which it is not possible to say, at least not so immediately, this is imitation, but if I want to set out to emulate a letter of Caro's, the same will not be true. Please, Mr Giordani, do not think me foolhardy, because I have told you what I felt so frankly and with so little concern for my own insignificance. Do not be disdainful of convincing me. It will be a small task in itself, but it will be an act of charity, and worthy of your fine heart.

About my Cantica,[9] and the affinity between Greek and Italian, and the very useful advice you give me (and which I will soon put into practice) to read and translate Herodotus and

[8] Horace, *Satires* I, iv, 43: *soul divine.*

[9] *Appressamento della morte*, see [2], n. 7.

the other three,[10] I would have a thousand things to say, but seeing to my dismay that this letter goes on for ever, and feeling very, very shamefaced at my boundless tactlessness, I leave them to another occasion; I hasten to say that I would thank you, if I could find the words, for examining my Cantica, and that there is no need to return the manuscript to Stella, who has no need of it, but if you think there is some friend of yours there who might not disdain to look at it, you can give it or not as you think best; that I have seen only the title of Cesari's *Terenzio*,[11] and that I would like to know if you think Cicognara's work might be useful to me,[12] because I do not bother now to read or see anything except what can be really useful, because time is short and the harvest immense.

As for the Belcari, I am making a great effort to find you subscribers and to show you how very eager I am to be of service to you as best I can.[13] I am writing and having other people write to Macerata, Tolentino, Rome and other places, warmly recommending the project. However I hear that many people are asking about the price, and I would like you to give me a rough idea of it. I will do what is possible, but I am very sorry to say that I have no great hopes: because as far as lovers of good language [*buona lingua*] are concerned, if I spoke to anyone here about it, they would think it was a question of some fine pig's tongue [*brava lingua di porco*];[14] and as for the pious people you say will prefer to read something well written rather than something ill written, this I venture to tell you is not true. For all my lack of years, I have a great deal of experience of pious people,[15] and I know that on the contrary they are singularly attached to books that turn our stomachs, first on account of a special taste they have, which experience has taught me does really exist and is not a fairy-tale; and then because the poor things are not quite up to certain concepts that are not really elevated but are not utterly pedestrian either, lastly (and this reason is all-powerful) because if the language has anything about it at all that is not commonplace, it is as though the book were written in Hebrew, since no pious person understands what 'Dantesque' is, because you must understand that here everything which is not broth, or even if it *is* broth is not too watered down,[16] is called Dantesque; so that Salvini, for example, is Dantesque; Segneri, Bartoli,[17] and all those who are not bad are Dantesque, and as well as those who are not bad, even my translation of Virgil. And these are not just the opinions of the common people, but of the very learned and the very literary, so much so that in the capital of our *molto excellentissima et magnifica provintia*, there is one important man of letters in whose writings the

[10] Giordani had urged him to read Herodotus, Thucydides, Xenophon and Demosthenes.

[11] Antonio Cesari (1760–1828), *Le sei commedie di Terenzio recate in volgare fiorentino* (Verona, Merlo, 1816).

[12] Leopoldo Cicognara (1767-1834), author of a *Storia della scultura* (Venezia, Picotti, 1813-1818).

[13] Giordani had asked him to find subscribers for the *Vita del Beato Giovanni Colombini da Siena fondatore de' poveri Gesuati* by Feo Belcari (1410-1484); it was to be reprinted in Verona that year, and would be of special interest to devout or pious readers.

[14] There is a play on words between the two meanings of *lingua*.

[15] Notably, of course, his mother.

[16] Leopardi is playing on an Italian idiom, in terms of which broth (in comparison with the meat from which it is made) is already not worth much, and watered-down broth is worth even less.

[17] Anton Maria Salvini (1653-1729); Paolo Segneri (1624-1694); Daniello Bartoli (1608-1685).

form *e'* is the only trace of Tuscan, who when he happens to use *mi pare* unfailingly attaches it to *e'*, and everybody says of his style that it is too exquisite, to which he modestly replies that yes, sixteenth-century style is a fine style. Here I really do recommend you to keep a tight hold on your sides if you don't want to die laughing like Margutte.[18] But as they believe Belcari and Scaramelli and Ligorio[19] are similar sorts of thing, then until the book appears *e'* will go down very well. That is enough: I shall do what I can, and the same goes for the Palcani;[20] I read it with real pleasure as something you liked and that comes from you; it has an elegance which is certainly very rare in scientific subjects, which would be truly enjoyable treated in this way, whereas now they are bristly and horrible.

My father thanks you for your good wishes, and warmly reciprocates. And what can I say to you, my dear Mr Giordani, to comfort you for the misfortune that afflicts you?[21] except that I suffer it too and that I pray to God that he make you as happy as it is possible to be in this world? I cannot give you any comfort with my beggar's eloquence. Your great learning and true philosophy will give it to you surely and abundantly. Do not think of writing to me (if you wish to continue doing me this favour) except in your leisure moments, and even then only when it is convenient. In short give no more thought to it than to things of no consequence, because if I see you doing otherwise, I shan't write to you, and so I shall be deprived of this pleasure too. In truth it would distress me greatly if you chose to stand on ceremony, in the first place with me, and then in something which does not merit it, indeed does not call for it.

How shall I set about asking your forgiveness, Mr Giordani, for having written you a tome instead of a letter? I am really blushing and do not know what to say, and nonetheless I ask your forgiveness. Your third letter had aroused a maelstrom of thoughts in my mind, your fourth doubled it. I delayed answering in order not to trouble you so often, but once I had picked up the pen I could not hold back any longer. I have answered a scant page of your thoughts with a sheaf of mine. This is the first time I have opened my heart to you: how was I to check the flood of my thoughts? Another time I shall be briefer, much briefer. I would not want you to be irritated by my being so tactless: certainly anger would be quite justified, but I trust in the goodness of your heart. Forgive me again, my dear Sir, and know that you are always in the thoughts of your most eager servant,

Giacomo Leopardi.

[18] The character in Pulci's *Morgante* who died laughing.

[19] Feo Belcari (see note 13); Giovanni Battista Scaramelli (1687–1752); Alfonso Maria de' Liguori (1696–1787; canonised in 1839).

[20] Luigi Palcani (1753–1802); Giordani had sent a copy of Palcani's *Le prose italiane* (Milano, Silvestri, 1817) with a preface by himself.

[21] Giordani's father had recently died.

4

Leopardi had written a 'Hymn to Neptune' and passed it off as a translation of an authentic classical text newly come to light. This letter explained his motives for doing so in the context of his recent 'conversion' from scholarship to literature.

To Pietro Giordani • Milan

[Recanati, 30th May 1817]

My dear Sir. The erudition you found in the notes to the *Hymn to Neptune* is in truth very commonplace, and I thought it appropriate to write those notes in Italy, but in Germany or in England I would have been ashamed to.[1] For a time I searched out the most arcane and recondite erudition, and from thirteen years of age to seventeen I was deeply immersed in these studies, with the result that I have written six or seven volumes (and not small ones) on learned subjects, and this labour is the very thing that has been my ruin; and a certain foreign man of letters who is in Rome and whom I do not know, on seeing some of my writings, was not disapproving of them, and urged that I should become, as he put it, a great philologist.[2] For a year and a half now, almost without realizing it, I have devoted myself to literature, which earlier was of no interest to me, and all the things of mine you have seen, and others you have not seen, have been done in this time, so that, having always looked after the branches, I have not been like the oak-tree which *A vieppiù radicarsi il succo gira, Per poi schernir d'Austro e di Borea l'onte*;[3] I have now turned all my attention to doing this. And so I wrote the *Hymn*, and the notes and the rest, a year ago: in recent months I could not have stood the strain. From this you will see, if you have not done so already, that the story I spread about the discovery of the *Hymn* is invented. Being in love with Greek poetry, I wanted to do as Michelangelo did when he dug up his Cupid, and then produced the missing arm for those who thought it was an ancient statue unearthed. And I was forgetting that he was Michelangelo and I am Calandrino;[4] as well as the fact that the strict need to imitate, or (better) to copy and remove from the composition its air of robust originality (so that, like a very fine veil, or rather a net placed over the imaginary text, it leaves all its muscles and features visible, and in short leaves it almost naked in order to deceive), so clogged and slowed down my mind that no doubt what I have produced is anything but poetry. I would dearly like to know what you think of the *Hymn* and the two *Odes*,[5] and what people there

1 The *Hymn to Neptune* had been published on May 1st in the *Spettatore Italiano* (a Milanese periodical edited by Antonio Fortunato Stella) with extensive notes.

2 The foreign philologist was the Swede D. G. Akerblad (1763-1819), who died before Leopardi was able to meet him.

3 *by dint of sending its roots deeper, circulates its sap, so that it then scorns the buffettings of North and South winds.* The lines come from Alfieri's sonnet *Già dell'ali sue calde il franco volo*, in V. Alfieri, *Opere*, XXII (Piacenza, Maino, 1811), p. 365.

4 Calandrino is the foolish character who thinks he is clever in Boccaccio's *Decameron*.

5 The *Odae adespotae* which he had written at the same time as the *Hymn to Neptune*.

think of them, because it is part of my luck to have my things printed and never know what is said about them, whether they are liked or not liked, whether they are judged to be mediocre or dreadful, so that for me a book of mine in print exists as though it were still in manuscript, except that the manuscript is free of errors, and the printed version is swarming with them, because at this distance I cannot supervise the printing. And in truth the 54 blunders they have adorned my little book with have made me blush for my poor honour, and made me feel quite sick. I would never have given my manuscript to Stella for him to crucify among all those foul things in his journal, if he had not promised me plainly that he would have another separate edition of it done at the same time; nothing will come of it. But while there is doubt, then so that he suffers no harm because of me, if the deception is common knowledge there (as I believe it is, for these tricks have a stale air and do not work any more) there is no need to do anything; if it is not, I would ask you kindly not to reveal it for the time being, which will be easy for you because no one will be interested in talking about that wretched thing. [...][6]

I ought not to want you to get to know me in person, because you will surely find me much less than you perhaps think; but I love you so truly and greatly that just the thought that next year I will see you and speak to you, if the hope you have given me does not prove vain, is driving me crazy. And equally I ought not to want a person I love so much to come looking for boredom and nausea on my account, yet all these considerations cannot stop me from wanting it fervently, and indeed I earnestly entreat you to put your charitable plan into effect. I'll take care of finding board and lodging for you, and I think that as far as the *friendliness* of your hosts is concerned you will not do badly, and as for *cleanliness* they will do their best.[7] Do not disappoint us, my dear Sir, and do not cheat my expectation and my father's; he sends his regards, and is very eager to see you.

If the word teacher makes you feel so uncomfortable, as you say, I shan't use it any more. I meant Counsellor and guide in my studies, and I hope you will not refuse to act this part for me, even if you reject the title. I am very distressed when I think that perhaps I turned your stomach by attributing the Juvenal translation to you. But not having read it or even seen it, I could not know that it was unworthy of you, and my memory tricked me about the author's name. So please consider me excused. Is the translation by Luigi Uberto Giordani by any chance? A letter of his that I have seen on the Book of Job seemed to me very fine and well-judged. I am certainly curious, or rather very, very keen, to see his *Panegyric* and his other things, if you have any of them. I do not know whether they are so bulky that they cannot be sent by post. If they are, then should you wish to make me such a splendid gift, you can hand them to Stella for him to send me along with other things I shall order from him.

When I said that Cicero, once my mind was so disposed as to desire intense and strong impressions (as happens), seemed to me (and this was in a philosophical treatise) slower and heavier than suited my desire at that moment, I did not mean that he and other great prose writers make me feel cold and slow. This would be a great misfortune or more truly stupidity.

[6] A list of misprints follows.

[7] Giordani had said in his previous letter that the only two things he required as a guest were *amorevolezza* and *nettezza*.

Though perhaps by natural inclination I am more drawn to poetry, yet I read and study prose writers as I can, and in reading them I am not forcing myself, but I feel an infinite and most exquisite pleasure. And although I believe one should not try to excel in many genres, this does not mean I think that even though I cultivate poetry, I must leave prose to one side, because it would be a very poor man of letters who could write nothing but verse. And therefore I try to cultivate both kinds of writing together, and with almost equal care. What I prattled about in my last letter à propos of Horace's *divine soul* I later thought might (because of the way I put it) have aroused your anger, and, quite justifiably, your revulsion. It is true that until then I had spoken about myself in particular, but there I was making a general point, because my mind has as much to do with what Horace meant and wanted as chalk with cheese and night with day. After you pointed out to me the affinity between our language and Greek, I began to reflect on it seriously, and I opened a few Greek prose writers, and found to my very great pleasure that your comment is quite true and worthy of a master, so much so that some passages in fourteenth-century authors seemed to me like a translation from the Greek. It is no wonder that I had not been aware of this very obvious relationship earlier (and without your pointing it out my intellect probably never would have become aware of it) because until now I have tended to have sixteenth-century prose writers and others to hand rather than fourteenth-century ones. As soon as I have managed to store up in my mind a little of their manner, which I think has the same purity and sweetness, I want to act immediately on the advice you gave me to make a point of studying and translating some of the oldest Greek prose-writers, an activity I think should be singularly enjoyable and useful.

[...] Among your prose pieces I most especially liked the one on the paintings by Camuccini and Landi, in which I admired the extraordinary charm and delicacy, and that propriety and power so very necessary and so very difficult when describing a painting in words and putting it in front of one's eyes. It is a truly tremendous test, and one to frighten anyone less bold and able than you are, to set the arts of writing and painting so openly in competition with one another. And you succeeded wonderfully. In this exquisite piece of prose I found an opinion about which I would have something to say. You remind young painters as a general principle that where there is no pressing historical need one must never depict the ugly (and even when there is such a need, it must be done judiciously and decorously). Since, you add, the function of the fine arts is to multiply and perpetuate images of those more attractive or desirable things or actions which nature or men produce: and what counsel or what pleasure is there in increasing the number or duration of disagreeable things with which the world is already too well-supplied? My opinion would be that the function of the fine arts is to imitate nature in lifelikeness. And since abstract general precepts which are valid for painting must be valid for poetry as well, so, according to your judgment, Homer, Virgil and the other great writers must be thought to have gone wrong countless times, and Dante, who depicted the ugly so often, more than all of them. For what are tempests, deaths and a hundred thousand calamities if not disagreeable, indeed very painful? And the great poets have multiplied and perpetuated these countless images. And tragedy would have to be condemned almost entirely by its very nature. Certainly the arts should give enjoyment, but who can deny that weeping, trembling, being horrified are enjoyable when reading a poet? indeed who does not know that they are very enjoyable? Because the enjoyment comes precisely from wonder at seeing nature imitated so well, for what is non-existent or dead or distant seems to us alive and present. And so it happens that beauty which gives us only moderate pleasure when seen in nature, that is to say in reality, when seen in poetry or painting, that is to say as an image, gives us endless pleasure. And so the ugly imitated by art derives its capacity to give pleasure from this imitation. If a man is incredibly deformed, portraying his deformity would not be a wise decision, even though it is real, because the arts must persuade us and make us believe that the invented is real, and the unbelievable cannot be made believable. But if the deformity is lifelike, I think that seeing it portrayed naturally must be a source of no small pleasure. It goes without saying that it must be in the right place, because if it is out of place, as it must be in the painting you speak of, there is nothing further to discuss. I have said all of this to obey you, and so that you learn not to give me orders again in these matters. And if I have used bold and unseemly words, you are to reprimand me, as is your duty.

I was well aware of what you tell me about Florentines and Tuscans who are not illiterate, and I knew it not only from their writings, but also from other things. But I was intending to learn from the illiterate or rather to familiarize myself through them with the countless turns of phrase used in speech which very often go extremely well into written works, and that propriety and vividness which the common people naturally preserve so wonderfully in their words: thinking of what Plato says of the people having been and having to be Alcibiades' tutor in speaking well, and of the simple Athenian woman who recognised Theophrastes as a foreigner by the way he spoke, and of Varchi who says that even in his time to learn Florentine speech one had from time to time *to mix with the the scum of the common people* of Florence. But since you do not think that illiterate Florentines can teach me anything of value, I shall accept your judgment. And as for accent I shall tell you something about Recanati that you will have to take on trust from me: because it may be that I speak too harshly of my birthplace (and yet I am not sure if that is possible) out of too much hatred, but I certainly cannot speak too well of it out of too much love. You cannot imagine how attractive the pronunciation of this city is. It is so smooth and natural and so far from any trace of affectation that Tuscans I think, judging by the very little I have been able to observe speaking with some of them, speak in a much more affected way, and as for the Romans there is no comparison. Certainly the few outsiders who stay here acknowledge this and are amazed at it. And this pronunciation, which has nothing of Tuscan preciousness about it, or Roman arrogance, is so much Recanati's own that you only have to go two steps outside its territory to become aware of a noticeable difference, a difference which in a few places not very far from here is not just noticeable but very great. But what seems to me most worthy of comment is that our common speech is rich in pure Tuscan turns of phrase and sayings and proverbs, so much so that I am amazed when I find in writers a vast number of these expressions and idioms that I learned as a child. And I am no less amazed at hearing on the lips of peasants and the lowliest folk words that we do not use when we speak in order to avoid affectation, judging them to be appropriate only for writers, words such as *mentovato, ingombro, recare, ragionare* and many others, and some even more singular ones that I cannot call to mind. It will be my singular pleasure to point out these turns of phrase and these words, my dear Sir, if you fulfil the fine hope you have given me;[8] and this will be one of the very few or none-at-all things (forgive me this barbarous expression) that I shall be able to show you in Recanati. And it could very well be that, because I have never left my birthplace, what I think peculiar to Recanati is common to the whole of Italy or to many parts of the country, and then you would put me right.

With this hope, albeit remote, I leave you, my dearest Sir, and I hope I shall have no need to remind you that I am, with all my heart, your most devoted

Giacomo Leopardi.

Stella writes that he has received a package from you for me. If it contains as I hope some work of yours, thank you a million times over, and I promise you that by reading it at once I shall imagine that I am in your company, with you present and speaking, a thought that will be most agreeable to me.

[8] Giordani had promised to visit Recanati.

5

In anticipation of Giordani's visit Leopardi took the intiative in suggesting they might address each other in the more intimate 'Voi' form rather than the formal third-person 'Ella'.

To Pietro Giordani • Milan

Recanati, 20th June 1817

My dear Sir. Not much in this letter, because I shall write another one straight away in which I shall explain the comments I made on your book defending the *Dionysius.*[1] I plan to use it as the preface to my translation (à propos of which I say nothing, because I imagine that Mai, to whom I wrote about it, will have spoken to you), provided you give me explicit permission to do so and tell me with utter and perfect sincerity your opinion of it as regards both substance and style. I shall publish it just as I send it to you, except for what your judgment or my revisions may change, because haste in writing may well make me say many things that do not stand up in print. In that letter I shall address you as *Voi* (because the third person form of address seems to me stylistically very awkward), and I would always do so if I were not afraid you would not reciprocate, because in truth when I speak to you I would like to talk tête-à-tête and without there always being this 'Sir' between us listening to me. If you promise to do the same to me, I promise that where you are concerned I shall put an end to 'Sir'. I am convinced that friendship does not consist in this nonsense, but when one usage is more convenient and advantageous than another I think it should be preferred.

[1] Angelo Mai had published a fragmentary historical work by Dionysius of Halicarnassus; his edition had been criticised by Sebastiano Ciampi, and defended by Giordani. Leopardi had translated the work into Italian.

You can be quite sure that I listen to the advice you give me about looking after my health, and I set great store by it and follow it as much as I can. I hope we shall agree about the board and lodging. All you have to do is make up your mind to come and as soon as you can, something my father (who sends his regards) wants me to encourage you to do each time I write. I am glad to know that Luigi Uberto Giordani is a relative of yours. I have long considered him one of the small band, but in spite of asking many people I had never managed to find out anything about him.

In the other letter I hope to include your subscription card for the Belcari reprint, for which I have appointed eight searchers in different cities, and yet I am ashamed to think that having promised very little I will give you even less. But what can I say if some searchers have forgotten to search even in their own wallets? Yet I would not want you to stop making requests, because I hope that another time perhaps with no greater effort I shall have better luck. As the subscriptions are on several sheets I shall send you just a copy, keeping the originals to send to you or to Cesari, when you tell me you need them, and what I could do not to inconvenience Cesari by sending them through the post. Dear Mr Giordani, do carry on being fond of your very loving

Giacomo Leopardi.

6

Now using the 'Voi' form of address, Leopardi reported on the success of the 'Hymn to Neptune.'

To Pietro Giordani • Piacenza

Recanati, 14th July [1817]

Thank you for banishing 'Sir'. My dear Giordani, I love you most tenderly. I knew you were going to Piacenza, and do you know how? from the gazette, where I always cast my eye over the *Departures* looking for you. Nonetheless I'd thought it safer to send my views on the *Dionysius* to you in Milan,[1] as I did in a long letter together with the note of the Belcari subscribers, on the 11th of this month, a few minutes before receiving your letter of the 3rd. I'm sending this by the first post, but I doubt it will find you in Piacenza, because your letter, as you see, reached me late. I'd very much have liked you to read my other one immediately, but I see that you won't get it immediately. I haven't received the *Panegyric*, but don't be amazed, because here to receive a book from Milan other than by post, after it is sent, very often takes three or four months of preparation, never less than one. Well then, we'll have to wait a year before seeing you. My dear Giordani, if I were my own master, chains and iron bars wouldn't keep me from flying to you. But I'm like Mahomet's mountain: everything can move except it, and people must come to it. Hopes with no basis where I'm concerned, because apart from the fact that I'm not suitable terrain for this, please don't make of my life

[1] See [5], n. 1.

a more valuable asset than I do, who count each day as something gained. Adieu, my dear Giordani. Thinking of you is a great comfort to me in this (for various reasons, and for some time now) most unhappy and horrendous life of mine. *Di, meliora piis:*[2] a better life for my sweet friend Giordani!

Yours, Leopardi.

The *Hymn to Neptune* has done well in Rome where it least should have. They are doing all they can to find the Chamberlain, who out of fright immediately ran off and went to ground, and huddled down with me so that we have become one and the same person. And since there not everyone is up to reading, they think the Vatican supplied me with the hymn (when I deliberately said it was a small library with very few manuscripts) and the Librarian of the Vatican swears he will find out who removed it without his knowledge.

[2] Virgil, *Georgics* III, 513: *Heaven grant a happier lot to the good.*

7

Adopting the more intimate form of address seemed to unlock a new capacity for analysing his feelings, or perhaps a new willingness to share them (although on the matter of his low spirits he told Giordani 'there is no need for you to answer me on this point'). The account given here of his daily routine is a first disturbing intimation of the fragility of his health.

To Pietro Giordani • Venice

Recanati, 8th August [1817]

When a young man says he is unhappy, my dear friend, one usually imagines certain things that I would not want imagined about me, and especially not by Giordani, for whom alone I would wish to be virtuous even supposing there were no other witness and no other reward for virtue. So I want to tell you that although I desire many things, and passionately too, as is natural in young people, no desire has ever made me nor could make me unhappy, not even the desire for glory, for I am quite certain that I would laugh at infamy, if I had not deserved it, just as some time ago I began to feel contempt for other people's contempt, and don't imagine that there can be any lack of that. But it is the want of good health that makes me unhappy in the first place, because, apart from my not being the sort of philosopher who has no interest in life, I find myself forced to abstain from the thing I love, which is studying. Alas, my dear Giordani, what do you think I do now? Get up in the morning, and late, because now (a diabolical thing!) I like sleeping more than being awake. Then immediately set out walking, *and continue walking without* EVER *opening my mouth or seeing a book* until lunch time. After lunch, keep on walking in the same way until dinner: except that, often forcing myself and often breaking off and sometimes giving up altogether, I read for an hour. I live and have been living like this except for very brief intervals for six months. The other thing that makes me unhappy is thinking. I believe you know, but I hope you have not experienced, how thinking can torment and torture a person who thinks somewhat differently from other people, when it has him in its power, I mean when the person has nothing to amuse or distract him, or has only studying, which, because it fixes the mind and holds it still, does more harm than good. For a very long time thinking has given me and still gives me such torments, for this reason alone, that it has had me and has me entirely in its power (and I repeat, without my desiring it), that it has clearly harmed me and it will kill me if I don't change my situation first. Be quite certain that living as I do, I cannot enjoy myself more than I do, for I do not enjoy myself at all. In short, solitude isn't suited to those who burn and consume themselves all on their own. In recent days I've been much better (though anyone who is well, lapsing into this better, would think he had died) but it's the usual truce that has returned after a long absence, and already seems to be coming to an end, and this is how it will always be for as long as I remain in this state, and I have experienced this continuously now for six months and intermittently for two years. Nonetheless this truce had given me some hope of being able to refashion myself by changing my life. But life doesn't change, and the truce comes to an end, and I go back to being, or more truthfully I remain, what I was. Let's stop this idle talk, and there's no need for you to answer me on this subject; talking about it is tedious and above all exceedingly pointless.

I would dearly love you to define for me your *perfect Italian writer*,[1] because I am convinced that to become mediocre one must aim at excellence. But what wouldn't I like hearing about from you, especially concerning Literature, which I think about day and night, and I have no one to talk about it with, when all men naturally desire to talk about what matters to them, and often like me scorn all other talk. I think that if we see each other, I'll say nothing to you for a few days, from not knowing where to begin. You'll be lucky if I leave you room to eat and sleep, and don't beseige you continuously with my talking. I'm spending as much time as I can with fourteenth-century writers, in love with their writing, and it's not just that I understand, but I see and tangibly feel, that whereas Latin style carried over into Italian can only be very harsh, and (as we commonly say) all of a piece, Greek style adapts and accommodates itself to Italian, and is so soft, sweet, natural, easy, and quick, that in short it is in its right place and seems made deliberately for our language. And lo, at this point a flurry and frenzy of thoughts; I'd like to say: I'll save them for when we see each other. I have great sympathy for your difficulties and troubles. They are what the Greeks called *ἄϑλους*. This word is often on my lips, and I like it very much now that, if I were to endure an *ἆϑλος*, it would be my last. Except that it is also a terrible *ἆϑλος* to endure the days and the months in this way as I do. What Italian word would we use to translate this Greek word? *Travaglio* has the loathsomeness but not the greatness and vastness. Yet I daren't venture to assert that the word cannot be translated into Italian, so little do I trust my knowledge of this supreme immense all-powerful language of ours. I am sorry you have not received my letter about the *Dionysius*, only because in it, in order to clarify the question, I put forward some new comparisons; I would not want some foreigner to come up with them before Italians, nor for Visconti to think of them; I tell you frankly that I don't like him

[1] Giordani had said that Leopardi himself could be 'that perfect Italian writer I have in mind' [M65].

at all, because he seems to me to have forgotten Italy (leaving aside the fact that it is his birthplace, what does an antiquarian not owe it?), having abandoned not only the country but the language. You will tell me he writes his things in French so everybody can understand them. I reply that these things that are meant to be European should not be written in French or in Italian (as Visconti did when he was in Italy) but in Latin, and I'd put forward many proofs, but you know them already, and I don't want to be too long. I am sending back the note of the Belcari subscribers, but I'm sorry that you're getting it without my other letter, in which I entreated you once again to forgive me the modest number, which dwindled cruelly in my hands. Since in the meantime you have not had any thanks from me for your book on the *Dionysius*,[2] I'll tell you that I'm hugely beholden, and that I liked it enormously, with the result that I've read it through twice from beginning to end, and dipped into it on many other occasions, and that in my other letter I thanked you particularly for the trouble you took to send it to me as soon as it was published. My father sends his fond regards. And I embrace you and leave you, my dear Giordani. Let your heart tell you how much I love you. If it is not as much as you deserve, I think that is only because so much is not possible. Adieu, my dear and most gentle Giordani. Your good friend,

Leopardi.

[2] See [5], n. 1.

8

The unreliability and delays of the post increased his frustration and sense of isolation.

To Pietro Giordani • Piacenza

Recanati [29th August, 1817]

Dear, dearest, best-beloved Giordani. I'd sent two letters to you addressed to Venice before I received your letter of the 10th. Don't think that I could stay so long without writing to you. [...][1] I ended by begging you, as I beg you or rather entreat and command you, not to be miserable in any way on my account, for I'd willingly always be miserable in order for you to be always cheerful. As for my present affliction, I must be very brave and bear it, and as for the harm that may come of it, what's to be done? It's enough that it won't be my fault. You see that I cannot say I am healthy: but I make an effort to be cheerful for love of you. I have a great need for distractions, but I have none: alas, they would give me back health and life. Meanwhile the truce my afflictions have allowed me has not been brief. You be cheerful and love me, and that way I shall be cheerful too. I am cutting some things from the dissertation, adding others, and I am sending it to the *Spettatore*.[2] Tell me if I am doing the right thing or

[1] Here Leopardi gives a detailed précis of the two letters ([7] and another not included here), in case they have gone missing in the post.

[2] Stella's literary journal *Lo Spettatore Italiano*.

not. We'll laugh about Ciampi.[3] I don't know how one can make such a noise after being treated so well, whether he's right or not. What people! Let's keep to ourselves, dear Giordani, for there are very few of us in the world who have a good heart, and very few of you who have a good head. I am waiting with open arms for your *Panegyric*, which must have been sent three months ago. Another packet of books sent to me from Milan four months ago still has not arrived. I have no news about an order placed three months ago. In short one is living among animals and it's impossible even to find out what people are writing. Be assured that it's enough to make you despair. When you write to Mai and Cesari give them my warm regards. I'd like to see Mai's new works, I'd like to see Cesari's Lectures, but it's no use even ordering them. I'll read them in Milan, if God grants I ever get there. I may die in Recanati; I certainly shan't live here. My father sends his regards. Tell me if the article on Visconti's judgment in the *Spettatore* is really by you as I thought. I received your last letter after 15 days. Letters from Milan reach me in five. Perhaps it will be better if you address them directly to Recanati. Goodbye, dear Giordani. *Sufficit talem amicum habuisse.*[4] God preserve him for me, because any misfortune of his would be my death. Adieu adieu.

[3] Sebastiano Ciampi had criticised Mai, who had been defended by Giordani; see [5], n. 1.

[4] *It is enough to have had such a friend.*

9

Giordani's letters became a lifeline for Leopardi at times of despair: he was kept going only by 'my spirit and your letters.' In this letter he described his brother Carlo, one year younger than himself, who was later to become one of his most intimate correspondents when he was away from home.

To Pietro Giordani • Piacenza

Recanati, 26th September 1817

My dear friend. I'm replying to your letters of the 1st and the 9th. Our friend Mai has written to me with his usual courtesy. I've answered: but he won't have received the letter if he has set out on the trip you spoke of. It really is a fine habit the *Spettatore* has of altering other people's writings as they please. They have done me this service so many times that I've sworn never to let them have another syllable of mine; but because it is convenient to have a journal at one's disposal, as this one has been for me until now, I'm afraid I may go back on my word at some point. My health could be worse these days. There is absolutely no question of being able to get away from here. What is happening to you is what will happen to me if I ever see the world: being bored by it. Then perhaps I shan't dislike, and perhaps I shall even like, this retreat I loathe. And when I say world I mean this ordinary world, because perhaps if I wanted them I would not get them, but I certainly *don't* want titles or honours or positions; and God protect me from the prelacies they'd like to muzzle me with, God protect me from Giustinian and the *Digest*, which I couldn't digest for ever and ever.[1] I certainly don't want to live among the crowd; mediocrity scares me to death; but I want to raise myself and become great and immortal by intelligence and application; an arduous and perhaps futile enterprise for me, but men must not lose heart and despair of themselves. But if I allow you to be tired of the world, I won't allow you to be tired of or any less passionate about your studies, which I want you to pursue enthusiastically and passionately for my sake too, for in this cursed city I must get all my strength from my spirit and your letters. So don't speak to me of these things listlessly, for you dishearten me. There is no need to blame the shortage of books. You don't have to learn, but to let what you've learnt bear fruit. If you think I am in a good position where books are concerned, you're very much mistaken. If you knew that there are Classics I don't have! If I were to name one of them, you'd blush for me: and certainly when you come here you'll call me a blockhead. But my income is not enough to buy them: and I don't want to use other people's beyond a certain point. I think you'll be fully convinced that one isn't better off here than in Piacenza for government or anything else. This is the capital city of poor people and thieves: but there are no vices (except for thieving) because there are no virtues. Be so kind as to tell me at least the names of the distinguished men you have in your native city. Here we have seven thousand of them all distinguished for their patience in living in Recanati, which many nobles are losing. The women haven't got much more than what nature gave them, or do I mean they've got a little less, as can be said accurately of most of them? I don't think the graces have ever been here, not even stopping briefly at the inn. Among members of my household, which is not small, you can hear some real gems every day which are astounding. But I've got used to it and they don't hurt me any more. Except that now with these foul fevers around, I'm sometimes afraid they may play some trick on me and ruin my digestion: but I trust it will be as sound as it has always been, morally no less than physically. Of my many siblings I have one I have been brought up with since childhood (he being just one year younger than me) so that he is myself all over again, and will always be (along with you) the dearest thing I have in the world; and he has a most excellent heart; and ability and application about which I could say a great deal if it were my place to do so; he is my confidant in all things and shares my studies and reading a little; I say a little, because we disagree a great deal – not in our inclinations, for he loves the same studies as I do, but in our opinions. He loves you, as is natural, as anyone does who gets to know you in some way, and he is the one and only person to whom I open my mouth to talk about my studies; which we do often, and would do more often if we could do it without arguing; our disputes are brotherly but heated. I am terribly sorry about your *Panegyric*, which still hasn't arrived. People who are impatient, and who cannot bear to wait when they passionately want something, really ought to come here. I once had these faults myself, but I can tell you that this hell tames all strong feelings. The riding you recommend would certainly help me, and it is one of the few forms of exercise I could take; swimming and ball games and suchlike, which not long ago would have given me life, would kill me now, supposing I were able to try them, which is quite impossible. I could ride, I mean, if I had *many things* I do not have.

[1] His father and his uncle were encouraging the idea of an ecclesiastical career.

Dear Giordani, I am counting the days and the months I must pass before I see you. Meanwhile write to me often, as you do, to comfort me and cheer me up, and if you can, write a long letter. You cannot be short of subject matter, knowing how I long to hear you talk about the studies we love. But if your troubles still persist, write me a short one. Adieu, my dear friend. My father, who only had to read two or three of your pieces to love you forever, sends his regards. I embrace you with all my soul. Adieu.

I don't know if you know that in Rome they are preparing a magnificent reprint of Caro's *Aeneid*, paid for by the Princess of Wales. Tell me what you think of the Sonzogno edition, and if you had any hand in it. I'd barely written when the Rome gazettes arrived, and I see Devonshire instead of Wales, and the pointlessness of my giving you news that is already public. I see they're also promising to print the *Dittamondo* and Baldi's translation of Quintus Calabrus.

10

Not hearing from Giordani for any length of time caused acute distress.

To Pietro Giordani • Piacenza

Recanati, 21st November 1817

My dear, kind Giordani, I embrace you with all my heart and soul. What is this new way of beginning? Oh God! you don't know how I've suffered these last few days on your account. You can imagine why. From the day I last wrote to you, until I received your letters of the 1st and the 6th (which came together) I've been in a frightful state of anxiety, seeing no letter from you. In short, I thought about you the bitterest things it's possible to think about a person dearer than one's own life. I felt a heartache so painful that I don't remember ever having felt anything like it in my life. And because in recent months my health has been much better, as there are only two things that can take away my peace of mind (I mean my own ill health, and the misfortunes of those dear to me), I despaired lest, just as I was in some way emerging from the one unhappiness, I should plunge directly into the other, which weighed on me all the more heavily because in the former, if I did not have any relief, at least I *could* have some; but in the latter, if I had had any, I would have abandoned it, because every hint of relaxation caused me nausea and pain. To free myself from this torment, having written you three letters, and not being able to do anything else (for I would have done anything I could), I wrote an anguished letter to Mai, entreating him to give me news of you at once: I've had no reply because I wrote it for the post that crossed with the one that brought me your last letters. And perhaps Mai will laugh at me, and will call me a silly woman and a simpleton, and who knows if you won't do so too: but if you do, think that I am not like that and I have only been like that because of you. But couldn't I imagine what it was? couldn't I imagine that you'd gone to the country? I could and I did, but the thought was not enough. Forgive my love if I thought that even in the country you would not forget me and you'd write. And as for forgetting, I'm sure I was not mistaken: as for writing, I'm not complaining that you didn't do so: I can't complain except about this love of mine, which configures the most ordinary and natural things as very strange and wondrous. But if I can't complain about you, I won't complain about this, and equally I'm not complaining about the anguish I felt, because it was for you, and above all because it was groundless. Now God be blessed that you are mine: and in truth when I received your letters, I challenged all the misfortunes in the world to befall me and shake me up if they could. Because certainly I live with you always, and in my thoughts I'm with you, and I study in order to please you, and because of this wretched fear, I thought I no longer had any reason for studying, and thinking of the future I did not see how I could live, unless in a state like that of a soul divided from the body, which philosphers say is violent. So now that this anguish is over, I beg you for God's sake to think that I am no more I than I am you, so that there can be no misfortune of yours which is not mine in equal measure, and that if just the fear of it was able to do all this, it is impossible to say what the certainty might not do. So have some thought for one who loves you more than he loves himself, and if you do not want him to die, live, and if you do not want him to live very unhappily, live happily. I'm telling you this while I'm rational, because I wouldn't want to fall back into past distress.

Don't bother about settling the differences between my brother and me, because you wouldn't succeed. Let me tell you that this rogue won't hear of differences, and doesn't even admit that there really are any between us; you see how much in agreement we are. These disputes themselves can't be written down, because they're endless, and they spring up all day like mushrooms. All you need to know is that on Carlo's side the causes are: not much love for his country, not much for the ancients, a great deal for foreigners, a very great deal for the French. On my side, *you* tell *me*. As for the line of poetry you add, since I think you have not forgotten what I said about our brotherly love for one another, I consider no answer is required.

I thought from the style that the Caro dedication must be by you: that's why I asked. Nonetheless my conjecture was timid, and so I did not declare it. But now I see that I hit the mark, I consider myself worth something, and I wager that you wouldn't manage to conceal yourself from me in your writings. From what I heard, I wasn't convinced that the *Dittamondo* was much good: and I thought that no fourteenth-century poets, apart from the two supreme ones,[1] were good for anything except vocabulary.

We're so closely in agreement about my choice of state that we couldn't be more so.[2] I made up my mind a while back not to make up my mind until God knows when. As for love of glory, my precept is this: love glory: but, first, only true glory: and so not only do not accept undeserved (let alone insincere) praise, but reject it – not only do not love it, but loathe it; second, be quite sure that in this age you will be praised by very few people for doing good, and try always to please these few, leaving other people to please the crowd and be smothered in praise; third, pay no more attention to criticism, malicious talk, insults,

[1] Dante and Petrarch.

[2] A reference to his father's and uncle's desire that he should take holy orders with a view to a career in the church; see previous letter. Giordani's response had been one of approval of his refusal to do so.

ridicule, or unjust persecution than you do to things which do not exist; when it is justified, be distressed only at having deserved it; fourth, do not envy men greater and more famous than you, but respect and praise them as best you can, and love them sincerely and strongly besides. If these conditions are observed, the love of glory does not seem dangerous to me. *Κἀγὼ μὲν οὕτω πως ὑπείληφα.*[3] When you have time, tell me your opinion, and although I am young, think that to learn from and follow your teachings, I'll try hard to seem mature.

Not long before receiving your last letters, I had begun to read Tasso, and your advice about the prose works I should read was very timely, because his pedantries and sophistries were already putting me off. Thank you for it, and I shall make use of it.[4] Now I'm with Demosthenes, Cicero, Segneri and *your* Tasso. Fine and very delightful company, but we miss you. *Erit ne quum te videbo?*[5] I surely hope so: and if it were up to me, it would not be a question of hoping: but since now it is only up to you, I must be content with hoping. If you love me, think about cheering me up. My father and Carlo send their regards. Adieu adieu.

I know that you were to write one of those lives of famous Italians that are being published by Bettoni. Tell me if you've written it, and which one.

3 *That's roughly the way I see things anyway.*

4 Giordani had advised reading Tasso's letters, the *Dialogo del Padre di famiglia*, and the *Risposta di Roma a Plutarco* [M84].

5 *Will the day come when I shall see you?*

11

Leopardi's relationship with his father, which he here described to Giordani for the first time, was complicated by his extreme reluctance to ask him for money. His sensitivity to his fellow townsmen's patronising perception of him was already acute.

To Pietro Giordani • Piacenza

Recanati, 5th December [1817]

My dear friend. I replied to your two letters of the 1st and the 6th of November with a long letter, and now I'm replying to your other one of the 22nd. I spoke to you in my last letter about my big brother (not little brother as you call him: he is tall and burly enough to frighten me, whereas I am slight and sickly). All I can tell you about my present work, about which you ask, is that, as my health has taken a turn for the worse again, I'm reading my Classics, Greeks in the morning, Latins after lunch, Italians in the evening; and I think I'll go on like this for another year or so, not writing anything except for a few trifles I have in my head, and polishing two or three others that are already done, after which, when I've become very familiar with Greek and enriched myself with the gold of the Classics, I plan to enter the field with a grand translation (as grand as I can make it)[1] and then leave it to inclination and luck.

But this really is drawing up the bill without the inn-keeper, and would require that two things which in me are very inconstant (my health and my will) should change their nature. Last July, reading fourteenth-century writers made me want to write a treatise for which I had prepared and ordered and abandoned the material years ago. I wrote the beginning of it and then I put it aside till a more favourable time. If it had been possible for this letter to reach you before you left for Milan, I would have asked you to get Stella to give you a few copies of Book II of the *Aeneid* to give to some of your friends, warning them that it is an unpolished work, which the author has corrected and altered in countless places since it was printed, and in particular that he's abolished the whole of the very laboured preface. It is certainly the case that very few people know my name now, but these very few know nothing but those wretched things that are a cause of shame to me; and if something of mine is to be known, this is the only thing, imperfect as it is, that I care to have known. But so that everything may go as I wish, I can truly say that having it printed was of no use to me apart from my giving exactly and precisely three copies of it as gifts, since I count as nothing the fifty or so copies of it I've scattered among the worthless common people of the March and Rome. In short, it is completely unknown in your parts, and yet I see that people there are talking about a hundred other translations which in conscience I can't say are any better. And the result is that, as I don't have any literary contacts, I cannot by myself put any work into circulation (mine or anybody else's), not even by giving it away. And since for the reason I've explained I wasn't able to give it away, Stella, who had promised to take care of distributing that little book as though it were his own, leaves it sleeping undisturbed, as is natural and as I saw in a note he sent me. And may it sleep in peace, for it is better that I was not able to put you to this trouble.

You did exactly the right thing with the Arici.[2] I want you to know that I don't have tuppence to spend, but my father supplies me with everything I ask him for, and is eager and insists that I ask him for what I want. But when it's a choice between not having and asking, I choose not having, except when the requirements of my studies or my too-passionate desire to read some book compel me. And I say desire for some book, because I have never asked him for anything other than books, apart from just one and a half pairs of post horses, which he won't give me, because he's convinced of something I'm not convinced of, that is to say that I should act the gentleman in his house. But getting back to books, when an occasion arises spontaneously to ask for them, like the one you've just offered me, I feel no reluctance at doing so; and so every time you happen to use my name in this way, you'll be pleasing me (for I shall have another good book to read) and not displeasing my father at all. I'd willingly try to find you subscribers, if I could. I won't stop telling you that in truth these towns are sterile and difficult, but anyone else taking half the trouble I do could still get much more out of them than I could. In the end I'm a boy and I'm treated like a boy, I don't mean at home, where I'm treated like a child; but outside, anyone who knows anything about our family, on receiving a letter from me, and seeing this new Giacomo, if he doesn't

1 Probably the *Odyssey*; but see the opening lines of the next letter.

2 Cesare Arici (1782-1836) was the author of a volume (*Pastorizia*) for which Giordani had put down Leopardi's name as a subscriber.

mistake me for the soul of my grandfather dead these 35 years, who had the same name, takes me for one of the children of the household, and reckons that for him a grown man (even supposing he is a steward) to reply to me a lad is doing me a favour, and so fobs me off with two lines, one of which conveys his regards to my father. As for Recanati, there I'm considered what I am, just a boy and no more, and most people add: little know-all, philosopher, hermit, and goodness knows what. So that if I venture to encourage someone to buy a book, either they laugh at me by way of reply, or they get all serious and say that the time is past, that I'll see it myself in due course, that at my age they had this same mania for buying books, that it passed with the coming of sound judgment, that the same thing will happen to me: and then I, boy that I am, cannot raise my voice and shout: dolts, if you think I'm going to end up like you, you're completely wrong; I shan't stop loving books except when I lose my judgment, which you never had, and which you certainly didn't get when you stopped loving books. So you see, as well as the picture of my present happiness, how utterly incapable I am of doing anything useful for you and for literature in this respect and in others of this kind.

You can see how much I respect Arici by reading the awful piece of prose I used as preface to Hesiod's *Titanomachia*, published months ago in the *Spettatore*. Yet I'll tell you frankly that I don't feel any enthusiasm for that melancholy Epistle of his in the *Biblioteca Italiana*, all verses and imitation of Pindemonte, nor for his discourse on the Epic, as narrow-minded and wretched a thing as can be imagined, nor for his plan for an epic poem on a subject he's scraped up somewhere, which is of no great interest in itself, humanly speaking, and does not arouse any great enthusiasm, in my opinion, in someone reading the story. As for your articles on the *Pastorizia*, as well as a few others of the ones you've published in the *Biblioteca Italiana*, before I loved you as much as I love you now (for I loved you from the moment I knew you in your writings), I'd noted down a few small points that I'll write to you about or else tell you about, *si tanti*,[3] when we are together. I leave you, dear Giordani, embracing you with all my soul. Adieu adieu.

[3] *if it's worth the bother.*

12

Defending himself from Giordani's over-hasty reproaches,[1] *Leopardi revealed the care with which he chose the phrasing of his letters, and took his friend to task for misreading him. Giordani when he replied disarmingly acknowledged that he was at fault [see Introduction, p. 10].*

To Pietro Giordani • Milan

Recanati, 29th December 1817

As I've replied to your letter of the 13th, all I need to do as far as the Xenophon is concerned is thank you again and ask you again to give my regards to our friend Mai. As for the translation you ask about, *nondum matura est res*,[2] I don't mean the work, which is not even begun, but the thinking, and so I can say nothing about it, as I've not even quite made up my mind what I'd translate. And besides I think I've realized that translating in this way for practice should really be done before one writes one's own things, and that it is necessary or very helpful for becoming an accomplished writer; but that to become an accomplished translator one should first have written something and be a good writer, and in short that a perfect translation is the work of an old man rather than a young one. So you see that I'm not even quite certain if I'll do a translation. The treatise I began and then abandoned was on *popular errors of the ancients*, a subject on which I have a mass of material I assembled a few years ago: but this means little or nothing, because selecting will almost be more difficult for me than collecting it was. I haven't written more than a few pages of the actual treatise.

Here follows the defence of Giacomo Leopardi accused of playing childish politics with a friend. I really don't know how on earth it can have got into your head to get defensive because of an innocent phrase I'd used simply to indicate the time when I'd noted those small points in your articles. Put yourself in my shoes for a moment and be kind enough to tell me what you would have written to indicate that time. *When I didn't know you*, no, because I don't know you in person even now, and I already knew you then by reputation and by your writings. *When I didn't love you*, no, not this either, because it would have been a lie, since I loved you from the moment I knew about you. What, then? *When you didn't love me*, or *before I wrote to you*, or *before receiving your first letter*? They would have been phrases more clumsy than I am capable of. So I wrote: *when I loved you less than I do now*: and I promise you that in choosing this phrase my mind followed exactly the train of thought I've just reported. But supposing, as you think, that I regretted noting those errors of yours (as you call them), I'd still like to know what obliged me to confess this sin, and what's more promise you that I'd write to you about those small points or tell you about them in person. Now since you are such a great preacher of frankness and openness between friends, I want you to know that I reproach you for a lot of things in that paragraph of your letter. In the first place, that very fault you accuse me of, I mean being over-careful with friends. You call me a

[1] M93.

[2] *the thing is not yet ready.*

very shrewd politician for a comment which, taken as you took it, was childish if not worse. This truly would be a fine compliment to pay a friend: I want you to know, my dear friend, that when I did not love you, I noted your errors, but now, Heaven forbid! In the second place, I reproach you for setting out on purpose to prove certain things to me: if you don't think me as convinced of them as any man on earth, you're wrong to love me. Then, for having so easily thought your friend foolish or vain or discourteous, and for having taken offence over such a slight thing. Further, for calling yourself a good friend of people who consider you to be quite the opposite of what you are, so that they are either stupid or malicious, and it is not possible that you respect them: now I can't and I don't think a person like you can love someone you don't also respect; and so as I respect very few people, I love so few that if I were to count them on my fingers, one hand would be more than enough. Apart from that, what you say about arguing with friends is more than true. Indeed I believe arguing is reasonable and useful only with one's friends, or with people who could easily be one's friends. My beloved Alfieri says quite rightly in his *Life* that he never argued with anyone he was not in agreement with about general principles. And I think this is the practice of the truly wise: so that I, trying to become wise, and not agreeing with anyone in Recanati about general principles, never argue, and I stubbornly let people come out with blunders that would make a dog sick, without ever opening my mouth; naturally they all take me to task for this, and say that one must state one's opinion, and other fine things; but they are wasting their breath.

I'll write down my brief comments on your articles some time when the page is less full. But they are trifles, sometimes à propos of a word, sometimes a line of verse, and so on; so don't expect the mountain to give birth. If I were not afraid you might think it childish curiosity, I'd ask you what books you are reading, that have the power to keep you in Milan; knowing this would serve as guidance for my own reading. Adieu, my dear friend. Be happy, and love me and write to me to make me happy. I'll write to Sartori at the beginning of next month. Adieu, adieu.

13

Giordani's silence induced a state near desperation.

To Pietro Giordani • Milan

Recanati, 13th February 1818

Why have you stopped writing to me, dear friend? Did something in my last letter perhaps upset you? If so, you already know for a certainty that it upsets you much less than it does me; but I don't know what it can have been: I do know that you can't have felt angry without cause, nor I have offended you except unwillingly and unwittingly. But won't you forgive a friend a first failing or even a third or a fourth? and a friend such as I am? and a failing which was without any doubt involuntary, because even reflecting on it I can't work out how or if I am at fault. But even if you want to punish me, punish me in some other way than by silence, and don't use on me the ultimate penalty. Will you abandon me too, alone and abandoned as I am? and when I need consoling to bear this unhappy life, will you, by continuing to remain silent, continue to make me infinitely disconsolate as you do? Or am I suddenly gone from your memory, and is it possible that you have completely forgotten someone who (you know it) if he can remember as he dies, will remember you as he dies? Or is there perhaps some other reason for your silence? For God's sake, write to me about it, and at once; and whatever it is and however things are, write to me, and do it as you please, for as long as you write to me I shall be happy.

14

Not yet twenty, Leopardi had become tragically aware that 'seven years of mad and most desperate study' had irrevocably ruined his health. Just a year after the correspondence with Giordani had started, this letter took stock of the situation and saw that worse was to come.

To Pietro Giordani • Milan

Recanati, 2nd March 1818

Pay no mind, my dear friend, to what melancholy managed to make me say, and my immense love much more, and from now on write to me in your own good time and briefly and just as you please: I don't want your friendship with me to add to your troubles and difficulties, which it should lessen if it could. The packet reached Ancona on the 17th of February: I was informed immediately, but my father, putting it off from one day to the next, still hasn't sent for it: when it comes I shall write to you and to Mai, who will probably be irritated with me, yet I don't want to appear ungrateful. I don't know anything about the Belcari's, if they're not with the Xenophon, as I think they aren't, because you didn't tell me they were. If you give the letter on the *Dionysius* to Stella, I'd like you to let me know; if you no longer think it a good idea to give it to him, for any reason at all, there is no need for you to tell me, and do as you think best. You ask about the subject of the other long letter I said I wanted to write you. But do you know you're an inquisitive fellow? Yet because uncertainty creates or increases one's expectations, and I am always afraid that *Parturient montes*,[1] I'll tell you: it's the *Fronto*. As for my health *sic habeto*.[2] For a long long time I firmly believed that I must die within two or three years at most. But in the last eight months, that is to say more or less from the day I entered my twentieth year, *ἵνα τι καὶ δαιμόνιον ἐνθῶ τῷ πράγματι*,[3] I've come to realize and I am convinced – not deluding myself, dear friend, and not deceiving myself, for deluding and deceiving myself are alas for me impossible – that there really is no necessary cause for

[1] Horace, *Ars poetica*, 139: *the mountains will give birth*, a ridiculous mouse will be born.

[2] *so be it.*

[3] *to introduce something superhuman into the matter.* The allusion is to Socrates and his *daimonion*, or guiding spirit.

me to die soon, and that provided I take infinite care of myself, I shall be able to live, although dragging my life along in my teeth, and using myself for barely half of what other men do, and always with the risk that every small incident and every tiny blunder may harm me or kill me: because in short I've ruined myself by seven years of mad and most desperate study at the time when my constitution was forming and should have grown strong. And I've ruined myself unhappily and without redress for my whole life, and made my appearance wretched, and quite contemptible that large part of a man which is all that most people take into account; and it is with most people that one must have dealings in this world: and not just most people, but anyone at all is compelled to desire that virtue be not without some external adornment, and finding it absolutely bare, grows sad, and by force of nature which no wisdom can conquer, almost lacks the courage to love the virtuous man in whom nothing is beautiful except his soul. Fate has placed these and other wretched circumstances around my life, giving me a mind acute enough for me to see them clearly and realize what I am, and a heart open enough to recognize that cheerfulness does not suit it, and, wearing mourning as it were, to take melancholy as its eternal and inseparable companion. Thus I know and see that my life cannot be anything other than unhappy: yet I am not frightened, and just as I shall make sure that I bear it without cowardice, so may it serve some purpose. I have passed years so bitter that it seems impossible that worse could come; nonetheless I do not despair of suffering even more: I've not yet seen the world, and when I first see it, and have experience of men, certainly I shall have to withdraw bitterly into myself, not because of the misfortunes that may befall me, against which I think I am armed with a resolute and robust indifference, nor even because of those countless things that will wound my self-esteem, for I am quite determined and almost certain that I shall never bow to anyone on earth, and that my life will be a continuous contempt for contempt and a deriding of derision; but because of those things which will wound my heart: and especially I shall suffer when, given all the circumstances I've described, the cruellest thing of all happens to me, as it necessarily must, and already in part has; I say nothing about it now.[4] As for the necessity of getting away from here; what with that same studying that wanted to kill me, with my keeping myself shut away all on my own, you see how wise it is, to leave me to melancholy, and to leave me to myself, my own most pitiless executioner. But I shall bear it, because I was born to bear it, and since I've lost my bodily strength, I'll bear losing as well the strength that all young people have: and I'll console myself with you and with the thought of having found a true friend in this world, a thing I gained before I ever hoped for it. Your last letter is dated the very same day on which a year ago I wrote you my first. So a year of our friendship is over: a friendship which, unless we utterly change our natures, cannot be ended except by the thing which brings everything to an end. My comfort is in you: take care of yourself, and reflect that, as you are no more yours than you are mine, if you love me you are not allowed to neglect yourself. I shall be waiting for your visit; never mind that it cannot now be in May: but I hope you will make up for the delay by staying longer. And when I've seen you, I'll be able to say that not all the most passionate desires I have felt in my life have been in vain. Adieu.

4 The 'cruellest thing of all' is probably unrequited love.

15

Giordani had asked for information about a fodder crop a lady friend wished to try to grow to feed her horses on.[1] *Leopardi's reply, with its charming willingness to put himself out for his friend, reflected his eagerness to please.*

To Pietro Giordani • Vicenza

Recanati, 1st June 1818

My dear friend. You don't want me to leave the house on your account and that of a lady, and she a person you speak highly of and a relative of yours? I'd go to the stake for her, not just leave the house, especially since I stay in the house so willingly, as you know. I've asked about *sulla*,[2] I've asked about *lubaco*, I've asked about *lupinella*, which many people confuse with your crop, as Cavaliere Filippo Re confirms, and nobody here has been able to tell me anything about it. They all came out with *crocetta*, which is the true *lupinella* or *sainfoin*. Re quotes his own *Annali di Agricoltura*: if I had it, I could perhaps see in what part of the March *sulla* is found, but I don't. So that as far as the March is concerned, the case is pretty well hopeless. But as I see from Filippo Re that *sulla* is grown around Urbino as well, I questioned someone from those parts, where it's as common as any other native plant; and this person told me what I wanted to know, and you shall have as much seed as you like, either here in Recanati or else in Piacenza, if you want me to have some sent directly from Romagna: tell me to whom I'm to send it. It grows especially around Urbino and Pesaro; it needs firm, clayey, white soil, and Filippo Re notes this as well; it likes a sunny position; in Romagna it never dies out, though elsewhere it doesn't usually last longer than forty years; but since it grows, as you know, in places sown with wheat, it comes up every other year, because the wheat year it barely sprouts, the same here as everywhere else. After the harvest it prefers rainy weather, but it doesn't need watering, and the only other job is mowing it. It's mown at the end of May, although Re says April, but I read somewhere else that in some places they start harvesting in May when it's in flower, and they go on the whole of June. In Romagna the custom is not to give it fresh, they make hay-stacks of it as they do with other hay and they give it in winter. You can see clearly that there's no place for this crop here, because the land is never left fallow; as you'll be aware, they only divide and rotate; one year wheat, the next maize and other fodder. As for sowing it, since in Romagna it never dies out, I wouldn't know what they do when they want to introduce it to a piece of land. Elsewhere I hear that they sow it around harvest time, either before or after, but before burning the stubble; and all they do is scatter the seed on the ground; then they burn the stubble, and the ash covers the seeds sufficiently with no further labour. Since you ask me for instructions about growing it, if what I've told you and what Re says (which isn't much) is not enough, I could

[1] M113.

[2] *Sulla, lubaco, lupinella, crocetta* and *sainfoin* are all names of varieties of crops used as fodder for horses; the first two are alternative names for the same plant (Hedysarum coronarium), as are the last three (Onobrychis sativa or Onobrychis viciaefolia).

have information copied from other books which speak about it in more detail, and send that to you, but I'm ashamed to do so, because I imagine that this Lady of yours who studies agriculture already has not just Filippo Re's works, but many others, and even if she hasn't, both she and you are in towns where there are many more books than there are in Recanati.

I wrote to you a week ago, to this address, that is to say to Vicenza. Adieu. I'm waiting for you: how eagerly? just imagine it, if you can. Be healthy and happy, and think about coming. Adieu.

16

A few months later, Leopardi had turned twenty and Giordani's visit was imminent.

To Pietro Giordani • Bologna

Recanati, 14th August 1818

My dear friend. I'm astonished that by the 6th you still hadn't received my letter of July 31st which I sent to Bologna care of Mr Brighenti,[1] as you instructed me. All it did was send my regards and ask you to let me know, as long as you could do so without inconvenience, when you were close. I am waiting for you very impatiently, consumed by melancholy, bursting with desires, weary, angry, just getting through these days that are bitter or utterly insipid, without a trace of sweetness or any flavour that could enthuse anyone. Certainly, as I've waited for your visit for such a long time, now that it's close each day seems a century, and not knowing how to fill them (and even if I knew how to ordinarily, everything must seem pointless to me compared with talking to you) I'm making very heavy weather of getting through them. You will say: and what about your studies? These days I'm like someone whose bones are aching from exhaustion or from a beating: my spirit is so slack and broken that I'm no good for anything. I'm glad you still like Bologna so much that you don't know how you'll manage to leave. Imagine that it is Recanati. Then *Il pigliarvene subito un puleggio, Un zucchero parravvi di tre cotte.*[2] But when you're in Recanati, imagine that it's Bologna. Meanwhile love me and, as I said, if you can manage to without inconvenience, before you arrive write to me. Adieu. Adieu.

1 Pietro Brighenti will become one of Leopardi's long-term correspondents and friends: a somewhat dubious figure, he is now known to have acted as an informer for the Austrian authorities.

2 *Leaving it immediately will seem a real treat*; from Lorenzo Lippi (1606-1665), *Il Malmantile racquistato*, I, 80.

17

Giordani had to postpone his visit because of a friend's illness.

To Pietro Giordani • Bologna

Recanati, 31st August 1818

I forgive you, my dear friend, that as you've not yet seen me, and therefore do not know me well, you were afraid that I was weary of loving you: since I'm very sure that when you've seen me and got to know me, even if you happened to spend a whole year without any letters from me, even if by begging, entreating, threatening, you didn't manage to get a word in reply, you'll believe all impossible things before believing that my will in respect of you has changed. As for your ills, or those of a friend of yours, I don't sympathize with them, I suffer them; so that, no matter how much I burn and ache to see you, no matter how impatient I've become, as I said in one of the letters that went missing, and for all that the days seem like centuries to me and I really don't know how to endure them, nevertheless I can't ask you to hasten to comfort me. It will be enough that when you can, you remember my love, and listen to your love. In the meantime I'll wait for you, and with me a small work that cost me a great deal of effort;[1] although, as it is to come out, it would rather not wait for long, and I'm even quite concerned about it; in any event I don't even want to touch it unless I've heard your judgment first, and conferred with you about whether it should be published or not. Be happy and be fond of me; there's no one in the world who deserves it as much as I do; nor will there be, because, my dear friend, as I am now so I shall be until I die, and if love for our loved ones endures beyond death, so I shall be forever. And I call on you yourself as witness that you haven't yet found and don't hope to find another person who loves you as fervently and steadfastly as I do: and just as I would wish that there might be such a person, equally, considering myself, I'm utterly convinced that no such person exists. I hope we will talk at greater length, in accordance with what you tell me, in a few days time. For now I leave you and embrace you. Adieu. Adieu.

[1] The *opuscolo molto sudato* referred to here is a matter of debate.

18

Giordani finally came to Recanati in September 1818 and stayed for five days. The visit marked a turning-point in Leopardi's relationship with his father, who thought (mistakenly) that his son's liberal sympathies dated from this time, and bitterly regretted Giordani's influence. Leopardi felt increasingly thwarted by his relatives' unwillingness to cooperate in helping him to leave Recanati.

To Pietro Giordani • Piacenza

Recanati, 19th October 1818

I've no doubt that my letter of the 5th addressed to Bologna, which included regards from Marquess Antici and especially from Carlo, and two lines from my father, has failed to arrive as usual. But tell me: two letters of Canova's[1] that I also sent to Bologna by the same post and didn't enclose in mine (foreseeing that they'd be at risk), so that if mine went missing the others might be saved – haven't they arrived either? In mine I informed you that just before receiving your last one dated the 1st, I'd sent you two other letters to Rome (one from Brighenti, the other from Perticari) enclosed in another one of mine, which I hoped wouldn't go astray, as I'd entrusted them to Canova. You told me in your last letter that if I wanted to write to you after the middle of the month, I should direct them to Piacenza. So that's what I'm doing; and since the one I wrote to Bologna didn't reach you, I repeat my uncle's regards, I repeat my father's regards, I repeat and renew Carlo's embraces, and I add regards from Pieruccio and from Paolina, who had given them to me for the other one as well, but I forgot and she was cross about it and scolded me for it.[2] With this letter you will receive a little work of mine in manuscript.[3] I would like you to have it printed there in Piacenza or where you think best, but in duodecimo or some other small format, because as the cost is to be met from my own income, it must be very slight, and even then it will be difficult; and you'll see that whether the format is large or small, there mustn't be more than one sheet. You'll see likewise that I dedicate the little work to Monti. I'd like you to write to him asking for his permission. I'll write to him when I send him a copy after it is published. I'd like the paper to be of middling quality. You be the judge of whether it's a good idea to have a few copies printed on wove paper or suchlike. Forgive my putting you to this trouble. I wanted to say: you do the same to me; but you can't, because for me it wouldn't be a trouble but a very great pleasure to be of service to you in some way. Except that I'm no good for anything, as you've seen sometimes from experience. I'm more than very eager to have the books you indicated. But as for me, I think Belisarius[4] was richer (if what they say about him is true, for

1 Canova was a friend of Giordani's, the half-brother of the sculptor Antonio Canova; see [67].

2 Carlo, Pieruccio and Paolina were his brothers and sister; Marquess Antici was his uncle Carlo, in whose house in Rome he would be a guest in 1822-3; all would be future correspondents of the poet.

3 The manuscript contained the two patriotic canzoni *All'Italia* (To Italy) and *Sopra il monumento di Dante* (On the Monument to Dante); see [21].

4 A Byzantine general whom the emperor Justinian deprived of all his possessions and reduced to begging.

I don't want you to think me an ignoramus); and as for my father, I've become extremely reluctant to ask, and I can't bring myself to do so any more on any terms.

Things are going from bad to worse with us; and when we tried to put into effect the plan we'd formed together about how to go to Rome, and proposed a means of doing it so simple that it didn't seem possible to pretend there was a difficulty even if they wanted to, the very people[5] we'd asked to speak to our father about it, and who should have been most concerned to help us, and who were the very same ones you counselled, abandoned us, ridiculed us, treated us like ignoramuses, fools, scoundrels; and we are calmly mocked by our father as children, so that, convinced at last that we must behave like desperadoes and put our trust in ourselves alone in all the world, we are now resolved to see what we can do. Be fond of us, dear friend, and grant us something that costs nothing, and yet we do not have it from a living soul here or anywhere else, except from you: I mean compassion. We embrace you with all our heart. Adieu.

5 Presumably relatives (including his uncle Carlo Antici mentioned earlier in the letter) who had been asked to intervene on their behalf with their father.

19

The unreliability of the post continued to cause anxiety.

To Pietro Giordani • Piacenza

Recanati, 27th November 1818

In short, I realized some time back that I am terribly unlucky in everything and in every way, and that there's nothing I care about that doesn't go wrong for me. While my bad luck keeps us so far apart, so that we cannot feed our friendship except on letters, lo! the confounded unreliability of the post deprives me of this one way, and I really am in despair, because as well as being stuck with living in this prison, I can now see the only window which could give me some light and air closing, and so at last I must get by in perfect darkness. On the 19th of last month I wrote you a letter which mattered to me, because it was accompanied by a manuscript, and I know for certain that that one is lost.[1] I wrote another one on the 9th of this month and I don't know if that one's lost, I do know that six days later, that is on the 15th when you wrote your last letter to me, it hadn't arrived. Thank goodness the post looks after all of yours, so that I wouldn't mind much about mine going to the devil, if that didn't give you grounds for thinking, and reproaching me, that since I've got to know you in person I've written to you less frequently. Now if you'll count your two from Bologna and two from Piacenza, and set against them the one I wrote you in Rome which reached you in Bologna, the other I sent to Bologna, the two I wrote to Piacenza, and this one which is the fifth, you'll find that I'm in credit by one letter. And if besides arithmetic you want to have a

1 See previous letter, n. 3.

quick run through geometry to measure our letters, you'll see clearly that each of mine equals three of yours, so that I'm so much in credit that if I were to demand repayment in full I'd ruin you, because in short yours seem like sweetmeats that melt in the mouth before they can even reach the throat, whereas mine fill the stomach. So make a solemn confession in the first letter you write me that you were wrong to think that I'd become more severe, and similar nonsense, or else expect three or four of mine without fail by every post: they'll make you beg for mercy or bury you alive under a heap of paper. I sent Canova's two letters to Bologna and I wrote to you in Bologna as well by the same post: you received mine, and in your last letter from there you said that Canova's had got lost: so now that they've been delivered to you in Piacenza, you're astounded that there's no accompanying letter from me. The manuscript I sent you was dedicated to Monti, and I asked you to have it printed there in Piacenza, and to write to Monti asking his permission to dedicate it to him, adding that I would write to him when I sent him a copy, once it was printed. The manuscript went missing along with the letter. *Sic te servavit Apollo*,[2] but only as regards having it printed, since I'm asking you again to write to Monti, as I've had another copy made of the little work and sent it to Rome, where I won't have it published until I know you have obtained permission as I said.

As for the Vida, I think you will have regretted spending the couple of hours you mentioned on it: but I haven't read it, and I'm speaking on the basis of what I've heard about it. You ask me what I'll read this winter: *scilicet*, old books, because modern ones don't reach here, and even though at present I spend all my time reading, I'm completely ignorant about things in the literary world. But I'll immerse myself up to the chin in the Greek, Latin and Italian Classics. If this letter were not too long already, I'd tell you about some plans I've formed. For now I'll only say that the more I read the Latins and Greeks, the smaller our own writers become, even those of the best centuries, and I see that not just our eloquence, but our philosophy, and our prose – in every respect, inside and out – must be created. A large field, which we'll enter, if not with great strength, certainly with courage and love of country.[3]

Be fond of me, and spare me your complaining, for now that you've met me, I'm not at all so ready to forgive you. Carlo embraces you, we both send our heartfelt best wishes, and we want you to carry on being well. Adieu, adieu.

My sister is urging me to send regards in her name. I already did so in the letter that went missing. Now that we know what happened, she wanted me to put it right in this letter.

[2] *Thus were you saved by Apollo*; cf. Horace, *Satires* I, ix, 78, where the poet thanks Apollo for having freed him from a bore.

[3] We, i.e. himself and Giordani.

20

Leopardi asked for advice about putting his work into circulation.

To Pietro Giordani • Piacenza

Recanati, 14th December 1818

My dear friend. I received your letter of November the 19th when I'd already written and sent mine of the 27th, from which you will have seen what the manuscript is that you were asking about.[1] Now, as I've sent it to Rome to be printed at my own expense, and as all the copies of it should therefore be at my disposal, and as I don't want more than a very few copies distributed in Rome, I'd be grateful if you could tell me how they can be put into circulation especially in Lombardy, into the hands of booksellers and such like, not in order to recover my costs, but simply to achieve the purpose of having them printed, that is to make them go *per manus hominum*.[2] I'm very ignorant about these things, I have no literary dealings with anyone, and with all these copies at my disposal, not wanting tuppence for them, I don't know what on earth to do with them. I would like a word or two from you about this, for I'll have them held in Rome until you've given me an answer on this point, as well as on what I wrote you about Monti in my last letter. And since I'd like to use this opportunity to become known to some of the cleverest Italians, friends of yours, I'd like you to tell me where Rosmini, Mustoxidi and Strocchi are at the moment, as I don't know for sure.

However as they write from Rome that it could happen that the manuscript though very small might nonetheless not manage to pas through the censor's sieve (and this would not be the last of my things not to get past the Roman censor), I'm writing to Rome that, if it doesn't pass, they're to send it directly to you. If this happens, then here I am putting you to trouble again, and repeating what I said in the letter that went missing: that as the cost must be met from my personal income, the format, the number of copies and the paper should ideally be such as not to exceed 35 or 40 *lire* in cost, especially bearing in mind that, as there cannot be more than one sheet, increasing the format size would increase the cost correspondingly. I would like just a few copies to be on wove paper or blue paper or something similar,[3] the others on the best quality the limited finances will allow; the printing to be done there in Piacenza or wherever you like. Forgive me this trouble, and if the manuscript should arrive, give it no more thought than to your least pressing business.

In your last letter you seem very mournful, and you can believe that I don't know how to comfort you, except by begging you to allow something to the illusions which essentially come from nature the universal benefactor, whereas reason is the executioner of the human race, it is a torch that should illuminate but not burn up, as unfortunately it does. I would really like our love to be able to comfort you, for if you were to be happy in proportion as

1 See [18], n. 3.

2 *into men's hands.*

3 'Wove' paper and 'blue' paper are better quality papers than ordinary 'laid' paper, and would be used for complimentary copies.

our love is great, I don't know if anyone in the world would be happier than you. As for us two wretches,[4] that feeble ray of light has vanished, and there is nothing left to hope for from any living soul apart from ourselves. Love us, my dear friend, for we shall always be yours whatever our situation. Adieu. Adieu.

4 Himself and Carlo.

21

Leopardi was deeply disappointed with the printed version of his two canzoni, published in Rome by Bourlié at the end of 1818. His continuing attempts to find some way of leaving Recanati reflected his increasing desperation and his sense of betrayal by the older members of his family. Carlo too was hoping to leave, whereas for Paolina marriage was the only possible escape route.

To Pietro Giordani • Piacenza

Recanati, 18th January 1819

My dear friend. You can imagine how much your letter of the 5th comforted me after your long silence. I am sending you a copy of the manuscript printed in Rome;[1] it is the one I had them send me by post unbound just as you see it, because I am expecting the other bound copies from one day to the next, but so far they have not arrived. And as soon as they do, I shall immediately hand them over body and soul to the grocer, as I don't want anyone to see this disgraceful piece of printing: I am ashamed of my poor verses when I read them in this form, for when they are dressed in rags like this I think they are even worse than they are. Add the fact that they have only printed 24 copies on this paper, calling it royal wove paper,[2] the rest are on ordinary paper, and I'm waiting to see how it can be any more dreadful. And the cost was several times higher than what I was expecting and what they had told me, so that as it was paid out of my own resources (which as you know are so abundant) it has completely ruined me, leaving me with these poems unpublished, since I'd much rather not be read than be read in this filthy form that would obliterate even the writing of an angel, let alone mine. And you can act as if this copy I'm sending is in manuscript, and, if you have mentioned anything to Monti, apologize to him if I am not putting my plan into effect,[3] since, unless you think differently, I have made up my mind that I must not have the shame of having allowed his name to be read so very ill written.

I shall perhaps write to you another time about my plans concerning Italian prose, if you have the patience to read me. I am not thanking you for offering to write and put in a good word for me with Mai, and to write to Borghesi and Perticari likewise asking them to put in a good word for me with Mauri, in order not to show either that I expected any less of your

1 See [18], n. 3.

2 See [20], n. 3; 'royal' is a size of paper.

3 He had planned to dedicate the canzoni to Monti; see [18].

love, or that I think any thanks can repay the favour. You ask for my agreement, which is whole-hearted, and for our part[4] we'll try to make the most of your good services, and to back them up by taking whatever steps are appropriate. You cannot believe how unknown I am in Rome; and I am not saying I don't deserve it, I am just saying that countless others who deserve it as much as I do are incomparably more well known and respected and praised and honoured than I am; I don't mind about this at all, nor should I mind about it in itself, but it puts me at this disadvantage, that, as I have no reputation, I cannot derive from it those real benefits that people who have it derive from it, however they come by it. So there is no doubt that your good services can help me a very great deal.

You say, couldn't Cardinal Mattei do something?[5] wouldn't it be possible? wouldn't it be easy? If just one of the people who have us in their power genuinely wanted it and were prepared to act, certainly what is easy for twenty others in this very city, and a thousand in this province, would not be impossible for us – with wealth and rank and connections very, very inferior to ours, they support themselves or support their children in Rome. In short, if only the person who ought to want it had wanted it (and as he does not want it, he tells other people and himself as well that it is not in his power), it is obvious that we would have got what we wanted a long time ago. But they do not want it and never will unless we force their hand, they are happy to see us in this state, they would wholeheartedly like us to die in this state, they regret having let us study, they say expressly in our presence that they have learnt the harm that knowledge can do, they deliberately and openly give our younger brother[6] a carpenter's upbringing and talent and tools, and our desires seem eccentricities, and crazy intolerable whims; to whom? I am not talking about the others who have lived and live as they would like us to live, I mean our uncle, who at the age of twelve went as a page to the court in Bavaria, came back at eighteen, lived mostly in Rome until he became provincial delegate to Napoleon and was put forward as a senator, became a knight, then a baron, then a chamberlain, went twice to Paris and to the court, has now set up house in Rome, moved his whole family there, and pursuaded all his brothers and the whole family of a sister much less comfortably off than ours to move there, and had the gall to tell me of his own accord more than once that he knew he could not bring his children up properly except away from here, and then to write me a long letter to prove to me that I am behaving like an ignoramus and a fool when all I think about is leaving Recanati.[7]

The plan involving the Turin militia is the very one that Carlo has for some time considered the only one suited to him, and he intends to make this clear when with a manly and determined refusal he declares to his father (who still says nothing and is still convinced that with a word he can dissuade him from his resolve) that he absolutely must abandon any hope based on the sacrifice of his son's liberty and happiness.

My sister sends her regards again, and, since you ask me, her name is Paolina. As for finding a husband for her in a distant town, I do not think they will raise any objection; and

4 i.e. his own and Carlo's.

5 Cardinal Mattei was a relative of his uncle's wife; see n. 7.

6 Luigi; see [90, 137].

7 His uncle is Marquess Carlo Antici, a native of Recanati; see [18], n. 2; and [83]. His letter is M143.

equally they will not attach too much importance to the question of rank, just as they will not entirely overlook it; but as it is a question of a girl leaving home, they will settle for a tolerable breeding, whereas if it were a question of a girl entering the family, they would be extremely particular. I think they are not proposing to give her more than forty thousand *lire* in dowry, but they think they will get that back from Carlo's wife's dowry; if that goes up in smoke, I don't know what steps they'll take. Certainly, though, if some suitable match came your way, you would be doing us nothing but a great favour by letting us know, and we would see if we could make something of it. Adieu, my dear friend. If you are fond of us, write to us often, and if you don't think you can stay with us for as long as you said in your last letter, do as you please, for we will be satisfied even with a little. Your two dear friends love you, embrace you and send their regards. Adieu, adieu.

22

As his majority approached, when in theory at least he would be independent, Leopardi was thinking hard about the practicalities of living away from home, given his father's unwillingness to offer financial support.

To Pietro Giordani • Piacenza

Recanati, 26th March 1819

Best-beloved. Be resolute in blaming everything on the post, which is appalling and contemptible, to use Demosthenes' word. And if you had any doubts on my account, though you show no sign of it, let this serve as an example to reassure you that, no matter what, where you are concerned I'll always be as attentive and thoughtful as it is possible to be, and more punctual in replying to your letters than anyone else, without any doubt. And if I were not able to because of illness, Carlo would certainly do it for me, as you say. [...]

But your letter of the 13th is so affectionate that I don't understand how I've managed to earn your love in such measure. Except that my amazement diminishes a little when I think of the love I feel for you, and the anguish I've experienced several times when your letters took longer than usual to arrive. In short, I acknowledge your superiority in everything, but certainly not in this: don't think that I am outdone or ever could be by you or by anyone else.

Perticari is probably right, and I'm convinced of it too, that in Rome everything good is for the priests. But I don't understand what he goes on to say next. Does he perhaps think I'm looking for somewhere to live in Rome? and in the meantime I'm not leaving Recanati because away from here I don't have anywhere to stay? or if I found enough money to live in the Ecclesiastical Academy, I'd want to curtail my liberty, when I can enjoy it entire? And as for hopes, we're back where we started, since positions as nuncio and suchlike will always be for priests, even if they are given to the ones who are members of the Academy. Now living in the academy is not cheap, and the 14 *scudi* a month covers barely half of what they need, and they have to supply the rest from other funds, which comes to almost twice as much for all of them, and for many of them a lot more. But even if it cost the smallest amount imaginable, in my case it's not a matter of looking for where, but for how. My father is absolutely determined not to give me a penny away from home, that is to say anywhere, given that even here he never gives me money, he just provides me with the necessities as he does the rest of the family. He does allow me to look for a way of leaving here without it costing him anything; and I mean allows me, for he doesn't lift a finger to help me; he'd rather do his utmost to hinder me. Now you can see what I can do, given that nobody knows me, and that I've always lived in a place that you have to look up in a reference book to locate, that I'm looked down on as a child, and take it as a very great favour to get a one-line answer in which they say they have no time to attend to me. I'll say another thing. The fact that all the best things go to priests seems to me rather to be in my favour than against me, bearing in mind that I certainly don't want to be a priest, but I've worn clerical dress up to now and I can go on wearing it for a bit longer, and in Rome, especially in the early stages, that is all they ask for.[1] The fact is that any place that gives me enough to live on very frugally will suit me very well, and I don't think I'll be able to leave this cavern without giving up many comforts that do me no good without fresh air and light; I mean seeing and being in contact with the world and the men among whom I was born, and talking to people who show some signs of life and, more important, of intelligence, for if there aren't many people in whom intelligence shines brightly, there certainly can't be any in whom it is as rusty and neglected as it is around here.

Carlo would like to know, not in detail – because we quite understand that even you cannot know it in detail – but in general terms, if you think that the Turin militia you suggested to him a short while back would be able to provide him immediately with enough to live on, even if very frugally, at any rate without lacking the necessities. But I'm ashamed now of talking so much about us. I'd like you to tell me how your troubles are and your melancholy moods. Dear Giordani, I feel my spirits rise again at the return of spring; certainly two months ago I was so stupefied, downcast, and senseless that I was amazed at myself, and I despaired of finding any comfort in this world. I certainly hope you feel better too, contemplating this innocent nature, in the midst of men's wickedness; I don't see, my sweet friend, that you should be so concerned about them if they want to be scoundrels. It is enough for you to be more different from them than light from dark, and for there to be someone who, loving you more than he loves himself, is determined while he lives to imitate you. So God save him from the plague, and may what ought to prosper not be spoiled with time, I mean the seeds of virtue one has tried to gather in youth. I only wrote briefly about your *Discorso* because any day now I am going to set about saying what I can about it in an article to be sent to Perticari in Rome, as I told you; he wants me to be one of the contributors to his Journal.[2] What with sleeping and studying I haven't a moment to spare, and I have become a real Isocrates, but only in this, that I write two lines in a day spent working hard on them without interruption. Paolina sends her fond regards. Adieu, dear friend. Let me know if the letters and poems I mentioned have arrived. Adieu: I must leave you at last, but I embrace you most tenderly as a man without compare and unique. I'm not worthy of your loving me, but love is not governed by reason. And so love me, as you've begun. Adieu. Adieu.

[1] Leopardi wore cassock and tonsure from the age of 12 to 22.

[2] The *Giornale Arcadico*; on Giulio Perticari, already mentioned in [21] and earlier in this letter, see [32, 51].

23

Leopardi was now addressing Giordani in the intimate 'tu' form.[1]

To Pietro Giordani • Vicenza

Recanati, 26th April 1819

My sweet friend. Your letter of the 20th comes to comfort me following on your other one of the 10th, which I answered on the 19th. Dear Giordani, you are still a man without compare and alone of his kind, such as a few years ago I imagined all men to be: now it seems scarcely believable to me that in reality one such is to be found. But as for me, give no thought to anything except loving me, since my comfort is all in that, and in the hope of death which seems to me the only way out of this wretchedness. Because apart from these two things, I find nothing desirable in this life, except the delights of the heart, and the contemplation of beauty, which is utterly denied me in this wretched state. Besides which books, and especially yours, dishearten me, teaching me that beauty is hardly ever found together with virtue, in spite of seeming to be her companion and sister.[2] This makes me yearn and despair. But how many times am I, as it were, dragged most unwillingly to curse this same virtue along with Brutus on the point of death. Unhappy man, for his own virtue is called into question because of those words, when I see from my own experience and am convinced that they are the strongest proof he could give of it, and we could put forward in his defence.[3]

Since finding some way of supporting myself immediately on leaving here is not possible, as you make me certain, rest assured and take it as an article of faith that I shall never ever leave Recanati except begging, before my father's death, which I do not want before my own. Consider this to be just as much beyond question as the love I feel for you: that neither your eloquence, nor that of Pericles, Demosthenes, Cicero or any great orator, nor of Persuasion herself, could make my father change his mind. And since the Ecclesiastical Academy would require a greater outlay than I would need somewhere else, it is (if there can be a comparative within the superlative) the more hopeless course of action: whereas what I am asking for, which is not to live like a Gentleman, or comfortably or without inconvenience, but only to live away from here – obtaining this is not even conceivable.

My brother and sister send their fond regards. Adieu, dear beautiful soul. I am writing to Trissino again, as you wish.

1 Giordani had spontaneously used 'tu' in M186.

2 This quintessentially Leopardian theme, already touched on in [14], will inspire the canzone *Ultimo canto di Saffo* (Sappho's Last Song).

3 Brutus and his dying words will inspire the canzone *Bruto minore* (The Younger Brutus); on the poem's lasting importance to Leopardi, see [185].

24

With Giordani's encouragement Leopardi sent copies of the two canzoni printed in Rome (see [21]) – both of them on patriotic themes and intended to stir his fellow-countrymen to a sense of their country's past greatness and its present decadence – to other intellectuals. A letter of thanks from one of them, Giuseppe Montani, prompted him to write back reflecting on the state of Italian literature and the responsibilities of writers to their country. The letter was intercepted by Leopardi's father, who, suspicious of Montani's political sympathies, began to exercise a 'domestic censorship' over his son's correspondence (as soon became apparent to Leopardi himself, see [27]). The letter was never sent. Leopardi was still not twenty-one.

To Giuseppe Montani • Lodi

Recanati, 21st May 1819

Dear Professor. Although your very charming letter of the 5th is not of the kind that absolutely requires an answer, in any event having found a writer so courteous and so passionate a lover of this poor country, I cannot rest unless I do my utmost to confirm his benevolence towards me. Even had I felt an icy indifference towards my native land, your words would have set me on fire: and certainly I do not presume to be able to do more than very little: yet I'll not let anything I can do remain undone, and I shan't fail to respond to your exhortations. To my mind it is not something Italy can hope for until she has books suited to the times, read and understood by the common reader, and available from one end of the country to the other; a thing as frequent among foreigners as it is unheard of in Italy. And it seems to me that the very recent example of other nations shows us clearly how much truly national books can do in this age to rouse the slumbering spirits of a people and produce great events. But to crown our ills, from the seventeenth century on a wall has arisen between men of letters and the people, and it grows higher and higher, and is a thing unknown in other nations. And while we have such a great love of the classics, we do not want to see that all the Greek classics, all the Latin classics, all the early Italians wrote for their time, and in accordance with the needs, the desires, the customs and above all the knowledge and understanding of their compatriots and contemporaries. And just as they would not have been classics if they had done otherwise, so we shall never be classics either, if we do not imitate them in this (which is of the essence and necessary), much more than in a hundred other trifling details on which we concentrate most of our attention. And meanwhile Italian eloquence, and poetry which is truly full of feelings and emotions, are things unknown, and there is no Italian man of letters who has a reputation beyond the Alps, when we hear about so many foreigners famous throughout Europe. But you put it very well when you say that we shall have great poets when we have great citizens, and I add that that is when we shall have eloquence as well, and when we have eloquence and books that are really Italian and loved by the whole nation, then we shall have some grounds for hope. Now with citizens in such short supply, and hence people capable of eloquence and stirring and generous poetry, I would not want you, who show yourself to be one of the leaders, to let your pen be idle when all our faith is placed in writings. And rest assured that if your words alone have roused me, it is not possible that your example should not fire me. I want it passionately and I entreat you to let me witness it, and when I've seen it I long for many people to follow it, because the more writers there are, the more justified our hopes shall be: but it is not easy for one person alone or a few people (excellent though they be) to achieve a great deal.

In your letter you as good as invited me to write back to you, and from this letter you will realize that I have not turned a deaf ear, on the contrary I have been very attentive in picking up and interpreting your words. But should the candour and the tedium of this letter force you to regret the invitation extended to me, please at least do not regret the love you granted me and do not cease for any reason to consider me,

truly yours.

25

Leopardi's eyes had started to cause problems and he was able neither to read nor to carry out the many plans he was making.

To Pietro Giordani • Vicenza

Recanati, 4th June 1819

There's no need for me to tell you if your letter of May 24th saddened me.[1] For God's sake, write to me or have someone else write how you feel, and take the greatest possible care of yourself, for you'll be taking it not just of you but of me as well in exactly equal measure. I wrote to you once before that no happy or troubling thing can happen to you that does not happen at the same time to your good friend: so if you are fond of me, take care as best you can that nothing disagreeable ever happens to you, for you would give grounds for great distress to me, to whom I know you would like to give every cause for contentment. You know how very delicious I find the fruits of your studies; but you also know that I want you healthy and happy (as much as a man can be, and you who are not made for it), much more than I want the enjoyment your labours cause in me.

I wrote to you on the 28th of last month by the same post that brought me your last letter. When you write to Roverella and Mai, and when you speak to Trissino, don't forget to give them my regards as affectionately as you can; do me this favour. I think Montani got my second letter: I know he did not get even the second copy of the *Canzoni.* He wrote me a very charming letter with protestations of fervent patriotism; so thank you for introducing me to him, for he really is worthy with a few others of being known and loved, and one of the people I'm looking for. I replied soon afterwards[2] and I hope he will not disdain being in contact with me. I've had several letters from Brighenti in the interim in which he alludes to

[1] Giordani's letter had spoken of his tiredness and ill health.

[2] The previous letter; as yet Leopardi had no inkling that his father was intercepting his letters; see [27], n. 1.

what you write to him about me.

You ask for news of my studies, but for two months I haven't studied, and I don't read anything any more, on account of an eye complaint, and my life is consumed sitting with my arms crossed, or walking from room to room. Plans accumulate in my head, but I can barely jot them down hastily so as not to forget them. I repeat that I'm longing for news of you: don't make me wait a long time. But I don't want you to exhaust yourself writing to me: though this is the only comfort I have left, two lines will do. Adieu. Carlo and Paolina send their regards again and you know with what feeling. Adieu. I'm here not just without a Journal but without even a newspaper. I've heard that a journal in Lombardy, I think the *Biblioteca italiana*, has criticised me (I'm still missing the whole of number 18 and the current one). It's of no great consequence, but in any event if you know anything, I'll be grateful if you write me two words about it.

26

This letter, written just a week before Leopardi attained his majority, showed evident signs of desperation about his situation and his prospects.

To Pietro Giordani • Vicenza

Recanati, 21st June 1819

Best-beloved. I'm replying to your letter of the 4th, which was the day I replied to your letter of May the 24th. I continue to entreat you, out of pity for me, to take the greatest possible care of your health. In the last lines of your letter I thought your handwriting was showing signs of strain. You know very well how much I want letters from you: but if writing is painful, do me this favour, don't suffer for my sake: it will be enough for me to know your news as best as may be. I never write to Brighenti without talking to him about you, but I certainly don't believe he's faithfully passed on all the regards I've sent through him. I'm more careful about my health than mine or any man's deserves. Since March I've been a prey to a very persistent weakness of the ocular nerves, which not only prevents any reading, but also any mental application. Apart from that, I'm well in body, and in spirit, as passionate and desperate as I've ever been, to the point that I could eat the very paper I'm writing on. And that poor friend of yours?[1] How sad for us, how sad. I have no peace of mind any more, and I make no effort to have it. Will I ever do anything great? not even now that I go stumbling around this cage like a bear? In this town of friars (that's exactly what I mean), and in this cursed house, where they'd pay a fortune for me to become a friar too, and give me no choice but to live like a friar willy nilly, and at the age of twenty one, and with this heart of mine, you can be quite sure that very soon I'll burst, if I don't change from a friar into an apostle, and escape from here begging, as the thing will surely end.[2]

[1] A friend of Giordani's had died at the age of 25.

[2] In less than a month Leopardi will try to run away from home.

A few days ago Compagni's *Cronica*, the *Life of Giacomini*, and *The Naple's Conspiracy* arrived from Bologna. But as for reading them it's all the same. I only managed with some pain to read Lorenzino de' Medici's *Apologia*, and my opinion was confirmed that the most eloquent writings and passages are those where a person talks about himself. See if he seems like a contemporary of those wretched sixteenth-century writers who had a reputation for eloquence in Italy in their own day and later, and if it seems credible that he followed the same form of eloquence as them. I mean the Greek and Latin form, which those poor wretches by dint of toil and travail carried over into their writings in such a disjointed and strained way that it was exhausting, whereas he carries it wholesale, fine and alive, and dominates it and is master of it, with a natural grace and ease in the most refined artifice, in the arrangement, in the transpositions, in the embellishments, in the feelings, and in the style, and in the language (which in the others is so angry and harsh because of the very affected Latinisms) that he seems – and is – no less original than the early writers, yet he's as like them as two peas, not only in their strengths, but in every aspect of those strengths. Because a person who is talking about himself has neither the time nor inclination to engage in sophistry, and search for commonplaces, for then every narrowest vein gives enough water, and the writer draws everything out of himself, he does not get it from a distance, so that it is spontaneous and adapted to the subject, and warm and passionate as well, and study cannot cool it, but can shape it and make it beautiful, as it has in this case.

My dear and only friend, be fond of me, take care of yourself, give my regards to count Trissino, and don't mind about my saying I love you, and Carlo and Paolina remember you.[3]

[3] Giordani's letter [M205] had ended: 'Comfort me by saying that you're fond of me.'

27

Leopardi began to suspect a 'domestic censorship' of his letters.

To Pietro Giordani • Milan

Recanati, 26th July 1819

From your letter of the 2nd of this month, and from one of Brighenti's, I see that my letter of June the 4th went missing and with it the news I gave you that I'd had a letter from Montani, and found it very engaging and full of patriotic feeling. I answered it, but I never had a reply, and it's two months and more. Either the post is to blame or else (as I suspect) a domestic censorship recently set up for letters that go from here;[1] and this because *cum horrore et tremore* they've realised that I *ἐλεύθερα φρονῶ περὶ τῶν κοινῶν*.[2] You urge me not to give up my studies. But it is four months since they gave me up because of the weakness of

[1] Leopardi's suspicions were well-founded: the letter to Montani was intercepted by his father and was never sent.

[2] *I have a liberal attitude when it comes to politics.*

my eyes, and my life is terrifying. At an age when constitutions normally grow stronger, I have less strength every day, and my bodily faculties are abandoning me one by one. This comforts me, because it has made me despair of myself, and realize that as my life is no longer worth anything, I can throw it away, as I shall do shortly,[3] because if I cannot live except in this condition and this state of health, I don't want to live, and if a different way of life is possible, it must be attempted. And to make the attempt as best I can, that is, desperately and blindly, does not cost me anything any more, now that the old illusions about my own worth, and about hopes for a future life, and about the good I could do, and the things to be achieved, and the glory to be won, have vanished before my eyes, and I have no opinion of myself, and I know I am worth much less than many of my fellow citizens, whom I used to hold in such profound contempt.

But what troubles me is hearing that your health is still no better. I can't urge you to take care of yourself more strongly than I did in my last letter and in the one that got lost. God grant that all ills fall on me (as I'm already no use to anybody) and spare the only man I know. Keep on loving me, and accept Carlo's and Paolina's regards, they never forget you and never will. If you write to Trissino and speak to Mai, give them my regards. The Porzio you write about in your letter, and the Nardi and Compagni as well, are still untouched, because I cannot read or write or compose a page without pain.

[3] Another allusion to his planned attempt to escape from home.

28

Leopardi had attained his majority on June 29th 1819; now in theory at least his own master, he resolved to run away from home. Needing a passport to travel outside the papal state, he wrote to a family friend in an attempt to obtain one without his father's knowledge.

To Saverio Broglio d'Ajano • Macerata

Recanati, 29th July 1819

My dear Count. I would like to be able to serve you in a matter of greater moment than this one about which you write to me so courteously. I am sending back the Pindar circular with my subscription, and I am extremely sorry that I cannot send the Bergalli collection with it: I have searched for it in vain among our books. I greatly appreciate the affectionate concern with which you advise moderation in my studies: as it was lacking at the appropriate time, however, it is now beside the point, because for many months I have not been able to engage in studying or reading of any kind on account of the weakness of my eyes.

To show you how much I value your precious offer of friendship, I want to be the first to benefit by it. In order to obtain a passport for the Lombardo-Veneto Kingdom (or, if one needs to specify the place, for Milan) from the Delegate's office in Macerata, I don't know if it is necessary to apply in person, or present some document, and of what kind. If it is possible to get one without that, I would ask you to obtain one for me, and send it to me, advising me of the costs incurred. If it is not possible, you would be doing me a very great favour by telling me what is required. Should it be possible to get a passport straight away for within the papal state, with no need to go in person or send a document, I would like you to get me one, since with that it won't be difficult, I think, to obtain the other one at the border.

My family send their very best wishes, and in particular my father, who will also be beholden to you for the favour I am asking of you. Forgive me this first inconvenience that your kindness has brought on you, and in return give me your instructions, if you consider me capable of being of service to you in some way; but above all believe me with a true heart your most obliged, most affectionate servant and friend,

Giacomo Leopardi.

P.S. The passport (if I have not expressed myself clearly) is to be for me.

29

He confided in no one, but wrote letters for his brother and father which they were to read after he had gone.

To Carlo Leopardi • Recanati

[Recanati; no date, but end of July 1819]

My dear Carlo. I am leaving here without having said anything to you, firstly so that you are not held responsible for my departure by anybody; and then because counsel helps an irresolute man, but can only harm one who is resolved: and I knew that you would disapprove my resolve, and place me in new difficulties by trying to dissuade me. I am weary of prudence, which could only lead us to the loss of our youth, a blessing one does not get back. I turn to boldness, and I shall see if I can draw greater advantage from that. Yet this is not a sudden decision; although made in the heat of feeling, I have allowed many days to pass while I pondered it; and I have never had cause to regret it. And so I am acting on it. It was all too clear that if we did not wish to remain forever in the state we loathed, we had better take this course of action; and all the time that has passed has been nothing but a mere delaying. There was no other way than this: a choice had to be made, and you know very well that the choice could not be in doubt. Now that the law makes me my own master, I did not wish to put off any longer what according to our principles had to be done. Two reasons were immediately responsible for my decision: the terrible ennui that resulted from the impossibility of studying, the only activity that could keep me in this town; and another reason that I do not wish to put into words, but which you can easily guess.[1] And just imagine if this

[1] Damiani, p. 161, suggests that this second reason may be his physical deformity and the humiliation of being known locally as 'the Leopardi hunchback' [*il gobbo dei Leopardi*]; see [163].

second reason – which, because of my mental and physical make-up, was capable of bringing me to the extreme of desperation, and made me take supreme pleasure in the idea of suicide – must not be capable of leading me to abandon myself blindly into fortune's hands. Be well, my dear Carlo, and be happy on my account, because I am doing what I should have done a long time ago, and the only thing that can lead me to a life, if not content, at least more tranquil. And so if you love me, you must be glad: and if all I were to gain was to be completely unhappy, I would be satisfied, because you know that the middle way is not for us. I am taking my papers with me, but since it could happen that they might be examined, I don't want to compromise myself, much less the people who have written to me, by carrying some which might be suspect. I have picked out all those of this sort, both mine and those of others (that is, letters written to me) and put them all together on the chest of drawers in our room. There are also some which I did not wish to bring because they were of no use to me. I entrust them to your care: look after them and defend them: you know that I have nothing more precious than the products of my mind and my heart, the only blessing nature has granted me. If letters come for me from Giordani, open them and answer them, and remember me to him, and inform him of my resolve. Brighenti is owed 8 *paoli* for Compagni's *Cronica*, 3 *paoli* for Giordani's *Prose*, and 16 *baiocchi* miscalculated on the money sent for the *Eusebius*. In total 1.36. See to it that he is repaid, and ask Paolina to forgive me if I've taken with me the 3 *paoli* she gave me for the Giordani, and the 16 *baiocchi* as just explained, hoping that she would not have denied her brother this last gift, if he had asked her. O how dearly I would like my example to serve to enlighten our parents about you and our other brothers and sister! Most assuredly I have some hope that you will be less unhappy than me. Adieu, remember me to Paolina and the others. Men's opinion does not matter very much to me, but if an opportunity presents itself, defend me. Be fond of me forever; you can count on me until I die. When I find myself in a place where it is possible to give you news of me, I shall write to you. Adieu. Embrace this unlucky wretch. Depend upon it, you won't be like this. O how much more deserving you are than me! What am I? A man quite worthless. I see and feel it most acutely, and this too has made me resolve to do what I am about to do, in order to escape from thinking about myself, which sickens me. For as long as I had self respect, I was more cautious; now that I despise myself, I find no other solace than to throw myself on chance, and seek out danger, as a thing of no value. Hand over the enclosed to my father.[2] Ask his forgiveness, ask my mother's forgiveness in my name. Do it from the heart, I beg you, and I do so too in spirit. It would have been better (humanly speaking) for them and for me if I had not been born, or if I had died a long time ago. Thus has our misfortune decreed. Adieu, dear Carlo, adieu.

[2] The next letter.

30

This letter to his father was never seen by its intended recipient, because the attempt to escape from home was foiled; but it was not destroyed. The analysis of his father's character and modus operandi is pitiless.

To Monaldo Leopardi • Recanati

[Recanati; no date, but end of July 1819]

Signor Padre. Although when you learn what I have done you may think this page unworthy of being read, at any event I hope in your kindness you will not refuse to hear the first and last words of a son who has always loved you, and loves you, and is infinitely grieved that he must cause you displeasure. You know me, and you know what my conduct has been up to now; and perhaps, if you were to put aside all local considerations, you will see that in the whole of Italy, and I am tempted to say the whole of Europe, no other young man will be found who, in my situation, even at a much younger age, perhaps with intellectual gifts decidedly inferior to mine, has used half the prudence, abstention from every youthful pleasure, obedience and submission to his parents that I have. For all that you may have a poor opinion of those few talents heaven has granted me, you cannot entirely refuse to trust those estimable and famous men who have made my acquaintance and formed the opinion of me that you know, and which it is not for me to repeat. You are not unaware that all those who have heard about me, even those who are perfectly in agreement with your principles, have judged that I must turn out to be something quite out of the ordinary, were I to be given those means which, in the present state of the world, and at all other times, have been indispensable in enabling a young man who gave even modest hopes for himself to come to something. It was amazing how anyone who made my acquaintance even fleetingly unfailingly expressed astonishment that I should still be living in this city, and how you alone among all of them were of the opposite opinion, and persisted in it immovably. Certainly you are not unaware that not just in any city that is at all lively, but in this very city, there is practically no young man of 17 years of age whose parents do not aim to find him a position of the kind best suited to him: not to mention the freedom *all* those in my position have at that age; barely a third as much freedom was granted me at 21 years of age. But leaving that aside, although – if I am not mistaken – I had given proofs of myself that were sufficiently rare and precocious, yet it was only much beyond the usual age that I began to reveal my wish that you should make provision for my destiny, and the welfare of my future life in the way suggested by what everyone was saying. I saw several families in this very city, much (indeed incomparably) less well off than ours, and I knew of countless other families from other parts as well, which in response to some glimmering of intelligence perceived in some young family member, did not hesitate to make the heaviest sacrifices in order to find him a position that enabled him to use his talents to advantage. Although many people thought my intellect gave forth somewhat more than a glimmer, you nonetheless judged me unworthy that a father should make sacrifices for me, and you did not think that the welfare of my present and future life justified any alteration to your family plan.[1] I saw relatives of mine toy with the positions they obtained from the sovereign, and, hoping that they would be able to take steps to some effect on my behalf as well, I asked that at the least I should be found some livelihood suited to my circumstances, without my family having to support me as a consequence. I was laughed at, and you did not think that your connections, in a word your efforts, should even be employed to find a decent position for your son. I was well aware of the plans you had for us, and of how, to safeguard the happiness of a thing I do not know, but I hear called home and family, you demanded of us *two* the sacrifice not of possessions nor of attentions, but of our inclinations, our youth, our whole life. As I was certain that you would never manage to get this from Carlo or from me, there remained no thinking to be done about these plans, and I could not be guided by them in any way. You knew as well the very wretched life I led because of the terrible depressions of spirit, and the torments of a new kind that my strange imagination caused me, and you could not be unaware of what was more than obvious: that is, that there was absolutely no other remedy for this, and for my health which was very visibly suffering because of it, and had done so since my wretched constitution was formed – no other remedy than powerful distractions, and everything which in Recanati could never be found. Yet in spite of this you left a man of my character for so many years either to wear himself away in deadly studies or bury himself in the most terrible ennui and, in consequence, melancholy, which resulted from the necessary solitude, and from a life with nothing to occupy him, as especially in these last few months. It did not take me long to realize that any possible or imaginable reason was quite powerless to make you change your mind, and that the extraordinary inflexibility of your character, masked by constant dissembling and the appearance of giving in, was such as to leave not the faintest shadow of hope. All of this, and my reflections on the nature of men, persuaded me that although I lacked everything, I must put my trust in myself alone. And now that the law has made me my own master, I had no wish to put off any longer taking charge of my own fate. I know that man's happiness consists in being content, and therefore it will be easier for me to be happy begging than amidst all the material comforts I may enjoy in this place. I hate the base prudence which chills us and binds us and makes us incapable of any great action, and reduces us to being like animals who calmly attend to preserving this unhappy life with no other thought. I know I shall be thought mad, as I know that all great men have had that reputation. And since the career of almost every man of great genius has begun from desperation, so I am not dismayed that mine should begin like this. I would rather be unhappy than insignificant, rather suffer than be bored, all the more so because tedium, which causes me deadly depressions of spirit, harms me much more than any physical discomfort. Fathers usually judge their sons more favourably than other people, but you contrariwise judge us more unfavourably than anyone else, and therefore you have never believed that we were born for anything great: perhaps you do not recognise any greatness other than what can be measured by arithmetic and the rules of geometry. But as for that, many people are of a different opinion; and as for us, since despairing of oneself can only be harmful, I

[1] On Count Monaldo's *piano di famiglia* and its effects on family life, see E. Gioanola's *Leopardi, la malinconia* (Milan, Jaca Book, 1995), ch. 2.

have never believed that I was made to live and die like my forebears.[2]

Having given you such reasons as I have been able to for my decision, it remains for me to ask your forgiveness for the upset I am causing you with this letter and what I am taking with me.[3] If my health had been less uncertain I would rather have gone begging from house to house than touch a bean of yours. But being as weak as I am, and as I can no longer hope for anything from you – going by the statements you have deliberately and casually come out with on this subject more than once – I have been obliged to behave in the way I have done, in order not to expose myself to the certainty of dying of hardship on the road on the second day. I am supremely sorry for it, and this is the only thing that troubles me in my decision, thinking that I am causing you displeasure; I know your great goodness of heart, and the trouble you have taken to make us live satisfied in our situation. I am grateful for it from the bottom of my soul, and I infinitely regret that I may seem infected by the vice I detest almost above all others, that is ingratitude. Difference of principles alone, which could not be overcome in any way, and which must necessarily lead me either to die here of desperation or to take the step I am now taking, has been the cause of my misfortune. Heaven for our punishment decreed that the only young people in this city who had thoughts that went somewhat beyond Recanati should be yours, as a test of your patience, and that the only father who considered these sons a misfortune should be ours. What comforts me is the thought that this is the last trouble I cause you, and that it serves to free you from the continual irritation of my presence, and from the many other inconveniences which my person has brought upon you, and would bring upon you much more in the future. Dear Father, if you allow me to call you by this name, I go down on my knees to beg you to forgive this creature unhappy by nature and by circumstances. I would like my unhappiness to have been mine alone, and no one else to have had to suffer for it, and so I hope it will be from now on. If fate ever makes me master of anything, my first thought will be to give back what necessity now compels me to avail myself of. The last favour I ask of you is this: if ever the memory of this son who has always revered and loved you returns to you, do not spurn it as hateful, and do not curse it; and if destiny has not decreed that you feel able to praise him, do not refuse to grant him that compassion which is not denied even to wrongdoers.

2 This is the essence of the quarrel between father and son, repeated in the next letter.

3 A small sum of money.

31

The escape attempt having failed, Leopardi felt the need to explain himself to his unwitting accomplice in obtaining the passport. The account given here of his father's behaviour and motivation is even more damning.

To Saverio Broglio D'Ajano • Macerata

Recanati, 13th August 1819

My dear Count Xaverio. As I have reason to believe that what I am about to relate has reached your ears by another route, and as my good name is involved, I decided to write to you so that other people's accounts did not make you think something other than the truth. I am sure you are already aware that I deceived you when I pretended that the passport I asked you for was also desired by my father. I knew that by asking you for it in any other way I would reveal my intention to my father, to whom you would immediately have written about it. If it is a sin for a poor young man, who could not hope for help in any other way from any living soul, to have tricked you with no harm to yourself, and little or none to anyone else, I confess that I am guilty: but I ask for your forgiveness, and I hope for it from your good-heartedness.

My dear count, although fate condemns me to have you of necessity against me, I don't despair of acquainting you with the cruelty of this fate. The decision I had made was neither rash nor recent. I had made up my mind to do it a month before, and I had first thought of it when I became aware of my own condition, and my father's immutable principles, that is several years ago. I do not regret it, and I have not changed. I have desisted from my plan for now, not constrained, and not convinced, but touched and tricked. I could not be convinced, just as I could not convince, because our principles are opposed, and so I avoid all talk on this subject, since talking cannot reach agreement when the fundamentals are at odds. If they oppose me with force, I shall win, because someone who is resolved to find either death or a better life has victory in his hands. My resolutions are not fleeting, like those of other people, and as I believe my father has convinced himself, in order to sleep soundly, as they say. I do not want to live in Recanati. If my father will provide me with the means to leave, as he has promised, I shall be grateful and respectful, like any good son; if not, what should have happened and did not happen is merely postponed.

My father believes that I, an inexperienced youth, do not know men. I would like not to know them, villains that they are. But perhaps I am further ahead than he imagines. He should not think he can deceive me. If his dissembling is deep and eternal, I want him to know that I do not trust him any more than he trusts me. Let him boast, if he wants to, that he has deceived me, telling me plainly that he did not want to force my hand in any way at all, and took no steps to intercept the passport. I thought I saw his heart on his sleeve, and I did what I had not done for many years: I trusted him, I was deceived, and for the last time. But he must think me very callow if he thought that so gross, and self-evident, a deception would last, and that I would not realize that your sending the passport to my father was not chance but collusion. All the more so because, although your letter was deliberately written so that it could be shown, he only showed me part of it, four days after he received it, and only out of a need to ensure that some subterfuges he had used with other people to safeguard not my reputation, but his own, in this affair, matched up with the replies I might give on the subject. As for the passport, he did not give it to me and he is holding on to it. And I am glad of it because in my hands it was more useless to me than it is now locked away with a hundred keys, and it bound me indissolubly to good faith, from which I am now free. Equally I want you to know that I am well aware that you will send this letter to my father, or inform him of its contents. I do not mind, nor am I afraid of the new obstacles he will be able to place in the way of my plans: indeed I don't go out if he opens doors for me, but if he shuts them: and my father is well aware of this, and therefore makes a show of not placing any obstruction in my path. But trying to deceive me is not the same as opening doors for me, and from now on I consider this to be a new bolt.

What I mind most of all is knowing that they are blaming this long-standing resolve of mine on a few men of letters I've met recently.[1] If I may be allowed to on this occasion, I swear to you by everything that is holiest that none of them has ever dreamed of giving me this advice. Indeed if I had revealed my decision to them I am quite certain they would have done their best to talk me out of it. I am offering to let my father read every one of the letters they have written me. My father really must believe himself to be the only sensible man on earth, since he thinks that people experienced and practised in the ways of the world would choose to get embroiled in someone else's family affairs, and bring down on their own heads the hatred of a third party, whatever the benefit might be for one of their friends. Especially since they would be very well aware, and are aware, that by leaving here I would deprive myself of my inheritance; so that it would make much more sense to them for me to stay here waiting and suffering, since they would not suffer anything with me. As for their principles, I am not deceiving myself, but I know them, so much so that I profess them too. I am not unaware that their aims may not be disinterested, but I distinguish cause from effect, and as for the latter, i.e. the principles, if they did not realize that these were my principles before I even knew the names of these men of letters (who, since they do not think like men from the Marches, must naturally be villains), they should not boast of that shrewd knowledge of men that they make such a great show of.

It is very odd that people should want to believe that unless I was *put up to it*, as they say, by men of letters, I would not be capable of a decision that any sensible person in my circumstances would see to be the only one left to me. My dear Count, you know the world: find me another young man in any town you like who has reached the age of 21 and lived as I have done. Does my father think that with a passionate character, with an extremely sensitive heart like mine, I have never had occasion to feel the desires and emotions that all young people on earth feel and seek out? does he think I haven't felt them, and much more often and more violently than other people? does he think they weren't capable of pushing me to the most terrible decisions? does he think that if until now I have led a life that one would not ask of a 70-year-old Capuchin friar, in the fullest sense of the words (and I call on the

1 Giordani and Montani. Leopardi's reading of his father's view of the situation is entirely accurate: Count Monaldo is on record as referring to Giordani as a 'wicked seducer' [*scellerato seduttore*] (cited by Damiani, p. 185).

whole of Recanati, which is amazed at it, and on my father himself as witness), that that comes from the coldness of my nature? I am asking if this is the reward I was to expect: I ask if there is another father in Recanati itself, in circumstances much less comfortable than my father's, who having a son as promising as I was, would not have made every possible effort to obtain for him what to everyone who knows me seemed natural and necessary, except to my father: I am asking if the Galamini, if the Giaccherini,[2] if the many others of this sort who at 16 already had more freedom than I have at 21, are better than me: I ask if I have lost the best part of my youth, toiling and labouring incredibly productively, shunning all other pleasure, ruining my health entirely and forever with my studies, in order to live in Recanati and obtain what all my fellow citizens obtain: I ask if after all this suffering and all this harm I am to form for my future life no other hope than what is left to the Galamini and the Giaccherini, who spend their youth as everyone sees. And if my father, loathing any notion of the great and the exceptional, regrets having let me study, is distressed that heaven did not make me a mole, and, in any case not only does not allow me anything out of the ordinary, but denies me what any father anywhere regards as his duty to allow children who show even a glimmering of intelligence, and is resolutely determined that I must live and die like his ancestors[3] – is a son rebelling if he does not submit to this law? If you do not believe my father has the intentions I have stated in regard to me, rest assured that that is the way it is, and if he shows himself to you in a different light, believe me that he is deceiving you, believe me that he is deceiving other people too, knowing as he does that few people are entirely in agreement with his principles – believe a young man who, though young, has a deep knowledge of the character of the people he has lived with since he was born. And I know for certain that he has declared that we shan't leave here while he is alive. Now I, who want him to live, and want to live myself, and live as a young man and not an old one (when I'll be no use to myself or anyone else), will throw myself in desperation into the hands of fate, and if fate is against me, as I have no doubt it will be, I shall be one more man lost, and the millionth example of men's wickedness.

Add to this the endless, deadly depressions of spirit that are inevitable given my character and a life like the one I am forced to lead. They ruin my health, so that any ailment I suffer once never goes away again, on account of the supreme power of a mind all afflicted and enclosed in its sorrow over a very weak and tormented body; anyone can see that there can be no other remedy for this than powerful distractions that are capable of making the spirit take on a habit different from its previous one.

I'll say one other thing in conclusion. I have always been in love with virtue: what I wanted to put into effect was no crime: but I am also capable of sin. Shame on them that I can say that virtue has always been no use to me. The warmth and the strength of my feelings could be directed to good, but if they want to turn them to evil, they will succeed. For a long time I have known the way to be less unhappy in this world, and I see examples of it in this very city. Don't let them force me to take that path.[4] I have no great opinion of myself: yet a

2 Two local families.

3 Cf. [30], n. 2.

4 The reference seems again to be to the example provided by the feckless Galamini and Giaccherini.

person who, having loved virtue from birth, gives himself in desperation to sin will always seem remarkable to me.

Forgive me for the tone I have adopted for the first time in this letter, and which in part I regret having used. I would not ever want to forget my duties, I want myself alone to be unhappy, and I swear to you that if anything troubled me about the decision I had taken, it was not the dangers I was exposing myself to, nor other people's censure, which means nothing to me, nor the death which hardship and poverty would quickly have brought for me, to my consolation, but only the thought of causing my parents to feel displeasure. I have always loved my father and I shall go on loving him: and it pains me that he wants to treat me like other men, and thinks deception works to greater advantage with me than candour, whereas I think I have given sufficient proof of the opposite. I repeat that all I want is to be always grateful and respectful to him, and so I certainly shall be in reality, if I cannot be so in appearance as well. I do not regret my past behaviour, and I do not want to change it. All I ask is that he should have some consideration for my inclinations, which can now no longer be changed naturally, and which if they are thwarted will make me unhappy for as long as I live, and perhaps worse than unhappy. Forgive me the tedium I have caused you by writing at such length, and the hasty, untidy handwriting, caused by the huge difficulty I have with every kind of concentration. If you do not disdain to be my friend, I shall continue always to love you, while not expecting you on that account to refrain in any way from opposing me in all that might be required by the need for prudence accepted among men, and the friendship which ties you to my father. Believe me, your most obliged, most devoted servant and friend,

Giacomo Leopardi.

32

Leopardi wrote to Giordani telling him of the failed escape attempt.

To Pietro Giordani • Milan

Recanati, 20th August 1819

I feel my own troubles little now, since I hear that yours are somewhat abated. Try as hard as you can always to give me better news. Just think that I don't have Arici's six cantos, they're not available here, where nobody even knows who Arici is;[1] and even if they were available I couldn't do anything with them, as I'm incapable of reading anything. The same goes for Monti's work, and not only the third volume, but all the earlier ones, which no citizen of Recanati has even seen the cover of. I took the initiative in writing to Perticari this February on the occasion of the small poems I published.[2] A *month* later he replied in a very friendly way, and I thought I'd gained a friend. He invited me to answer, and I did so; on getting no reply, I wrote again a month and a half later, and equally to no effect. Since then I've not

[1] The first six cantos of Cesare Arici's *Gerusalemme distrutta.*

[2] The two patriotic canzoni; see [18], n. 3 and [21].

wanted to trouble him further. I have gone back to writing to Montani in Varese, to see if the post might actually manage to deliver some of my letters.

I was escaping from here forever and they found me out. God did not choose that they should use force: they used prayers and grief. I no longer hope for anything, although they have promised me a great deal: but I trusted only in myself, and now that I am not myself any more I trust in no one. Carlo is left with the same hopes, perhaps even less, because in him they have not yet recognized a desperation capable of deciding on some disagreeable action. But they won't take long to realize.

If you like, remember me fondly to Mai. Give me news of yourself, especially your thoughts, and your state of health. Paolina and Carlo wish you every cause for cheerfulness. I am the one who will always be your chief admirer, and the more men and scholars I get to know, the more I admire and value you, and I love you as a very dear thing that I didn't deserve, unless perhaps on account of this very love which no one in the world can outdo. Adieu. Be fond of me.

33

Leopardi had been corresponding since April with Leonardo Trissino, a liberal friend of Giordani's, whom he now told of recent events.

To Leonardo Trissino • Vicenza

Recanati, 27th September 1819

My dear Count. You could give me no greater comfort than what you have given me with the news of the good progress of your strange and painful illness,[1] which Giordani told me about when he was in Recanati, and I was very concerned about it, although I did not venture to ask you about it directly. You cheer me up of your own accord, and I thank you with all my heart, and I am as pleased about it as can be, and I want you to carry on giving me other news of this kind too.

Sir, you write to me with an affection that beguiles me. The more I become acquainted with the wickedness and baseness of men, the more enthusiastic and fervent I become towards noble and worthy hearts like yours, thinking it a supreme and very rare good fortune to find them, and much more so to be deemed worthy of their love. If you wish to take into account any other good quality, you had better seek out other people on whom to place your affections; but a heart as candid and tremulous and impassioned as this, and certain to reciprocate with equal and greater affection, will not be so easy to find, and in this respect I do not judge myself unworthy of your having begun to love me, and I beg you fervently to carry on doing so.

As for the things you ask me about,[2] I want you to be convinced, and to consider it quite

[1] A herpes infection, which Trissino apparently suffered from all his life.

[2] Trissino had enquired about the progress of his studies.

certain, not only that I am worth very little, but that for all that I passionately want to put all of that little to use for the benefit of my poor country, fate without a shadow of doubt will prevent my doing so. It began to do so from the very beginning of my life with every kind of obstacle, domestic, geographical, physical, and every other kind imaginable. But in the last six months it has prevented any use of my eyes and my mind because of an extreme weakness of the ocular nerves, which prevents me not just from any reading or studying, but from any slightest mental effort. And so, deprived of the only consolation that was left me in a city like this, and in my condition, you can imagine what kind of a life it is that I am leading. I was about to give in to fate, putting into effect a decision which would have brought me in a short time to the common end of all ills, but I was found out, and prevented, not by force, which could not do it, but by prayers.

I too am very concerned about Giordani, having had no news since August the 4th. Continue to count me among those who are fond of you, and cheer me up with your letters, and with the evidence of your love; if I can be sure I have got that and can keep it, I shall consider that in this my fate has abandoned its usual practice. Your most grateful and most affectionate servant,

Giacomo Leopardi.

34

The failed attempt to leave home, and worsening health problems, which by now had made him unable to read or write for eight months, precipitated a crisis which Leopardi described in this letter to Giordani in terms that suggest a nervous breakdown.

To Pietro Giordani • Milan

Recanati, 19th November [1819]

I am so stupefied by the nothingness which surrounds me that I do not know how I have the strength to pick up the pen to reply to your letter of the 1st. If at this moment I were to go mad, I think my madness would be to sit forever with my eyes staring, my mouth open, my hands between my knees, without laughing or crying or moving except when forced to from the place where I happened to be. I no longer have the energy to conceive any desire, not even for death, not because I have any fear at all of death, but I no longer see any difference between death and this life of mine, where not even pain comes to comfort me any more. This is the first time that tedium not only weighs on me and wearies me, but it torments me and tears me like a terrible pain; and I am so terrified by the futility of all things, and by the condition of men when all passions have died, as they are spent in my soul, that I go out of my mind, thinking that my desperation too is nothing.

As for the studies you affectionately urge me to continue, for the last eight months I have not known what such studies might be, as the nerves of my eyes and my head are so weakened that not only am I unable to read, or pay attention to anyone reading anything at all to me, but I cannot fix my mind on any thought of great or little consequence.

My dear friend, although I no longer understand the words friendship and love, still I beg you to go on being fond of me, and to remember me, and to believe that I love you as best I can, and I shall always love you, and I want you to write to me. Adieu.

35

A month later his depression had not lifted, but had induced in him a more generalized sense of the wretchedness of the human condition.

To Pietro Giordani • Piacenza

Recanati, 17th December 1819

I thought that the capacity to love like the capacity to hate was extinguished in my soul. Now your letter makes me realize that it is still alive and functioning. The world must be something, and I not entirely dead, since I feel fired with affection for that fine heart of yours. Tell me, where shall I find a man like you? tell me, where shall I find another I can love as I love you? Dear soul, the only one *infandos miserata labores*[1] of this wretched creature, do you perhaps think that I am moved by the compassion you show me because I am its object? I am touched by it now because I see no other life than tears and compassion; and if sometimes I find myself a little less disconsolate, then I have the strength to weep, and I weep because I am happier, and I weep for the wretchedness of men and the nothingness of things. There was a time when the wickedness of men and virtue's misfortunes moved me to contempt, and my grief sprang from contemplating iniquity. But now I weep for the unhappiness of slaves and tyrants, oppressed and oppressors, good and bad, and in my sadness there is no longer any spark of anger, and this life no longer seems to me worth the fighting. And much less do I have the strength to harbour ill feeling against the foolish and the ignorant; on the contrary, I try to merge with them; and because the tenor and the habits and the events and the places of this life of mine are still those of my childhood, I cling with both hands to these last remnants and these shadows of that blessed and blissful time, when I hoped for and dreamed of happiness, and as I hoped and dreamed enjoyed it, and it has gone and will never come back, surely never again; seeing with extreme terror that along with childhood the world and life are finished for me and for all those who think and feel; so that the only people who live until they die are those many people who remain children all their lives. My dear friend – the only person I see in this terrifying desert of the world – I feel I'm dead already, and although I have always believed myself to be good for something out of the ordinary, I have never thought that fate would allow me to be anything. So do not be distressed on my account, for where there is no hope there is no place for anxiety: rather love me serenely as someone not destined for anything at all, but on the contrary sure that his life is already over. And I shall love you with all the warmth left to this frozen and shivering soul. Carlo and Paolina send their fond regards. Adieu.

[1] *Aeneid* I, 597: *who has felt compassion for the unspeakable suffering.*

36

Leopardi had been corresponding for some time in a desultory way with Angelo Mai.[1] *In October 1819 Mai had been appointed librarian to the Vatican Library, where he found a copy of a lost work of Cicero's, the 'De re publica'. Leopardi's enthusiasm and excitement at the discovery, and his eagerness to work on the newly discovered text, account for the slightly obsequious tone of this letter.*

To Angelo Mai • Rome

Recanati, 10th January 1820

Dear Sir. Since your arrival in Rome I have more than once wanted to intimate to you how happy I was to have you closer now than previously, and to refresh your memory of this honest admirer and servant of yours. But fear of being a nuisance, and distracting you from better occupations, has always dissuaded me. Finally the acclaim for the new marvels you are performing does not leave me the strength to restrain myself any longer, and when the whole of Europe is about to celebrate your precious discovery, I do not have the heart to be among the last to congratulate you on it and show the joy I feel, not only in common with all scholars, but also particularly because of the esteem and respectful affection which I profess especially to you. You really are a miracle in a thousand things – intelligence, taste, learning, industriousness, tireless study, unprecedented and unparalleled good luck. In short, you take us back to the time of the Petrarchs and the Poggios, when every day was lit up by a new classical discovery, and the astonishment and delight of men of letters never ceased. But now, when erudition and criticism shine so brightly, when there is such a wealth of libraries, such a host of philologists, you alone, in manuscripts which for centuries have been accessible to the investigations of any scholar, in libraries frequented by every sort of learned man, you alone discover treasures lamented as lost without hope of recovery since the first renascence of letters, treasures which men of letters in their most idle and fleeting hopes had never thought could come to light again: this is a marvel to beat all the wonders of the fourteenth and fifteenth centuries.

Some time ago I lovingly and carefully prepared the materials for some letters, to demonstrate, in a manner which if not beautiful or good was at least my own, the real and deep usefulness and value of your discoveries, with a quantity of critical observations on the details of each of them. But my utterly ruined health, and in these last nine months an extreme weakness of the nerves of my eyes and head, which actually prevents my fixing my mind on any thought whatsoever, has deprived me of the possibility of carrying out my plans. In any event, because the acclaim and the splendour of your most recent discovery is such as to arouse the sleepiest and the weakest, I too have felt myself spurred by a desire not to remain idle on such a propitious occasion. And having made up my mind to gather all my almost vanished strength, for a study (perhaps my last) on the great work which you are about to publish, I pluck up the courage to make a request which will seem improbable to you, unless

[1] See [2], n. 3.

you should wish to take into consideration the confidence inspired in me by your extraordinary kindness, and the many proofs of affection you have not disdained to give me at various times: and it is that when the work is at the printers, you should be so good as to send me the sheets as they are run off, so that my labours should have more room, since they cannot be other than very slow for the reasons I have stated. And should I by this means manage to do something, always with the proviso that it be subjected to your scrutiny and judgment, you can imagine how the boundless gratitude I profess to you must grow as a result. But it will grow in the same manner if, judging that you are unable to satisfy me in this, you tell me so frankly, reassuring me in this way that you still consider me your special servant and friend.[2]

I would dearly love to find an opportunity to prove to you how fitting this last desire of mine is, and I mean how I remain always what I have been since the first moment I knew you. Be so good as to provide me with such an opportunity, and to forgive my temerity. Your most devoted, most obliged true servant,

Giacomo Leopardi.

[2] Mai did not agree to the request to see the pages as they came off the printing press.

37

Studying (no longer possible) was now described as a source of comfort.

To Pietro Giordani • Piacenza

Recanati, 14th January 1820

My letter of December 17th, in answer to your very affectionate one of the 8th, can't have reached you, since I've had no reply. Not even the slight consolation of talking to you about our misfortunes; to you, the only person who can understand me. In this letter I'm answering yours of the 22nd. You are all too right to say that perhaps I would not be aware of, and certainly would not feel, all the nothingness of humanity, if I could still occupy myself with my studies. I've never found a more lasting and reliable source of distraction and forgetting, nor a less fleeting illusion. The words of your last letter give even further confirmation to the notion I always had of your matchless heart. There is no need for me to talk to you about myself. You wouldn't be the man you are if you could doubt my love, which is deeper and more intense all the time. I would dearly like to prove it to you by my actions, but fate denies this proof to both of us. Let's be satisfied with words and the mutual certainty of our affection. Paolina and Carlo return your fond regards. Adieu.

38

Early in the new year Leopardi wrote to Brighenti asking him to arrange for the printing of three canzoni, including a new one he had written to celebrate Mai's discovery.[1] *The meticulous attention to detail is characteristic.*

To Pietro Brighenti • Bologna

Recanati, 4th February 1820

Dear Sir. As long ago as last October, thinking an opportunity for delivery by hand safer than the post, I gave a letter for your good self to a Gentleman from here, who on setting out for your parts promised to deliver it to you; but as I have never had a reply, I think he must have forgotten his promise. Now I am going to trouble you with a request which your kindness alone gives me the courage to make. With this letter will be a small manuscript of mine which I am sending by post, insured. I would ask you to be so kind as to arrange to have it printed at my expense there in Bologna, in 12o or 16o format so as not to exceed two printed sheets, on ordinary paper, except for a dozen I'd like printed on good quality paper, either wove paper or what you consider most suitable; and as for the overall number of copies, I want it not to exceed between two and three hundred. As for the binding, I'd like you to have it done in coloured paper, or else printed white paper, as you think best. But most importantly, as the printing must be done in my absence, I would ask you to be so kind as to give the task of proof-reading to a person who would do it with all the care necessary in these small editions, where every tiny error is a cause for shame, and often also badly damages the work itself and the author's honour. And so the proof-reader should not overlook even the punctuation, which I have tried to set out in the manuscript with absolute precision, since I think that it too plays no small part in the good or bad quality of the style, especially in this sort of writing.

Should you be so kind as to oblige me, informing me of the cost, my gratitude towards you will be boundlessly increased. But my chief desire is that you should excuse my boldness, attributing it to the trust I have in your kindness. And with great and genuine respect I have the pleasure of remaining your most devoted, most obliged, servant and friend,

Giacomo Leopardi.

[1] The canzoni are: *Nella morte di una donna fatta trucidare col suo portato* (On the Death of a Woman Killed with her Unborn Child); *Ad Angelo Mai quand'ebbe trovato i libri di Cicerone della Repubblica* (To Angelo Mai, on his Discovering the Books of Cicero's *De re publica*); *Per una donna inferma di malattia lunga e mortale* (For a Woman Suffering from a Long and Fatal Illness). Brighenti subsequently suggested [M253] that he reprint the two patriotic canzoni (already published in Rome at the end of 1818, see [21]) as well.

39

After almost a year of continuous ill-health, the arrival of spring seemed to signal a revival in Leopardi's spirits, prompting him to reflect on the respective roles of reason and nature in human existence.

To Pietri Giordani • Piacenza

Recanati, 6th March 1820

My dear friend. Since the 10th of December I've written you two letters to Piacenza to no effect: I don't know about the third, because on the 15th of February when you last wrote to me it could not have arrived. I too am fervently longing for fair springtime as the only hope of medicine left for my exhaustion of spirit;[1] and a few evenings ago, before going to bed, I opened the window of my room, and seeing a clear sky and bright moonlight, and feeling the warm air and hearing some dogs barking in the distance, there stirred within me certain old images, and I thought I felt an impulse in my heart, whereupon I set to yelling like a madman, begging nature for mercy – nature, whose voice I seemed to be hearing after so long a time. And at that moment, casting a glance at the state I'd been in, and to which I was sure I'd return immediately afterwards, as indeed happened, I felt an icy fear, not being able to understand how life can be endured without illusions and intense feelings, and without imagination and enthusiasm, things which a year ago took up all my time, and made me so blissfully happy in spite of my troubles. Now I am stiff and withered like a dry reed, and no feeling finds its way into this poor soul, and for me, at the age I now am, the eternal and supreme omnipotence of love itself is annihilated. Meanwhile I tell you these things I'd tell no one else, since I'm certain you will not think them fanciful, as you know how I detest above all else the cursed affectation that corrupts everything beautiful in this world, and you know that you're the only person who can understand me; and so, as I cannot talk to anyone else, I talk to you about these feelings of mine, which for the first time I don't call pointless. For this is the wretched condition of man, and the barbarous teaching of reason, that as human pleasures and pains are mere illusions, the anguish that comes from the certainty of the nothingness of things is always and only right and true. And although if we were to lead our whole life in accordance with this feeling of nothingness, the world would come to an end and we would rightly be called mad, at any rate it is logically certain that it would be a madness that was reasonable in every respect, indeed that compared with it all wisdom would be folly, since everything in this world is done out of a simple and continual forgetting of this universal truth, that everything is nothingness. I would like these considerations to bring a blush to the faces of those wretched would-be philosophers who take comfort in the boundless increase in reason, and think that human happiness consists in knowing the truth, when there is no other truth than nothingness, and this thought, and having it continually in mind, as reason would wish, must lead us necessarily and directly to that frame of mind I spoke of, which would be madness according to nature, and absolute and perfect

[1] Giordani on the 15th of February had written expressing his impatience for the arrival of spring [M252].

wisdom according to reason.

My nerves are in their usual state. I hug and kiss you, and hope your efforts to put a little more life into your native city turn out well.[2] Adieu. Paolina and Carlo love you and send their regards.

[2] Giordani was trying to set up a gentlemen's literary club which would supply copies of gazettes and scientific journals for members to read, thus enabling his fellow townsmen to stay in touch with contemporary thinking.

40

Leopardi explained to Giordani his sense of what remained to be done in Italian literature, and lamented his own inability to do it.

To Pietro Giordani • Piacenza

Recanati, 20th March 1820

My dear friend. I'm replying to your letter of February 23rd, having already replied to your other letter of the 15th on the 6th of this month. I'm delighted at the good you are trying to do for your native city, and I fervently hope your plans have a happy outcome.[1] I knew about the books of the *De re publica*, and as for the worthlessness of Italian eloquence you write about, what can I say? There are still so many things to be created in Italy, that I sigh to see myself so constrained and fettered by bad luck that the little strength I have cannot be put to any use. But as for plans, who can count them? Lyric poetry to be created (and this in all nations, because the French too say the ode is the sonata of literature), so many kinds of tragedy, because from Alfieri we have just the one kind; poetic, literary and political eloquence, philosophy truly of its time, satire, poetry of every kind suitable for our age; even a language and a style that, while being classic and old, yet seem modern and are easy to understand and as pleasing to the people as to men of letters. In short, the course to be run is boundless; and I who had perhaps received from nature some little strength to take part, and achieve something, am always imprisoned by fate, and now have no hope of showing Italy something that at present she cannot even dream of. But you, my dear friend, take heart, and take comfort from the comparison between your riches and others' poverty, and the sight of the vast field that lies before you, and all empty. You ask me what I'm thinking and writing. But for a long time I've not thought or written or read anything at all, because of the persistent weakness of the nerves of my eyes and head: and perhaps I'll only leave sketches of the works I'm thinking about, and in which I've been exercising as best I can the creative faculty which is now extinguished in Italian minds. And for all my knowing the small thing that I am, yet I'm terrified at having to leave what I have conceived unexecuted. But now I really have become unfit for anything, I despise myself, I'd hate and loathe myself if I had the energy, but hate is a passion, and I no longer feel passions. And this is the only

[1] See previous letter, n. 2.

reason I can find for not having torn my heart from my breast a thousand times. I see that everything contradicts me, and I'm rebuffed on all sides, and it's enough for me to want something for the opposite to happen; I don't know what I'm doing in this world.

As for the *Canzoni* you ask about, the first and last were written a year ago, and so you won't find what I'm feeling today except in the second, which came from my pen by a miracle in the last few days.[2] I've written to Brighenti to send you the three copies you were kind enough to ask him for, and another two that I'm asking you to give in my name to Count Pallastrelli and Count Calciati there in Piacenza. And should you want any more, you'll be doing me a favour by telling Brighenti directly. Paolina and Carlo are well and very eager to see you. I've no doubt it isn't necessary to ask you to go on loving me, and I think it's equally superfluous to tell you I love you above all others. Adieu.

[2] The new canzone is *Ad Angelo Mai*, inspired by Mai's discovery of Cicero's *De re publica*; see [36]. It is the first of Leopardi's poems of patriotic commitment to introduce more personal themes.

41

In response to Brighenti's request for payment to cover the costs of the edition of the canzoni, Leopardi explained his financial embarrassment and tried to abort the project.

To Pietro Brighenti • Bologna

Recanati, 7th April 1820

Dear Sir, Patron and Friend. It would always be extremely indelicate, and more so than ever in these times, to demand from a friend the loan of a sum of money, whatever the amount. And it was therefore my intention to send you the money required for the edition in advance, as was right and proper, once I knew for certain that it was to go ahead at my expense. But you perhaps know that I am a dependent son, and when I first asked you about this edition I still did not actually have the money needed for it, but I was convinced that I would have it any time I wanted it, and I think everybody who knows me here or elsewhere must have thought the same thing. After your very courteous letter of the 22nd I found out that I was mistaken, having utterly failed to scrape together the full amount.[1] I do not choose to abase myself, and it has never been my habit since misfortune brought me into this world. And fate may even make me lack food and clothing, but not force me to ask for them even from my family. Therefore I entirely renounce any plans in connection with this or any other edition; and since I'm not very clever – and no matter how clever someone is, it's never any use at all in this world – I am resolved to sacrifice my intelligence entirely to the immutable

[1] Count Monaldo had refused to give him money for the edition, pleading the family's financial difficulties, but in fact alarmed by his son's political sympathies; see Damiani, p. 180f., for an account of the whole tortuous episode.

and eternal wickedness of fate, by burying myself even deeper in the terrible nothingness in which I've lived until now. Please do not think of me any more unless as the most desperate man to be found on this earth, and only a whisker away from removing himself forever from the perpetual unhappiness of this cursed life of mine. And I thank heaven especially for having convinced me of my impotence before a friend such as your good self had yet undertaken anything on my behalf which might deprive me of the possibility of putting an end to the matter as I do at this time.

I would like you to tell our friend Giordani, who must once again be a witness to the cruelty of the hellish fury of my fate in everything connected with me, right down to my dealings with the post, that in addition to the letters of mine already lost of which I advised him this February, I realize that another one has gone missing as well, which I had written him on the 6th of last month, and I think the same thing will happen to the last one I wrote him on the 20th. But tell him that his don't go astray, at least in the ones I've been getting I find no indication that others have got lost. And just as I have broken off my contacts with everyone else, so I see that not I but the post will completely break off my contact with him as well. [...]

Please excuse the trouble I have put you to; thanking you warmly for the deep and undeserved kindness you show towards me, I assure you of my unfailing affectionate gratitude. Your most devoted, most obliged servant and friend,

Giacomo Leopardi.

42

On finding out that his father had written to Brighenti – although he could only have known about the projected edition by reading through his son's private papers – Leopardi expressed his anger and contempt. The desire to circumvent his father's interference and have full control over his own works would lead to secrecy and subterfuges in the future.

To Pietro Brighenti • Bologna

Recanati, 21st April 1820

Dear Sir, Patron and Friend. Before receiving your letter dated the 12th of this month, I knew nothing of my father's letter, just as I still do not know anything more about it than what you write. I do not even see how my father can have found out about something I have never spoken of to him or anyone else (as I have few friends outside Recanati and none in this barbaric town), unless he has been through my papers, which does not surprise me; and I do not complain about it, because everyone follows his own principles. As for my father's misgivings, I reply that just as I shall always be what I choose to be, so I want to appear to everyone what I am; and I am certain that I shan't be forced to do otherwise for roughly the same reason Cato in Utica was certain of his liberty.[1] But it is my fate to seem a bloody fool

[1] Cato killed himself for liberty: Leopardi is saying he will kill himself rather than compromise.

to all the people who have dealings with me on a daily basis, and they think I know nothing of the world and men other than their complexion, and that I don't know what I'm doing, but am letting myself be led on by the people they say,[2] without understanding where they are leading me. So they reckon they must enlighten me and keep watch over me. And as for *enlightenment*, I thank them kindly; as for *keeping watch*, I can assure them they are wasting their time.

As for my *canzoni*, I am putting them in the large bundle of all my words or deeds or writings from my birth on, which my detestable fate has stamped with everlasting pointlessness. I have forgone all the pleasures of young people. From 10 to 21 years of age I have kept myself to myself, meditating, writing and studying books and things. Not only have I never asked for an hour's respite, but I have never asked for or got any other help in those studies than my patience and my own hard work. The fruit of my labours is to be despised in a way that is remarkable given my situation, especially in a small town. After everyone abandoned me, good health was pleased to follow suit. In 21 years, having begun to think and suffer while still a child, I have run the gamut of misfortunes of a long life, and I am morally speaking old, or rather decrepit, because even feeling and enthusiasm, which were the companions and the sustenance of my life, have faded for me in a way that horrifies me. It is time to die. It is time to give in to fate; the most terrible thing a young person (normally full of fine hopes) can do, but the only pleasure left to one who after prolonged efforts finally realises that he was born with the sacred and indelible curse of destiny.

I beg you most earnestly not to send the manuscript to my father.[3] If you happen to have sent it already, and he were to send it back to have it printed with any alteration however tiny, I beg and entreat you – with whatever authority I can have over writings that I persist in thinking of as mine – to reply that I have entirely given up all thought of publishing those *canzoni*, and that I have told you so quite unambiguously. Should he send them back without alteration, or should he write telling you to have them printed without having seen them, you are to do as you think best, I being in that case completely indifferent.

Those who reacted unfavourably to my *Canzone* on Dante were wrong, in my view, because I am telling you in so many words *that I did not write it to displease such people*, but partly out of love for the pure and simple truth, and hatred for pointless favouritism and prejudice; partly because, as I could not name the people these people would have liked me to, I introduced other actors as a pretext and to stand in their place.[4]

2 Giordani and Montani.

3 Brighenti [M266] had offered to approach Count Monaldo on Giacomo's behalf to try to obtain his consent to publication.

4 Brighenti had reported trying to reassure Count Monaldo (who thought the poem dangerously liberal in its sentiments) that in fact some liberals in Bologna had not liked *Sopra il monumento di Dante* because of its anti-French polemic. The people Leopardi has not named are the Austrians (restored to power in the Lombardo-Veneto after the Congress of Vienna); both Austrians and French represent foreign domination in Italy. Monaldo's views on liberty are summed up with admirable succinctness in his *Autobiography*: 'One can be free, indeed anyone who is not base must be free, but the foundations and limits of true freedom are faith in Jesus Christ and loyalty to the legitimate Sovereign. Outside these limits, people do not live freely, but dissolutely.' [*Si può esser libero, anzi deve esserlo chi non è vile, ma le basi e i confini della vera libertà sono la fede di Gesù Cristo, e la fedeltà al Sovrano legittimo. Fuori di questi limiti non si vive liberi, ma dissoluti.*]

I would go to the stake for Giordani, but I am so terrified by the futility of my actions, to which I have been condemned since I was born, that I barely have strength left to write to him again. Yet I shall certainly do so, although to no purpose, and I won't submit to my misfortune in this respect.

I am as cheered by the gracious offer of your friendship as I am saddened by the story of your misfortunes. In short, in this world one only has to be undeserving of ills to have a plentiful supply of them. I am no use even to myself, but if my destiny ever allowed me to help or encourage you in any way, you can be sure that I would give heartfelt thanks to fate for it, and I would take the opportunity to do so with whatever strength I had left. Love me, and be assured that I love you in return, and forgive me for the trouble I must have caused you with this business. This will end up falling into nothingness too along with all my things, and with myself. Your most devoted servant and friend,

Giacomo Leopardi.

43

The unreliability of the post continued to make writing seem futile.

To Pietro Giordani • Piacenza

Recanati, 24th April [1820]

In short, I'm splattering ink on paper pointlessly when I write to you, and I think you will have heard from Brighenti how many other times I've done so to no effect.[1] But this is the one thing I won't grow weary of doing. If we were living in ancient times, you would be frightened by me, seeing me so perpetually cursed by fate, and you would think me the wickedest man in the world. I throw myself onto the ground and writhe,[2] asking how long I still have left to live. My misfortune is assured forever: how much longer shall I have to bear it? how much longer? I'm on the point of cursing heaven and nature who seem to have brought me into this world on purpose to suffer. I think it almost impossible that you can love me. At any rate I have to force myself to believe it, and in regard to you I cannot doubt it, but only in relation to my own bad luck. For certainly if you love me, you are the only one on this earth who does. Brighenti writes to me about a Discourse of yours on the Marquess of Montrone's poems. I've no idea if it's old or new. If it's old, why have you never spoken to me about it? if it's new, why don't you send it to me? But perhaps you realize that I have become less than nothing, and worse than dead, and the services one performs for the living are no longer appropriate for me. Paolina and Carlo send their regards and love you very much, and so do I with all my remaining strength. Where is the man more desperate than me? what pleasure have I enjoyed in this world? what hope is left me? what is virtue? I don't understand anything any more. Adieu.

1 Yet another reference to letters which had gone missing in the post.

2 Cf. *La sera del dì di festa* (The Evening of the Holiday), written this year, l. 22-23: 'here I throw myself on the ground, and cry out, and tremble' [*e qui per terra / Mi getto, e grido, e fremo*] .

44

Rage at his father's interference was expressed with biting sarcasm in this letter to Brighenti, whom he had asked first to arrange and then to abort the printing of the canzoni.

To Pietro Brighenti • Bologna

Recanati, 28th April 1820

Dear Sir, Patron and Friend. I reply to your letter of the 22nd of this month. I thank my father (whom I have always respected and truly loved) for the permission he grants me to print *my* canzoni.[1] But he does not want the two Roman ones to be reprinted. He is quite right. He wanted you to tell him the titles of the unpublished ones. He did the right thing. He does not want the first one printed. Again, quite right: not to my mind, to be sure, but it is quite right that *in my writings* his opinion should prevail, because I am and always will be a child, and not capable of making decisions for myself. That leaves two canzoni. For these two (about which at last and by chance it is my turn to have a say) I say there is no need to put the printers to the trouble, and so let's put an end to the matter, and the bother I must have caused you.

My father has seen only the title of the first unpublished one, just as he had seen it by chance here as well, while I was writing it, a year ago; and he immediately imagined a thousand filthy things in the execution of it, and a thousand improprieties in the subject, which can come into the mind of a person who, although very intelligent and quite well read, yet has no idea of the literary world. The title of the second unpublished one was luckily found to be quite innocent. It's about a Monsignor. But my father cannot conceive of someone for whom all subjects provide an opportunity to speak of what matters most to him, and he has no inkling that under that title is hidden an Ode full of horrible fanaticism.[2]

Thank you for your offer to print my canzoni, or what's left of them, in the *Abbreviatore*. But it has always been a bad experience for me publishing in journals things not written expressly for them, and I have seen that they are read by very few people, and read or not read are immediately forgotten. Do as you please with the manuscript without sending it back to me, all the more so because I too am now beginning to agree with the whole world which despises me, and to think I have thrown away the labours of all these years at this best time of my life, and lost all the blessings of this life fruitlessly, though irreparably, in order to manage to write things that are not worth a fig. What you say to me in your own name à propos of my canzone *Nello strazio di una giovane* is I think absolutely right, and I thank you for

[1] See [38], n. 1.

[2] The title of the first of the new canzoni (on a current local scandal involving a young woman who had died from an abortion) had, perhaps not surprisingly, caused Count Monaldo some alarm. The second, addressed to Mai, who was a Monsignor, seemed guaranteed *ipso facto* to be innocuous. The reference to 'horrible fanaticism' seems ironical, but was certainly unwise. Brighenti may have felt impelled to denounce Leopardi to the Austrian authorities (for whom he worked as an informer), and the poem was in fact subsequently banned in the Lombardo-Veneto region [M481].

it above all the rest;[3] and I consider it to be a sure proof of what I've said; because my own poor judgment, and the experience of writing that canzone about uneducated women and people, in the way I usually do, and its having gone much better than on other occasions, had convinced me of the opposite. I realize now that I was mistaken.[4]

I am most grateful to you for the affectionate invitation you extend to visit your fair and learned city. But what would my personal unhappiness consist of (I say my personal unhappiness, because no one is spared the unhappiness we all share, least of all I who was born to feed on it) if I were my own master, and free to go wherever I pleased? You probably do not know Recanati, but you surely do know that the March is the most ignorant and uncivilised province in Italy. Now the citizens of Recanati themselves all admit that my city is the most uncivilised and dead in the whole of the March, and away from here people have no idea of what life here is like. I want you to know then that I have never left nor will leave Recanati, I do not know a single man who is well known, except for poor Giordani who came on purpose to visit me, and consequently I am sure I shall never be able to attain even that celebrity which the most insignificant scribblers achieve, and which you do not get except through knowing people, and through a life lived in the world, and not completely cut off from it. It being unfortunately true that the rarest and most sublime intelligence (even supposing I had any of it) is not enough even to make one's name known, without the help of indispensable circumstances. Music, if not my chief passion, is certainly a great passion of mine, and must be for all souls capable of enthusiasm. Entertainments and distractions, even if they were not to my liking, are – as all those who know me feel – the only remedy left for my already ruined health, without which I am going to perish and inevitably soon waste away.

Love me, and take care of yourself, and give my fond regards to Giordani. I remain your most devoted servant and friend,

Giacomo Leopardi.

I answer my father's objections to my first unpublished canzone with a single example among the millions available, that I happen to have in mind. Goethe's *Werther* is about an episode which was widely known in Germany, and Caroline and her husband were alive and well when that famous work was published. Well then? But if we wished to follow the grand principles (cautious and typical of the March) of my father, who, as I have said, has nothing to do with the literary world, we would always write about subjects from Biblical times, and our writings would not even fail to pass the censorship of the Spanish Inquisition that was. My intellect is weary of chains imposed from within the family and from outside.

3 Brighenti, caught in the middle between father and son, had suggested [M269] that this poem was not the best of the three, and that he publish only the other two. The version of the title used here and in the next letter (On a Young Woman's Torment) is an alternative to that cited in [38], n. 1.

4 This deferring to the judgment of others also seems to be ironical.

45

The correspondence about the projected edition of the canzoni continued.

To Pietro Brighenti • Bologna

Recanati, 26th May 1820

My dearest Sir. No, for God's sake no, do not write that I have cooled in my friendship towards you. I write with a heart so closed and trembling with despair, that I do not know what I am putting down on the paper, and I start by saying this so that you will excuse me any inadvertent blunder I might commit. Returning to the subject, if I wrote to you bitterly, it never entered my head that the bitterness might fall on you, rather than on the people I was talking to you about. As for your judgment on my canzone *Nello strazio*, etc., I don't know how you could have thought that I wished to reproach you or complain about you. Giordani can bear witness to how much I want to defer to my friends in everything I write; he knows that at a hint of disapproval from him I have thrown aside works already finished on which I had worked long and hard. I'll tell you frankly that having a particular fondness for that canzone, it upset me to see that you did not judge it favourably, but in the same way that it is upsetting if a hail storm wipes out a capital asset; if this happens we don't complain about anyone, unless we are mad, because it is not something that someone chose to do. I thanked you for having revealed your opinion to me, and I did so sincerely and warmly, because my friends can do me no greater favour than show me the faults in my little works, or even the futility of all of them.

As for your kind invitation to visit Bologna, what else did I reply, except that I was always chained up here in Recanati by the will of my family. By saying that, I did not think I was offending you in any way; rather, as a sign of trust and gratitude, I was sharing with you one detail of this barbarous situation I am in. And how could I have any cause for complaint about your affectionate concern? I am very grateful to you for it just as I am to Giordani, who in any case has known for a long time how free I am to make decisions about my own movements.

Do not be amazed if my father does not answer your letters. He does not do it out of a wish to be rude, but out of laziness, and because it is his habit to start things with enthusiasm, and stop them out of lukewarmness. He has stopped corresponding with a hundred other people who do not deserve to be neglected in this way, just as he has with you. And it is an old habit of his, that when he has failed to reply once or twice, then feeling himself to be at fault, he does not even open letters from that person any more, wishing to *enjoy* his *blessed peace* entirely. For this *blessed peace* of his he makes me *enjoy* this terrifying life.

I am very distressed to see that the withdrawing of my commission causes you inconvenience.[1] Do bear in mind though that I was not in a position to foresee it. You made no difficulty about halving the edition, indeed more than halving it:[2] I thought the difficulty

[1] Brighenti claimed he had already bought the wove paper for the special copies [M273].

[2] By printing only two poems instead of five.

involved in doing that must at least be considerable, if not as great as in withdrawing it entirely. You kindly proposed as well to publish my *canzoni* in the *Abbreviatore*, and in consequence to abandon the idea of printing them on their own. That made me think I was still in time to cancel the commission. But now that you inform me of the inconvenience you suffer as a result, I reflect that I cannot publish the canzone *Nello strazio* etc. in opposition to my father's wishes, much less with his money. On the other hand, even if the Canzone is not very good, it came from the heart, and I do not want to abase myself by asking my father for money for the other two, after he has wrought havoc with the first three, and that out of childish fears, and for antiquated principles. It remains for me to print the Canzone to Mai at my own expense, and for this reason I am asking you to inform me of the outlay necessary to publish it in the form and on the terms already agreed on for the others, and using the letter I enclose as a preface.[3] And on receipt of your reply I believe I shall be able to send you the money by return post. You could have a larger number of copies than we previously agreed on printed on fine quality paper, so as to use up the paper obtained for printing a more substantial work. The title will be *Canzone di Giacomo Leopardi ad Angelo Mai*, and on the back of the title page will come the letter I mentioned, which I enclose. But please be so good as to make the following small corrections to the Canzone. [*Four small textual corrections follow.*]

Please excuse me for all this trouble, for which I cannot make it up to you. But love me, for I love you, and from the heart, and being so unlucky, I would be mad as well if I chose to lose through my own fault the very few true friendships that fate offers me in a moment of distraction, when perhaps she leaves off thinking about me, in order to attend to making some person of exceptional virtue unhappy. Your true and steadfast friend,

Giacomo Leopardi.

[3] The dedicatory letter to Leonardo Trissino.

46

In this letter to Giordani Leopardi rehearsed some of the ideas (the status and role of illusions in human life, the relationship between nature, reason, and truth) that he would explore at greater length in the 'Zibaldone', and which lie at the heart of his thinking in these years.

To Pietro Giordani • Piacenza

Recanati, 30th June 1820

O my dear, sad friend. Your letter of the 18th makes me disconsolate because I realize that you have fallen into that same sickness of soul that afflicted me in recent months, and from which, though I am not truly recovered, yet I know and feel it is possible to recover. And the causes were the very ones that are now producing the same effect in you: extreme weakness of the whole body and especially of the nerves, and utter sameness, idleness and enforced solitude, and worthlessness of the whole of life. These causes acted so that I did not think but *felt* the futility and tedium of things, and I utterly despaired of the world and of myself. But although even today I feel my heart to be like a dry stick or thorn, nevertheless I am improved in this respect, that I am resolutely of the opinion that I can get better, and that my anguish comes more from the feeling of my personal unhappiness than from the certainty of universal and necessary unhappiness. I believe no man on earth in any circumstances should ever despair of the return of illusions, because they do not come from art or reason, but from nature, which *expellas furca, tamen usque recurret, Et* MALA *perrumpet furtim* FASTIDIA *victrix.*[1] What shall I do for you, my poor friend, or what can I do? Change the world? not even comfort you? If nothing else I can love you, and that boundlessly, as I do. I become a child again, and I think love is the finest thing on earth, and I feed on empty illusions. What is barbarity if not the state in which nature no longer has power over men? I do not consider illusions to be insubstantial, but as things which in some way have substance, since they are not personal caprices of this person or that, but natural and inborn as part of our being in everybody; and they make up the whole of our life.[2] How shall we think we go astray if we follow nature? And why do we choose rather to rebel against nature who gave them to us, and wanted us to live by them, as all other animals live, indeed in a sense all things do? since everything which exists is not unhappy to exist, except for us who are no longer what we were meant to be and what we were at the beginning. Seneca used to say that reason must observe and consult nature, and that living happily, and in accordance with nature, is one and the same thing. But modern reason, unlike ancient reason, does not observe or consult anything but truth, a very different thing from nature.

I do not think that the wicked live better than us. If true happiness could be attained in some way, the reality of things would not be so terrifying. But good and wicked swim effortfully in this sea of troubles, where no other haven is to be found than what comes from our fancy and imagination. And in this respect I think the condition of the good is better than that of the wicked, because great and splendid illusions do not belong to the wicked: so that confined to the truth and bareness of things, what else are they to expect if not infinite and everlasting tedium?

You see that, desperate as I am, I still take on the role of comforter. From that you can get the measure of the love I feel for you. But I really am speaking from the heart and not pretending; on the contrary I think you ought to pay more attention to me than to anyone else, because people who have no experience of misfortunes, or any special and present cause for sadness, imagine the world to be a fine thing, and reckon that everybody thinks or ought to think as they do at the time. But I lie motionless with misfortunes heaped upon me, where no ray of hope shines through. Paolina and Carlo entreat you to cheer up, and to have some thought for yourself and for us. Give in to our prayers. You see that I weep for you. Weeping is a comfort for misfortunes too, and I would like you to be able to experience it with us. Give me news of your health, embrace me, and think of me often, but only this, that I love you above all else and as no one else does.

[1] Horace, *Epistles* I, x, 24-5: *even if you chase her out with a pitchfork will always come back and triumph secretly over tiresome troubles.*

[2] Cf. *Zibaldone* I, p. 78, on the universality, centrality and value of illusions in human life.

47

Again he explained his father's unwillingness to support him or help him find a position which would enable him to be self-supporting.

To Pietro Brighenti • Bologna

Recanati, 28th August 1820

My dear friend. I am very sorry about the new complaint which is giving you trouble. Take care of yourself, and another time be less willing to go along with parties of friends, and if they invite you to bathe, answer like the English Lady invited on a tiger hunt: having already been in great danger on one, she said *I've done that.*

As for the Bologna chair, I'm telling you that you have no idea what my father is like. There is nothing he is less interested in than those matters which are his concern. He does not want to support me away from home entirely at his own expense, but he would not lift a finger to secure a livelihood for me somewhere else that might release me from this despair. I have no doubt I'll get his consent after the event, but it would be easier to move a mountain than get him to do something for me himself. This strange lethargy of his is well-known, wondered at, and has been put to the test millions of times. Nonetheless be so kind as to tell me the stipend of this chair, and who is principally responsible for the appointment.

You are quite right to say that the nobility are the dead body of society. But unfortunately I cannot see what can be called the living body nowadays; because all classes are plagued by an egotism that destroys everything fine and everything great; and a world without enthusiasm, without greatness of spirit in its thoughts and nobility in its actions, is more dead than alive.

Giordani too spoke to me about Abbé Farini very approvingly. Do me a favour, tell me the name of the person who received my Canzone, and whose idle talk I should despise. And I would like to know if you are writing about this in general terms, or because he has spoken ill of me, and in what way. I tell you honestly that I don't think I'll encounter hatred or hostility, because they are felt towards one's equals, and nobody will deign to think me his equal; but I do expect scorn and contempt, and I get them from everyone I have dealings with or see; and so whatever you related to me could not upset me; and I want to know out of sheer curiosity and for amusement.

You tell me Count Trissino did not receive my reply to his letter of July 28th. But I must confide to you a fear that occurs to me. In the dedication I spoke of that excellent gentleman with a kind of familiarity which seems to be customary in literary matters. His letter of July 28th was extremely kind. But he still had not received my little book. It troubles me to think that having seen it he may have found my tone over-familiar. I asked his forgiveness already when I wrote to him, and I am writing to him again. But because my letter may easily go astray, do me the favour of telling him about these misgivings of mine, and ask his forgiveness in my name.[1]

The wickedness of women terrifies me, not for myself to be sure, but because I see the wretchedness of the world. If I were to become rich and powerful, which is impossible, because I have too few vices, women would certainly try to ensnare me.[2] But in the state I am in, scorned and derided by everyone, I have no qualities to attract their flattery. Besides which I have a soul so frozen and withered by continual unhappiness, and also by the wretched knowledge of the truth, that before I had loved I lost the capacity to love, and an Angel of beauty and charm would not be enough to set me on fire: with the result that, young as I am, I could serve as a Eunuch in any harem.

Adieu, be fond of me, and give me news of your health. I love you and embrace you. Tell me to whom I am to send the money for the *Foscolo.*

[1] In fact Trissino (see [33]) was not best pleased to have *Ad Angelo Mai* (banned in the Lombardo-Veneto) dedicated to him. The dedicatory letter had concluded: 'But remember that it is fitting that the unfortunate should wear mourning, and likewise that our odes should resemble funeral dirges [...] I won't say that weeping is natural to me, but I am constrained to weep by the nature of the times and by our fate.' [*Ma ricordatevi che si conviene agli sfortunati di vestire a lutto, e parimente alle nostre canzoni di rassomigliare ai versi funebri* [...] *Io non dirò che il piangere sia natura mia propria, ma necessità de' tempi e della fortuna.*]

[2] This worldly-wise tone is adopted in response to Brighenti's comments in the same vein.

48

The correspondence with Giordani continued to be a lifeline.

To Pietro Giordani • Piacenza

Recanati, 4th September 1820

I've just got your letter of August the 23rd which distresses me and tears my soul, showing me that you're still having trouble with your health. I'd rather complain about fate for anything else at all than the misfortunes of friends, especially yours. It would be no slight comfort for the pain I feel if I could, as you say, come and live closer to you,[1] see you often, talk to you, and if not cheer you up and comfort you, at least lighten your ills in the presence of friendship and love. Things will turn out as my dismal fate disposes. You mustn't think there's a day of my life when the memory of your virtues and your misfortunes doesn't make my heart ache with affection and compassion.

Brighenti wrote me that he had sent you some copies of a canzone of mine, as I asked him to; and he was convinced you'd already received them. But perhaps he was mistaken about this, or you were not able to read. If you've got them, or when you get them, I'd like you to arrange for Count Pallastrelli and Count Calciati to have a copy each, in remembrance of the kindness they expressed towards me last year.

Be fond of me. Let's console ourselves for the unworthiness of fate. In the last few days, as though to take revenge on the world, I've devised and sketched some short satirical pieces in prose.[2] You see what comes into my head to write to you. Simply as a pretext for talking to you longer. Adieu adieu.

[1] Giordani was hoping to help get Leopardi appointed to a teaching position in Lodi.

[2] This is probably the first germ of the *Operette morali.*

49

To Pietro Giordani • Piacenza

Recanati, 20th November 1820

Your letter of the 5th consoles me somewhat because you seem a little less troubled. Brighenti had already written to me about your new publication,[1] and had promised it to me. When you can, I want you to write to me at greater length, as you say in this last letter you want to, because whenever I lack news of you, and the comfort and support of talking to you, I'm like someone who is alone and without a star on a sea that is boundless, but stubbornly and painfully motionless, so that not even a storm breaks the silence and the tedium. I'm reading and scribbling with difficulty, and my studies are now not of words but of things. Nor do I regret having on purpose first studied how to speak, and then how to think, the reverse of what other people do; with the result that now if I have something to say, I know how it must be said, and I don't have to store it away, waiting until I've learned how to express it. Besides which the faculty of speech is incredibly helpful to the faculty of thought, and smoothes and shortens its path. Indeed I have realized from experience that a knowledge of several languages also contributes wonderfully to ease, clarity and exactness in thinking. I've almost forgotten poetry, because I can see but I don't feel anything any more. Carlo and Paolina send their fond regards. Take care, and love me with all your heart. Adieu.

[1] An edition of a seventeenth-century text, Pietro Sforza Pallavicino's *Arte della perfezione cristiana*, with an introductory essay on the author's life and works.

50

'I reckon four lives would not be enough.'

To Pietro Giordani • Piacenza

Recanati, 5th January 1821

My dear friend. Your letter of the 24th of last month confirms what I supposed, that mine in reply to your other letter of November 5th had gone missing. I'm sending this one to Brighenti, and asking him to have it delivered to you by the Bologna post.

There is nothing you could have told me that could give me such great comfort as the news of your improved health. But don't use it while it will still be easy for you to abuse it. Wait until it is consolidated, even if by inactivity and boredom. I beg and earnestly entreat you.

I am tolerably well in body. My mind, after very long and very fierce resistance, is finally tamed, and obedient to fate. I would rather not live, but if I have to live, what good does it do to kick against necessity? Necessity cannot be conquered, except by death. I swear that I would have won a long time ago, if I could have been sure that death was a matter for me to decide. As I could not be sure, the only course left to me is to give in. Nor do I now find that any other virtue is needed, except for patience, which I was not born to.

I read and write and make so many plans that if I wanted to fill out and complete just the ones I've not only jotted down but drafted in outline, I reckon four lives would not be enough. Although I understand or rather feel the pointlessness of human affairs continuously and intensely, nevertheless I feel distress and anguish at the thought of how much needs doing, and how little I shall be able to do. Especially that this one life nature grants me is made sluggish and is fettered by wretchedness; and I see it slipping from my grasp and fading away; so that whereas my plans would need many lives, I shall barely even have one.

My brothers and sister embrace you and send their regards. Write to me if you are fond of me, and as much as you can manage without discomfort or inconvenience. Adieu dear soul. I love you as much as you're capable of conceiving.

51

Leopardi had been corresponding with Giulio Perticari, a minor writer and son-in-law of Monti, since 1819. He now tried to mobilise his support to find a position in the Vatican.

To Giulio Perticari • Pesaro

Recanati, 30th March 1821

My dear Count. Asking is hard, and asking someone who owes us nothing – indeed to whom we are very much indebted – is worse. But on the one hand your exquisite kindness, on the other the desperate state of my life, compel me to ask and beg, or rather entreat you. And first of all I ask you to forgive the roughness of my writing, because gloominess of spirit and wretchedness of circumstance leave me neither time nor space for considering words.

I think you know (because of the kindness you have shown in finding out about my affairs) that from 10 years of age, with no help at all except the ignorance of anyone who has ever talked to me, the contrary example of my fellow citizens, and the indifference of everybody, I gave myself furiously to my studies, and in these studies I have consumed the best part of human life.[1] But perhaps you do not know that so far I have gathered from my studies no other fruit than suffering. Frailty of body; deepest and everlasting depression of spirits; the scorn and contempt of all my fellow citizens; and finally, the only consolation I had left (I mean imagination, and the powers of the heart) practically extinguished as well, along with bodily strength and any hope of happiness; these are the rewards I have obtained from my most unfortunate labours. Fate has condemned me to a life without youth: because from childhood I passed in one bound to old age, or rather decrepitude both of body and mind. From the day I was born I have never experienced a single pleasure; hope, for a few years; for a long time now, not even that. And my life (outer and inner) is such that even just dreaming

[1] i.e. youth.

about it would make men grow ice cold with fear. And my parents, who see that I am wasting away and destroying myself in this prison, and that, living forever buried in a town where even the word literature is unknown, even supposing I had the genius of Dante and the wisdom of Solomon I could not attain the tiniest part of the fame that the most idle and worthless get – my parents are implacably resolved never to let me leave here, unless I find some position that allows me to be self-supporting. And they reward me for my way of life (which is of a kind not to be described or believed, at my age, of anybody in the world) by stubbornly declining to help me get the very thing they point out and prescribe as necessary for me. They allow me only the miserable option of procuring for myself – with almost no contacts, and from a distance – what is difficult to obtain with a great deal of help and patronage, and on the spot.

An approach has been made on my behalf to the Secretary of State for the position now vacant of professor of Latin language in the Vatican Library. But his Eminence does not know me except as that very obscure and quite unknown man that in reality I am. I am assured that if Monsignor Mai were to put in a word for me with the Secretary of State, the business would have a favourable outcome. I am writing to Monsignor Mai, with whom I have been corresponding for some time. But equally they tell me (and I had already formed this impression myself) that he is a cold person, and needs to be pushed hard to put himself to any trouble for anyone at all. Now I can certainly request his help, but not deserve it, either speaking in general terms, or (given my situation) in the eyes of anyone in particular.

My dear Count, it does not matter if I live, and no one need trouble themselves to ensure that I do; I do not want to, indeed I would much prefer not to live; but since I cannot die (for if I could, I swear to you that I would not finish this letter, or rather I would be long dead), I ask for pity from nature which brought me into the world on purpose to see me suffer, I ask for pity from my very few friends, to help me bear, not life any more, but the years. I do not know if you are on terms of intimacy with Monsignor Mai: but knowing that you are famous and respected, throughout Italy and abroad, and especially in Rome, I thought that perhaps you would be able to help me in whatever way you please, and I have made so bold as to ask. But forgive me if I make you share my wretchedness with this odious complaining. Wanting to try to defeat my dark destiny, I have broken the rule I imposed on myself a long time ago: that no one, apart from myself, should know of my unhappiness. Forgive me; and if you can do nothing else, and whatever happens, continue to think kindly of me; so that, if nature condemns me to the contempt I deserve, and fate condemns me to be hated by many people, which I do not deserve, I still have the love of a very few people as a final source of comfort. Yours,

Giacomo Leopardi.

52

He wrote to Mai at the same time about the same position.

To Angelo Mai • Rome

Recanati, 30th March 1821

Most reverend Monsignor. Asking is always difficult, both for the person who asks and, especially, for the person who is asked. But much more so if the person who asks has no right to the help, and takes the initiative in asking; which is the situation I now find myself in. Because ever since I had the good fortune of making your aquaintance, I have never had either the opportunity or the ability to be of service to you, except in my desires, whereas you have always been extremely gracious towards me. And now instead of being able to reciprocate, I find myself compelled to implore another favour. But this is what happens to the obscure and insignificant, in their dealings with the eminent and distinguished; we can only communicate with them through reverence and gratitude.

An application has been made on my behalf to his Eminence the Secretary of State for the position of professor of Latin language, now vacant in the Vatican Library. But his Eminence does not know me except as the very obscure and quite unknown man that in fact I am. I have been assured, Sir, that if you deigned to volunteer a word in my support to his eminence, the business would be certain to have a favourable outcome. And I am sure that that is true, taking into account the fame and glory (unparalleled, it may be said) which you enjoy, both in Rome and everywhere else.

I could never have brought myself to trouble you with this request, and to put your kindness to the test with this perhaps rash and presumptuous familiarity, if on the one hand I had not known from a thousand proofs the exquisite goodness of your heart, and on the other the unhappiness of my life had not violently dragged me to it. You, Sir, who have more than once been so kind as to take an interest in my affairs, will know how from ten years of age I have of my own accord dedicated myself to studying with the result that, at my present age of twenty-two years, when youth should be beginning, for me it is already finished and gone. For by dint of persistent and immoderate application, I have ruined my developing constitution, weakened my health, and seen old age come upon me, just when it was time, through my youth, to gather the fruits of my past labours. Besides this, my parents have always been, and still are, firmly resolved not to allow me to leave here, unless I find a position which allows me to support myself. For me such a position can only be of a literary sort. Having always lived in a small town, I have no aquaintances, friends, or contacts of any kind. So that having lost all of life's other advantages, I find myself reduced to losing utterly even that last fruit of studying, the conversation of distinguished men, and that small measure of celebrity that every insignificant man flatters himself he can achieve and wants to achieve. But a person who lives buried in a town like this can never hope to become, I do not say famous, but even well-known in any part of the world. All the hard work, all the suffering, all the losses I have borne are to no avail. I see myself here scorned and disparaged by everyone; all the hopes of my childhood are gone; and I almost weep for the time I have spent on my studies, seeing myself mingled with the lowest scum of the idle and the ignorant. These reasons have compelled me to implore your mercy. I shall not disguise the fact that I am speaking to you with my heart on my sleeve, and with all the artlessness of a tender and respectful trust. I shall be indebted to you for a great deal more than my life, because life is not in itself a blessing; unhappiness and utter despair with life is a supreme misfortune in this world; and a person who frees us from this frees us from something a great deal worse than death.

I bow with all my soul to you, Sir, to entreat you to forgive my importunity. In the end, I am a man worth nothing; and if I lose all the fruit of my life, if I am destined never to experience, as I never yet have, a drop of good on this earth, it is of no consequence; and I confess that it is not in any way unfitting to my deserts. But we are naturally inclined to attribute great importance to our own affairs: and especially when it is a matter of almost our whole existence, we do not baulk at being a nuisance, and even appearing foolhardy, to anyone at all. Forgive me, I earnestly entreat you; and if I put myself in your hands, accept me as your servant, unhappy or not as the case may be – a servant who can be counted on, and who is steadfastly devoted and attached to your person and your singular virtues.

53

The correspondence about the Vatican chair continued.

To Giulio Perticari • Pesaro

Recanati, 9th April 1821

Dear and longed-for friend. I would not want to pester you with words. But as I think that your most elegant and friendly letter does require some answer, I am answering.

I do not thank you for the compassion you show towards me, although it is very rare in this world, and almost unique in relation to me, because what thanks could equal your goodness? You affectionately urge me not to allow myself to be overwhelmed by sadness, and to take refuge in wisdom. My dear count, there is truth in the saying that the man who has not been unhappy knows nothing; but it is equally true that the unhappy man can do nothing: and for just this reason (that he was always very unhappy) I think Tasso sits below rather than alongside our three greatest poets. All the blessings of this world are illusory. But take away these illusions: what good is left us? where can we take refuge? what is wisdom? what else does it teach us apart from our own unhappiness? In short, the happy man is not happy, but the wretched man really is wretched, for all that even the most wretched wisdom tries to comfort him. There was a time when I put my trust in virtue, and despised fate; now after a very long struggle I am tamed, and prostrate, for I am in the position that if many wise men have recognized the sadness and futility of things, I, like several others, have also recognized the sadness and futility of wisdom.

The courts, Rome, the Vatican? Who doesn't know that den of superstition, ignorance and vice? But practically the whole world is purgatory. Here is really hell, where you need to be careful not to reveal that you can read; where all people talk about is the good and bad weather, or else women (in the language of the tavern and the brothel); where on the one hand a clever man has no other occupation than studying, no other relaxation than studying, yet on the other hand, being so far away from any civilised town and any civilised mind, studying does not even give hope of glory, that last illusion of the wise man. Because if he wants to write, leaving aside the fact that the poor wretch's thoughts and words are like the unvarying screeching of night birds, in the situation I am in the purpose and fruit of writing are missing, since in the first place it is not possible to have things printed, or if they are printed to circulate them.

I wrote *professor* to you just as they wrote to me from Rome. I too took it to mean *writer,*[1] and I was not mistaken, judging by what you tell me. A lowly position: but what is lower than my life? which is now wholly futile; and if I could spend one half of it throwing the other half away, I would be much better off. I certainly cannot aspire to more important positions with so few means at my disposal. Besides, if by whatever means I had become my own master, and if I were in a place where I could see and speak, I would perhaps attain, not high office or wealth or such things, which I have never hoped for nor cared about, but a situation such that my life was not indistinguishable from death.

My reply to your kind and thoughtful invitation[2] is that, unless I find paid employment, I shall never be able to see heaven or earth except for those of Recanati, until that event which nature commands me to fear, and which in any case, in the natural way of things, will happen when I am old; I mean my father's death. All he cares about where I am concerned is leaving me to live in that room where I drag out the whole day, the month, the year, counting the strokes of the clock.

But I am ashamed of talking about myself at such length. I explained at the beginning my reason for doing so; that is to say, so that silence should not seem like ingratitude or indifference to your advice and your love. Thank you from the bottom of my heart for your generous offer that I should make use of you for my own advantage. Be fond of me: if I ever manage to shake your hand and embrace you, you will see a man defeated but not spoiled by bad luck, and one whose mind is defeated but not his heart, nor his capacity to feel, although it is enfeebled.[3] Your fond and devoted

Giacomo Leopardi.

1 i.e. amanuensis or clerk.

2 Perticari had invited him to stay in Pesaro for a time.

3 In the Moroncini edition the closing words read: *and one whose body and mind are defeated, but not his heart,* and a note says that the words *né la facoltà degli affetti, sebbene illanguidita* (the last words of the sentence as printed by Flora and translated here) are cancelled. The tinkering with the phrase provides a good example of the care with which Leopardi composed his sentences.

54

The correspondence with Giordani resumed after an interval of almost six months.

To Pietro Giordani • Milan

Recanati, 18th June 1821

I hear that you are in Milan, and in the hope that the postal service to Milan may be more reliable than to Piacenza, I am breaking the silence that our friendship has observed for such a long time. I got the letter you wrote supporting me, and the reply. I thank you as best I can for both of them, that is in a way that falls far short of the sense of indebtedness I feel towards you, recognizing you to be a splendid and unbelievable man, more concerned about someone else's welfare or harm than about his own. Give me news of yourself, though I tremble to ask, fearing it must be the usual sorry story. But tell me, couldn't you change from being Heraclitus to being Democritus?[1] That is what is happening to me, who thought it quite impossible. It is true that Desperation disguises itself with a smile. Yet laughing at men and at my own misfortunes, as I am growing used to doing, although it does not come from hope, does not come from suffering either, but rather from indifference, which is the last refuge of those unhappy people necessity has tamed by stripping them not of the courage to fight, but of the last hope of winning, that is the hope of death. My health is not good but tolerable, and such that I should not despair on its account of living to some purpose. I am slowly reading, studying and scribbling. I spend all the rest of my time thinking, and laughing to myself. I am working on the plan and material of what I would like to call a small work, but the material is growing by the day so that I'll be forced to call it a work *tout court.*[2] When I have finished preparing it, God willing, I shall set about composing it, and I think it will be soon. I have chosen to write you this chit-chat to satisfy the affectionate interest that makes you want to be kept informed about my affairs. You do the same for me; and God grant that in giving me news of your condition you may confound me, and prove me a bad fortune-teller. Adieu adieu.

[1] Heraclitus's melancholy philosophy caused him to be contrasted traditionally with Democritus, who was known as the 'laughing philosopher'.

[2] The project is described in [56] and [153], and was to consist of a comparison of five languages.

55

To Pietro Brighenti • Bologna

Recanati, 22nd June 1821

My dear friend. Your last letter filled me with sorrow and compassion. Would you expect me to preach courage and confidence? And yet I do: indeed I insist you be in good spirits and be confident. The person who said that man's life is a war said something at least as true in the secular sense as in the religious. We are all fighting against each other, and we'll fight to our last breath, without truce, without treaty, without quarter. Each man is the next man's enemy, and has no one but himself on his own side. Except for those very few people who were granted the capacity to feel, who can have on their side some of their own number: and you in this respect are superior to countless others. What is more, whether vanquished or victor, one must never weary of fighting, and struggling, and charging and riding roughshod over anyone who gives ground even for a moment. That is the way the world is, not how they painted it to us poor children. I live here, scorned, spat on, kicked around by everyone, leading my whole life in one room, in a way that makes me shudder if I think about it. And yet I am getting used to laughing, and I manage it. And no one will triumph over me until he can scatter me over the countryside, and amuse himself by making my ashes fly through the air. I beg you with all my heart to take courage, not because I don't feel your misfortunes, because I feel them more than my own: but because I think that this life, and this business of fighting ferociously and forever, is the destiny of man and every living creature, allotted to it by nature.

I wrote to Giordani on the 18th of this month, to Milan. I'll see if my letters in that direction have better luck. You wrote to me months back of a Latin translation of my Canzone to Mai; I've heard nothing else about it, before or since. If you still have it, I'd like to amuse myself a little by seeing how I have been understood, and you would be doing me a favour posting it to me. It certainly won't leave my hands. Give me some news about your edition. I am not aware of the inflated style of your *Babini*, in fact it seems to me very restrained. Love me, dear Brighenti, and let's laugh together at these bloody fools who possess the whole earthly globe. The world is made the wrong way round like those damned souls in Dante who had their arse in front and their chest behind; and their tears trickled *down the cleft*.[1] And it would surely be more ridiculous to want to set it straight, than to be content with just looking at it and whistling in derision. Yours,

Leopardi.

[1] *Inferno* XX, 24.

56

Leopardi was still pondering the issues of language, literature and nationhood.

To Pietro Giordani • Milan

Recanati, 13th July 1821

Your letter had the usual and expected effect of distressing me.[1] It was not like this once, when I had no greater source of comfort than your letters. Would to God that your friends' distress brought some benefit to you. But you despair of your health, and I don't think you should. For a very long time I have had to regret having a brain in my skull, because I could not think of any least thing, for even the shortest time, without a spasm and pain in my nerves. But as one does not live except thinking, so I regretted that, as I had to exist, I was not a plant or stone or anything else at all whose existence is not accompanied by thought. I say nothing of my eyes, which had reduced me to the nature of owls, hating and shunning the day. And yet these ills, although they have not disappeared, are diminishing. I hope the same will happen with yours as well, and if my affection for you means anything to you, I'd like you to be hopeful about it as I am, for not long ago I was in despair just as you are.

My sister Paolina will be married this January in a city in the Urbino region which is not large or beautiful, but to a suitable person, very liberal, and humane. Carlo enjoys excellent health, and is easy in his mind and ready for good fortune or bad, or indeed for neither, which is perhaps the worst situation for men, or certainly for young people.

My essay will be on languages, and especially the five which make up the family of our Southern languages, Greek, Latin, Italian, French and Spanish. There has been and still is a great deal of discussion about language in Italy, nowadays especially. But the best people, to my way of thinking, have remembered and preached philosophy rather than practised it. Now this subject demands all the profundity of thought the human mind is capable of, given that language and man and nations are almost the same thing. I don't flatter, and I have no reason to flatter, because no one would be pleased by my flattery. I say that I think your letter to Monti is the most philosophical of all the writings published in Italy in recent years on the subject of language, and perhaps the finest piece of Italian prose of this century, except for one small fault, which you share with almost all the great early writers. That is a sort of obscurity that comes not from any affectation, or from carelessness, or from any bad habit, but rather from the good qualities of the writing; as from the very carefully wrought and tightly structured sentences, which are somewhat tiring for the reader, and from time to time force him to re-read some sentence, if he wishes to follow the line of argument, and follow your ideas which are abstruse and remote from common usage. This perhaps happens because, especially in philosophical and scientific and didactic writings, we are too accustomed to a loose, broad manner of speaking, which aids ease of understanding as much as it jeopardizes strength and beauty.

Getting back to the point, it is futile to build if we don't begin from the foundations.

[1] Giordani's letter had spoken of his continuing ill-health and depression.

Whoever wants to do some good for Italy will first of all have to show her a philosophical language; without that I think she will never have a modern literature of her own, and without a modern literature of her own, she will never ever be a nation. Thus the effect I chiefly wish to achieve is that Italian writers can be philosophers, inventive and in tune with their times, which is as much as to say writers and not copyists, and so they ought not to be barbarians where language is concerned, but Italians. Many people have aimed at this, no one has achieved it, and no one, to my mind, has tried hard enough. Certainly it can never be achieved by any book that does not, in addition to exhorting, give a noteworthy example not just of good language, but of subtle and hidden philosophy; and not just of philosophy, but of good language; for both these means are necessary to achieve this end. I shall also try in this essay to smooth the way to its being possible then to treat philosophical subjects in this language which has never treated them; I mean philosophical subjects as they are today, not as they were in the age of innate ideas.

I've written at length, my dear friend, as you see, to comply with your wishes. And if you want me to do as you wish with regard to your last request as well, that is to repeat what you are very well aware of, just imagine that I can repeat what I've already said on other occasions, but can never say as much as I'd like to, nor enough to express the love I feel for you, and the distress I am feeling on your account. For a long time you have been as it were the measure and the form of my life, and I, with my eyes fixed always on you, do not live and do not feel any consolation if I see you disconsolate and dispirited. For God's sake try to bear up if you don't want me to give up on myself, for all my living and all my thinking and all my striving is almost for no other purpose than to be loved and valued by you. Adieu.

57

Paolina's wedding plans were proceeding. Leopardi was 'making many plans, doing very little.'

To Pietro Giordani • Milan

Recanati, 26th October 1821

Could I wish for anything more welcome than a letter from you, and one with good news about your health? Nothing, I think, unless to hear that you were stronger than Atlas, and happier than goodness knows who. Come on, let's take heart. If I had to imagine something that would make me very happy, I don't think I'd have thought up a greater source of consolation than the one you've given me. You really have cheered me up. Do look after yourself, and if you are content to imitate me in this, be hopeful. Oh, if only I could see you again. After just three years, you would scarcely recognize me. Not young any more, no longer resisting fate, a stranger to hope and fear, a stranger to the least fleeting pleasures that everyone enjoys; but all the warmer towards you, the better I have come to know you, from my experience of other people, for that very rare treasure that you are. Paolina will be married to a Mr Peroli in Sant'Angelo in Vado, but not before January, as I wrote to you already, and perhaps in spring.[1] She sends her regards, and so does Carlo, and they send their heartfelt congratulations. I get by, making many plans, doing very little, needing only to distract myself and enjoy myself, and never leaving the house. But being tired of waging war against the invincible, I let rest take the place of happiness, from habit I've grown accustomed to tedium, which I thought I could never get used to, and I have almost finished suffering. My health is in God's hands, sometimes worse, sometimes better; I still cannot concentrate for long, and I am still determined not to lose the little I can do by forcing myself to do too much. You are not mistaken in thinking that I remember you every day to my nearest and dearest, of whom there are not many. In the last letter I wrote you to Milan towards the end of July, I sent you regards from Marquess Antici, whom you met in Recanati in 1818, and who is here now, and reads your things with incredible relish and approval. His regards must have gone missing with the letter; I never heard that you got it. Be fond of me and carry on giving me good news. I embrace you, I love you, I pray for all earthly blessings for you, and I remain inseparably with you. Adieu. Paolina and Carlo are not happy with what I said in their name; they want me to give you their regards again, and to urge you on their behalf as well to take heart.

[1] In view of these plans Leopardi started composing *Nelle nozze della sorella Paolina* (On his Sister Paolina's Wedding). In fact, as we shall see [66, 67], the plans came to nothing.

58

A year later, in November 1822, Leopardi finally managed to leave Recanati, travelling with relatives to Rome where he was to be a guest in the house of his uncle Marquess Carlo Antici, his mother's brother. This short letter to his mother told her of their safe arrival.

To Adelaide Leopardi • Recanati

Roma, 23rd November [1822]

Dear Mother. We have reached this point safe and sound with no mishaps, and find all our relatives equally safely arrived. I am writing in haste because the post is about to leave, and I pass on regards from Uncle Carlo, Uncle Momo, Aunt Marianna and all the others, who are very well. Please pass on my respectful and affectionate regards to Father, to whom I already wrote from Spoleto, and give a hug to my brothers and sister, assuring both him and them that I shall write at length, and give them my news, when I am free to do so in less of a rush, and when I have found my own head again. I am well, and the discomforts of the journey far from harming me have notably helped me. I kiss your hand with all my heart, and full of deep affection, and missing you, I remain your very fond son,

Giacomo.[1]

[1] His mother's reply [M431] is worth quoting: 'You know how sincerely I love you, and what a thorn it has been in my heart to see you always discontented and bad-tempered [...] Take great care of yourself, and don't mix with unworthy people.' [*Sapete quanto io vi amo sinceramente, e qual spina mi sia stata al cuore il vedervi sempre malcontento e di mal'umore* [...] *Abbiatevi moltissima cura, e non trattate persone indegne.*]

59

Writing from Rome to Carlo, his confidant from infancy and his natural ally against his parents, he was able to speak with a frankness unmatched even in the letters to Giordani. This first letter to his brother, written just a few days after his arrival, already expressed a profound disappointment with what he found in Rome, in relation to both his literary and his sentimental (or sexual) expectations.

To Carlo Leopardi • Recanati

Rome, 25th November [1822]

My dear Carlo. If you think the person who is writing to you is your brother Giacomo, you are much mistaken, because he is dead or senseless, and in his place is someone who barely remembers his own name. Believe me, my dear Carlo, that I'm beside myself, not from amazement, because even if I were to see the Devil I wouldn't be amazed: and I don't take the slightest pleasure in the great things I see, because I know they are amazing, but I don't feel it, and I assure you that their vast size and there being so many of them began to bore me after the first day. And so if I tell you that I have almost ceased to recognize myself, don't think of amazement, or pleasure, or hope, or anything happy. I want you to know, Carlo, that during the journey I suffered what it is possible to suffer,[1] as is the lot of one who travels at someone else's expense, and that someone a person who at every turn seeks out and insists on his own most exquisite comforts, whether or not they are compatible with those of other people. But in spite of that, on the whole journey the only thing I enjoyed, and greatly enjoyed, was the suffering itself, and the lack of consideration for me, and the adopting of quite new and different ways of doing things every moment. And yet I still had that thread of hope that I am capable of, which without arousing enthusiasm or even pleasure is still enough to sustain life. But having got here, and seen this horrendous muddle, confusion, nothingness, unbearable small-mindedness, and unspeakable untidiness, and the other terrifying qualities that reign in this household; and finding myself utterly alone and naked in the midst of my relatives (though I lack nothing), I swear, Carlo, that my patience and self-confidence, which from long experience I had thought invincible and inexhaustible, have not only been defeated but destroyed. As I am very unfamiliar with the streets, I can't leave the house, or go anywhere, or stay there, unless I'm accompanied by some member of the family; and in consequence, no matter how strongly I might wish not to, I am absolutely obliged to lead the life of the Antici household; that life which we two, talking together, did not know what it might be like, or what it might consist of, or how it might be tolerated, or whether it was a life in any sense at all.

Yesterday I visited Cancellieri, who is a bloody fool, a stream of gossip, the most boring and exasperating man on earth; he talks of absurdly frivolous things with the greatest interest, of supreme things in the chilliest way possible; he smothers you with compliments

[1] Compare the bland comment to his mother in the previous letter. They are his mother's relatives he travelled with and stayed with, and of whose household he now goes on to give such an unflattering description.

and extravagant praise, and he does it in a way so icy and with such indifference, that to hear him it seems as if being an extraordinary man is the most ordinary thing in the world. In short, such a profound melancholy has taken hold of me that once again I have no other pleasure than sleeping: and this melancholy, and being always exposed to the outside world, in complete contrast to my long-standing habit, oppresses me, and does away with all my faculties so that I am no good for anything any more, I no longer have any hope, I want to speak and don't know what the deuce to say, I don't feel myself any more, and I have become altogether and in every respect a statue. Have Father read this letter; I don't know what I wrote him from Spoleto: because you ought to know that I wrote at a table surrounded by a riff-raff from Fabriano, Iesi, etc., who had already made enquiries about me of the waiter, and already knew my name and condition *of poet*, etc. etc. And a rascal of a very sly priest who was with them decided to make fun of me too as he did of all the others: but believe me that at my first reply he quickly changed his tone, and his party became very good and polite like so many sheep.

Listen, Carlo, if I could be with you, I would think that I could live, I'd get back a little energy and courage, I'd have some hope, and I'd have a few hours of consolation. In truth I have no company at all: I have lost myself; and the other people around me will never ever be able to be company for me. Write me a long letter, and tell me in detail about your state of mind; I have many misgivings about it that are tormenting me. Love me, for God's sake. I need love, love, love, fire, enthusiasm, life: the world doesn't seem made for me: I've found the devil far uglier than he is painted. Roman women, high class and low, are really stomach-turning; the men arouse rage and pity. But you write to me, and love me; and talk to me at great, great length about yourself and the rest of the family. Kiss Father's hand for me, and Mother's; I'll write to them by the next post, if I can still write. Remember me to Paolina and Luigi and Don Vicenzo.[2] We absolutely shall take heart; and habit will take over and put everything right. Adieu, *caro ex carne mea.*[3] Adieu.

[2] Don Vincenzo Diotallevi, tutor and member of the Leopardi household, always remembered by Leopardi when away from home.

[3] *flesh of my flesh.*

60

To his father his tone is more circumspect.

To Monaldo Leopardi • Recanati

Rome, 29th November [1822]

Dear Father. I have received your very affectionate letter of the 25th, from which I gather that the letter I wrote you from Spoleto on the 20th must have gone missing. It is not one quarter of the bitterness that our separation causes your fine spirit that I feel, but at least as much as you do:[1] indeed in the first days after my arrival, my dismay at finding myself isolated and a long way from those dearest to me was such that I did not think I could endure in this state without great and continuing distress, as I wrote to Carlo, asking him to have you read my letter at once. Now, although my having become accustomed to it, and some acquaintances I have made, have soothed and calmed my spirit a little, yet they have not compensated for, and nothing in the world will compensate me for, the closeness and the present and visible love of my parents and my brothers and sister. It is a great comfort to me to think that you pray to the Lord for me, that he may deliver me from the dangers of the world, which certainly are great; and that you bless me from a distance, and consider me your good and loyal and very loving son. But so that you may have peace of mind on my account (to the extent that such a thing is possible when one loves), I shall tell you that I have found in Rome much greater foolishness, fatuity and worthlessness, and less wickedness, than I was expecting; and I shall repeat what I said to you shortly before I left, that is that I am much more stubborn than fickle, and much more apt to despise than to admire: and notwithstanding my limited experience of dealing with men, I nonetheless expect (and some experience confirms me in this flattering notion), that I shall uncover at least a large part of the stratagems that are used to seduce, deceive, deride and ruin young people and every sort of man. Cousin Melchiorri sends his warm regards; you must believe me that he is really not a bad young fellow, indeed he is good more than three times over, and much more deliriously infatuated with literature than I have ever been. The uncles send their regards, and so does insufferable Aunt Marianna, who is fond of me – whatever that means. I kiss dear Mama's hand; my regards and a hug for my brothers and sister. Towards you I shall forever profess the deepest gratitude and the warmest filial affection. Love me, dear Father, for I love you with all my heart, and I want to serve you and please you and obey you in everything. And I am glad that fate has given me a tender and loving heart for almost no other reason than that I can direct my tender feelings towards you. Your most respectful and affectionate son,

Giacomo.

[1] His father had written hoping that if Giacomo didn't feel all the pain of separation as intensely as his father did, he might at least feel a quarter as much.

61

Leopardi was already disenchanted with the vast size of Rome when he wrote to Paolina ten days after his arrival.

To Paolina Leopardi • Recanati

Rome, 3rd December 1822

Dear Paolina. What do you want to know of my doings? If I like Rome, if I'm enjoying myself, where I've been, what kind of life I'm leading? As for the first question, I don't know what to answer any more, because everyone asks me the same thing a hundred times a day, and as I don't want always to give the same answer, I've used up my stock of phrases, and Rabbi's Synonyms. Speaking seriously, you can be quite certain that the most stolid citizen of Recanati has a greater measure of common sense then the wisest and most serious Roman. Rest assured that the frivolousness of these fools is beyond belief. If I wanted to tell you about all the ridiculous things which serve as subject-matter for their talk, and which are their favourite topics, a whole folio volume wouldn't be enough. This morning (to mention just one example) I heard them talk solemnly and at length about the good voice of a Prelate who sang Mass the day before yesterday, and about his dignity of bearing in performing this function. They asked him how he'd managed to acquire these fine abilities, if at the beginning of the Mass he'd felt at all awkward, and similar things. The Prelate replied that he'd learnt by assisting in the Chapels over a long period, that this practice had been very useful to him, that it is a necessary training for people like them, and that he had not felt at all awkward, and a thousand very witty things. I found out later that several Cardinals and other bigwigs had congratulated him that the sung Mass had gone so well. Reckon that all the subjects Romans talk about are of this sort, and I'm not exaggerating at all. The physical fabric of Rome would have some point if men here were five yards high and two yards wide. The whole population of Rome wouldn't fill St Peter's Square. I saw the cupola, with my short sight, from five miles away, as I was travelling, and I saw it quite distinctly with its ball and cross, as you can see the Appennines at home. All the great size of Rome only serves to multiply distances, and the number of stairs you have to climb to find anyone you want. These huge buildings, and these streets that in consequence are never-ending, are so many spaces thrown between men, instead of being spaces that contain men. I can't see what is so attractive about putting chess pieces of normal size on a chess board as long and wide as the piazza of the Madonna in Recanati.[1] I don't mean that Rome seems uninhabited, I mean that if men needed to live as spaciously as they live in these buildings, and as they walk in these streets, squares, churches: the world would not be enough to contain the human race. There's your answer to the first question. I'll answer the others when I'm in less of a hurry. Give my regards to Papa, kiss his hand for me, tell him I received his letter of the 29th of November, that I'll carry out his instructions as regards Countess Mazzagalli and father Trachini, that the other business concerning Fusconi the lawyer is already seen to, that

[1] The main square in Recanati as it then was.

Marchioness Roberti's money and cloth were handed over days ago, that I'm well, as are all my hosts, who send their regards to him and to Mama, and especially the uncles. I've received Mama's letter too: give her my regards as well, and give her a kiss. Tell Carlo that whatever the trunk is that Luigi is talking about, my head wasn't on the trunk; but that I had another trunk (the one I'm talking about) behind me the whole time.[2] All best wishes for health and happiness to Luigi, Pietruccio and Don Vincenzo etc. I haven't carried out your instructions, but in due course it will all be done. Be fond of me, and be well. I'm expecting a letter from Carlo by this post, and one from you in a week. Adieu. Marietta sends her regards. Adieu.

[2] 'Trunk' (*baule*) is a jocular way of referring to a hunched back.

62

Carlo's first letter to Giacomo, not seen by his parents, had suggested that his brother write to him under a false name ('Please write to me under the name Sofia Ortis').[1] This Leopardi now started to do, establishing a pattern of secrecy and subterfuge with his parents that would come into operation whenever he was away from home.

To Carlo Leopardi • Recanati

Rome, 6th December [1822]

My dear Carlo. The misgivings tormenting me were certainly not that you were going to forget me, because even supposing that could happen or had happened, I was quite sure that it could only be for a matter of moments. But I was very, very trepidatious about your state of mind in relation to yourself, and your circumstances, and this thought caused me endless anxiety that first day when I left you, and when in my imagination I pictured all the blackness, all the coldness, all the deadness of finding yourself thus abandoned. And as there was nothing else I could do, I urged the wife of the farm manager in Tolentino, should she have the opportunity, to pass on news of me, and my regards, to you and the rest of the family. Believe me, Carlo, if our love for one another could grow, it would grow on my side, not just because of our being apart, which in minds like ours usually causes a great desire for the loved one, but because of the very living in the world and its turmoil, and because of the very distractions and the obstacles I have to thinking only about you. For me in truth there is no greater solitude than being in the company of many people; and because I don't like this

[1] M430. Carlo's original reason for the suggestion was amour propre: he had told the postman that letters would be arriving for him (from his cousin Marietta in Rome, whom he was courting) under this name; but she had not co-operated. By getting Giacomo to use the name, Carlo avoided losing face with the postman. Having established that the system worked, the brothers used it frequently, often adding a line or two to family letters to allay suspicion. The choice of name is revealing, suggesting the influence of Foscolo's *Ultime lettere di Jacopo Ortis*.

solitude, I then wish to be solitary in reality, in order really to have company, that is your company and that of my heart. Listen, my dear brother; don't call me a misanthrope, or a coward, or a bigot; but rather be assured that what I am about to say to you is dictated by experience, and by knowledge of your mind and mine. I say that in truth, if you were somehow able to arrange a life for yourself there that was less dependent and less poor than the one you're now leading, you wouldn't have to think and reckon that you are giving in to fate, and leaving to it the greater part of happiness; but you'd have to convince yourself completely that you are, if not in the best, certainly in one of the best states possible to man. Ask me if in the two weeks since I've been in Rome I've ever enjoyed even a moment of fleeting pleasure, of stolen pleasure, foreseen or unexpected, outward or inward, stormy or calm, or in any shape whatsoever. I'll answer with a clear conscience and swear to you that from the moment I set foot in this city, not a drop of pleasure has ever fallen on my spirit; except in those moments when I've read your letters, which I tell you with no exaggeration have been the best moments of my stay in Rome: and for me those few lines you put at the bottom of Mother's letter were like a flash of light breaking through the thick, silent and deserted gloom surrounding me. You'll say I don't know how to live; that for you, and for others like you, it would not be like this. But listen to the arguments and the facts. Man absolutely cannot live in a large sphere, because his power or capacity to relate is limited. In a small city we can be bored, but in the end man's relationships with his fellow-man and with things do exist, because the sphere of those relationships is limited and in proportion to human nature. In a big city man lives without having any relationship at all to what surrounds him, because the sphere is so large that the individual cannot fill it, cannot feel it around him, and so there is no point of contact between it and him. From this you can surmise how much greater and more terrible is the tedium experienced in a big city than that experienced in small cities: since indifference, that horrible feeling, or rather absence of feeling, in man, truly and necessarily has its headquarters in big cities, that is in communities which are very extensive. Man's sense faculties, in these places, are limited just to sight. This is the only sensation individuals have, and it is not reflected in any way within them. The only way of being able to live in a big city – and everybody, sooner or later, is forced to adopt it – is by creating a small sphere of relationships for oneself, while remaining completely indifferent to the rest of society. That is to say by constructing around oneself so to speak a small city within the big one, with all the rest of the big city remaining useless and indifferent to the person in question. To do this, there is no need to leave small cities. This is truly a falling back on smallness by force of nature. Let's come to concrete proofs. I leave aside the fact that I see boredom on the faces of all the worldly people in Rome. I shall say just this. You know that the only source of pleasure is self respect; and that this self respect in the final analysis comes down to either ambition or feeling. As for feeling, you can imagine if a dissolute multitude that never thinks about itself is capable of it. As for ambition, you must accept that in a big city it is quite impossible to satisfy it. Whatever distinction you lay claim to – beauty, learning, nobility, wealth, or youth – in a big city there is such a superabundance of all this that no one pays any attention to it. Every day I see men who would fill Recanati with themselves, and here nobody takes any notice of them. Attracting other people's attention in a big city is a desperate business; and really cities of this kind are made only for monarchs, or for such men as can immeasurably surpass the greater part of humanity in some distinction which for the most part they have by luck, such as immense wealth, rank close to that of a prince, and similar things. Apart from these cases, you cannot enjoy Rome, and other big cities, except as a pure spectator; and a spectacle in which you can have no part bores you after a moment, no matter how beautiful it is. Leaving aside wit and literature, which I'll tell you about another time (since I've already met quite a few Roman men of letters), I'll restrict myself just to women, and the success you perhaps think it is easy to have with them in big cities. I assure you that actually quite the reverse is true. Out walking, in church, going along the streets, you won't find an old hag who gives you a glance. I've gone and go around Rome often in the company of very handsome, well-dressed young men. In their company I've often passed very close to young women: they have never raised their eyes; and it was perfectly clear that it was not out of bashfulness, but out of utter and habitual indifference and lack of interest: and all the women you meet here are like that. Getting down to business, it is as difficult in Rome as in Recanati to stop and talk to a woman, in fact much more so, on account of the excessive frivolousness and dissolute living of these foolish females, who in any case don't inspire a flicker of interest, are full of hypocrisy, only like going around enjoying themselves heaven knows how, and don't *deliver* (believe me) except with the endless difficulties one experiences in other towns. It all comes down to prostitutes, who I find are much more wary now than they once were, and in any case are dangerous as you know. I'm running out of paper. I wish I could go on talking to you forever. They are all asleep: I steal these moments from sleep, because during the day they don't leave me a moment's freedom. Give my fond regards to Paolina. Please, my dear Carlo, for my sake, when you write to me, make an effort to make your handwriting bigger, and leave a bit more space between the lines, for the sake of my poor eyes. Marietta is well, and seems to pay a lot of attention whenever the talk is about you.[2] You can write to me freely under my own name, without covering letters etc. because I don't show anyone your letters or anyone else's, and the people here in the house are incapable of tampering with the letters that come for me.[3] This evening I met some learned Germans who cheered me up somewhat. Adieu, I kiss you, be in good spirits.

2 Carlo was infatuated with his cousin Marietta, who had spent the previous summer with her family in Recanati.

3 But three months later Carlo wrote [M495]: 'I raced to the post to see if there was anything for Sofia [...] So in your next letter tell me a name under which I should write to you when I have something important to say.' Carlo's fear now was not interference by members of the Antici household, but by the postal authorities.

63

Leopardi complained to his father that antiquarianism was the only subject valued by Roman intellectuals.

To Monaldo Leopardi • Recanati

Rome, 9th December 1822

Dear Father. All the letters I receive from home, and yours especially, comfort me and cheer me up above anything else, because in truth I always had and always will have a need to share my heart and feelings; this I cannot find in my hosts, although they do not let me want for any other necessity or comfort. But the strange and quite anomalous principles and elements that make up their characters, and the unbelievable and inconceivable muddle which reigns in the daily life of this family, do not allow me to be anything but an outsider with them. [...] As for men of letters, about whom you ask, in truth I have met few of them, and those few have destroyed any wish on my part to meet others. They all expect to achieve immortality in a coach and pair, the way bad Christians think they can get to Heaven. According to them the summit of human wisdom, or rather man's sole true science, is antiquarianism. I still have not managed to meet a Roman man of letters who understands by the term literature anything other than archeology. Philosophy, ethics, politics, knowledge of the human heart, eloquence, poetry, philology: all this is foreign to Rome, and seems child's play, compared with finding out whether some bit of copper or stone belonged to Mark Anthony or Mark Agrippa. The joke is that a Roman who has a real mastery of Latin or Greek is not to be found; without a perfect knowledge of those languages, you are well aware what the study of antiquity can amount to. They gossip and argue all day long, they jeer at each other in the journals, they form cabals and cliques, and that is how Roman literature lives and moves forward. As for me, some of them knew of me before my arrival, others did not. The former treat me very well, the latter not very well, as happens to a new man, especially one who has never bothered about becoming known in this city, and who does not know how to talk about their favourite subject, or who is bored talking about it. Cancellieri is insufferable for the extravagant praise he bestows with supreme indifference on anyone who goes to see him: and he is famous for this unattractive habit, which makes his conversation completely meaningless, since it is impossible ever to believe him. Monsignor Mai is quite the opposite of this rogue; he is very courteous to everyone, very obliging in his words, a politician in his actions; he makes a show of wanting to satisfy everyone, and does what suits himself in the end; but as for me, not only do I have no complaints, on the contrary I have to say that he really has obliged me in all my requests, and that he treats me almost with respect. His *De re publica* came out after my arrival;[1] it is a fine thing, and much praised by those who understand it, just as it is criticised by the faction opposed to Mai. The *Fronto* will come out soon, enlarged to twice the size it was in the Milan edition, so that a large part of his works is now complete and without gaps. I have met Cavaliere Marini, Director General

[1] Mai had discovered a manuscript of this previously lost work of Cicero's; see [36].

of the Land Registry, a very cultivated man, who immediately spoke to me about you, and that business of yours at the time of the victualling-board, which he was involved in too, as he told me; and he showed great respect for you.[2] He has a very rich library, which is, it may be said, at Melchiorri's and my disposal. It is not open to the public. Here we mostly spend a good part of the morning, and normally we are alone. At the Minister for Holland's (he asked after you, and wanted your work on our Mint, having seen it announced in the *Effemeridi*[3]) I have met some foreign scholars (a very different thing from Romans). One of then came yesterday expressly to call on me, and on his own initiative; and he asked me to tell him about some observations I am about to have published; he commended them, and asked me at what time he could come back to *chat*[4] with me. He is a professor of Greek literature in Munich, a famous man, whom I had already known by name for some years.[5] I have taken up your time with these trifles because I believe, and you assure me, that you are pleased to be kept informed of my doings. I hope your new appointment causes you as little inconvenience as possible: I hope and trust that our native city will benefit by it.[6] Please give my regards to all the family, especially to Mama, and my respects to Marchioness Roberti. Bless me: there is no need to tell you that I await your instructions; please do let me have them, so that I may have the consolation of being of some service to you insofar as I am able. Your loving son,

Giacomo.

2 Marini would quickly become a prospective husband for Paolina. The victualling-board business is described by Count Monaldo in the final chapters of his *Autobiography*.

3 A Roman newspaper, in which excerpts had appeared of a study Count Monaldo had written of the Recanati mint and coinage.

4 Leopardi uses the invented verb *côsare*, i.e. French *causer*.

5 The Minister for Holland was F. G. Reinhold; the Professor of Greek was F. G. Tiersch.

6 Count Monaldo had just been elected by his fellow-townsmen to serve as *gonfaloniere* for Recanati on the town council.

64

This letter to Carlo (addressed to 'Sofia Ortis') was clearly not meant to be seen by his parents, as it spoke freely of dissolute living, women and literature in terms that they could not have approved of. After sending it Leopardi suffered an anxiety attack that it might have fallen into their hands, as he wrote to Carlo ten days later in a letter not included here: 'I have a terrible suspicion that my letter was intercepted and opened at home, and not given to you... I talked about almost nothing except women and silly stories.'[1]

To Carlo Leopardi • Recanati

Rome, 16th December [1822]

My dear Carlo. If you are not convinced by what I tried to prove to you in my last letter, *n'en parlons plus.* I assure you that not only have I not felt any pleasure in Rome, but I have always been sunk in deepest despondency. I don't deny though that this comes largely from my own particular moral and physical make-up. I assure you too that where women are concerned there is absolutely nothing more to be done here than in Recanati. I assure you that spectacles and entertainments are much more boring here than in Recanati, because in them no one shines, apart from the spectacle and entertainment itself. That is the only thing that can shine, and one does not go to a spectacle except purely to see the spectacle (a very tedious thing), or else to pass the time with the few people who form one's own small circle: and this small circle exists much better in small cities than in big ones, and certainly in big cities is more restricted than in small ones. But let's move on to more cheerful things. In the first place I haven't met any guard or any member of the Spada family.[2] I *have* met that odd fellow Menicuccio Melchiorri, and I spend time every day with that bloody fool Peppe, who is inviting half the world to give him cuckold's horns five feet high. But no matter how frightful an idea you may have of his wife, you simply cannot conceive of the sort of wretched, worthless woman she is. Imagine a common servant girl, very stupid, very ugly, very clumsy, with no charm in her eyes or in her bearing or in any part of her person, with nothing to say for herself, in short lacking any conceivable attractive quality at all; and all this on top of being a whore, or at least a flirt. I don't know high class whores, but as for low class ones, I swear to you that the ugliest and shabbiest little flirt in Recanati is worth all the best in Rome. I've met several of these crafty, clever fellows. They're more outspoken and more articulate, but as for knowing how to behave and getting somewhere, the Galamini[3] would beat the lot of them. A Condulmari[4] would eat the whole of Rome alive in one bite. Be confirmed in your opinion that a good and well-bred man from the March can take on half the

[1] M450.

[2] This is in response to a comment of Carlo's about their cousin Peppe [M441]: 'This fool wants to know if you've met Spada, the guard'.

[3] A Recanati family.

[4] The Condulmari were another Recanati family.

world. I realized it as early as Spoleto, comparing those people from the March who were at our table with others from other parts, young and gallant though they were. Cancellieri amuses me sometimes with spiritual stories, for example that Cardinal Malvasia of blessed memory used to put his hands down the dresses of the Ladies in his circle, and was a *débauché* of the first rank, and sent the husbands and sons of those who resisted him to the inquisition, etc. etc. Similar things about Cardinal Brancadoro, similar ones about all the Cardinals (who are the most disgusting people on earth), similar ones about all the prelates, none of whom get anywhere except through women. The saintly Pope Pius the Seventh owes his becoming both cardinal and pope to a Roman flirt. After going into raptures, he amuses himself presently talking about the loves and lusts of his Cardinals and Prelates, and he laughs about it, and offers them *bons-mots* and compliments on the subject. His favourite set consists of some lay people, professional buffoons, whose names I was told, but I don't remember them. A daughter of some artist or other, formerly Lebzeltern's favourite, obtained through him, and currently enjoys, a pension of seven hundred *scudi* a year, with the result that when her first husband died she got married again to a prince. The Magatti woman, Calcagnini's famous whore, is in exile in Florence and has a pension of 700 *scudi* from the government, obtained through the prince Royal of Bavaria, her former lover. He is the prince who made that miraculous and unexpected recovery from deafness (as one read in the papers), while remaining deafer than ever. What do you think of that? All the same you can be certain that on the essential point (where women are concerned) there is much more to be done in Recanati than in Rome, if you take into account their respective populations, and leave out what is done wholly and solely for money, which no doubt is a great deal, indeed most of it. But it takes a lot of money, because here there's no shortage of it, and we're not talking about trifling sums. I've spoken to you only about women because I don't know what to say about literature. Horrors and then more horrors. The most sacred names profaned, the most egregious nonsense praised to the skies, the best spirits of this age disparaged as inferior to the most insignificant Roman man of letters, philosophy despised as an occupation for children; genius, imagination, and feeling, words (I don't mean things, I mean words) unknown and alien to professional poets and poetesses; and antiquarianism placed by everyone at the pinnacle of human knowledge, and considered unfailingly and universally to be man's only true study. I'm not exaggerating. On the contrary it's impossible for me to say enough. In Rome man of letters and antiquarian are exactly and precisely the same thing. If I'm not an antiquarian, it means I'm not a man of letters, and I don't know anything. And then, I'm disheartened by seeing people even more fanatical about literature than I ever was; by that wretched trafficking in glory (since here people don't talk about money, which would at least be worth making the effort to pursue), and in glory envied, contested, snatched from one person's mouth by another; by those continual factions, which you cannot have any idea of if you're not on the spot; by that endless talking about literature (like Massucci, for example, about his business dealings), and talking about it very foolishly, as though it were a real profession, making plans all day long, criticising, promising, blowing their own trumpets, glorifying people and writings that are pathetic; all this disheartens me so that if I did not have the haven of posterity, and the certainty that with time everything takes its rightful place (an illusory haven, but the only one there is, and an absolutely necessary one for a true man of letters), I'd send literature to the devil a thousand times. As for the jealousy to be aroused, leave it to me; and already I haven't missed some opportunities. As for the jealousy you're feeling, I know that distance kindles it and stirs it up, but it truly, truly is out of place.[5] Aunt Marianna has told me and repeated several times that I'm to send you regards particularly in her name. This is the first and perhaps the last time I do as she asks. Give my regards to everybody. I'm well. It's hellishly cold, because the wind is blowing from the north. Apart from days of heavy snow, it's never as cold as this in Recanati. Good night. Be cheerful, if you can; be fond of me, and write.

[5] A further reference to Carlo's infatuation with his cousin Marietta.

65

Leopardi confided to Carlo his hopes that he might find paid employment with a foreigner – English, German or Russian – who would take him abroad.

To Carlo Leopardi • Recanati

Rome, 22nd January 1823

Dear Carlo. I'm on my feet, and I can say recovered, after exactly two hundred hours in bed.[1] I'm answering your last two letters, as I promised. Don't be misled into thinking that my effusions etc. come more from calculation than from any other source,[2] although it cannot be denied that distance somehow revives sentiments either dulled or dead, firstly because it is distance, then because man always needs someone he thinks takes an interest in him, and he feels this need particularly when he is living among people who are strangers and foreigners and for the most part unknown. I gave Father an account of De Romanis's plan[3] purely out of a wish to chat and fill up the page, and because, firstly, it never occurred to me that Father would have the misgivings about it that he did, nor that he'd be afraid I might stay away longer, when, it may be said, he'd suggested in so many words that I should obtain some position that enabled me to live away from home; secondly, the thought that gave rise to Father's uneasiness (that is, that what I make from this project might be enough for me to live on in Rome) was and is very far from my mind. Just imagine what a handsome income five or six hundred *scudi* in all would be, in the five or six years it would take to complete a huge work like that. A hundred *scudi* a year at most would already be a big return. So that I've never pinned any of my hopes on this project, and I told Father about it as a thing of no consequence, and he has become agitated about this thing of no consequence, and has written to me as you can imagine. Thank you very much for the clarifications you gave me on

[1] He had taken to his bed with an acute case of chilblains.

[2] Carlo had been surprised at Giacomo's expressions of affection towards his parents, assuming that they were calculated for effect rather than being entirely genuine.

[3] The publisher De Romanis had planned a translation of all Plato's works; the plan came to nothing.

this matter, which will be useful to me as a basis for my reply. Apart from that we have almost reached an agreement with De Romanis. I'm still hesitating though, I haven't committed myself, and I'll take my time making up my mind: because it's a great deal of work, the profit is small, the time required by the project is long, and I have many better things to spend it on, if I want to write.

If you ask me what hopes I have, where it is leading, and what benefit I think to gain from this trip, here we go. Seeking employment in the State is almost a waste of effort. The closer the view one has of the court, the more one despairs of getting anything from it. I'm fairly friendly with Cavaliere Marini, the Director General of the Land Registry. A slight commitment on his part would perhaps be enough to get me a position as a Keeper of records in the tax office (entirely in his gift), as soon as there is a vacancy. Uncle Carlo tells me it's a sure thing, that I'm to cultivate Marini and not think about anything else. I let him prattle as I've always done. Marini isn't a man to commit himself, and he has a thousand people pulling strings to get these positions etc. etc. My plan is to get myself taken off by some foreigner, English, German or Russian. Cancellieri tells me it will be very easy (I've told only him, and no one else, about this plan of mine), and as he knows many of these people, he has promised to support and help me. One mustn't take what Cancellieri says too seriously, but I can see that the thing really isn't difficult, I know that Italian men of letters are still being taken on, I know the names of several Roman hacks who have done very well or who at least get by comfortably in those countries; I see others, and know some in person, who have been to Germany, to England etc., with their journey there and back paid for, and they were treated very well there and urged to stay; I know that some Italians have been invited by Italinski the Russian minister and other such people, to move and settle in their countries, with stipends, etc.; and finally I can see with my own eyes how little it takes to do very well with these foreign gentlemen, what modest abilities they pay a high price for, how highly they value any modest literary accomplishment one is able to show. You ought to know, though, that philosophy, and everything connected with genius, in short, true literature, of whatever kind, counts damn all with foreigners; as they have almost no knowledge of Italian, they wouldn't give a damn for the finest works they might be shown in this language; and they take no interest in someone who excels in a discipline that is beyond them. So I've changed my clothes, or rather put on again what I wore as a child. Here in Rome I'm not a man of letters (a title which, if true, is useless with Romans, useless with foreigners), but I'm a scholar and an expert in Greek. You can't think how useful to me those scraps of philological learning have been that I've gathered and scraped together from the memory of my boyhood occupations. Without them, I'd be nothing with foreigners, who usually respect me and give me many signs of approval. And because in a big city where there are *some* people who read, it is very useful, in fact necessary, to bring out something to make yourself known, and this, for good or ill, unfailingly does make you known, as I have become very aware; I've therefore chosen to write a few trifles (all scholarly) which are about to come out, and you will be the first to have a copy of them. This will be my first step; after which (as I see from many examples, indeed on a daily basis) it is probable that various foreigners, ministers, etc. will want to make my acquaintance, and then we shall endeavour to get somewhere. In Rome, although much less so than in other capital cities, there is some life; and many trifles help, and there are various ways of earning money and going forward along one road or another. Indeed, if I were to settle for certain rather humble occupations, I would already have found various opportunities for earning money (not with the government, but in private employment), and with literature alone I could expect to survive in Rome – not live as a gentleman, but survive. That's enough, we'll see: and meanwhile French, which they tell me I speak well, is indispensable to me; and in truth speaking it doesn't much bother me; but you can't believe what a dreadful strain and effort it is to understand it when it is spoken by foreigners, who pronounce it so throatily that it completely alters and distorts what the words seem to be, so that they reach your ears all different from the ones you know. They speak it very fast, and you always have to concentrate very hard with your ears and your mind, and not be interrupted even for a moment; it's frightfully hard work. Believe me, the difficulty really is huge; to get over it, it's not enough to know the language well. But with practice it will all come right. It goes without saying that you're not to tell anyone these things. I take good care not to give the slightest hint of my intentions to my hosts. Dear Carlo, you can well believe I love you, and how I feel about even the thought of leaving you behind. But perhaps it is a dream, and I'm well aware that you would like it to have some substance. I tell you truthfully that even supposing I'd already achieved it, I wouldn't feel any sense of cheerfulness; but although I'm already quite incapable of enjoyment, and incapable forever, Rome has at least given me the advantage of perfecting my insensitivity towards myself, and making me look at my whole life, for better or worse, as if it were the life, for better or worse, of some other person. Thank you especially for the information you give me about yourself, and you see that I am paying you back with interest. I'd like you not to grow weary, not to get bored with carrying on. But how much more I'd like, I won't say to know that you're happy or contented, because for us those are dreams; but to be with you, and share everything of yours, and you everything of mine, as we have for our whole lives up to now. And surely we shall for as long as we draw breath, if you don't doubt me. But this is the rarest thing of all about our friendship, that neither of us has any doubts that the other one could ever doubt him. I kiss you.

66

Paolina's marriage plans had come to nothing. Her low spirits prompted Leopardi to write consoling her, showing complete empathy for her situation, and the characteristic seriousness and respect with which he responded to her feelings. He accepted that leaving home was her only way of finding happiness, and continued to make efforts to arrange a match.[1]

To Paolina Leopardi • Recanati

[Rome] 28th January [1823]

Dear Paolina. Your letter was very welcome, as the letters you write me always will be, but I'm still very sorry to hear that your imagination is causing you such distress. I don't say imagination, meaning to imply that you're wrong, but what I mean is that all our ills come from there, because in fact, humanly speaking, there is no real good or ill in the world except bodily pain. I'd like to be able to comfort you, and obtain your happiness at the cost of my own; but as I can't do this, I assure you that at least you have in me a brother who loves you from the heart, who will always love you, who feels the awkwardness and the anguish of your situation, who feels for you, who in short shares in everything that concerns you. After all this I won't repeat to you that human happiness is a dream, that the world is not beautiful, in fact is not bearable, unless it is seen as you see it, that is from a distance; that pleasure is a word, not a thing; that virtue, sensitivity, greatness of spirit are not just the only consolations for our ills, but also the only possible blessings in this life; and that these blessings, if one lives in the world and in society, are not enjoyed and not put to good use, as young people usually believe, but are lost entirely, and the mind is left in a terrifying void. You already know these things, and you don't just know them, you believe them; and yet you need and desire to see them from your own experience; and this desire is making you unhappy. This is what happened to me, this is what happens and will forever happen to all young people, this is what happens to grown men too and even to old people, and this is nature's way. So you see how far I am from telling you you are wrong. But I want you for my sake to make an effort, to benefit a little from philosophy, to try to cheer up somehow or other, as I know from long experience one can even in your state, no less than in any other. And finally I don't want you to despair; because in the space of a day the cause of your low spirits can disappear, and it is very likely that this will happen; or rather, it is more than likely; in fact, if things go in the natural way, it is quite certain. What I can do for you, you must believe I will do. Meanwhile enjoy yourself. Do you think I'm enjoying myself more than you? Certainly not. And yet in these last few days I've had, and continue to have, a life with many distractions. But take as true this precept recognized by all philosophers, which will be able to comfort you in many eventualities; it is that each man's happiness and unhappiness (leaving aside bodily pains) is exactly equal to that of every other man, in whatever condition or situation either of them happens to be. And so, strictly speaking, the poor man, the old man, the weak

[1] See [69, 72].

man, the ugly man, the ignorant man, have as much pleasure and as much pain as the rich man, the young man, the strong man, the handsome man, the learned man: because each one in his state fashions his own blessings and his own ills; and the sum of blessings and ills which each man can fashion for himself is equal to what anyone else can fashion.

Perhaps, wanting to comfort you, I'll have bored you with so much philosophising. In any event, be as cheerful as you can, and wait for me to comfort you in person; if you haven't by then already been comforted by fate. Give my regards to our parents, our brothers, Carlo especially. I'm well, and I love you. Adieu.

67

Leopardi complained to Giordani too about the state of literature in Rome, and reported interesting contacts with foreigners.

To Pietro Giordani • Piacenza

Rome, 1st February 1823.

My divine friend. You can't think what a comfort it was to me to see your handwriting again after such a long interval; although it makes me infinitely disconsolate to hear that you're still having trouble with your nerves, contrary to what I was hoping and almost expecting. Whenever I think of you (as I do every day), and especially reading your letters, I'm seized by an incredible desire to see you again and embrace you again and have long talks with you, and show you my heart and contemplate yours; and if not console you for the harshness of fate, shoulder some part of the troubles and the sadness that weigh you down. Do believe that this is my greatest desire and that I am determined to fulfil it in any event, as soon as I have something to call my own. I have several times seen Monsignor Mai, who asked after you the first time he saw me, saying he had had no news of you for a long time. I'll see him again very soon and give him some. He has done me many acts of kindness, and I hear he is in the habit of speaking very well of me. I'll certainly see and call on Abbé Canova[1] on your behalf. The gentleman you speak of must have many enemies here. They say he is a hypocrite, self-seeking, and a spy for the government, and for some ambassador or other. I know nothing. What shall I say about Canova? You see that I am unlucky, as usual, because just when I had managed, after so many years and so much desperation, to leave my poor birthplace and see Rome, the great Canova – on whom my desire was chiefly fixed, and with whom I hoped to talk intimately and, through you, to form a true and lasting friendship – went and died, scarcely a month before my arrival in this city that is full of him.[2] And death took pleasure too, when I was almost on the point of making a move, in killing off some other people who were here, and who on seeing me again against all hope (theirs or mine)

1 A half-brother of the sculptor Antonio Canova (mentioned later in the letter), and a friend of Giordani's.

2 Canova the sculptor died in Venice in October 1822.

would have been delighted, because of the affection they felt for me, and it would have given me heart to see them and be with them.[3]

Roman literature, as you are very well aware, is so wretched, base, stupid and worthless that I regret having seen it and seeing it, because these wretched men of letters give me a distaste for literature, and the contempt and pity I have for them works in my mind to the detriment of the great conception and the great love I had of literature. I've brought some small bits and pieces here that I've worked on for a long time, which I could manage to have printed in this city (not without difficulties and obstacles); but I'm very undecided because I think that everything published here, if it is not absolute vanity and folly, is thrown away and lost. For the most part I don't bother with Romans and Italians; I talk with foreigners: we now have some who are very distinguished and famous.[4] I think it very unlikely that I'll find a position either in Rome (where it would be difficult for me to spend the hot months) or in the papal State. Nonetheless this is what I would like. A very modest income would do me. I don't care about wealth, only about freedom, which someone who has nothing of his own to live on cannot possess. I don't care about capital cities either. I'd be content with a medium-sized city. But this little that I desire I have almost no hope of obtaining in this country, especially as I have very little boldness in asking for it. I've been thinking a good deal about finding a position with some rich foreigner who can take me to his country, where (who knows) I might manage to live tolerably well by working and writing. I know that the foreign ministers who are here at court are looking out for men of letters and scientists to send to their own countries; that they have made this offer to some people who have not accepted it, to others who have accepted it and today find themselves quite comfortably placed, and yet they are people who have little talent, and whose learning is what they have been able to get in Rome, since I'm speaking only about Romans. I know that the plans I've conceived and. the sketches I've made in all this time of solitude, cannot by any means be filled out and completed in Italy, or, even if they were filled out and finished, they'd have to remain on my desk; and on the other hand, I more or less don't want to write except in accordance with those plans, or in keeping with their kind or nature. Please tell me your opinion; if you think it possible to get away from here and live well away from here; if you think this is what I should do; if you think the benefit is greater or less than the difficulty and the disruption needed to bring it about.

My uncle's translation was of a German work by Count Stolberg, which contains the Gospels more or less. My uncle had added a preface, not in the style of Passavanti, but suited to his time.[5] He sent you his work as a testimony to the memory he still has of you, and

[3] Leopardi's aunt, Ferdinanda Melchiorri, who lived in Rome and with whom he felt a special bond and had corresponded for some years, had died the previous summer. Her letters to him are extant; his to her, sadly, are not.

[4] Contacts formed with foreign diplomats and scholars were one of the most satisfying aspects of Leopardi's Roman sojourn, and had lasting consequences: Barthold Georg Niebuhr would try to use his influence to help him find employment [70]; Carlo Bunsen would become a long-term correspondent [83, 92, 209, 210].

[5] Passavanti was the fourteenth-century author of the *Specchio di vera penitenza*. This was a barbed comment: his uncle had failed to match the purity of Passavanti's style, while nevertheless producing something which was so backward in spirit as to seem medieval.

of the very great esteem he professes for you. Both are genuine and unchanging, and I can bear witness to that myself, as you don't yet have his gift and his letter. He sends his regards, and has already written to arrange for the packet to be redirected to you. Carlo and Paolina enjoy good health, and will be very pleased to have news of you, for I'll pass it on at once. Paolina never did get married. She wanted (and I confess it was on my advice and Carlo's) to make a fashionable match, that is a 'good' match, taking that gentleman who was very ugly and very dull, but not set in his ways and reputed to be rich. It then turned out that this last quality was attributed to him erroneously, and the negotiations, which had already been concluded, were broken off. She and Carlo love you, and remember you all the time, not believing it possible (as I do not) that they will be able to find in their whole lives a heart and a spirit like yours. Hearing from you that you still love me, although I did not doubt it, is so sweet that I don't know what other sweetness and what other satisfaction I would not exchange for it with all my heart. But that you continue to suffer saddens me much more than I could ever express. For a long time I have been of the opinion, and almost had the feeling, that my life and fate and yours are as it were one and the same, and that I must be very happy for your happiness, and very unhappy for your unhappiness. Write to me as often as you can, because your letters always bring me a sense of life which for several years I've not been used to feeling, one can say, ever. You see that I'm doing as you ask and writing about myself at greater length than I ever would to anyone else, or even to you, except to please you. Go on loving me as you do. I embrace you and take my leave with all my soul. Adieu, dearest and only friend. Adieu.

68

He reported to Carlo on his hopes for a position in the Land Registry, and on a visit to the Opera.

To Carlo Leopardi • Recanati

Rome, 5th February [1823]

Dear Carlo. From the tone of your letter I think I can see that you're more cheerful than usual, and I wouldn't think it unlikely that you owed that to the talks you've been having with the beautiful singer, and to the feelings you are experiencing for her, which I think resemble love. I congratulate you with all my soul, and I share your feelings at a distance, just as I shared the chilblains of the *aimable chanteuse*; but as for her bed, you are the only one who can share that, if you can, which I doubt.[1] Thank you for your sonnets; à propos of which I almost have a suspicion that you want to become a new Alfieri, with the difference that he set out to study and write for the first time when he was older than you are, and you

[1] Carlo had been writing sonnets for the singer Clorinda Corradi, then performing in Recanati, who had taken to her bed for the same period of time as Giacomo and with the same complaint (chilblains). Carlo had joked that Giacomo would not have minded sharing the bed with her.

at your younger age would not be beginning your studies, but taking them up again, or rather continuing them. Certainly your verses are very much in the Alfieri manner, without your perhaps realizing it; and your reason for writing poetry would be the same one as Alfieri's, that is love or something of this sort. You can believe, Carlo, how willingly I'd do anything for you, that is to say for me, since you and I have been and always will be one and the same consubstantial person, and there is no need to repeat it. It is true that Marini has some influence on positions of employment in the land-registry. It isn't true that he is in charge of them: that's one of uncle Carlo's usual dreams and fanciful notions, as I wrote you. He and I are quite friendly, but it is one of those cool friendships you can have with busy people, who see vast numbers of folk every day, and who have been successful by dint of working hard, and in consequence have become used to being self-centred, that is to working only for themselves, since if they had worked for other people, they would not have been successful. Anyway he is a very courteous man; there might perhaps be a side of him that could be taken and won over, and if I can get something out of him for you, I shan't fail to do so. I congratulate you on the impressions and the tears Rossini's music caused you, but you're wrong to think we've got nothing similar. We have the *Donna del Lago* at the Argentina;[2] the music performed by remarkable voices is a splendid thing, and I could weep too, if I hadn't temporarily lost the gift of tears, since I'm aware that I haven't lost it entirely. But the length of the performance (it lasts six hours) is unbearable and deadly, and here the custom is not to leave one's own box. It seems that these Roman buggers, who've made their buildings and streets and churches and squares on a scale fit for giants to live in, want to make their entertainments on the same scale as well, that is gigantic, as if there were no limit to the amount of entertainment human nature, bloody stupid though it be, can tolerate and enjoy. I won't tell you about the spectacle of the procession, which really is beautiful and worth seeing (I mean the Carnival procession); nor of the impression made on me by the dancing seen with a *lorgnette*. I'll tell you in general that a woman cannot beguile a man by singing or any other means as much as by dancing: it seems to impart to her form something almost divine, and to her body a strength, a power more than human. You've seen this dancing at parties, but there's no comparison with the dancing of the least good dancers in a theatrical piece. The waltz they sometimes perform is considered a thing of no account and a fill-in. In short believe me if you were to see one of these dancers in action, I have such a notion of your anti-erotic resolutions that I think you'd be infatuated straight away. And before and after your letter I let slip quite a few of those artless and unwary remarks that you'll forgive me for. To help your cause I also related the fair lady's exploits at dinner.[3] The heartless one was very attentive, as usual. Don't think that she has many distractions: at least to my mind the distractions she has can't amount to much. You can be quite sure that she's not making a tiara for you,[4] because she really follows the same routine as my hosts: go out, see, come back home: a hellish life, which they want me to be part of – as if I were a boot

2 Rossini's opera, composed in 1819, was being performed at the Teatro Argentina in Rome.

3 He was trying to help his brother's cause with his cousin Marietta in Rome by making her jealous of his dealings with the singer back in Recanati.

4 i.e. being unfaithful to you, the 'tiara' being a joking allusion to the cuckold's horns.

wider and longer than Italy.[5] They come home more bored than when they went out, and take it out on one another by making fun of each other, and with a hundred fine merry jokes which it's a delight to witness, as is my lot: but I've become hardened to it.[6] Giordani, who has written to me after a year and more of silence very enthusiastically, asks after you and Paolina with infinite concern and sends his regards. I send my regards too and embrace you from the heart. Don't tell me again to look after myself, because I am better and as fit as a fiddle thanks to having done things my own way, that is not using any bloody medicines, as they were insisting, and staying in bed as long as I saw fit, which they were unanimously against. Adieu, adieu, it's lunch time, and we'll go and hear some real gems, as usual.

5 'Boot' (*stivale*) is a colloquial term for fool, simpleton; cf Stendhal, *Rome, Naples and Florence*, translated by Richard N. Coe (London, John Calder, 1959), p. 273: 'Oh, the coals of fire that shall be heaped upon my head for this unwary pronouncement! I shall be *bue, stivale e somaro*.'

6 There were six children in the Antici household. Their boisterousness and talkativeness must have contrasted oddly with Giacomo's habitual silence (interpreted by many as taciturnity, but possibly the result of his weak chest), described in a letter from his uncle to his father six weeks earlier: 'His silent manner is in any case still the same, and I am sure that if at table I did not drag some monosyllable out of him from time to time, he would not speak any more than he spoke at his father's table. But that should convince you that his silence (so painful for you) did not come from a hostile spirit, but from a long-standing habit which can no longer be overcome [...]' (cited in Moroncini II, p. 197, n. 1).

69

The problem of finding a suitable match for Paolina continued to occupy the family. The moving account of a visit to Tasso's tomb reflected Leopardi's lifelong interest in the Renaissance poet with whom he felt a particular affinity and whose destiny he had long pondered. The tomb, and the experience of going to it, provided a touchstone of true values and true achievement (simplicity, truth, the dignity of honest labour, poetic distinction), amidst the falseness, grandiosity, and intrigue of fashionable Rome.[1]

To Carlo Leopardi • Recanati

Rome, 20th February 1823.

I've just received your letter of the 9th, in which you give the lie to my insulting imputations against your constancy and your experience in love, and you leave me nothing to reply. I don't know who wrote to you about Mai's lunch. I wrote to you about it in another connection, but that was at a later date than your letter. In truth I could feel few consolations equal to that of seeing the plan you describe concerning Paolina's marriage put into effect.[2] I'm

1 By contrast, Leopardi would be unmoved at the sight of Dante's tomb on a brief visit to Ravenna in 1826; see *Zibaldone*, 14th March 1827, for his reflections on the significance of the difference between the two poets' personalities and destinies.

2 There was a new prospective husband in view.

sure that on your side you won't fail to do anything that might help bring it about. I don't know, and no one can know, if Paolina will be happy in her new state, and with this companion; but we all know for certain that for her there is no better course of action, or rather no course of action, except that of getting married soon, and if possible to a younger man. Give her my warmest regards, and express my feelings to her as you think best: give me news of this business again later on.

On Friday the 15th of February 1823 I went to visit Tasso's tomb, and I wept there. This is the first and only *pleasure* I have experienced in Rome. The street that takes you there is long, and you don't go to that spot except to see this tomb: but couldn't one even come from America to savour the pleasure of tears for the space of two minutes? And yet it is quite certain that the huge sums of money I see spent here simply in pursuit of one pleasure or another are all wasted, because instead of pleasure all they achieve is boredom. Many people feel indignant seeing Tasso's remains covered and marked by nothing except a stone about a foot long and wide, and placed in an out-of-the-way corner of an insignificant little church. I absolutely would not want to find his remains under a mausoleum. You understand the host of feelings that arise from contemplating the contrast between Tasso's greatness and the unpretentiousness of his tomb. But you can't have any idea of another contrast, that is the one felt by an eye accustomed to the boundless grandiosity and vast size of Roman monuments, comparing them to the smallness and bareness of this tomb. One feels a sad and angry consolation thinking that this lack of ostentation is still sufficient to interest and inspire posterity,[3] whereas the most magnificent mausoleums contained in Rome are gazed at with perfect indifference towards the person to whom they were erected, whose name is not even asked, or else is asked not as the name of the person but of the monument. Near Tasso's tomb is the tomb of the poet Guidi, who wanted to lie *prope magnos Torquati cineres*,[4] as the inscription says. He did the wrong thing. I didn't even have a sigh left for him. I could hardly bear to look at his monument, fearing to stifle the sensations I'd felt at Tasso's tomb. Even the street that leads to that spot prepares the spirit for the impressions of feeling. It is all flanked by houses destined for artisan work, and it resounds to the noise of looms and other such implements, and the singing of women and labourers busy at their work. In an idle, dissolute, disorganised city such as capital cities are, it is a fine thing to contemplate an image of life which is thoughtful, orderly and engaged in useful occupations. Even the expressions and the behaviour of the people one meets in that street have something simpler and more human about them than those of other people; and they reveal the habits and the character of persons whose life is based on truth and not on falsehood, that is who live by hard work and not by intrigue, imposture and deception, as the greater part of this populace does. I've run out of space: I hug you. Adieu adieu.

[3] The deliberate echo *povertà* [lack of ostentation] – *posterità* is lost in English; on *povertà* and creativity in Leopardi's thinking, see D'Intino, p. lxxxi.

[4] *near the great ashes of Torquato.*

70

In spite of his 'aversion to the priesthood', Leopardi briefly considered – and quickly rejected – the possibility of compromise in order to obtain a position in the papal Court. (It is clear that by this time he had lost his religious faith.)[1] *Niebuhr, the Minister for Prussia and an admirer of his philological work, acted as intermediary with the Secretary of State.*

To Carlo Leopardi • Recanati

[Rome] 22nd March, 1823

My dear Carlo. Many, many thanks for your letter of the 13th which reached here two whole days later than usual, and for the other one dated the 16th which I received straight away. You must surely laugh at philology, as I do; I make use of it here in Rome only for the reasons I told you of once before,[2] and as I use it, I become increasingly aware of its triviality. In particular the article I sent you is a piece of foolishness, but although the method I followed is precisely the one used by the Germans, you must not on that account think that the Minister, praising the article, had only or chiefly the method in mind. Indeed he didn't even mention it to me; but he did talk about other qualities he finds in it, which it is not worth elaborating on. A few days after the first *entrevue* I had with the Minister, I received a note, in which in the most courteous and considerate way possible, he told me in brief: that he had spoken about me to the Secretary of State, that this gentleman was not disinclined to find a position for me, that understanding my aversion to the priesthood, he had asked if I'd be prepared to wear Court dress, which would open the way for me to employment and honours.[3] He advised me to send him without delay a formal request for the Secretary of State, and he concluded by calling me his philologist colleague. I don't know what you think about taking holy orders.[4] At this point we're considering abandoning the beautiful in favour of the useful. A career in holy orders at present really does offer very great advantages, especially to someone of noble birth, because there is a great shortage of Gentlemen who embark on this career, and the Secretary of State likes certain functions to be carried out by noblemen. So that one can hope for a Delegation in a short time, and perhaps even straight away, and then rapid advancement, etc. etc. I found myself very confused, as it is a matter of deciding *de agenda vita*, and of making a choice of state, and that in a few hours. I told my two uncles about the note, and I can't deny that their views were helpful, if only because they could talk dispassionately. All three of us talked the matter over together, so that at least I shan't be able to regret not having given it enough thought. In short it is almost certain that if I'd wanted to become a prelate, you'd have heard shortly afterwards that your brother in

[1] Leopardi had tried to reconcile his philosophical system with Christianity in a long entry in the *Zibaldone* two years earlier (9–15 December 1820), but the attempt was not very convincing and in any case was superseded by his developing thinking.

[2] See [65].

[3] Court dress indicated a status midway between priestly and secular. Niebuhr's note is M499.

[4] Carlo's reaction was understandably one of horror.

his clerical cape was going off to govern a province. The great outlay required to become a man of the cloth would have been covered by a loan, which it would have been easy to find here, once the position was obtained or guaranteed. I looked around me, and decided I didn't want anything to do with it. The reasons, which I could tell you, are many: I think you agree with me; if that's not so, at least be assured that I did not make this decision out of indecisiveness and lack of courage: but because a long time ago, and before coming here, and much more so since coming, I made up my mind that my life must be as independent as possible, and that my happiness can only consist in doing what suits me. My nature is like that, and it has been confirmed for me by so many experiences that I cannot doubt it any more. So given that I had to seek a lay position, after passing them all in review, we ascertained that there was none that suited me except Keeper of records in the Tax office. All the positions of this kind are filled, but it is in the power of the Secretary of State to free one of them, transferring the holder to some other position among the huge number available in this government. I called on the Minister that same evening; we reached an agreement, and having then sent him the formal request, in which he wanted me to make a few changes, he sent it back to me, as we had agreed, with a letter and recommendation from him to the Secretary of State, and with a note from him for Abbé Capaccini, who takes the minutes etc., who was to present the request. After a whole day sweating it out, and no lunch, I walked up Monte Cavallo street four times in the dazzling sun, and in the end got nowhere; finally the next morning having got up at dawn, and walked twice up the same street, I managed to see Abbé Capaccini, and hand him the packet, about which he gave me cause to feel hopeful. My uncles say I can't fail to get a position: I'm treating the whole thing as a joke, and I hope that if that is what it proves to be I'll be more content than before.[5] Meanwhile Abbé Capaccini has been informed about a position that could become vacant in June, to which it won't be difficult to transfer one of the present tax office record keepers.

I've told you this whole story in such detail – needless to say you're not to mention it to anyone in the family or outside – to abide by the agreement we have with one another to tell each other about all our doings. Carlo, if you love me, believe that I love you no less, and that truly with every passing day I want your company more and more, and feel I need you. It would perhaps be futile for me to try to convince you of it, because you know yourself well enough and you know me equally well, and you know there's no one like you, and that I'm not one to talk to people who don't understand me, much less to love people who don't love me. I could say endless loving things to you; or rather, I'd like to say them, but I wouldn't know how; and on the other hand our love is so real and natural that it seems to avoid or not to care about being put into words. I live here very indifferently, I have no dealings with women; and without them no activity or circumstance of our life has the right to earn our affection or to please us.[6] I am sure of this from experience, and I can swear to you that I have conceived a deadly hatred for conversation, witty or witless. Everything is dried up except our heart: and that is never exercised: let society go to the devil. Adieu, Carluccio. Give my regards to everyone.

5 In fact nothing came of this attempt.

6 Cf. M512, also to Carlo: 'Certainly talking to an attractive girl is ten times more worthwhile than walking, as I do, around the Belvedere Apollo or the Capitoline Venus.'

71*

At the end of April 1823 Leopardi returned to Recanati. In a letter to a young foreign man of letters he had met in Rome, the Belgian A. Jacopssen, from which the following excerpt is taken, he reflected on the problem that the richness of one's inner life incapacitates one for action in the real world, and the paradox that an encounter with the object of desire in the real world can never match up to one's experience of it in one's imagination.[1]

To A. Jacopssen • Bruges

Recanati, 23rd June 1823

My dear friend. [...] In love, all the enjoyments that ordinary souls experience are not worth the pleasure given by a single moment of rapture and profound emotion. But how to make this feeling last, or recur often in life? where find a heart that responds to it? Several times I have avoided for several days meeting the object which had charmed me in a delightful dream. I knew the charm would have been destroyed approaching the reality. Yet I thought continually of that object, but I did not consider it as it was in itself; I contemplated it in my imagination, as it had appeared to me in my dream. Was that a folly? am I a romantic? you be the judge.

It is true that the habit of reflecting, which is always characteristic of sensitive spirits, often takes away the capacity to act and even to enjoy. The superabundance of the inner life always pushes the individual outwards, but at the same time has the effect that he does not know how to engage with what is outside himself. He embraces everything, he would like always to be filled; yet all objects elude him, precisely because they are smaller than his capacity. He demands even of his slightest actions, his words, his gestures, his movements, more grace and perfection than it is possible for a man to attain. Thus, never being able to be satisfied with himself, or to cease examining himself, and always mistrustful of his own powers, he cannot do what other people do. [...][2]

* The letter is in French.

1 The reflections may have been prompted by his failure to find emotional or sexual fulfilment in Rome. On the subject of Leopardi's sex life, or lack of it, it is impossible to assert anything with confidence, though the lucidity of his analysis of the conflict between the intensity of the inner life and the capacity to function successfully as a social and sexual being seems to spring directly from his disappointments and disillusionment in Rome.

2 In retrospect, the Roman sojourn was described by Leopardi as a period in which he was unable to function either outwardly or inwardly, and consequently lost all self-respect: 'Having gone to Rome, the need to live with men, to direct myself outwards, to act, to live on the outside, made me stupid, inadequate, dead on the inside. I became completely devoid of and incapable of inner action and life, without for that reason becoming more capable of life directed outwards. [...] That state was perhaps the most painful and mortifying I've experienced in my life; because, having become incapable inside and outside, I lost almost completely any good opinion of myself.' (*Zibaldone*, December 1828)

72

Giordani was brought up to date on his news, and enlisted in the cause of finding a husband for Paolina.

To Pietro Giordani • Piacenza

Recanati, 4th August 1823

My dear angel. Before leaving Rome I'd begun writing you a long letter, which I had to break off suddenly along with everything else, because the person with whom I was to make the journey[1] wished to leave earlier than I was expecting. So I brought the letter I had begun with me, and when I reached here I meant to finish it and send it to you, but I was held back by the thought that from Recanati no letter of mine is ever fated to reach you: among the many miseries of living here this for me is the main one. By the last post I got your very sweet letter of July 10th, which was sent on to me from Rome. And since you are so eager to hear my news, let's hope to goodness this one I'm writing doesn't go astray. So much by way of excuse for my past silence, if needs be, because you must believe that I don't and never will want or enjoy anything more than your company, face to face if possible, and when that is not possible, in my thoughts and writing. Well then, my dearest and saintly and divine friend, I left Rome three months ago and came back to my poor birthplace – having enjoyed little or nothing, because of all the arts, the art of enjoying myself is the one I least understand, and feeling no regret at returning to the tomb, because I have never known how to live. In truth it was too late to begin to get used to life, never having had any inkling of it, and my habits are so deep-rooted that no force can eradicate them. When I already felt old, or rather decrepit, before I had ever been young, I had to demand of myself the functions of the youth I had never known. But youth could find no place in this soul. And so, from experience of myself, I am satisfied that nature or habituation have so inclined me that all I can be is worthless. I don't deny though that this entombment is rather more irksome to me than it was before, especially because I do not have that freedom I experienced away from here for a few months. And the presence of men, towards whom I no longer know how to behave, is, as you know, much more tiresome in small cities, and especially in one's birthplace, than in capital cities, where people can live right out in the public squares as though in a desert. For this reason I was very eager that the steps taken by the worthy minister for Prussia should lead to something; he put in a word for me with the Secretary of State, and couldn't have recommended his own brother more warmly. And the last time the Cardinal[2] saw him (because the Minister left Rome, as you will know) he promised him explicitly, and unprompted, that steps would be taken to make provision for me; the promise is all we have got so far. Meanwhile the Pope dies, and with the Pope goes the Secretary of State, and with the Secretary of State goes his promise. The Cardinal had the Minister suggest to me that I wear

[1] The same uncle Girolamo with whom he had travelled to Rome the previous year.

[2] i.e. the Secretary of State, Cardinal Consalvi.

Court dress,[3] pointing out that this did not oblige me to become a priest; but I wanted some employment found for me so that I could be free and follow my own inclinations, I did not want to put aside my inclinations and my liberty in order to be found employment.

If I were ever to become my own master, do you know the main reason I would be glad about it? Because I would be able to come and see you and spend some time with you. Believe me that I want this as much as I ever wanted anything, especially now; and I want it more with every passing day. I would not hope to cheer you up or comfort you, or even pass the time of day with you agreeably, though you know how much I want that. But I would be with you, however it was; and my mind settles on this thought and takes pleasure in it, and does not look beyond it.

You ask about my studies, which now have no fixed goal; and I confess to you too that having observed at close quarters the falseness, the ineptitude, the foolishness of literary judgments, and the absolutely universal inability to recognize what is truly good and excellent and carefully thought out, and distinguish it from the bad, the mediocre and what is dashed off, has made me regard the perfection in writing that I used to aim at as almost pointless – that perfection in every tiny detail that one labours to achieve, and without which writing is of no interest to me, and which I plainly see would never be felt or enjoyed by anyone, except for two or three people in all. I had put together a small volume of poems[4] similar to the few you know, and added to them some prose pieces on related subjects; and contrary to what I was expecting and other people were predicting, I had permission from the censor in Rome to print it. But of those two things which get in the way of *τὴν παῤῥησίαν*,[5] I mean fear and hope, the first has never bothered me, the second took me by surprise for the first time just as I was arranging for the printing. So what with that and with having to leave Rome, I put off printing my small collection of lyrics, and now, finding myself exiled here, I don't give it another thought.[6]

Uncle Antici got your letter and passed on your regards. I shall pass yours on to him and to Abbé Rezzi by letter. Carlo loves you, embraces you, is well, and not knowing what to do with himself amuses himself a great deal with the ladies. Paolina sends her fond regards as well. She is still here, for we never did find a match for her, and she has turned down various offers. My mother says I am to write to you to see if you might be able to find one for her in your parts. I doubt very much whether you would be able to, because the dowry is modest. Anyway, so that you know, I'll tell you that the dowry is seven thousand *scudi*. As for herself, both as regards her mind and upbringing, and her looks, I think there could be someone who would be satisfied. She is twenty-two years old; she would not attach too much importance to her husband's age (provided he was not too old) or rank. You see I've written you a

[3] As noted, court dress was a compromise between secular and ecclesiastical attire, and required of those employed by the Vatican.

[4] The canzoni written in the interim since the publication of *Ad Angelo Mai*.

[5] *speaking freely*.

[6] The canzoni (with the addition of *Alla sua donna* (To his Lady), written in September 1823) would be printed the following year in Bologna, where permission to publish, although it had been given by the censor in Rome, would initially be twice refused; see [77].

long letter, and only about my own affairs, showing myself to be infected by the vice I loathe above all others, and which I really think I perhaps ought to be a little less free of with the people around me. Think how much I love you, for to please you I don't mind seeming inept both to myself and to you, whose judgment means more to me than my reputation. You are to write to me just exactly when it suits you; or else find some way of letting me know that this letter has reached you, so that I can be confident about starting to write to you again. You say I'm to stop saying I love you. In truth I would have stopped, because I never knew how to put it into words adequately, and now less so than ever. I embrace you and take my leave; with how much affection, you know (who love me so) and I know (who am consumed by it), and no one else can understand. Adieu, dear and heavenly soul.

73

His cousin Peppe had been supervising the printing of Leopardi's 'Annotations on the Chronicle of Eusebius' in Rome: Leopardi was appalled at the final bill. He adopted a man-of-the-world air to cheer him up in his affairs of the heart.

To Giuseppe Melchiorri • Rome

Recanati, 19th December 1823

Dear Peppino. I received your letter of the 6th, together with the copy of the Eusebius, on which you very generously paid the postage, not remembering that you were sending it for my convenience and my benefit only.[1] I enclose the *Errata* list; in printing it please be so kind as to continue the favours you did me in printing the rest, making sure that it is accurate and there are no mistakes; in the *Errata* they would be more damaging than ever. I leave it in your hands. Although the *Errata* list, as you will see, is fairly substantial, nevertheless you can tell De Romanis that I was very pleased with the proof correction, because the mistakes are of no great consequence. I also enclose the design for the title page. I'll be pleased if you will ask De Romanis to leave out *Reprinted from the Roman Effemeridi* etc., if it is not against the regulations to do so, and if he wants to do me this favour. I mean please ask him not to put these words on the title page. As for the price of the copies, which all together is supposed to come to 17 *scudi*, I found it a little surprising. You told me that the printing of your Nibby *Esame* cost you four or five *scudi* all told. It's true that my little book contains roughly twice as many sheets: but there is a big difference between having to pay for the whole printing done from scratch, and paying only for the paper and for running off some copies. Your *Esame* was full of Greek like my little book, but even if that had not been the case, the Greek and any other difficulties come under the type-setting, the costs of which are not to be paid by me. You told me yourself that my outlay could not be more than five or six *scudi*. There's a big difference between 6 and 17. You inform me that 170 copies were printed. You are my witness that I ordered only a hundred, which in any case leaves me with some to spare. The other seventy

[1] Normally a charge was payable by both the sender and the recipient of a letter or packet.

are no use to me, and are not mine. There's no argument about this. As it's a matter of my having to pay only for running off the copies and for the paper, seventy fewer copies should reduce the total price by a good two fifths. This seems obvious to me too. Please pass these comments on to De Romanis. I'll pay punctually what in the light of all this you agree and settle with him. Please however tell De Romanis that I'd like him to give me a little time. Shortly before receiving your letter I'd contracted for the printing of my Canzoni in Bologna[2] (and I'm telling you this, because it can't be of any interest to De Romanis); this printing is costing me a notable sum. A *dependent son*, whose dependency on his family is never-ending, finds himself in difficulties for every small thing. I'll pay scrupulously and as soon as possible: you know very well what I am like: but I hope De Romanis will do me the favour of waiting for a while. As for the binding please give instructions for it to be done as cheaply as possible, in a very plain paper, like your Nibby *Esame*. Needless to say this binding is to be of one hundred copies only; or rather ninety-nine, because you've already sent me one of the hundred, and I'm holding on to it. If you're surprised that I am having my Canzoni printed in Bologna rather than in Rome, I want you to know that I am only doing so because in Bologna they'll have an easier reception than in Rome, and will be in a better position to circulate. Your letter, dear Peppino, was a great comfort to me, because I see that the misfortunes that you are complaining about, and which I was worrying about, are affairs of the heart. Love, even deep and desperate love, is always sweet. I am too persuaded, I don't say of your philosophy, because philosophy in these cases is no help, but of your good sense and your knowledge of the world, to think you capable of falling in love in such a way that passion can unsettle you. Dear Peppino, those times are long past. In the first flush of youth, this can happen to us; but after one has had experience of things, it's impossible or else it's too unreasonable. Don't think I am made of stone. A while back I was quite capable of a mad passion; I have felt them too, and to confess my foolishness to you, I'll tell you that more than once I've come very close to killing myself in a frenzy of love, even though in reality I had no other cause for despair than my own imagination. But having had the experience, I'm quite sure that I'll die and suffer for anything but a woman. I'd be doing a wrong to your good sense if I reminded you that women are not worth the trouble of loving them and suffering on their account. I can't believe that you'll reply that your lady is different from the others. This is the reply given by everybody in love, and it would not be worthy of you. You and I must hold it as axiomatic that there is not and cannot be a woman worthy of being really loved. In short I'm almost certain that someone like you is not capable of loving except for amusement. You tell me that Literature has caused your passion. So the object of your love is a Minerva. I don't expect to be told your secret: I've seen from experience that in affairs of the heart you are more mysterious and jealous than many people customarily are with their close friends. I content myself with congratulating you on your choice, supposing (for so I must suppose of an experienced man like you) that you did it only to amuse yourself. If this is the case I commend you and greatly respect you. Merrily, dear Peppino: let's laugh at the world, and especially at women, who are made on purpose for it. But should you find it more amusing to weep, I'm ready to weep with you, and sympathize: and if

[2] Brighenti was supervising this [77]. The book appeared in 1824.

confiding in me is any comfort, do so in whatever way you see fit. You know I love you; perhaps you also know my heart, and you know that it is capable of understanding, and sharing in the afflictions of true and close friends, such as you have been to me and always will be, if you so choose. Love me and write to me, and above all cheer up, because I could not give you a more useful or reasonable piece of advice or one more suited to anyone who has some experience of life, as you have. Indifference and cheerfulness are the only appropriate feelings not only for the wise, but for all those who have some experience of human affairs, and a talent for profiting from the experience. Adieu, adieu, I embrace you and wish you a happy Christmas. Give my regards to De Romanis and our other friends. You can tell De Romanis that as I have no other occupation now than studying, and as I've now at last put in order many small works that were holding me up, if he has something he can use me for, I'm in a position to be of service to him, and promptly as well.

74

Giampietro Vieusseux, a leading liberal intellectual based in Florence, was an important new contact, made through Giordani; he was to become a lasting friend and supporter, and open up new possibilities for Leopardi in Tuscany.

To Giampietro Vieusseux • Florence

Recanati, 5th January 1824

Dear Sir. Mr Pietro Giordani, who considers that he has derived great benefit and pleasure from having met you in person, and been able to witness your virtues, writes to me that you have already done a great deal of good for Italy, and are about to do even more, and he urges me warmly to convey to you the gratitude I owe you for this as an Italian and as someone who, while readily conceding my inferiority to everyone else in every other respect, does not consider himself inferior to anyone in love of country. I willingly undertake to do this, although I have not so far had the pleasure of your acquaintance in person or by letter. It is not my intention to encourage you to persevere in your noble undertakings, knowing that you need no urging, and that the convictions of those who have no authority or reputation can count for very little. I only want to show you that I share the respect and gratitude that good Italians profess towards you; and I think that this tribute, coming from someone you do not know, must mean more to you than if you did know me, because it must enable you to see that even those who do not know you, love you, and that your good work on Italy's behalf causes you to be appreciated and honoured even by those who do not have any other particular reasons for feeling warmly towards you. I am well aware that Italy has a very great need to be aided and assisted, as you, Sir, have taken to doing; I cannot say if she is worthy; but even supposing that no present merit of hers deserved it, yet the memory of her ancient merits could still make her deserving of it; and today her very unworthiness, which is no fault of hers, must move good minds to have pity on her and to help her out of compassion, if not because she deserves it.

Should you have occasion to use me to be of service to you in some way, do not spare me, because I offer myself to you from the heart for what I am worth, and I would like to be able to give you some greater evidence of the gratitude and esteem that have moved me to write to you, and to say that I remain your most devoted, most obliged servant,

Giacomo Leopardi.

75

Vieusseux had proposed that Leopardi might report in the 'Antologia' on newly published works of interest, and in particular that he might give an account of scientific and literary developments in the papal State. Unable to accept this offer, Leopardi explained to Vieusseux what he saw the function of a journal as being in Italy, if the nation were to benefit.

To Giampietro Vieusseux • Florence

Recanati, 2nd February 1824

Dear Sir. I have received your letter of January the 15th, and the last number of the *Antologia* you were kind enough to give me, along with the offprint of your prefatory Letter to the first number last year. Reading this offprint has greatly increased the admiration and love I felt and shall henceforth increasingly feel for your virtues and your nobility of mind. You are perhaps the first person in Italy who has understood what a real Journal ought to be, and certainly the first to form a plan for one, and to begin putting it into effect. You do not need to use many words to convince me of the huge difficulties you had to overcome and have continually to struggle against in your fine enterprise. I know Italy and Tuscany well enough in general to imagine all the obstacles that stand in your way. In any event, if your Journal, because of the shortcomings of Italian literature and circumstances, is still a long way from the point your refined judgment sees as its goal, and which several foreign Journals have reached, it is nonetheless the best periodical Italians have, and better than we could have hoped for.

To the kind invitation you extend, my answer – thanking you for the good opinion you have of my modest abilities – is that within the limits of what it is in my power to do, I am disposed for love of you and of Italy to put myself at the service of your Journal. But to my regret I find myself quite unable to do so in the manner you propose. I live here cut off from contact not just with literary men, but with men *tout court*, in a city where a man who can read is a rarity, in a veritable tomb, where no ray of light enters from any direction, and from which I have no hope of escaping. You will appreciate that someone who is out of the world is not in a position to give information about what is going on in it. In fact I never hear or see anything new, and I reckon that I live in a desert; you are much better informed about new developments in China than I am about literary and scientific news in this State.

On the other hand, even though my opinion can carry no weight, nonetheless to show you my way of thinking as one of the crowd, I shall tell you freely that my view would be that an

Italian Journal ought to teach what is to be done rather than report on what is being done. You are all too well aware of the difference between circumstances in Italy and those in other European countries. Foreign Journals are useful when they carry reports, because they always have worthwhile works to analyse, or things that are worth reporting on. But the books published nowadays in Italy are just foolish, uncouth, and above all stale rubbish, copies and repetitions. A journal that can only report on the occasional sonnet, the odd unpublished or reprinted language text, the occasional commentary on a classical author, on a stone, a coin and things of this sort, cannot contribute very much to the progress either of the human spirit or of the nation. Among the excellent precepts set forth in your prefatory letter, some of which deserve to be carved in stone, I find this one: that a Journal must chiefly promote the progress and spread of the moral sciences. Now these sciences, and all those included nowadays under the heading philosophy – a chief part of the present state of knowledge in all the rest of Europe, and especially characteristic of our age – are precisely, as you know, the area of study least cultivated in Italy; indeed they would be quite unknown there, if it were not through foreign books and translations. So that, if one wanted to give an account of recent Italian works, there would never be any scope for talking either about ethics or philosophy. Then the poverty common throughout Italy is much greater in these provinces, and especially in Rome, where the most important book published in the course of the year is the one we call *Cracas.*[1] If I were to tell you that in the capital city, in the space of several months, I was not so fortunate as to meet a Roman man of letters who made me desire the privilege of forming a friendship with him, you would perhaps think me arrogant or ignorant; the latter quality I acknowledge belongs to me, the former has always been quite alien to me. But I can say the same thing on behalf of all the foreign scholars I met in that time, among whom the former Prussian Minister in Rome,[2] a man (as you will be aware) of great learning, told me in so many words that he had never encountered a Roman man of letters with whom he had wished to speak a second time. If you think Roman Journals are not very interesting, you can be quite sure that the chief cause of that is not the Censor, who is much easier to deal with in practice than in theory. But a person who knows the spirit of the Editors and Contributors to those Journals knows what they would be capable of doing in whatever country in the world they found themselves. It would seem to me very useful, unless those wiser than I think differently, that an Italian Journal should devote a good deal of space to giving news and information about important works being published abroad, but do so in articles that are original and adapted to Italy's needs, both as regards the choice of works and the opportunities they could provide for talking about what is the right course for us.

You must forgive me the freedom with which I write, which perhaps has something wild about it, as of a man who lives outside all civilised contacts. If the occasional article of a philosophical kind seemed suitable for your journal, I could occupy myself writing some to the best of my ability; and since you, dear Sir, because of your judgment and because of your position, are much better placed than a solitary such as myself to know what is suited to

1 *Cracas,* also known as the *Diario di Roma,* was a bulletin of current events, published by a printer of that name.

2 Niebuhr, with whom Leopardi had become friendly in Rome, and was now corresponding; see [70].

present needs or tastes, if you had some subject which you thought might usefully be discussed, and suitable for your Journal, do not hesitate to propose it to me, because I would like to show you by my actions my willingness to do something to please you, and to take part, in accordance with my limited abilities, in putting your noble plans into effect.

I remain, always, your most devoted and most obliged servant,

Giacomo Leopardi.

76

Leopardi's cousin had asked him to write a poem commemorating the brother of a friend, who had recently died. Leopardi replied explaining that he could not write poems to order, and that inspiration must come of its own accord.

To Giuseppe Melchiorri • Rome

Recanati, 5th March 1824

Dear Peppino. You were not wrong to make a promise on my behalf, because you weren't to know that I wasn't like all the other people who write poetry. But I want you to know that in this and every other respect I'm quite unlike and very inferior to everybody else. And as far as poetry is concerned, it will be useful for you from now on to understand my nature should a similar occasion ever arise. In my life I've written only a very small number of short poems. In writing them I've never followed anything but an inspiration (or frenzy); when it came on me, in two minutes I formed the outline and plan of the whole composition. When that is done, it is always my habit to wait for another moment to come, and when it does come (which normally happens only a few months later), then I set about composing, but so slowly, that it is not possible for me to finish a poem, even a very short one, in less than two or three weeks. This is my method, and if inspiration does not come of its own accord, it would be easier for water to come from a tree trunk than a single line from my brain.[1] Other people can write poetry whenever they want, but I absolutely do not have this ability, and no matter how much you asked it would be to no avail, not because I did not want to oblige you, but because I could not. I have been asked many other times, and I've found myself in situations similar to this, but I've never written half a line on request, no matter who the person or what the circumstances. Prevail on Mr Carnevalini to accept these excuses of mine, thanking him for the opinion that he reveals of my poetic ability (as false as it is kind), and assuring him that along with all good men I weep from the heart for the death of his worthy brother: I think him very deserving of honour and of tears, and I am delighted that steps are being taken to celebrate and perpetuate his memory. My verses would have rather the opposite effect, but however he in his kindness chooses to judge the matter, it is certain that asking a difficult and unproductive nature like mine for a poem is the same as asking me for a bishopric: the latter I cannot give, and the former I cannot write to order. Do

[1] For similar statements by Keats and Shelley on the impossibility of willing inspiration, see Introduction, p. 20.

ask him to preserve his friendship for me, which I value and consider an honour, having a very vivid memory of the noble and generous temperament, and the quick, acute and lofty intellect which I discovered and knew in him in the very short time I had the pleasure of being with him.

I'll wait for the important news you promise in your last letter and which you promised, if I'm not mistaken, in your other one a month ago as well. But if you want to delay giving it to me for another while, have it embalmed first, so that it doesn't go sour. Joking apart, I love you, and want to have news of you. As for seeing you again, it will be, at the latest, in the valley of Jehosaphat. Adieu, adieu.

77

The publication of the 'Canzoni' in Bologna was causing problems with the censors, who had twice refused permission for the printing, evidently worried by the political and religious implications of some parts of the text. Leopardi answered these objections in this letter to Brighenti, who was supervising the project.

To Pietro Brighenti

Recanati, 3rd April 1824

Dear friend. I've received your two very charming letters of the 17th and 27th of last month. I have a very bad habit, dear friend, and it is that I don't ask the Friars for permission when I think or when I write, and that is why, when I want to publish, the Friars do not give me permission to do so. Thank you no end for the trouble you've taken over my Canzoni: I feel doubly indebted to you, for the thing in itself, and for the distress that having to argue with people like that must have caused you. You are quite right to say that theologians are a sort of person as stubborn as women. It would be easier to pull out all their teeth than to extract an opinion from them. I do think it is better to deal with women, and even with the devil, than with them. Besides I don't see how offence is given to monarchs in my *new* canzoni, and if in the prose passages virtue is said to be worthless, I say in so many words to anyone who is capable of reading, that what I am talking about is human virtue, and I am not discussing the theological virtues. I mean that at the beginning of the prose passage[1] that gave rise to this reprimand, it is written that virtue is etc. etc. *humanly speaking*, and at the end of the same passage religion is touched on in a way that no one, apart from a friar-censor, could find reprehensible. I'll greatly appreciate it if you will be so kind as to arrange to publish the canzoni in some other place following the guidelines I have already explained in detail.[2] I'll be very beholden to you, indeed I thank you as of now for this suggestion, and I leave it in

1 The *Comparazione delle sentenze di Bruto minore e di Teofrasto vicini a morte* (A Comparison between the Pronouncements of the Younger Brutus and Theophrastus when they were Close to Death). The fate of Brutus had long preoccupied Leopardi; see [23], and [185].

2 In a letter of December 5th, 1823 [M565].

your hands. I have not seen Professor Orioli's Journal, because you know I am very out of touch. And that is why my letters don't reach our friend Giordani; but I've always written to him, and in particular I answered his most recent letter of February 16th at once. If you have an opportunity to tell him so, embracing him on my behalf, I'll be very pleased. I love you, and pray for every happiness for you, and I wish I could obtain it for you by some other means than prayers. Don't forget, if you think I can be of service to you in any way, to make use of me as your person, and continue to love me. Adieu adieu. Your very good friend

Leopardi.

78

In this letter of advice to his Milanese publisher Stella, Leopardi described the low standards of scholarship in Italy in critical editions of classical texts. He was clearly hoping to be invited to Milan to supervise the projected edition of Cicero.

To Antonio Fortunato Stella • Milan

Recanati, 13th March 1825

Dear Sir and Friend. Your letter of the 5th of this month was very much appreciated, inasmuch as it shows me the memory you still have of our old friendship, which meant and always will mean a great deal to me on acount of the personal esteem I conceived for you and for your character when I came to know you at close quarters.

I come at once to the project you speak of, and which I have learned about from the circular you enclosed for me. In general I could not commend your idea enough; it could not be more worthy of you nor bring more honour to Italy. You propose, in addition to the Italian translations, to give us all of Cicero in the original. In enthusiastically commending this plan as well, I'll tell you that, especially as it is a question of such a vast and costly project, I would consider the recension of the text to be of the utmost importance, that is to say the choice of the *truly* best editions, the accuracy of the readings, and in short the philological aspect of the project. I say this because I judge it to be very difficult in Italy, indeed I am quite sure that without special care and exceptional attentiveness on your part, the edition will be very imperfect in this respect. We have very recent examples of this, that is of very well-printed, very expensive editions of Latin classics, produced in Italy, which could not have been done worse as regards the recension and reading and choice of texts, that is to say of editions to be followed; which is greatly to the detriment of the publishers, who because of this fault will certainly not be able to find outside Italy those sales their editions would undoubtedly have found had the case been otherwise. I say this not just as my opinion only, but as the opinion of many foreign philologists with whom I have had the opportunity of discussing the subject. In general foreigners are convinced that in Italy no one knows how to produce an edition of a classical author in which the recension and the text are not worse than faulty; and truly I don't think examples can be found to date that can be cited to prove them wrong. I certainly would not be capable of doing a great deal in this respect.

Nonetheless if industriousness, and a little experience I have had in these studies, and some small comments already made on various passages and books of Cicero, were of some use, I would willingly take on the task, in whole or in part, of critically reviewing the text for your edition, if I were there on the spot. But being so far away, and in a city quite lacking in modern books, especially on philological subjects, I cannot even indicate to you in detail the sources I would prefer. It is enough to have touched on this point in general, and in short I think that if your edition presents a collection of all Cicero's original works with a really accurate text, this project will benefit very considerably by it, not only in Italy, but also abroad.

As for the translations, I'll tell you frankly that among those published to date, I do not think you can find even one which (leaving other aspects aside) does not make frequent and serious errors in understanding the text correctly and interpreting it, and which can bear comparison with the translations of various classical authors published recently in England and especially in Germany; translations which leave absolutely nothing to be desired in terms of accuracy and acumen in understanding the authors' true meaning as reflected in the smallest turns of phrase in the ancient languages.

As for your proposal to entrust some of the translations to me, I cannot give you a definite answer, talking in general terms. But if you will be so kind as to indicate which work in particular you wish to have translated afresh, I shall be able to take a close look at the work and at my abilities, and in the light of this scrutiny give you a definite answer.

Do tell me if there is anything I can do to be of service to you, and continue to feel towards me the good will you have already demonstrated. I am with all my heart your most devoted Servant and Friend,

Giacomo Leopardi.

79

Brighenti had suggested that Leopardi come to Bologna, but with no offer of help with finances or with finding employment.[1] *Leopardi told Giordani he saw no prospect of leaving.*

To Pietro Giordani • Florence

Recanati, 6th May 1825

My dear Giordani. Brighenti is offering to forward my letters to you from Bologna, if I send them there.[2] Finally I'm ashamed and angry at such a long silence with my only friend. Allow me to call you by this name, dear Giordani, and to go on living with the conviction that I have one person in the world who loves me and whom I love. I know that at present you are very busy. So I don't want you to write me a long letter: I'm not asking about what

1 M652.

2 Leopardi's letters to Giordani continued inexplicably to go missing. This one reached him via Brighenti.

you are doing, your thoughts, your work. In the last few days I've had occasion to talk about you several times with people who had come from places where you are talked about, because here no one talks about you except me, to myself, every day. The more men seem to me to be plants and stones because of the tedium I feel when I am in their company, the more every passing day confirms my idea that there still exists one man, living and talking with whom I would think I was living and talking with a being like myself or (to put it less arrogantly) with a man: and that person is you; you are the only man (I swear it) who could make company seem sweeter to me than a desperate solitude. If I did not have you to think about, the world would really be a desert to me, where I would be on my own, unrelated to anything. If it pleases you to write to me, tell me you are well, that you still love me, that I – already nothing to the world and less than nothing to myself – am to you what I always was, and this will be enough for me. I work day and night for as long as my health permits. When it cannot tolerate it, I walk about the room for a few months; and then I go back to working; and this is how I live. As for the kind of work I'm doing, just as I am changed from what I was, so my studies have changed. Anything that is affectionate and eloquent bores me, seems a joke and absurdly childish. I no longer seek anything but the truth, which I once so hated and loathed. I take satisfaction in ever more clearly discovering and tangibly feeling the wretchedness of men and things, and in experiencing a cold horror, reflecting on this unhappy and terrible strangeness of life in the universe. I realize clearly now that when passions are spent, no other source and basis of pleasure is left in studying than idle curiosity, the satisfaction of which still has great power to give pleasure – a thing that previously, for as long as the last spark remained in my heart, I could not understand.

You wished to light up my darkness with those affectionate words you said about me to Capponi.[3] I certainly must thank you for having made me known for a moment to Italy, as has been confirmed for me on more than one occasion, in part feeling amazement, and in part distress at being thought to be better than worthless because of a friend's words, in the absence of any proof I myself have given or hope to give. But you are well aware that the time is past, and that even if I was born good for something, as so many are born, it is already determined and irrevocable that this promise shall come to nothing.

I am here with no hope of leaving. I would willingly throw myself on chance to live, making a modest living with my pen in some big city, but I do not have, and I see no way of having, enough not to starve to death the day after leaving here. Thus I content myself with not doing or hoping for anything at all. Adieu, my soul. Give my regards to Vieusseux, if you like; I've written to him several times and had no reply. Forgive me the tedium of this long letter where I don't know what I may have said. I love you with all the strength of my frozen heart. Adieu, adieu.

[3] Gino Capponi, co-founder with Vieusseux of the *Antologia*, who would become a friend in Florence.

80

Stella now invited Leopardi to come to Milan, offering to pay his expenses.[1] *Leopardi responded cautiously, making it clear that he had no financial resources at all. This letter showed his willingness to go into painstaking detail in the advice he offered on Stella's editorial projects.*

To Antonio Fortunato Stella • Milan

Recanati, 18th May 1825

Dear Sir and Friend. Your letter of April 30th is further proof of your kind and cordial character. And because I make a habit of readily taking into my confidence people who deserve it, and are kind enough to offer me sincere friendship, I shall tell you that coming to Milan and seeing you again and embracing you would be a matter for me alone to decide, and there would be nothing to stand in the way of it, if having what was needed for the journey and my stay were likewise for me to decide, but this I must never hope for as long as I remain what we call a *dependent son*, however modest a thing it is that I have grown accustomed to being satisfied with.

I shall tell you frankly that the Turin collection of Classics, which I have examined, and on which I have heard the opinion of several distinguished German and Dutch philologists, is dreadful, both in the choice of the editions that have been followed, and especially in everything regarding the notes and comments, and in the proof-reading as well. I must however advise you that when I was in Rome, the edition of Cicero's works was not yet begun, and Peyron, as far as I heard, had not yet made a start on the project. Since then the later volumes of the Turin collection have not come my way any more, and I could not tell you my opinion of them. Foreigners think very highly of Garatoni and his Cicero, and they are amazed at how little the man's memory is honoured by us. In truth his Cicero is very fine in many respects, and I think you would do something very worthwhile in itself, and very welcome to foreigners besides, if in your edition you decide to make considerable use of Garatoni's.

As for translating, if I were like many other people, I would have no difficulty in promising you my work. But as I have the bad habit and the weakness of wanting to publish under my name only things that satisfy me completely, and of always aiming at a kind of perfection in writing; and on the other hand as I have never made a real effort to translate Latin prose, especially Cicero; I am very, very unsure of myself, and so for the moment all I shall say is that in order to be of service to you, I shall try translating one of the shorter orations, namely the *post reditum ad Quirites*. When I have translated it, if I am not unhappy with it, I shall send it to you, and when I have heard your judgment on it, I shall decide whether to translate others or not.

I come now to the sample you sent me of your edition, and I shall tell you my opinion with

[1] M653.

all my natural frankness.[2] There is nothing in the argument that is not appropriate, except perhaps for a rather declamatory colouring, and a hint of criticism in it of one part of the oration. It would perhaps be possible to answer this criticism very satisfactorily, and in any case for my part I would not think it in any way appropriate to set about criticising Cicero, especially in the Summaries, because criticism of a great man admired by all the world, even if it is fair, requires a much more extended and carefully argued discussion. And it would not seem appropriate for your edition to take on the character of a *critical* edition, like Cesarotti's *Iliad* or similar ones, because for that different materials would be required, a different apparatus, in short either your edition would change its nature, or it would grow excessively large. And superficial criticism will always be contemptible, because everything superficial is.

On the notes and the *organization* of the edition, I shall tell you my opinion or advice honestly, setting it out under headings.

1. The text, in my view, ought to be taken word for word from one edition, the best available. When this edition has been chosen after mature reflection, it ought to be copied exactly and scrupulously as far as the text is concerned, with no changes, except for any misprints there might happen to be. Making changes of any other kind would be what foreign philologists call *giving a new text*, something which requires limitless knowledge and checking, and is absolutely alien to the kind of edition yours is, and I am even doubtful whether such a thing could be done tolerably in Italy nowadays. If the editor of the edition has some new variant to suggest, he must do it in the Latin notes; readings which differ from the edition chosen and followed (those that are truly significant and worthy of comment) should be noted there too. The choice of edition to be followed is a very important point, and here you need the guidance of a real (and competent) philologist. My view is that neither the Paris edition nor any other edition of the complete works of Cicero should be chosen. These works have been published individually with great care, different ones by different men of letters; and editions of individual works are often better than the editions of the complete works inasmuch as the editor has had the opportunity to make a better job of a more limited project. So that the works of which there exist good and careful separate editions should be reprinted by you based on a judicious and considered choice of these editions. Works of which there are not separate editions, or where the text has been established more perfectly in one of the collected editions, should be based faithfully on that collected edition. And in a general preface, or in individual prefaces placed at the beginning of each work, the reader should be given an exact and considered account of the editions chosen and followed.

2. The division into sections or numbered paragraphs: changing and improving this, as has been done in other recent editions, is a very good idea. But it is absolutely essential that the numbers of the old division are registered in the margin at the appropriate point (as has been done in other editions), because for more than a century all scholars, in the whole of educated Europe, have quoted Cicero according to the numbers of the old division, and they

2 The sample had been drafted for Stella by Niccolò Tommaseo, but Stella did not reveal the name of the author to Leopardi, whose frankness in expressing his opinion about its inadequacies made Tommaseo an enemy for life; see [211, 218].

will continue to quote him in this way in future. So that without those numbers your edition would be no use for checking and finding any quotation from Cicero.

3. Putting the analysis of the orations at the end, rather than at the beginning, is an excellent idea.

4. The Latin notes should be based on a selection made carefully and sensibly and tastefully from the various published commentators and annotators. They should deal only with i. noteworthy variants, or ii. matters of lofty and recondite grammatical and historical learning. Among others, Garatoni's notes are excellent, and much use can be made of them. Those of President Bouhier (Buherius) in Olivet's edition are also very good. I imagine Peyron's must be very commendable. Modern foreign philologists, editors of various works by Cicero, similarly have a large number of very valuable notes. The choice of these Latin notes is another very important point, and requires that the person given the job have a fine judgment and be exceptionally well-informed about erudite subjects. But the success of your undertaking outside Italy depends on this judgment and this knowledge, because I have no hesitation in affirming that a complete edition of all Cicero's works *cum selectis variorum*, based on really first-class editions, and with a really critical and sensible selection of Latin notes, would be very favourably received abroad. If the Editor or Director etc. of the Latin part has new notes of his own, which are interesting and valuable, these will only increase the standing and the value of the edition. Each note should have its author's name.

5. The notes concerning non-recondite history and grammar should, in my view, all be written in Italian. The reason is this. They are absolutely necessary for the common reader for comprehending the text, especially in certain works, such as the Orations, the Epistles, etc. But they are no use at all to scholars. The common reader will use your edition only in Italy, because foreign common readers already have very good editions, and many of them, at their disposal. Now Italian common readers, whether they want to understand the text or the translation, will always be in a position to use the notes written in their own language. Among foreigners your edition will be of use only to scholars (and you know how many of them there are in learned subjects in Germany, Holland, England, etc). And they, just as they will approve a selection of truly philological Latin notes, would scorn a selection where they saw included notes which pertain to a learning, whether historical or grammatical, which for them is trivial. Very many of the Latin notes I see in the sample you sent me are of this sort. If you want to do something perfect, I would think it appropriate to follow the observations just touched on regarding the *organisation* of the notes. Besides, the Italian notes would not exceed the Latin notes in bulk; in fact there would be a much better balance between the two.

6. There should be two general prefaces that are different from one another, or else two prefaces for each work, one in Latin, the other in Italian. In the Latin one a detailed account should be given of the entire procedure concerning the Latin part; in the other, the Italian part.

7. In the spelling of the text no edition should be followed blindly, but mostly the Latin spelling of Cellario and Forcellini should be adopted; they are the best and are mostly in agreement; and use should be made too of the fine and useful observations published recently by Niebuhr as an appendix to the Fragments of Cicero's *Repubblica.*

Here you have my opinion with complete frankness: I may be mistaken about many things, but certainly I have wished to deceive or dissemble about none. Please attribute my candour and my concern with detail to the true desire I have for the success of your fine and vast project. I would have said more, and I would have gone into greater detail, had I not been without the necessary books here, especially modern ones. You cannot doubt my love, considering your virtue and my knowledge of your merit and your heart. Continue to love me, and let me know of anything I can do for you as your true servant and friend,

Giacomo Leopardi.

81

Leopardi accepted Stella's offer to come to Milan. He arrived in Bologna on July 17th 1825, after a journey which took him through Senigallia and Pesaro. The first effect of the new environment on his health was very positive, and he was reluctant to leave.

To Monaldo Leopardi • Recanati

Bologna, 22nd July 1825

Dear Father. I have received your letter of the 15th. In my letter of last Monday I was very brief because I found my head bewildered by a thousand things that I am not used to. I also forgot to tell you that in Sinigaglia I saw Aunt Eleonora, who is well and sends her fond regards to you and Mama. In Pesaro I only had time to see the Cassi family, who are all well, and what they said about Schiavini in Recanati is wishful thinking.[1] On the journey and here in Bologna it has been terribly hot, and as I continually have to go about in the heat of the day I have gone and go around every day all in a sweat. The temperature here reached 29 degrees. With all of this, instead of getting worse, as I thought I surely would, in fact my health is so much better that no exertion harms me any more, I eat like a wolf, and the only complaint I suffer from is the exact opposite of in the past, that is constipation more severe than I have ever experienced in my life. My eyes too are much better. I was very tempted to stay here in Bologna, a very quiet, very cheerful, very hospitable city, where I have had a very warm welcome, and I would perhaps have a way of supporting myself here inexpensively, occupying myself with some literary work I have been offered, which would not require a great deal of effort, nor take up too much of my time. But Mr Moratti (Stella's agent) pointed out to me that Stella would have good reason to complain if I failed to keep to the agreement I had made with him, and as I was not able to convince him with my arguments, I was obliged almost against my will to consent to seeing Milan at Stella's expense. We still have not fixed on the day we leave or the means of travel, but I think it will be soon. So far I have not been able to see Uncle Raimondo, because, for all my enquiries, no one has been able to tell me where he lives. Anyway I shall keep on trying to see him, and if necessary I shall ask at the police station. I learned by chance that Don Rodriguez, whom Mama asked me to find

[1] Evidently a reference to something reported in his father's letter, which does not survive.

out about, is tolerably well, although in his eighties. I was and still am staying with the Conventual Friars, that is in my travelling companion's convent. In Milan I shan't take on any commitments that are too long-term, because, as well as not being to your liking, they would not be to mine either. Thank you for the advice you give me so affectionately, and I am proposing to follow it in every respect. If I have a moment, I shall write to you again before I leave, if not I shall write from Milan. Please give my fond regards to Mama and my brothers and sister, and please, please do love me and be convinced of the sincerity of my affection; I remain your very loving and very grateful son,

Giacomo.

I am writing to Uncle Ettore today as well.

82

Two weeks later he went on to Milan, albeit reluctantly, and hoping to stay for only a month (in fact he stayed for two).

To Carlo Leopardi • Recanati

Milan, 31st July 1825

My dear Carlino. I can't tell you how much your letter of the 25th upset me: I received it at the very moment I was climbing into the coach for Milan. I didn't write by the post I'd promised to write by, because as I'm still not familiar with the time-table of deliveries and collections (which in Bologna might as well be algebra), I thought I was still in time at an hour when the post had already gone. I hope that by now Papa will have received my letter of the 22nd and the other one of the 26th, and Uncle Ettore the one likewise dated the 22nd. I forgot to say that in Bologna I finally saw Uncle Mosca, who is well, although he complains about his nerves, and sends his regards to everyone. I arrived here yesterday evening, after a pleasant journey, which I made in the company of two English travellers. At first sight it seems impossible to me that I can last here even a week, but since experience has taught me that my forebodings aren't always rational and aren't always borne out, I'm still not venturing to assert anything, and I'm very quietly awaiting what time will bring. I am missing Bologna, though, where I was almost feted, where I made many more friends in nine days than I did in Rome in five months,[1] where people think only of living cheerfully without calculation, where outsiders have no rest on account of the attentions lavished on them, where men of talent are invited to lunch nine times a week, where Giordani assures me I'll live better than in any other city in Italy, apart from Florence; where I could support myself at very little cost, and I'd have several ways of meeting this cost already settled and agreed on, and in this respect etc. etc. there's no comparison between Milan and Bologna. Milan is a small

[1] Compare Stendhal's comment ten years earlier that he had made more friends in Bologna in a fortnight than he had in Milan in three years; Stendhal, *Rome, Naples and Florence*, translated by Richard N. Coe (London, John Calder, 1959), p. 175.

version of Paris, and arriving here you breathe an air that you can have no idea of if you haven't been there. In Bologna materially and morally everything is beautiful and nothing is grandiose; but in Milan the beauty (of which there is a great deal) is spoilt by the grandiosity and the calculation, even in entertainments. In Bologna men are wasps without stings, and believe me that to my boundless astonishment I've had to agree with Giordani and Brighenti (a good chap) that kind-heartedness really does exist there, indeed is very common, and that the human race is different there from the one of which you and I had a notion. But in Milan men are the same as they are *partout ailleurs*, and what makes me angriest is that they all stare at you and scrutinise you as they do in Monte Morello.[2] Apart from that someone who loves entertainment finds here what he couldn't find in any other city in Italy, because Milan materially and morally is all a garden of the Tuilleries. But you know how I hanker after entertainments. For now I say no more, because there'd be no end to the things I could tell you. Give me or get someone else to give me news of Uncle Ettore and pass on my regards to him. Give a hug to my brothers and sister for me. Give my fond regards to Papa and Mama, and if you write to me, give me news of everyone. It goes without saying that you're to talk to me about yourself in as long a letter as you can manage. If there were any possibility that you might doubt it, I'd say that near or far, you are always my same dear Carlo, who for me is something unique, because even in Giordani, with whom it may be said I lived in Bologna, I couldn't find another Carlo, and I'll certainly not find one ever in my life. Adieu, dear Carluccio. I'm well; my eyes are tolerably so. I'll stop, because I'm writing almost in the dark. In Milan there are alleyways too.[3] You know if I'm fond of you; adieu adieu. Give me news of Pietruccio[4] as well. I had a visit in Bologna from a Mr Astolfi who came to call on me at the request of Mr Antonio Condulmari;[5] I was touched.

[2] The far end of Recanati, where the Leopardi palazzo is located.

[3] The phrase is obscure and seems to be a private reference. Carlo's letter to which this is a reply does not survive.

[4] His youngest brother.

[5] The Condulmari, as noted, were an old Recanati family.

83

Impressed with Bologna, Leopardi now hoped to obtain a position there as secretary to the Academy of Fine Arts. Carlo Bunsen continued to intervene on his behalf in Rome (where there was the possibility of a university chair), as did his uncle Marquess Antici.

To Carlo Antici • Rome

Milan, 3rd August 1825

Dear Uncle. I was not able to thank you either for the passport you obtained for me in Rome, or for your charming and affectionate letter, or for your letter of recommendation to Alborghetti, or for your fine book and the kind mention you made in it of me; I mean I was not able to thank you before leaving Recanati, because I was prevented from doing so by a stubborn eye infection, which is still not better although somewhat alleviated. Now through Alborghetti (with whom I have talked a great deal about you) I have received your letter of July 21st, which I am answering at once, and by this same post I am writing to Mr de Bunsen along the lines you suggest. As for thanking you, I think it as well not to, in order not to repeat things I have already had to say a thousand times. As for Mr de Bunsen, please do express my gratitude to him more fully than I was able to do in my letter. Moving on to the Secretary of State's offer, I shall tell you in confidence that if the government will not give me or unequivocally guarantee me a decent and permanent position before I come to Rome, I shall not move from here, where I can settle for good, and live at someone else's expense; or else, if I do move from here, I shall settle rather in Florence, or else in Bologna, where I stayed for nine days and was welcomed with attentions and honours which I was as far from expecting as I am from deserving, and where among the many courses of action open to me I have an offer from a young Venetian gentleman,[1] very rich and very studious, who wants me entirely for himself to help him with his studies. I shall see what further steps the Secretary of State takes, and then I shall decide in accordance with your advice; please do continue giving it to me.

I shall tell you as well that at present in Bologna the post of Secretary to the Academy of Fine Arts is vacant; as everybody has told me, it does not require greater knowledge than the little I have, and it would leave me almost all my time free for studying. Living in Bologna would be much more agreeable and advantageous for me than living in Rome, because in Rome I could only mix with foreign men of letters (since there are no *Roman men of letters*), which is very difficult for me, as I have had no practice speaking their languages: whereas Bologna is full of Italian men of letters, and all of them good-hearted, and very well disposed towards me. If Mr de Bunsen were to suggest to the Secretary of State that he give me this post, perhaps the thing would succeed, and in that case I could serve the Sovereign with whatever works were to his liking, and the government would have no additional expenditure on my account, since it would only be keeping me in a post which in any case would have to be filled and paid for.

[1] Antonio Papadopoli, who would become a friend and then a correspondent [117, 118, 133].

I had Stella read your paragraph relating to Monsignor Invernizzi. Stella will be endlessly grateful to you and to that gentleman if he will allow us to use his variants, with the annotated edition etc. The variants will be published under the name of Monsignor Invernizzi, with all due honour. Stella will immediately instruct an agent of his in Rome to place at Monsignor Invernizzi's disposal a copy of any complete edition of Cicero's works, to be chosen by Invernizzi himself. If no edition which satisfies him is available in Rome, Invernizzi shall nominate the one he prefers, and it will be sent him from here.

Forgive me my rough and hasty writing. I am eager to read your new translation, which I could only glance at in Recanati, because my eyes could not stand the strain of reading. Please give my fond regards to Aunt and the cousins. Do continue to love me, and believe me without fail your most affectionate and most grateful nephew.

P.S. Monsignor Invernizzi can, if he so wishes, hand over his *variants* to Stella's agent mentioned earlier. This agent will be the book-seller Paolo Olmi, who will see to having them delivered safely to Milan.

84

Lack of news from home was a cause for concern.

To Monaldo Leopardi • Recanati

Milan, 24th August 1825

Dear Father. I am very confused, as I have received no letters from home since I have been in Milan. The last one I received in Bologna was from Carlo, dated 25th July. I wrote from here as soon as I arrived, giving my news and asking for yours. I was waiting for a reply, so the letters would not cross, because the postal charges here are really exorbitant, and even higher than what I wrote. But as nothing has come, I cannot put off any longer asking you to arrange for some news of you to reach me to allay my anxiety, although I do not think I can attribute your silence to anything but some mistake by the post-office. I am well, though the air, the food and the drink in Milan are the opposite of what I am supposed to need, and perhaps the worst in the world. I was counting on leaving here towards the end of the month, but I can see that without being rude to Stella I will not be able to set out until some time next month, by which time I hope I shall have done everything good manners requires me to do for him – not everything he would like me to do, because that would take several years, as he himself knows very well, which shows me clearly that he would like to keep me with him almost forever. But neither Milan nor someone else's house are good places for me to live. If I can be useful to him at a distance, I shan't fail to be so, and at a distance I will make him be useful to me too, because close to it all turns into flowery talk. Be so kind, dear Father, as to give everybody my fond regards, and believe that I love you as much as you deserve, that is with all my heart. Do not fail to write, for God's sake. I ask for your blessing, and I remain your most affectionate son,

Giacomo.

85

Paolina had written to say that her marriage would now take place in November.

To Paolina Leopardi • Recanati

[Milan, 7th September 1825]

My dear Paolina. I congratulate you, but half-heartedly, because when I get back you'll either already have left or be close to leaving, and so I won't be able to tell you all the stories, all the adventures, all the observations (philosophical, anthropological etc.) that I've made on this journey of mine towards the pole, and which I was storing up to make you pass at least four winters, as you passed two with my Roman chit-chat. And believe me, those were trifles compared with these; so you're losing a lot; but never mind. In the meantime I want you to know that I continue to believe you can be very happy with this husband, especially if you persist in your philosophical principles, and laugh at gossip and at men; believe me, it's not worth losing a quarter of an hour's sleep over them. I want you to know as well that I love you as much as before, which was not little, and perhaps even more than before, not the easiest thing. In Bologna Giordani must have asked after you and Carlo at least twenty times: had I written, had I sent his regards, had I said this, that and the other in his name. Then in Parma, where I waited for him at the inn until midnight, he asked me the same things all over again, and whether you two had answered. The day after receiving Papa's last letter, I got the other one dated the 19th. But I want you both to know that here the rates for printed matter are not much lower than for letters, and there are liable to be a thousand difficulties with the censor etc. as well, so don't resort to this expedient any more. Rather, write to me on fairly fine paper, because if the paper is a bit thick, here the letter immediately costs twice as much, and instead of eighteen Austrian *soldi* it costs thirty-six, as has happened to me some times. Give my regards to Luigi and Pietruccio. Tell Mama to be fond of me. Give my regards to the Curate and Don Vincenzo individually as well. Adieu, adieu. Be fond of me. I've been invited to Varese by Count Dandalo, the Senator's son, a young gentleman I don't like at all. Varese is the Versailles of Milan, thirty miles from here. Perhaps I'll be obliged to go there for a few days: in which case it could happen that I might be a little late in answering your letter in reply to this one. I'm warning you so you don't get anxious.

86

He described his impressions of Milan to Carlo.

To Carlo Leopardi • Recanati

[Milan, 7th September 1825]

My dear Carluccio. I've received your witty, clever and philosophical letter of the 17th. (By the way, I challenge all the men of letters and fine spirits in Milan to write half such a letter.) You've immediately noticed what very hard work it is, not just to make an impression, but to keep your end up with other people, even in a very simple high society salon. Believe me that it isn't just northerners who work at it like this, but the French much more so, and southerners, in short everybody, except for people from the Marches, who en masse are the only ones who give life its true value, and without exaggeration are the most philosophical and in consequence the shrewdest in the world. But you didn't properly understand the meaning of my letter. The awkwardness I spoke of came only from the trade atmosphere in this house, which at first sight I thought the worst lodgings that had been my lot on the journey. Then things settled down a little, and I got used to it, and from the first evening, although I thought I couldn't stick it out, I was nonetheless intrepid, because my patience knows no bounds. Apart from that, both in the house and in Milan, I've always been *très – à mon aise.*[1] That inquisitive and insolent spirit of observation you noticed in Sinigaglia I noticed there as well, and it seemed to me so blatant as to make even someone like me lose my patience; although I found the city already so crowded and noisy that it was hell. But you mustn't base your idea of capital cities on that. What I wrote you about Milan was an over-hasty observation on my part. The fact is that in Milan nobody is thinking about you, and everyone lives as he pleases even more freely than in Rome. Here as well (incredible, but true) there isn't even any social life apart from the promenade, that is to say brisk stroll, and the café; just the same as in Recanati, no more nor less. In this respect, both Rome and Bologna are Paris compared with Milan. So you see how far I was from feeling downhearted at not being able to make an impression in a place where nobody does, and where a hundred and twenty thousand men live together by chance, like a hundred and twenty thousand sheep. All the more so because I was not at all downhearted in Bologna, and because in truth I've never thought myself inferior to anyone in the societies where I've been, either in Bologna or here. I owe this to nothing but that perfect indifference we so longed for, and that I've finally attained and ingrained so that it isn't afraid any more. I'm very eager to leave here however, because I'm bored, and from Bologna I have pressing letters from a young Venetian gentleman, very rich and very studious, who seems to have set his sights on having me with him, and on saying that he made me come back to Bologna and stay there. I shan't tell you how much I long to see you again. If the position were secured,[2] I could see you again almost at once, because I'd leave here immediately, and I think the duties of the post would leave me

1 This phrase echoes one in Carlo's letter [M686].

2 The post of secretary to the Accademia di Belle Arti in Bologna; see [83].

plenty of time to come to Recanati, and often as well, and to spend a lot of time there. What you heard about the trunk is true, and it is a very natural thing, but I don't have enough room to explain it to you. Give my regards to Dr Prosperi, and tell me if he has received the book I ordered for him in Bologna. If you see Puccinotti,[3] do please give him my fond regards. I'll stop because I've run out of paper. I kiss you. Adieu Carluccio. Talk to me about yourself at length every time you write.

[3] A doctor from Urbino, one of Leopardi's few friends in Recanati; he left shortly after this to take up a chair in medicine in Macerata; he too would become a correspondent, see [105, 115, 119].

87

Leopardi returned to Bologna at the end of September, on a modest monthly salary from Stella, for whom he was working on various projects.

To Monaldo Leopardi • Recanati

Bologna, 3rd October 1825

Dear Father. I answered your last letter, which reached me in Milan and was dated 30th August, on September 7th, and so far I have had no reply. I left Milan on the 26th, in accordance with what I had written you about wanting to leave by the end of the month, and I arrived here after an excellent journey on the morning of the 29th. I would have liked to write to you at once, but at the inn I could not find an ink-well with ink. Here I have rented a small apartment for a month in the house of a very good and very friendly family, who also see to providing me with service and meals, because I do not like to avail myself much of the invitations I get to lunch away from home. Stella, who let me go very reluctantly, has assigned me ten *scudi* a month for work done and to be done, on account, without prejudice to any further sum my literary labours may earn in the course of the year. These labours are entirely at my discretion, that is to say I can occupy myself in writing what I choose, giving my works to him. For an hour a day that I spend reading Latin with a very rich Greek gentleman I get another eight *scudi* a month.[1] I pass another hour and a half reading Greek and Latin with Count Papadopoli, a Venetian nobleman, a very rich and very studious young man and a great friend of mine, with whom I do not discuss money, but I am sure that I will not be the loser by it. There, I have described my situation for you; I shall try it for a while to see how it suits me. All I am looking for is freedom, and the ability to study without killing myself. But in truth I do not find the freedom and the comforts of home anywhere; and so far here in Bologna I am feeling very melancholy. You can imagine on the other hand how very eager I am to see you again, and Mama and my brothers and sister. The only thing that induces me to put up with the inconveniences of my situation (which perhaps would not be

[1] Count Monaldo was unhappy both with the monthly salary and the payments for teaching: 'According to our old ideas and perhaps prejudices, this monthly remuneration seems somewhat humiliating to me' [M710].

inconvenient for anyone else, however) is having experienced for too long and become all too well aware that the more I try not to suffer, the more I suffer, because laziness, and studying without large and continual distractions, are the ruin of my health. Love me, and give my fond regards to Mama, my brothers and sister, and Uncle Ettore; I shall write to them when I am a little less pressed for time. I love you, as always and as I ought, with all my heart, and I am longing to have news of you and the family. And kissing your hand I remain, fondly, your very affectionate son,

Giacomo.

88

Missing Carlo badly, he gave him an account of his daily routine.

To Carlo Leopardi • Recanati

Bologna, 10th October 1825

My dear Carluccio. Tears come to my eyes writing your name. Who could tell you how much I love you, and how much I long to kiss you again! I talk about you as often as I can, and especially with this fellow Papadopoli; he's a young man almost the same age as you, and his principles are virtuous, generous and heroic like your own. He's a man capable of being a true friend, but no friendship will ever, ever equal ours, which is based on so many memories and goes back as far as we do, for if either of us were to ask the other for all his blood, the one would be quite ready to give it and the other quite certain of getting it. But come now, you tell me nothing about yourself. What are you doing, my dear Carluccio? why don't you write me all about yourself, happy or sad as the case may be? do you perhaps think I don't care? on the contrary I want you to know that I'm endlessly eager to know, not just out of affection, but out of real curiosity as well, because to tell the truth your news interests me and whets my appetite much more than news of anything else in the world, and it's a joy and a thrill for me when I open letters from home. – Here I'm treated by my hosts very well and affectionately, and also with great respect, because they consider me to be quite something. I get up at 7. I go straight down to the café to have breakfast. Then I study. At 12 I go to Papadopoli, at 2 to the Greek. I come back home at 3. At 5 I dine, mostly at home, and if I'm invited out it's tiresome. I spend the evening as God wills. At 11 I go to bed. There's my life for you. Those lessons that rip out the middle of my day are a horrible nuisance. Apart from that I've nothing to complain about. These literary men who at first, as I've been told over and over, looked on me enviously and very suspiciously, because they thought they were bound to find me arrogant and inclined to be overbearing, were then very pleased at my affability, and at seeing that I leave room for everyone; so far they speak very well of me, they come to call on me, and I feel they regard my presence as an acquisition for Bologna. Don't forget to tell me if Prosperi the surgeon has received the Tommasini book I had sent for him from here. Carluccio, write to me. I hug you, I love you as much as my own eyes. Adieu, adieu. What you can all see is a comet, have no doubt of it.

89

Paolina too was much missed.

To Paolina Leopardi • Recanati

Bologna, 10th October 1825

My dear Paolina. You write with your usual sensitivity, and you comfort me in three ways: because you show you're so fond of me, because you convince me that sensitivity does exist in the world, because you re-awaken mine which as you know is all too numb, not towards you in particular but towards the whole universe. If you're thinking of me in Recanati, don't imagine I have such distractions in Bologna that I don't think of you every day, and would do even if I were in Paris. À propos of Paris, I want you to know that I came from Milan to Bologna with three Frenchmen, and I went from Bologna to Milan with three Englishmen. You can see what a lot of material there is for observations and stories for our winter evenings, because you can imagine with what familiarity and intimacy one lives with one's companions when one is travelling, and therefore how much scope I had for observing the customs and characters of those gentlemen. I'm expecting Giordani here any moment, and I've already written to him about your betrothal. Keep on giving me the latest news of Recanati, for it gives me great pleasure to hear it, because I've become much more curious than before. Give Pietruccio a kiss for me, and Mama a thousand, and tell her to take care of herself. Give my fond regards to Luigi, and ask him from me to write me two lines giving me his news. I'll stop because it's 12 o'clock. Adieu, my dear, adieu adieu. I'll try and get news of Angelina.[1]

[1] A former servant of the Leopardi family; see [93, 95, 102].

90

Marriage had begun to seem the only possible escape route from home for Carlo as well as Paolina.

To Carlo Leopardi • Recanati

Bologna, 28th October 1825

My dear Carlino. Your letter comforted me and saddened me at the same time, as you can well imagine. Or rather you can't imagine how distressed I am thinking about your situation. Taking a wife would be absolutely the best thing for you: I can quite see the difficulties there are, I can see that you're not very keen, but I think this would be the best course of action for you and for everybody: if I could help bring it about in some way, I'd do so wholeheartedly. Tomorrow evening I'm expecting Giordani. I'll talk to him about this business. There's no one like him for sticking his nose into other people's affairs, and no one better informed, or more energetic, or more affectionate. I'll urge him warmly to give the matter his attention. I take comfort from a very sweet hope, and it's that of seeing you again soon. I got a letter today from Bunsen, in which he speaks of the post proposed for me, which is the combined chair of Greek and Latin eloquence at the *Sapienza*[1] in Rome: and it seems that if I accept it I can have it almost immediately. I'm replying and accepting this very day:[2] another thing that prompts me to do so is the beastly cold in this town, which has so cast me down as to make me feel despondent and despairing. I'm writing by the fire which is burning to spite me in a bloody fireplace that seems designed barely to warm my heels. I won't go on any longer because the post is leaving, and because I hope to hug you (would to Heaven!) fairly soon. My dear Carluccio, I kiss you. Adieu. Oh how I love you, how I want you, how I'd like to see you happy, or at least close to me.

My dear Paolina. Thank you for the news you give me from home, which is truly amusing. Do carry on giving it to me, for you'll be doing me a great favour. I love you with all my heart. From what I've written to Carlo you'll understand what you were asking about. Giordani sends his fondest regards to you and Carlo every time he writes. I wrote to Papa a few day ago. Give him my regards, and Mama too, and Uncle Ettore; I'd write to him, but I think Giovanni wouldn't give him my letter.[3] Give my regards to Uncle Carlo too, and Mariuccia, if she's still there. I hug you, my dear, and please be cheerful for God's sake, if you don't want to make me despair. Adieu, my dear, adieu.

My dear Luigi.[4] Thank you for your regards and for remembering me, for I certainly haven't forgotten you. Say hello to Pietruccio for me, hug him, kiss him, bounce him up and down for me. Be as fond of me as I am of you. Adieu, adieu.

1 The university of Rome.

2 But once more Leopardi's hopes came to nothing.

3 Giovanni was Uncle Ettore's servant.

4 His younger brother; see [21, 137].

91

Leopardi had to explain to Bunsen that if he were appointed to a chair in Rome he would not have the money to make the journey.

To Carlo Bunsen • Rome

Bologna, 28th October 1825

Dear Cavaliere. I have this moment received your very amiable letter of the 25th of this month, full (indeed overflowing) with courtesy and kindness. I think by now you will have received mine of the 24th, with the enclosed letter for showing.[1] Now I say that if you think the stipend for the combined chair of Greek and Latin eloquence is enough to live on decently in Rome, you can as of now take all the steps you think appropriate for my being appointed to it, since I am disposed to accept it and to go to Rome at the first nod from the government. Speaking to you in confidence and with the frankness which the friendship you show me allows, I add that I now find myself in such straitened circumstances that (not wishing to burden my family) the journey from here to Rome would be difficult for me to undertake, and therefore I would ask you to entreat his Excellence the Secretary of State to cap his kindness towards me by providing me with a sum sufficient for the journey, should his Eminence deign to honour me and help me by appointing me to the chair in question.

I do not write at greater length because the post is leaving. I read Cousin's Plato, and considering what one might have expected of a Frenchman, it seems to me a very thorough piece of work. I find it excellent as regards the philosophical part, and also for elegance and purity of style. I do not deny that I think some of his interpretations wrong, but that does not detract from the merit of the work in general. My desire to see you again, and to profit from your conversation and your understanding, is boundless. In the sweet hope of enjoying this blessing soon, and with the liveliest gratitude for the affection you have shown and continue to show towards me, offering myself to be of service to you in any way, I have the honour of remaining your most devoted, most obliged, most affectionate servant,

Giacomo Leopardi.

[1] Leopardi had sent Bunsen two letters, one private, the other to be shown to the Secretary of State.

92

Bunsen arranged for credit of 20 luigi to cover the travel expenses, should Leopardi make the journey to Rome.[1] *Leopardi never forgot this act of generosity. Here he explained why he preferred to remain in Bologna if possible.*

To Carlo Bunsen • Rome

Bologna, 16th November 1825

Dear Cavaliere. Each letter of yours is full of so much love and so much kindness that it makes me feel not just gratitude, but astonishment. The one I have just now received, dated the 12th of this month, is such that nothing in the world would have the power to make me forget, for as long as I live, the proof you give me in it of your true and very rare friendship. It is quite true that in exchange I can offer you only the deepest and most intimate feelings of a heart that knows and appreciates yours as it deserves. Be so good then as to accept these sentiments which are the only thing I can give, assuring you that they will last forever.

I fully recognize the wisdom of your advice to come to Rome at once, and I see, as you say, that this would be the sure way to be employed at last. But I must confess to you that at this time it would be absolutely impossible for me to set out, because to my other misfortunes is now added an intestinal complaint, a result of the heat I suffered on the journey to Milan this summer. This complaint, though so far not serious, is nonetheless very inconvenient for me, and makes motion unbearable for me, especially in a coach; and what is worse, it seems very persistent. This reason prevents my taking advantage of your offer which is as truly loving as it is generous and noble, and which I shall never remember without feeling moved. What you write me about the stipend of the vacant chair, combined with my earlier considerations on the unhealthiness of the Roman climate in summer, and the weakness of my physique and morale, which are not cut out for giving public lectures, makes me go back to my first wish to see myself settled for preference here in Bologna, where living decently costs much less than in Rome, where books are readily had from friends, and where the position of Secretary to the Academy would require little time and very little effort. Therefore, if the business of the chair is still, as you tell me, *res integra*,[2] I would greatly appreciate it if you would continue to employ your credit with his Excellency the Secretary of State to obtain the Secretaryship for me, or else some other small remuneration here in Bologna rather than somewhere else. If this were to prove impossible, let it remain settled that I shall accept the chair, provided the stipend is sufficient to live on, and I shall take myself to Rome at the first nod, as soon as my health allows. [...]

In the seclusion that my illness forces on me here, I have undertaken the translation of a Selection of Greek moralists, in which Plato's *Thoughts* are also to be included. Now I'm working on a collection of the finest fragments conserved in the Stobeo collection, a work too neglected, or rather completely forgotten, in the modern languages, as far as I know. The

1 M743.

2 i.e. to be decided.

circular for this Selection of Moralists will come out soon in Milan and the first volume as well, containing Isocrates' moral discourses which I had already translated a short while ago. Continue to love me, and be sure of the eternal gratitude of your most devoted, most grateful, and most affectionate friend and servant,

Giacomo Leopardi.

P.S. I must ask you not to mention my illness to anyone who might write about it to my family, from whom so far I have steadfastly kept it hidden, knowing that the news of it would throw my relatives into a state of great anxiety.

93

Leopardi had managed to track down Angelina, a former family servant.

To Paolina Leopardi • Recanati

[Bologna] 9th December [1825]

My dear Paolina. Thank Mama so very, very much for her gift, which I shall keep as a relic, and tell her that for me the comfort of seeing her handwriting was so great that I almost thought my eyes were deceiving me. Pass on regards a thousand million times from Angelina, who also sends them to Papa and you and Carlo and Luigi as warmly as it's possible to imagine. A few weeks ago, walking around Bologna on my own, as I always do, I saw *Via Rimorsella* written on a street corner. I remembered Angelina and number 488, which you wrote for me on a slip of paper the evening before I left. I went, I found Angelina, who on hearing that I was Leopardi turned as red as the rising moon. Then she said this was the greatest comfort she could have, that she dreams of Mama every night, and then a hundred thousand other things. She enjoys excellent health, and still looks younger and fresher than me; there's much more colour in her cheeks than before. She has a very nice apartment, and leads a very comfortable life. She's called on me several times since then with her husband, who, judging by his face, his clothes and his manners, seems a real gentleman. They've invited me to lunch very pressingly, and I've promised to go. I'll eat very well, because he's a good cook, and from what Angelina tells me they serve delicious food every day. Today I'm going to take her a Sonnet she asked me for, for a first Mass.[1] You can imagine that every time she sees me she asks after Mama: she can't stop talking about her, and about all of you. – Say a big hello for me to Luigi and Pietruccio, and tell Pietruccio I'm waiting for him to write to me, and that Setacci talked to me a lot about how well he carries himself in his new habit. Give me news of Uncle Ettore, and give him my regards if you think it appropriate. I'm much, much better, as I tell Carlo. But you don't tell me anything about yourself: I'm not pleased: from now on you're never to write to me without giving me your news, and telling me about your doings. Adieu, my dear: be fond of me: give my regards to Don Vicenzo as well.

[1] *Messa novella* is the first mass celebrated by a newly ordained priest. The sonnet does not survive.

94

Pierfrancesco, his youngest brother, was now 12 years old.

To Pierfrancesco Leopardi • Recanati

Bologna, 19th December 1825

Dear Pietruccio. This letter I'm writing you is to be absolutely your own property, and Paolina is to have no rights over it; indeed I'm putting it in trust, and I intend that it cannot be alienated, exchanged, sold, given away, on pain of being forfeited etc. etc. I'm pleased about your becoming an abbé, and when you're a rich abbé, whenever I need some money I'll turn to you.[1] I'm cheered by your fine style as well, and I assure you that if you continue like this, in time you'll become a good writer. I can't remember you when I go to dinner, because I don't go to dinner, but instead I remember you when I go to lunch, and when I have breakfast, because once I used to have it in the room where you studied. By the way, how's the grammar going? Give my warm regards to the Curate and wish him happy Christmas and New Year from me. The same goes for Papa and Mama, whose hands you're to go on kissing for me until they tell you to stop. Give my regards to our brothers and sister too, and wish Don Vicenzo happy Christmas and New Year, and tell him not to eat too many *cappelletti*,[2] which will be bad for him. I continue to feel better, thank God. Goodbye, and I leave you with tears in my eyes because I'm thinking that this year I won't taste the pastries, which are quite unknown here, just like so many other fine things from our parts. You eat your share and mine, and let it serve to remind you of me at breakfast and lunch too. Adieu, be fond of me and do me the honour of giving me your instructions. Adieu adieu. Yours,

Muccio.

[1] Pierfrancesco had become an abbé, i.e. had started wearing ecclesiastical dress (as had Giacomo in his time), in order to keep an ecclesiastical benefice, which brought in a modest income, within the family.

[2] Pasta in the form of small shapes stuffed with a meat filling.

95

To Paolina Leopardi • Recanati

Bologna, 19th December 1925

My dear Paolina. I'll do as you and Mama ask with regard to Angelina; I've promised to go to lunch at her house on the third day of Christmas. I'm very pleased at the better news you give me about Uncle Ettore; give him my warm regards. Tell Papa that I didn't answer his note of the 7th of this month, because I thought that by then he would have received a letter of mine I'd written to him a short while before, in which I told him about the news given me by Bunsen concerning the position promised me etc. Let me know if he received it or not. I'll write to you another time separately about what you say about yourself. Meanwhile don't stop giving me your news, and try to be cheerful for my sake. Tell Carlo to give my regards to Puccinotti, and to tell him that I'm very sorry to hear that he wants to abandon us. I remember that in a cup or bowl Mama had some snuff that Papa had no use for. If there was ever an opportunity, and he could send it to me, I'd be very pleased, because here it's a real nuisance finding wholesome snuff of a kind that suits me.

I still don't know what the theatres are like in Bologna, because performances bore me to death; so that I've preferred to be teased in a kindly way by the ladies who've invited me to their boxes, and after promising to go and not keeping my word, I told them all frankly that I'm not cut out for the theatre. The joke is that the wall of my room adjoins the Corso Theatre, so that I get to hear the play clearly, without leaving the house. Does Carlo know a chap called Tommasini di Castelfidardo, the eldest son of a Tommasini who has gout, a real *yokel* in his manners, and yet he has the cheek to pass himself off here as a Count? He came a short while ago on business, and the devil led him to take board and lodging with the same landlords as me. He tells me his family is connected with the Recanati nobility, and he drives me mad with his clumsy ways.

Do you know which theatrical company we have here for Carnival? The one we had in Recanati for San Vito in '24, that is Villani, Francanzani etc. Adieu, my dear Paolina. Tell Mama all the things you think I'd tell her if I could talk to her, or if I could express what I feel when I talk to her. Be fond of me and write to me. Adieu with all my heart.

96

Count Monaldo had raised the question of an ecclesiastical benefice which had become vacant on the death of Uncle Ettore.[1] *Here Leopardi specified the conditions on which he would be prepared to accept it.*

To Monaldo Leopardi • Recanati

Bologna 13th January 1826

Dear Father. Thank you very much for your thoughtfulness in sending me the snuff, which I shall arrange to have collected immediately, and which will certainly do very well for me. Similarly I must thank you for your affectionate offer of the benefice. Since you say you would be very pleased to give it to me, I am not averse to receiving it, just as I am full of gratitude for your kindness. If there had been no one at home to whom it could be given, I assure you I would have agreed to any conditions in order to secure it. But now that to my very great delight Pietruccio is in a position to be appointed to it, it is permissible for me to accept it on certain terms, which I hope you will find fair or forgivable. The first is that I would wish not to be obliged to assume any other *habit and tonsure* than what priests here

[1] M790. It was important to keep this second benefice in the family as well, as there was again a small income attached to it.

wear too, consisting of just a black or navy habit and a black neckerchief.[2] The second is that I would need to be exempted from the duty of divine office, because, as you are well aware, this duty would almost wholly deprive me of the capacity to study. I absolutely cannot read except in the morning. If I had to spend the morning saying the office there would be no time left me for my own affairs. It would be enough for me to be exempted from divine office even on condition of reciting an equivalent quantity of prayers, since, once the morning is gone, I have nothing to do all the rest of the day, and I would very willingly spend a few hours on specified prayers, provided they did not have to be read. I think it would be possible to describe the situation frankly, and the physical state of my eyes, to the person who can grant the exemption, and that this would be a sufficient reason for getting it. Besides, if I were sure of it, if for a few days at the beginning divine office had to be recited, I would have no difficulty with that. I leave the matter in your hands, and you will know better than I do whether and by what means a dispensation of this sort can be obtained quickly.

I am in tolerable health, thank God, and perhaps (or even without a perhaps) I would be well, if it were not winter, which for me will always be a serious illness. I am waiting for spring and invoking it at every moment. My fondest greetings to Mama and my brothers and sister. I am really not very surprised at their astounding cheek in cleaning out poor Uncle.[3] Do love me as I love you, which is as much as I know how to and am able to, and bless me; I remain your very affectionate son,

Giacomo.

[1] Count Monaldo was typically uncomprehending of Giacomo's reluctance to wear clerical garb: 'Anyway I cannot see what objection there could be to a way of dressing, it hardly matters whether clerical or priestly, which was adopted by so many saints and also by so many very great men of every kind' [M794].

[3] After his death uncle Ettore had left the family nothing because his servants had apparently persuaded him to make gifts to them of everything he owned, as Count Monaldo had explained [M790]: 'They cleaned him out of everything, in the full meaning of the word' [*Lo hanno pulito di tutto in tutta la estensione del termine*].

97

Leopardi was now able to decline the benefice tactfully, knowing that his brother Pietruccio could accept it.[1]

To Monaldo Leopardi • Recanati

Bologna, 25th January 1826

Dear Father. The very fair considerations you put to me in your letter of the 16th, and for which I can only thank you, fully convince me of the impossibility of reconciling my present life with the position of a person holding an ecclesiastical benefice. As for changing my state, although I am endlessly appreciative of the loving advice you offer me, and your reasons for it, I must confess to you with filial freedom and frankness that at present I feel such repugnance for it that it almost assures me that I do not have a calling, and also that I would prove ill-suited to the fulfilling of my new duties, were I to take them on. I foresee its not being impossible, indeed its being more possible than perhaps you yourself believe, that as I grow older my disposition may change completely, and may lead me to the decision to which at present I am so little inclined, but in this I think I must not anticipate the effect of time, by taking a course of action today that I feel would be entirely premature. As for the benefice, you can be quite sure that in seeing it bestowed on one of my brothers, I shall feel the very same satisfaction as I would have if I saw it in my own hands. In any event, however, I thank you again with all my heart for the kindness with which you chose to leave to me the decision on this point.

Here we do not have much snow, but severe cold, which is tormenting me in a quite extraordinary way, because the stubborn inflammation of my intestines and lower back prevents me from having a fire, from walking and from staying in bed for long. So that from morning to evening I find no rest, and all I do is shiver and shake from cold, which sometimes makes me want to cry like a child.[2] But apart from that, thank God, I am in good health. I long continually for spring and for the moment when I can kiss your hand in person, as I do now in my heart, asking for your blessing; I remain, with all possible fondness, your most affectionate son,

Giacomo.

[1] Count Monaldo replied saying that he would try to arrange for Giacomo to have the small income anyway for a few years, if he could persuade his wife: 'I have to negotiate between my heart and your Mother's great wisdom; she loves you tenderly, but thinks your Literature is a gold mine, which makes any other financial help superfluous' [M804].

[2] We know from the evidence of Brighenti that Leopardi suffered so badly from the cold in Bologna that he improvised a kind of sleeping-bag lined with feathers in which he sat throughout the day as he worked.

98

In view of the difficulties of dealing with Rome and the Vatican, Bunsen had proposed a university chair in Berlin or Bonn.

To Carlo Bunsen • Rome

Bologna, 1st February 1826

Dear Sir and Friend. I reply to your very kind letter of January 27th. Your opinion concerning the proposal of his Excellency the Secretary of State, relative to a position in the Vatican, is very shrewd and your German proverb is very apt. My affair, which you speak of with your usual kindness and affection, is further proof of how little (or rather not at all) we can trust this barbarous government of ours, whose most solemn promises are worth less than those of a drunken lover. I assure you that no idea could be more welcome to me and more flattering than the one you put forward of a chair in Berlin or Bonn. But unfortunately now my poor health is in such a sorry state that I dare not think seriously about a proposal which would in other respects be a cause for joy. Will you believe that I can barely tolerate winter in Bologna, and that I pass these days shaking continually and suffering in a way I cannot describe, because of my intestinal complaint, which is hugely aggravated by the cold? Now what would it be like in the climate of Germany? However, as my recovery is not to be utterly despaired of, and as the doctors promise me that in spring I shall be settled again and much better, I beg you warmly not to abandon the idea you spoke of, which I think does not have to be put into effect hastily and can bear postponement. At a more favourable time of year, consulting my health, I shall be able to give you a more definite answer concerning your proposal, which I greatly appreciate and which is extremely close to my heart, and perhaps I shall also be able to come to Rome and try to spend some time in your company. You are well aware that for now it would be impossible for me to undertake the journey to Rome, as you advise me, as I am obliged to spend the greater part of the day in bed to protect myself from this dreadful and deadly cold.

I hope to be able to send you some time soon a copy of the Manual of Epictetus which will be published shortly in Milan, recently translated by me with all possible love and care. I prefaced it with a very brief foreword on stoic philosophy, which I find I have embraced naturally, and which is very useful to me. But you cannot imagine how abysmal Bologna and Milan are where philology is concerned. Rome is a Leipzig compared with these cities and the whole of Northern Italy. Philology is a term quite unknown in these parts, and it is barely possible with huge difficulty to find Greek classics in old and very imperfect editions. In the whole of Bologna, a city of some 70 thousand souls, there are three people who know Greek, and God knows how. Nonetheless they wished to undertake a vast and fine work here, that is the printing of a complete *Variorum* collection of all the Greek classics, which they wanted me to supervise, on the literary side. Had it happened, I would sorely have needed, and eagerly sought, your advice and help. But the Turin printer Pomba who is undertaking a similar collection, for which he says he has many unpublished things ready, and among them some by Isocrates, has ruined everything. I am sure that Pomba's Greek classics will be no better than his Latin classics. It is possible though that the Bologna project may be resurrected. À propos of Plato, have you seen that philosopher's thoughts, selected, translated and published in Greek and French in Paris last year by Prof. Le Clerc, the editor of the Latin and French Cicero? The selection seems to me very bad, the translation worse, and the commentary worse still. Yet his book was meant to be used in schools in France.

I shall not fail to bear in mind what you say about sculptures for sale, etc. For now I could not say anything definite, but I shall look into the matter carefully.

I am longing to see you again, and to consolidate face to face the friendship that you through no merit of mine have been kind enough to grant me at a distance. Continue to love me as I love you; I revere you, and I am and shall forever be entirely yours, with all my soul; your most devoted, most obliged servant,

Giacomo Leopardi.

My compliments to Mr Niebuhr, if you have the opportunity.

99

Not hearing from his brother and sister caused anxiety.

To Carlo Leopardi • Recanati

Bologna, 24th February 1826

My dear Carluccio. Thank God, at last I have a letter from you; and I want you to know that your long, long silence had made me feel a kind of terror that you weren't at home any more, and that they were trying to hide from me what had become of you. The post before your letter I got the package, for which many thanks. My Farfa[1] was in reality in part our library, in part the Jew's coach, and in part Rome. I want you to know, though, that Cesari, who's considered the best judge in these matters, read the manuscript in Milan in my presence, and judged it to be authentically fourteenth-century, and that's what people think it is now in Milan and here. My other things (except for the circulars for Stella's Cicero, all of which I've got and could send you, but they're not worth the bother) are printed in the Milan *Raccoglitore*, and so I can't send them to you; but they're trifles.[2] I'll send you some other more important ones that are being printed now in Milan as soon as I have a copy of them[3]...So now you're paying the postage on the letters you write me? Don't ever do it

[1] Farfa was the name of the medieval abbey where Leopardi claimed to have unearthed a fourteenth-century manuscript which he published with the title *Martirio de' Santi Padri.* Most readers took it to be an authentic medieval text. On Leopardi's predilection for *falsi*, see [4].

[2] The 'trifles' [*bagattelle*] referred to so casually are the first six *idilli* (including *L'Infinito* and *La sera del giorno festivo*, as it was originally called) which appeared in the December 1825-January 1826 number of the *Nuovo Ricoglitore.*

[3] The pieces which were to form the first volume of the planned Selected Translations from the Greek Moralists to be published by Stella; this plan too came to nothing.

again, because, thank God, paying the postage on a letter is not a burden for me, I assure you; and it's certainly more of one for you than for me. If I wanted to tell you about my situation in detail, I'd have to write a much longer letter; but I'll just tell you that after the first month, that is at the beginning of November, I gave up the lessons (if I'd had to carry on with them, I'd have lost patience), and that I'm living here decently and quite free to do as I please;[4] and if I'm careful about what I spend, I even pass for rich with the people here where I live. If I wanted to and my health were good enough to work harder on literary things, I could even have something to spare, because there is no shortage of projects and offers from publishers here, and in Turin and elsewhere. The picture you paint of your state, painful as usual, increases my longing to see you again. I swear that in comparison with that, the pleasure of living in a big city rather than in Recanati would mean nothing to me; so that I'd leave at once, if reflection and reason didn't compel me first to seek to ensure that this absence of mine bore some fruit, and to make that fruit last. When that's done, I'll embrace you again immediately, and no doubt it will be soon. In truth, I'd like to make money, but not for myself: rather to be able to be of some use to you. This would be the greatest consolation that fate could give me, for which I'd willingly forgive all the troubles it has brought and will bring. Your expressions of love, if they were not mixed with pain, would raise my spirits. You, your love, the thought of you, are like the pillar and the anchor of my life. Every part of it has its centre there. And as I've said more than once to Giordani and Papadopoli, who understood this situation of mine very well, if I were to think for a moment that you didn't love me any more, or were not keeping faith with me, or might ever for any reason stop doing so, or that you might doubt my love or my keeping faith; in short if that theological faith, or rather that coexistence we share, were ever suspended; I'd no longer be the person I am now; my existence would no longer have its foundation; and the whole world would change its aspect for me at a blow, like a scene-change. Give my regards to Papa, Mama, Luigi and Pietruccio. Give my regards to Paolina and tell her to write to me, and not to pay the postage. Adieu, Carluccio. Believe me that if I didn't have the trust in you that you're asking of me, I wouldn't even have the strength to write this letter, or to open my eyes to face each new day.

[4] Stella had increased his allowance from 10 to 20 *scudi* a month on condition that he took on no other work.

100

To Paolina Leopardi • Recanati

Bologna, 1st March 1826

My dear Paolina. At last I get a letter from you: you know how much that means to me. I got it this very day, and I'm replying today; so Mama won't be surprised at not getting the velvet with this letter; but assure her that I'll do everything I can to do as she asks speedily and efficiently, and give her my regards and kiss her hand for me as fondly as you can. Thank you so much for the news you give me of the town, and I repeat that I very much appreciate it, and I want you to write to me often about it. I've never been to Florence, as far as I'm aware, and you can well imagine that I'd have had no reason to make a mystery of it. This autumn I meant to take a look at it, and had a convenient opportunity to do so, but I had to give up on the idea, because the journey would have been poison to my ailing health. It's true that this winter, although I went out every day, I led a retiring life, because of the usual laziness the cold brings on in me; but Ricci is talking about this November, when I was always surrounded by servants, a state in which you're well aware that I couldn't lead a very dissolute life. Anyway pay no attention to Ricci, who is a decent young man, but doesn't understand anything, and gets things muddled up and above all is a terrible bore, so much so that here, to get rid of him, I was obliged to instruct them that they were to tell him I wasn't at home: he used to come by every third day to ask me to help him make an impression in the literary world. Give my regards to Carlo, and tell him to write to me. Tell me something about Luigi as well: and how Pietruccio's studies are going and how he carries himself in his new habit,[1] which I'm keen to see him in. Giordani hasn't written to me or anyone else either for a long time, because he's turned into the laziest and most amused man in the world. As for the copy of my little works, have no fear, you'll have one all for yourself that belongs just to you without taking out a subscription.[2] I don't dream about you, because you know that away from Recanati I never dream (a thing that astonishes me, but is absolutely true); but I think of you when I'm awake, and I love you, if possible, more every day. But what does it mean that you don't give me any news about yourself? You've left out an essential part,[3] and so I condemn you to writing to me again, and telling me all about your affairs. If you see Aunt Mazzagalli and the cousins, give them my regards, *si bon te semblera.* Give my regards to the Curate and Don Vincenzo as well. Adieu, my dear Paolina. I say no more, because if I wanted to reply to your expressions of affection, and explain the feelings I have for you, I wouldn't find the words for it, and believe me, I wouldn't know how to express myself.

1 Pierfrancesco was now wearing ecclesiastical dress; see [94], n. 1.

2 Paolina had wanted to be included in the list of subscribers to an edition of his works being planned in Bologna.

3 i.e. her wedding plans.

101

Leopardi was distressed when, contrary to his intentions, three of the 'Operette morali' were published separately from the others in the 'Antologia' (no. LXI, January 1826).

To Giampietro Vieusseux • Florence

Bologna, 4th March 1826

My very dear Sir. Thank you for the honour you have done my dialogues by publishing them in your Journal, although I realize that I failed to explain my wishes in this matter to Giordani,[1] and I feel a little humiliated by the many dreadful misprints that have crept in (such that often when reading I did not understand myself) and the barbarous spelling throughout. Although the piece that concerns me bears the title a *first sample,* I believe it is not your intention to publish any further dialogues, and that you do not even have a copy of them, having sent me back the manuscript, for whose conscientious return I thank you very much. Should this not be the case, I would ask you, if you can do so without inconvenience to yourself, to suspend publication of them for now.

But above all I must thank you and I do thank you sincerely and warmly for your friendly letter. To your charming and cordial declarations I reply that for a long time I have held you in high regard and I love you with all my heart as a man valuable to Italy; I would willingly say of Italy what Agamemnon said of the Greek army à propos of Nestor, that it would be better off if it had ten such as you. And I add that when I see Giordani or write to him, I have never failed to ask him to pass on my affectionate regards to you.

I come to your kind invitation to write for your Journal, which I always praise, not just as the only Italian Journal, but as one that in many respects has the honour of not seeming to be a thing produced in Italy. Believe me that I would willingly spend all of that little (truly little) of which I am capable, in the service of Italy and of yourself, by helping you in this project in accordance with my abilities, and that I recognize and appreciate the honour you do me in judging me capable of being of use to you. But do believe me as well that at present I have such commitments with publishers in Milan and elsewhere, that they take up all the time I can give to studying; so that if I do not want to break my word and fail to fulfil my obligations, I cannot take on any other work; especially as I am no good at all at doing a lot of things at once. This is a circumstantial obstacle and circumstances may change. But your proposal that I should become your regular contributor will I think always be incompatible with my state, because my health, which certainly is not going to change, will not submit to any routine in the world, and does not allow me to commit myself to fixed deadlines. Enough: if this same confounded ill-health does not prevent it, this spring I want to make a quick visit to Florence, and then we will be able to talk face to face and resolve these details.

1 Leopardi had given the manuscript of the *Operette morali* to Giordani to take to Florence, but had never intended that they should be published except as a volume. Publication of an excerpt was intended to help get the book past the censors.

Meanwhile, because I do not know and never have known how to bear being thought more clever than I am, or capable of doing what I cannot do, allow me to elaborate. Your idea of the *Hermite des Apennins* is a very good one in itself.[2] But for this worthy Hermit to be able to lash out against our customs and our institutions, he would have to have lived in the world before withdrawing to his hermitage, and to have played a role neither insignificant nor incidental in the affairs of society. Now this is not the case with me. My life, first from necessity of circumstance and against my will, then from inclination born of habit that has become second nature and ineradicable, has always been, and is and forever will be solitary, even in a salon, where, to use the English expression, I am more *absent* than a blind man or a deaf man would be. This bad habit of *absence* is in me incorrigible and desperate. If you want to convince yourself of my uncouthness, ask Giordani: if needs be I give him full permission to tell you all the bad about me that I deserve and that is the truth. With these habits of mine and this character it naturally happens that in my eyes men are what they are in nature, that is to say a tiniest part of the universe, and that my relationships with them and their relationships with one another are of no interest to me, and as they are of no interest to me I observe them only very superficially. Therefore be quite certain that in social philosophy I am in every respect a real dunce. Rather, I am accustomed to continually observing myself, that is man in himself, and similarly his relationship with the rest of the natural world; for all my solitude I cannot free myself from that relationship. Therefore consider it settled that my philosophy (if you wish to dignify it with this name) is not of the kind that is appreciated and welcome in this age; it is useful to me, because it makes me despise life and consider all things as chimeras, and so it helps me to bear existence; but I do not know how useful it might be to society, and how suitable for someone who is to write for a Journal.

What I've said, which otherwise would have been very out of place and very unimportant, can serve to determine your opinion both of my abilities, and of the kind and degree of usefulness you can expect from my writings, for your enterprise.

You see that I have spoken to you no less frankly than you did to me. Indeed I think I outdid you in this, as easily happens to me. I hope I shall have the pleasure of paying my respects, and, if you will allow it, of embracing you in person, and I also want you not to neglect to encourage me and cheer me up from time to time with your letters. Your most devoted servant and cordial friend,

Giacomo Leopardi.

[2] Vieusseux had suggested that Leopardi write a regular report on matters of interest in the papal state for the *Antologia* under this pseudonym.

102

To Paolina Leopardi • Recanati

Bologna, 17th March 1826

Dear Paolina. Thank Papa and Mama for me so very, very much for the new gifts[1] they're sending, which will serve to increase the honour I've brought on myself here with the figs and the oil: people are still talking about how good they were. Then thank Papa in particular for the information about St Gerio: I hadn't realized he was the same as St Girio. The Urbino business can't come to anything, because a university chair isn't really the thing for me, as I have little or no desire to wear myself out.[2] And then, speaking in confidence, a provincial chair wouldn't be appropriate for a man of letters like me, besides the fact that it would be wretchedly badly paid. Congratulate Carlo from me on cutting off his side-whiskers, and tell him they weren't in fashion any more, and that not just the English but the French who travel in Italy too, women and men, laugh at Italians who wear them, as I've heard them do myself. If you think that all I need to look like Carlo is plumpness, cheer up, because I realize, and everyone tells me in amazement, that I've got much fatter; and I don't know how, for I don't eat anything any more, although I'm well. Angelina, who sends her warm regards to Mama, Papa, you and everybody, would like to have the certificates of baptism of her two brothers who were born in Recanati, one of whom is to be married shortly, but can't get married without the certificate. She's given me the names etc. on a piece of paper which I'm copying here *exactly*. Take note: *born on the 17th of January 1799 Antonio son of Adam* (as we all are) *Jobbi and Metilde Alesandrini. born on the 8th of February 1801 Giovanni, son as above, under* (above and under!) *the parish of St Agostino in Recanati and the parish priest mala zampa.* She asks you to let her know what it cost. Give my fond regards to Luigetto and Pietruccio, and as for the book, let me to wait a little and see if the Governor gives it back to you, because I've only got one copy left, which I shan't give away though until I know yours has been given back, and if that doesn't happen, I'll send it to you. My dear Paolina, you can well imagine how much I love you, and how much I want to see you happy and satisfied, and how willingly I'd do everything I could to bring that about. Carry on giving me your news, and kiss Papa's and Mama's hands for me. I'm waiting for the coach-driver to bring me Carlo's letter. Give my regards to the Curate and Don Vincenzo, and wish them a happy Easter from me: I'll spend it without hard-boiled eggs, without Easter pie, without any signs of festivity. Be fond of me: I hug you: adieu, adieu.

The day before yesterday evening Peppe Melchiorri called by to see me, but I wasn't in; he's racing off in triumph to Paris, as special Government courier to a cardinal whose name he left written down for me but I couldn't make out.

1 8 cheeses and 4 confections of dried figs had been promised in a letter from his father.

2 Elsewhere Leopardi explained his reluctance to take up a university post as being due to 'the great weakness of my chest' [*la grandissima debolezza del mio petto*] (and hence difficulty in making his voice carry when addressing an audience) and to 'my not being very cut out for dealing with a student body which is always insolent, given the natural timidity of my character' [*la mia poca attitudine a trattare con una scolaresca, sempre insolente, attesa la timidità naturale del mio carattere*] [M731].

103

To Carlo Leopardi • Recanati

[Bologna] 14th April [1826]

My dear Carluccio. Your letters always leave me with a feeling of sadness; because even supposing I had a thousand reasons for joy (and I don't have even one) I could never be cheerful thinking that the object that is far closer to my heart than any blessing of mine, real or imaginary, lives in such a state of despondency. I swear that the goal of my present life, the subject of my castles in the air, of my chief hopes, is just to see you again. I'm so bored with praise that I try to avoid it. You know that the other pleasures that might be available in a big city are not for me. So that I have no other prospect than that of your love, and of enjoying it again. I'll see you again as soon as I've finished a boring piece of hack work I'm doing for Stella, which I couldn't do in Recanati.[1] Apart from that I'm always brooding about how I could find a way of removing you from your desert, at least for a little while. If my health were better, and I could work harder, I'm sure I'd manage it. Yet I hope I may manage something even in my circumstances. You make my heart ache reminding me of the night we parted. My body felt so weak that my spirit didn't have the strength to consider its situation. I remember climbing into the coach with a feeling of blind and desperate resignation, as though I were going to die, or something similar; putting myself wholly into the hands of fate. But I shudder at the thought of the distress you must have felt, and of that dismal solitude in which I was leaving you without a comforting thought. So, my dear Carluccio, I made you suffer, without having been able to make you enjoy.

Not all of my short moral prose pieces are in the *Antologia*, but only a sample, which is being reprinted now in a journal and separately in Milan, where perhaps the whole work will be printed as well.[2] Spring was very lovely here too, but it produced in me that nervous restlessness that I usually have at this time of year, with the ailments consequent on it. But these are laughing matters compared with the sufferings of winter or hell,[3] and on the other hand the warmth does me a lot of good.

You speak of a fashion recently introduced in your parts. I understand what kind of fashion you mean; but I don't know anything about what's been happening in Recanati.[4] The Governor writes that he's expecting to be transferred shortly, and will I please write home so that he can be given a trunk in exchange for the one he gave me. I'm trying to find a way here of sending his own one back to him straight away once and for all, and I'm telling you so just to be on the safe side, in case he were to make the same request of you that he has of me. Take care of yourself, my dear Carluccio; my love for you is my whole life. Give my regards to everyone.

1 Leopardi was now preparing a commentary on Petrarch's *Rime* for Stella.

2 The three *operette* were reprinted in the *Nuovo Ricoglitore* and separately as an offprint. The original twenty written in 1824 were published by Stella as a book in 1827.

3 There is a play on *inverno – inferno*.

4 The fashion is for suicide, inspired by Goethe's *Werther*.

104

Once again Leopardi arranged to write to Carlo under a false name, so that he could send copies of his latest publications and be sure they would not fall into his parents' hands. He also reported a new and important friendship with a woman, though he did not tell Carlo her name. She was Countess Teresa Carniani Malvezzi.[1]

To Carlo Leopardi • Recanati

Bologna, 30th May 1826

My dear Carluccio. Paolina tells me you have some criticisms to make of my circulars for the Cicero. Why don't you write to me about them? You complain that I haven't sent you the verses I wrote for the Accademia. I want you to know that I'd already put them in the packet; then I took them out, because I wouldn't have wanted them to fall into any hands but yours and Paolina's, and I couldn't be sure of it. I'm sending you my things printed in the *Antologia* by post. But I don't want them to be seen by anyone except Paolina and you. When you read them, you'll understand why. So write me an invented name, care of which I can send them to you in Recanati. Do me the favour of giving Papa the enclosed slip of paper, and of telling Mama that Angelina told me that Don Rodriguez had been bed-ridden for some time, and was showing signs of wanting to peg out. Then yesterday she sent word that he'd got much worse, and that no one went into his room any more. If I hear anything more, I'll write at once.

What are you doing, my dear Carluccio? How do you love me? I talked about you a great deal with Gaetano Melchiorri, who is really fond of you, and really feels for you from the heart. Pour your heart out from time to time with me, dear, unlucky Carlo. I'll be there with you in two or three months without fail, unless my health were to make it quite impossible for me.

I've formed a relationship with a woman (Florentine by birth), married into one of the most important families here, a relationship which now forms a large part of my life. She is not young, but she has a charm and a spirit which (believe me, who until now had thought it impossible) make up for youth, and create a marvellous illusion. In the first days I knew her I lived in a kind of delirium and fever. We've never spoken of love except in jest, but we live together in a tender and sensitive friendship, with an interest in one another, and a lack of constraint, which is like love without restlessness. She has a very high regard for me; if I read her something of mine, she often weeps unaffectedly from the heart; other people's praise has no substance for me, hers all turns to blood and all remains in my soul. She has a great love and understanding of literature and philosophy; we are never at a loss for things to talk about, and almost every evening I am with her from vespers until past midnight, and it seems a moment. We confide all our secrets in one another, we reprove one another, we

[1] Teresa Malvezzi was a prominent figure in the social and intellectual life of Bologna, where her salon attracted noteworthy literary figures, including the poet Vincenzo Monti, with whom she had a long relationship. She had literary ambitions of her own, having just translated *The Rape of the Lock* when Leopardi met her. She seems merely to have hoped that her friendship with him would be useful to her, whereas Leopardi believed his strong feelings for her to be reciprocated. Sadly, this proved not to be the case; see [112, 114, 116, 117].

point out our faults to each other. In short this acquaintance forms and will form a clearly marked epoch in my life, because it has disenchanted me with disenchantment, it has convinced me that there really are pleasures in the world that I thought impossible, and that I am still capable of lasting illusions, in spite of my long-standing conviction to the contrary; and it has revived my heart, which has been asleep (or rather completely dead) for so many years.

Tell Luigi that I'll try hard to do as he asks about the music. Give my warmest regards to Papa, Mama, Paolina, Luigi, Pietruccio. Write to me, dear heart, and believe me that if I'm recovering my capacity to love, so too is growing day by day the strength and the tenderness of the yearning love I feel for you, which for such a long time was the only sign of life in my soul.

105

Francesco Puccinotti, a doctor who had now moved to take up a chair in Macerata, was one of the few friends Leopardi made in Recanati with whom he could discuss literary matters and with whom he remained in touch.

To Francesco Puccinotti • Macerata

Bologna, 5th June 1826

My dear Puccinotti. Believe me that if in my last letter I addressed you as *voi* instead of *tu*, it wasn't deliberate, because it will just have come to my pen like that; and if I didn't sign my name, that was really a sign of intimacy, because that's what I usually do with my close friends, as I reckon they don't need a signature to recognize me. How's your headache? how's your reading of Byron going? He really is one of the few poets worthy of the age, and of sensitive warm souls like you. Goethe's Memoirs[1] have many new and distinctive things, like all that author's works, and a great deal of other German writing; but they're written with such a wild obscurity and muddle, and reveal sentiments and principles so bizarre, mystical and visionary, that if I'm to tell you my opinion, I don't really like them very much. I'm amazed at what you write me about Costa, because as early as last November I handed over a copy of the canzoni to Giacomo Ricci to deliver to him, and he promised he would. Here I often talk and hear people talking about the Franceschi girl:[2] they're expecting great things of her. If your advice can influence her, as I think it can, urge her warmly, I don't say to give up poetry, but to cultivate prose and philosophy assiduously. This is what I make an effort to preach in this blessed Bologna, where it seems that man of letters and poet, or rather versifier, are synonyms. Everyone wants to write poetry, but they're all keener to read prose; and you are well aware that this age is not and could not be poetic; and that a poet, even a great one, would not be much acclaimed, and even if he were to become famous in his own country,

[1] Extracts translated into Italian had been published in the *Antologia* LVI, LIX and LXII in 1825 and 1826. Leopardi was replying to M905 in which Puccinotti talked of reading Byron and Goethe.

[2] Caterina Franceschi, a twenty-year-old from Macerata, whose poems Puccinotti had sent.

would scarcely be known to the rest of Europe, because perfect poetry cannot be translated into foreign languages, and because Europe wants solider and truer things than poetry. By cultivating verses and frivolities (I'm speaking here in general) we're doing an express service to our tyrants, because we reduce literature to a game and a pastime – and literature alone could be a sound starting-point for the regeneration of our country. The Franceschi girl, who has devoted herself to studying so precociously and with such brilliance, will manage to achieve immortality if she despises the easy praise of fools (praise shared with so many people, and so ephemeral) and if she applies herself earnestly to serious and philosophical things, as the most famous women of other nations have done and do, she will be a real honour to Italy, which has many poetesses but wants a woman of letters.

My Dialogues printed in the *Antologia* were meant to be just a sample, and that's why there were so few of them and they were so short. The selection was made by Giordani, who unbeknownst to me put the last one first. The complete manuscript is now in Milan, where it will be printed, if the Censor allows, which is very doubtful. I love you, and talk about you often with the praise and in the way you deserve. How are your lectures going? and what fine things are you reflecting on? Write to me, and love me from the heart; and if there is anything I can do for you, do make use of my services. Yours,

Leopardi.

106

The problem of getting the 'Operette morali' past the censor continued to occupy him.

To Antonio Fortunato Stella • Milan

Bologna, 16th June 1826

[...] I would have liked to do a preface to the *Operette morali*, but it seemed to me that their prevailing ironical tone, and their whole spirit, absolutely preclude a foreword; and perhaps when you think it over, you will agree with me that if ever there was a work that ought not to have a foreword, this one especially ought not to. Nevertheless I wanted to make good the lack with the Dialogue between Timander and Eleander, already printed in the sample extract,[1] a dialogue which is at the same time both a kind of preface, and an apologia for the work against modern philosophers. That is why I put it at the end. Here the spirit of the whole work is, I think, declared sufficiently, and the Dialogue could serve as a guide for the Censor, to form a general idea of the method followed in the book. – I earnestly urge you to act on your idea of handing the manuscript to the Censor privately,[2] and to be able to give me a definitive answer, from which I may know if the book can be published in Milan or not. Once I know this for certain, I will have some peace of mind, and should it not be possible to publish it in Milan, I shall decide on what I must do with it. [...]

1 The sample of three dialogues printed in the *Antologia* in January; see [101].

2 Leopardi's anxiety, as he had explained in an earlier letter [M885], was caused by his having been told that manuscripts which were rejected were not returned to their authors.

107

Carlo had voiced a suspicion that a letter of his to his brother had been intercepted by his mother.[1] *Leopardi again used a fictitious name in order to speak freely and send a copy of the 'operette' reprinted from the 'Antologia.'*

To Carlo Leopardi • Recanati

[Bologna] 21st June [1826]

My dear love. Your letter in reply to mine, which you speak about in your most recent letter dated the 19th, never reached me. You can imagine that your last one upset me a great deal, because for one thing I'd be sorry if Papa and Mama were to think badly of me. Opening your letter couldn't, I think, have done *you* any harm, but as for me, it could have put me in a bad light, a thing I greatly regret, because longing as I do to embrace you again, and to come back and be with you, it would be very distressing to find Papa's and Mama's minds ill-disposed towards me. But what upset me more than anything was that you talk of some unspecified physical weakness. So you're not well? My dear Carluccio, you know that our existence is one and the same thing: that if I am not fully informed of your state, I have no knowledge of my own; that if I am wondering about some ill of yours, I can't have a moment's peace. Write me everything, don't hide anything from me, in the name of that boundless and everlasting love we feel for one another. I'm racked day and night thinking of your gloominess and the unhappiness of your situation. I shan't tell you that mine's happy, or that I'm much more contented than I was at home: but I do believe that if you were in my present circumstances you'd be happier than me, or certainly less sad and desperate than at home. I'll certainly see you soon; but in the meantime try to find out what Papa thinks of me; raise the subject with him if you can, and write to me frankly. I'm sending this to you under the fictitious name. It is really very unwise to let my letters or yours fall into Mama's hands; I've always been very careful about it; from now on, make sure it doesn't happen again. I'm sending you, under the same fictitious name, the reprint of the prose pieces published in the Florence *Antologia.* I'm not sending you the poem I recited at the Academy,[2] because as it's a manuscript the postage would cost too much: I'll show it to you when we're together. I'll write to Paolina by the next post, and I'll send her the first volume of the Petrarch. My dear Carluccio, I was quite sure that you couldn't abandon me. I wrote the letter like that, suspecting that they'd opened my previous one, and might open that one too. With that misgiving, I had to choose expressions that were vague, and different from the ones my mind dictated. Tell me something soon about yourself, and what your state of health is. I'm feeling very bored and angry but my health is improving perceptibly with the heat. I love you above everything, and I don't love anyone but you, I have no other pain than your state, no other desire or hope than to see you. Take heart, for God's sake. I kiss you. Do make sure my book isn't seen, because it has some ideas that perhaps Papa wouldn't like.

[1] M916. The letter suggested a new fictitious name to be used by Giacomo (Livia Luosi), in case his mother had discovered the one he had supplied earlier (Marianna Bianconi) in response to the request in [104].

[2] He had recited his poem *Al conte Carlo Pepoli* to an audience at the Accademia dei Felsinei but the occasion had not been a great success; see Moroncini IV, p. 82 n. 1.

108

Leopardi assured his father that he would be home before the winter, and reassured him that in spite of reports about murders Bologna was less dangerous than he thought.

To Monaldo Leopardi • Recanati

Bologna, 3rd July 1826

Dear Father. Your letter caused me real joy, as talking with you always will, just as your long silence had distressed me and always will, except insofar as I shall think it may be caused by your more important activities, and that it saves you the bother. Certainly, God willing, I shall never again spend the winter in a climate colder than that of my birthplace. Unless my state of health is an insuperable obstacle, I am counting on being with you come what may at the very beginning of autumn, and as for staying, you will decide that at your pleasure. Meanwhile do not worry at all about my safety. The incidence of murders in recent days has been truly horrifying here,[1] but the course I have taken is never to go out at night except through the busiest streets and places in Bologna; so that, as long as they do not kill people right there in public (in which case the danger would be just as great by day as by night), nothing can happen to me for sure. I also have the advantage of living in the city centre and opposite a guard corps, so that to get home I am not obliged to go through dangerous places.

I did not put the name of Recanati on the title-page of the Petrarch, certainly not because I am ashamed of my birthplace, but because putting it on the title-page of everything I do would have seemed an affectation; and you see that no writer does so nowadays, whether his birthplace is illustrious or not.[2] When my works are printed all together in one volume, it will not seem an affectation to name my birthplace, and I shall do so without fail. Stella thought the Petrarch an excellent business opportunity, not only for abroad, but also because these studies or pedantic works predominate in Italy, and especially in Lombardy, where almost nothing else is known; so he thinks he is going to make a handsome profit publishing this work, and I am of the same opinion. Anyway the work was extremely demanding, long and boring. Nonetheless, although I had given him to understand that I would only finish it in autumn, I have already finished it and sent it all off as of now, and I would have finished it much sooner if I had not interrupted it for five months that were taken up partly with other matters, and partly with shaking from the cold, which made me break off all work completely.

Here it has been cloudless and hot for more than a week. We had good weather for the festival of the decorations, which I, who am not very fond of spectacles, thought a fine thing and worth seeing, especially in the evening, when a whole long road is lit up as though it

[1] Ten days earlier Leopardi had reported to Paolina [M921] that four people had been killed in different parts of the city in a single evening.

[2] Count Monaldo had expressed his disappointment that the name Recanati did not appear on the book [M825].

were daytime with crystal lamps and mirrors; it is splendidly bedecked, hung with pictures, full of hundreds of seats all occupied by elegantly dressed people, and seems transformed into a real salon.

My health is tolerable, thank God. Uncle Mosca, who sends his warm regards, would like to know what became of doctor Giordani, whom he has heard nothing about for a long time. My very fondest regards to Mama and my brothers and sister. My respects to the Marchioness Roberti and to Broglio, if you have occasion to write to him. Love me, and if it is not a burden, give me news of your health and your present activities. I shall bear in mind what you write. Be persuaded of the very deep and heartfelt love I feel for you, and of the immense gratitude that I have towards you and will have all my life. I kiss your hand with my soul, and, asking for your blessing, I remain your most affectionate son.

109

Leopardi corresponded intensely with Stella in this period about the commentary he was preparing on Petrarch, among other things. His luke-warm judgment on Petrarch, whose influence on his own poetry was considerable, is striking, as is his urgent sense of the need for Italians to have contact with foreign cultures.

To Antonio Fortunato Stella • Milan

Bologna, 13th September 1826

Dearest Sir and Friend. In reply to your letters of the 2nd and 6th of this month, the first of which reached me when I had already sealed my last one of the 6th: you are quite right to comment that after Tiraboschi and especially Ginguené, and now Foscolo as well with his *Essays on Petrarch*, it is very difficult to say anything new about this poet. All the same I would have something of my own to say on the subject, but certainly my thoughts would be completely out of place at the end of my commentary, and they would be directly in conflict with the edition's best interests. I confess to you that, especially after working on the *Petrarch* with the close attention required for interpreting him, I find in him only a very few (but really very few) poetic beauties, and I have come entirely to share the view of Sismondi, who at the same time as he recognises Dante as truly worthy of his fame, and even of greater fame if that were possible, confesses that in Petrarch's poems he has not managed to find the reason for their renown. My thoughts would all turn on this point, and you are well aware that such thoughts are not going to be well received in Italy in these times. Petrarch's Platonism seems to me a fable as well, because more than one place in his poetry shows very clearly that his love was like that of so many other people, a matter of feeling, yes, but not without its carnal goal. The good gentleman from Turin who writes to you cannot have read much of our *Petrarch*. He has seen that I sometimes note the case of nouns or the type of verb etc. and that is when at first glance it is not clear if the case is accusative or nominative, if the verb is active or intransitive, etc. Noting these things then serves to clarify the passage in a flash. But he thought I noted them in order to teach grammar. Here in Bologna, in Romagna and in

Tuscany, not just women, but the leading men of letters have given a different reception to my commentary; they have judged it not unworthy of being used by themselves; they have said an author could not be explained more fully and clearly, nor more succinctly; and some of them have confessed to me that with its help they have understood for the first time various passages which until then they had never understood, or else had completely misunderstood. Finally they went so far as to say that it should serve as a model for all commentaries; and in Bologna they would have set about reprinting it at once if they had not learnt that I would oppose it with all my power. The criticisms of the gentlemen from Turin and Verona require no answer, and I am not in the habit of taking notice of criticism. All the same, to oblige you, I shall write a very brief reply in the form of a conclusion to the work, which you are entirely free to put at the end of the commentary or discard altogether, as you see fit.

Before the copy of the Turin gentleman's paragraph I saw in your letter that something had been very carefully crossed out, which shows me that you wanted to conceal his name. If you know my sangfroid in these matters, and if you think me sufficiently prudent and also sufficiently fair-minded not to abuse your confidence, I would appreciate knowing (as long as you do not mind) the Critic's name, out of curiosity: he may in any case be a very fine fellow.

There are no articles suitable for the *Ricoglitore* among my manuscripts. As for the *Philosophical Dictionary*, I wrote that I had the material for it ready, which is true; but it is completely lacking in style, which is the most laborious thing, since it is all jotted down in words and phrases that are barely intelligible, except only to me. And what is more it is scattered through several thousand pages containing my thoughts;[1] and in order to be able to extract what belonged in any given article, I would need to reread all those thousands of pages, to mark the thoughts that would be appropriate, arrange them, order them etc., all things I shall do when you think it is a good idea that I should set about drafting this *Dictionary*; but which cannot be done for the moment, and for just one or two articles. Meanwhile for your *Ricoglitore* I have an idea that I think may be very timely. A short while ago in England they began to publish an English Journal, exclusively devoted to *Italian literature*. This Journal is unknown in Italy, and yet you know how curious Italians are about the judgments of foreigners on our books. I think that if the *Ricoglitore* were to include a selection of the best articles from this Journal translated into Italian, with a few notes, comments etc. by the translator where necessary, and where Italian literature might need to be defended impartially; the *Ricoglitore* would acquire a very high degree of interest, and also a great usefulness, from the civilised discussions it would give rise to between one nation and another, from comparing the literary opinions of the two nations etc. I will shortly be able to obtain and I shall send you the title of this Journal, with the necessary particulars. I am offering to take on both the selecting and the translating of the articles, and any notes that may be necessary. And if you follow this advice of mine, you will be able to have the English Journal sent directly to Bologna, to avoid delays by the Lombard Censor.

Today I received the first volume of the *Petrarch* and your magnificent *Cicero* from Brighenti. As far as I have been able to see at a rapid glance, I am really very pleased with the

[1] Leopardi had not yet prepared the index to the *Zibaldone*; he was to do so only in the summer of 1827.

Latin notes, which I find excellent and completely in keeping with the taste and practices of present-day philologists. As for the rest of the edition, I do not just like it, I am surprised at it. Your *Cicero* will without question be the finest and best *Cicero* Italy has ever seen. I also very much like the preface by Mr Soncini, a man I do not know except from a few things of his, which however seem to me very well written, and which reveal a more than ordinary intelligence and application. I shall send you the Errata for the 4th volume of the *Petrarch.*

I enclose my little Petrarchan apologia,[2] which I spoke about earlier. You be the judge, and do as you please with it.

I have been able to gather the necessary information about the English Journal I mentioned earlier. It is not devoted exclusively to Italian literature, as I thought I remembered. In the Prospectus (which I have seen myself) it promises to pay particular attention to our literature, generally neglected by other English Journals, and it states that the editors are in a position, through appropriate contacts, to receive fuller and more complete information about our literary works than is usually to be had in England. The title is *The Panoramic Miscellany,* that is to say *Miscellanea Universale.* It is published monthly in London by the printers Effingham Wilson. The first number came out at the end of last January, in octavo format – 9 sheets, price three shillings and sixpence. It contains various pieces relating to Italian literature, among others an outline history of it from its origins to the present day. I repeat that I think that to offer the articles from this Journal relating to our literature, from time to time and at regular intervals, either translated or analysed, with any appropriate notes, comments etc., should arouse great interest in and procure many readers for the *Raccoglitore.*

My best wishes to all your family, and to Mr Luigi in particular.[3] Love me and believe me always your most affectionate friend and servant,

Giacomo Leopardi.

[2] The *Scusa dell'interprete* can be found in *Poesie e Prose* II, pp. 698-99.

[3] Stella's son.

110

Leopardi decided to return to Recanati to avoid the rigours of winter in Bologna, and to work on compiling an anthology of Italian prose for Stella.

To Antonio Fortunato Stella • Milan

Bologna, 18th October 1826

Dear Sir and Friend. The few words you write about your good state of health, which is as close to my heart as the dearest things in the world can be, have really and truly consoled me. While you have been passing the time agreeably in the Gaggiano, I have been fighting off a rheumatic pain in my head, throat and chest, which made me feverish for several days, and which still gives me no peace even though the fever is gone. This circumstance, my fear of the bitterly cold weather in this city, the memory of last winter when, contrary to my habit, I was forced to be idle and was quite incapable of working; finally the desire once more to see my family, who want it, and are earnestly entreating me to do it, would have made me decide to go back to Recanati to pass the coldest months amid those comforts that cannot be had away from home, and with the help of which it has always been my habit to work more in winter than in summer. I say *would have made me decide*, because my final decision will not be taken until I have heard from you if there could be any reason for your minding. Work on the Anthology (which I shall make a start on immediately, as you like the idea) will be much easier for me in Recanati, in my own library, than it would be in Bologna, where I would not have with me even one of the very many books that would need to be consulted, or rather read closely for the project: and working in public libraries is absolutely impossible for me, because when there are other people around, I am not able to work. I shall wait for your reply on this matter, and if you do not mind, I shall leave for Recanati at the end of the month.[1] The volume, or volumes, of the Anthology, as I intend them, should correspond roughly to 600 good octavo pages, type and margins not too large.[2] I have enrolled Count Antonio Saffi of Forlì, who is now in Bologna, as a subscriber to your *Latin-Italian* Cicero. I had Brighenti give him the first volume. He wants to get the others in Milan, where he will be going shortly. He is a very studious young gentleman, who will come to call on you, and will perhaps talk to you about some translations of Cicero he is working on. If I happen to produce some article for my dictionary that I think suitable for standing on its own, I shan't fail to send it for the *Nuovo Ricoglitore.* I never did get to see Brancia's poetic Anthology, although I know it by name. My best wishes to all your family, and please accept my embraces, and continue to love me.

1 His father offered to help with the cost of the return journey if necessary, by sending money behind his mother's back, suggesting he write to him if he needed it using a fictitious name, *il signor Giorgio Felini* [M983]. Giacomo did not avail himself of the offer.

2 Four and a half months later he was able to report that the work was almost complete: 'All the passages have been copied by my own hand' [M1030].

111

Carlo Pepoli, another close friend Leopardi made in Bologna, shared his love of literature and his patriotic feelings. (Later he became the author of the libretto for Bellini's 'I Puritani', and in 1861 was elected to the Italian Parliament.) This letter seems to be in response to a request for biographical and bibliographical information to be included in a projected edition of Leopardi's complete works.

To Carlo Pepoli • Bologna

Bologna...1826

Dear Friend. I am sending you the not very remarkable details of my life, and I'm adding to it two small books[1] where, at the places marked, you will find things which may or may not serve your purpose. I'm sending back the second volume of the Buhle, which Countess Malvezzi has not read, as she says she doesn't think this is the moment to continue reading something so weighty, which demands more concentration and effort than she is able to give it at present. So don't worry about getting the other volume for her. Be fond of me: a heartfelt adieu.

'Born of Count Monaldo Leopardi of Recanati, a city in the March of Ancona, and Marchioness Adelaide Antici of the same city, on the 29th of June 1798, in Recanati.

Lived always in his birthplace until 24 years of age.

He had no teachers except for the first rudiments, which he learned from tutors retained for the purpose by his father in the house. But he did have the use of a rich library collected by his father, a man with a great love of literature.

In this library he passed the greater part of his life, for as long as and to the extent that his health, destroyed by his studies, allowed; these studies he began independently of his teachers at 10 years of age, and continued subsequently without any respite, making them his sole occupation.

Having learnt Greek, without a teacher, he gave himself in earnest to philological studies, and persevered with them for seven years; until, his eyesight ruined, obliged to spend a whole year (1819) without reading, he turned to thinking, and formed a natural affection for philosophy; to which, and to the fine literature associated with it, he has devoted himself almost exclusively until the present time.

At 24 years of age he went to Rome, where he refused holy orders and the hopes of rapid advancement offered him by Cardinal Consalvi, as a result of pressing solicitations made on his behalf by Counsellor Niebuhr, at that time Envoy extraordinary from the Prussian court in Rome.

Having returned to his birthplace, from there he went to Bologna, etc.

In the course of 1816 and 1817 he published various translations and original articles in the

[1] Probably the three *operette morali* printed separately and the *Versi* printed in Bologna in 1826.

Spettatore, a Milanese journal, and some philological articles in the Roman *Effemeridi* in 1822:

1. War of the mice and the frogs, translation from the Greek; Milan, 1816: reprinted four times in various collections.

2. A supposed "Hymn to Neptune, newly discovered, translated from the Greek", with notes and an appendix containing two supposed "anacreontic odes in Greek, newly discovered"; Milan, 1817.

3. Book II of the Aeneid, translated; Milan, 1817.

4. Annotations on the Chronicle of Eusebius, published in 1818 in Milan by Dr Angelo Mai and Dr Giovanni Zohrab; Rome, 1823.

5. Odes on Italy, and on the monument to Dante being erected in Florence; Rome, 1818. Ode to Angelo Mai, on his discovering the books of Cicero's De re publica; Bologna, 1820. *Canzoni* (that is, *Odes et non pas Chansons*); Bologna, 1824.

6. Martyrdom of the Holy Fathers of Mount Sinai, and of the Hermitage of Raitù, composed by Ammonio Monaco, a translation (in fourteenth-century Italian, supposedly) done in the good age of the Italian language; Milan, 1826.

7. A sample of short moral pieces; in the Florence *Antologia*, in the new *Raccoglitore*, a Milan journal; and separately, Milan, 1826.

8. Poems (various); Bologna, 1826.'

112

The relationship with Teresa Malvezzi had soured.

To Teresa Carniani Malvezzi • Bologna

[undated, but October 1826]

My dear Countess. The last time I had the pleasure of seeing you, you told me so clearly that conversation with me tête à tête bored you, that you left me no scope for a pretext to venture to carry on calling so frequently. Do not think that I am offended: if I had any cause for complaint, I would complain that your actions, and your words, though clear enough, were not even clearer and franker. Now after all this time I would like to come and take my leave, but I dare nor do so without your permission. I request it urgently, as I very much wish to tell you once more in person that I am, as you know very well, your true and cordial friend,

Giacomo Leopardi.

113

Leopardi returned to Recanati in November 1826. He was appalled to discover that Stella was now planning to publish the 'Operette morali' by instalments in a series whose title alone (The Ladies' Library) declared its inappropriateness for a work of some philosophical weight.

To Antonio Fortunato Stella • Milan

Recanati, 6th December 1826

Dearest Sir and Friend. In reply to your letter of the 29th of last month. The rest of the *Petrarch* still has not arrived, and therefore the corrections are not included with this letter. [...]

With the frankness of friendship, I confess to you that I am a little downcast at hearing that you are thinking of printing my *Operette morali* in the *Biblioteca amena*;[1] an idea of which I had hitherto heard no mention. Published works lose nothing when they are included in a Series; but I know from experience that unpublished works, if they come out for the first time in a Series, attract no attention, because they are considered only as constituent parts of a larger entity, and things that do not stand on their own. Then, a book whose subject is deep and completely philosophical and metaphysical, if it appears in a *Library for Gentlewomen*, can only be infinitely the loser by it in public opinion, which always judges more by titles than by substance. The lack of weight of a series of this kind is a merit in its own terms, but not when it is applied to my book. Finally, coming out in installments of 108 pages each will greatly harm a work which is meant to be judged as a whole, and as an organic structure, as happens with everything philosophical, although written with an apparently light touch. It is true that later you will put the whole book out in one volume, but the public's first judgment will already have been formed on the basis of the pieces that have come out a few at a time, and very slowly: and the first judgment is always the one that lasts. In spite of all that, if this is what it suits you to do, I will sacrifice my self-esteem and the particular fondness I have for the book; and I shan't stand in the way, though I certainly would have done so with anyone else in these circumstances. But if your only reason for including these works in the *Biblioteca amena* is to find a place for them, and apart from that it is a matter of indifference to you, and you see no benefit to yourself in publishing them some other way, I would ask you to be so kind as to send the manuscript back to me by some safe means: and I shall find some other opportunity to publish it, or else I shall more willingly hold on to it myself. [...]

[1] On the *Biblioteca amena ed istruttiva per le donne gentili*, see Moroncini IV, p. 209, n. 2 and p. 215, n. 3.

114

Leopardi wrote to Teresa Malvezzi just before he returned to Bologna in the spring.

To Teresa Carniani Malvezzi • Bologna

Recanati, 18th April 1827

My dear Countess. At last a book that comes to me from you shows me that you have remembered me, on one occasion at least, since my departure: and an address on the outside in your hand assures me that the book is not a posthumous work, and that it comes as a gift and not by way of a will or codicil. The many letters you wanted to write me, and promised more than once, are reduced to an address. If by any chance you were intending to begin now, that is after five months, I want you to know that you are not in time any more, because I leave for Bologna this week or, at latest, the beginning of next week.

So I shall say nothing to you about your book, in which I admire the sobriety and good sense of the preface, the purity of language and style, and the many difficulties you have overcome. I shan't even ask you for your news: because I hope that I shall soon be able to tell you in person everything you want to know, and ask you everything I want to know. Meanwhile love me, as you surely do, and I remain *your most faithful friend, or servant, or both, or what you like.*[1]

[1] The phrase in italics is in English in the original.

115

To Francesco Puccinotti • Macerata

Recanati, 21st April 1827

Dear Puccinotti. Shortly after receiving your last letter (this last February), I wrote to you, hoping to send my letter with Monsieur Pagliarini, who'd promised me he'd drop by before he went back to Macerata. But in fact Monsieur didn't put in an appearance; and as Lent had arrived, I didn't think it appropriate to send you a letter that talked about Carnival. Now I'm writing to you at last to say goodbye before my departure (which will be the day after tomorrow) for Bologna, whence I'm intending to go on to Florence, and stay all summer. I hope that from time to time you'll want to give me news of yourself and your studies: I know very well that any letter of yours will mean a great deal to me, because I still love you as a remarkable man, and I respect you as a rare intelligence. An article appeared here on a performance of *Saul*[1] in Macerata, in which some people thought they recognised your style. What am I to say? are they right, or not? For several months I've been completely cured of that digestive

[1] Alfieri's play of that name.

complaint; if it doesn't come back. I'm longing to escape from this confounded city, where I don't know if men are more fools or rogues: I'm well aware that they're all both. I say all, because certain exceptions who could be counted on one's fingers can be left out of account. Of the priests, though, I mean all of them without exception. As for me, the first time I'll have been out of the house in Recanati will be the day after tomorrow, when I get into the coach to leave: so they weren't able to bother me very much. Adieu, dear Puccinotti; be fond of me, and write to me; and give my regards to Miss Franceschi, if my regards are of any interest to her. Yours,

Leopardi.

116*

Leopardi returned to Bologna towards the end of April. The break with Teresa Malvezzi was now complete.

To Antonio Papadopoli • Florence

Bologna, 21st May 1827

My dear Papadopoli. I'm really grateful for your short letter that Rangoni gave me, and for your searching for the edition I wanted, and for your passing on my regards to Giordani. Hearing from you and from the Countess that you are well is a very great comfort to me. I too am well (since you ask) and I manage to enjoy myself. As for the dialogues,[1] what can I say? The printing is finished but for three sheets, and they're expected from one post to the next, but still aren't here: the Stella household is topsy-turvy because of the oldest son's wedding. How can it enter your head that I'm still calling on that Malvezzi bitch? May my nose drop off, if I've been back, or ever will go back, since I've heard the gossip she's been spreading about me;[2] and if I don't speak as ill of her as I can. The other day I ran into her, and turned my face to the wall to avoid seeing her. Give my regards to Giordani again, and tell him that if my health remains good, I'm quite determined to see him again this summer. Write to me sometimes, my dear Papadopoli, and give me news of your travels, your studies, your thoughts. Be fond of me always, and believe me that I'll be fond of you for as long as I live. Adieu, adieu.

* The text of this letter in Moroncini [M1062] is incomplete. The full text is in Flora.

[1] i.e. the *Operette morali.*

[2] One story which circulated was that when Leopardi went down on his knees to declare his feelings to her, she summoned a footman to bring him a glass of cold water.

117

In June he moved on to Florence.[1]

To Antonio Papadopoli • Milan

Florence, 3rd July 1827

My dear Antonino. I heard about your accident from the Countess, with great sympathy and sadness. It cheers me up to hear that you're feeling better, and to talk about you often with Giordani and your other friends and acquaintances here, who respect you and love you dearly. Perhaps by now you'll have been able to see Stella, who I believe is already back in Milan. I've been here for two weeks, treated very kindly by the Florentines, but wretched because of my poor health, and especially because of my eye complaint, which forces me to stay at home all day without reading or writing. I can't go out except in the evening in the dark, like the bats. I'll stay here all summer; winter in Pisa, if I don't feel too ill; in which case I'll go back to Recanati, as I want to die at home. I don't know why you choose to doubt my firmness of purpose in staying away from that woman.[2] I'm almost ashamed to tell you that when she saw I'd stopped calling on her, she sent to ask for news of me, and I didn't go; that after a few days, she sent me an invitation to lunch, and I didn't go; that I left for Florence without seeing her; that I've never seen her since you left Bologna. I mean I'm ashamed to tell you these things, because it seems as if I want to prove something to you that you do me a wrong to doubt. Certainly that witch's youth, her beauty, her charms are so great that it takes a great deal of strength to resist! If you see Ambrosoli, be kind enough to give him my warm regards. I still haven't read his article, because I can't read; but I've been told about it. Take care of yourself, and give me your news. I'm extremely eager to see you again in Venice, but when will my health allow me to travel? Yet I don't despair of coming to see you next year, in spring. Be fond of me always. You know how fond I am of you.

Leopardi.

1 Giordani had strongly recommended Florence before Leopardi returned to Recanati the previous autumn: 'do you want to go back and bury yourself in Recanati? [...] try Florence: there you'll find all the good one can have in this wretched world in these sorry times. You'll find you can use your pen profitably as well' [M934]. Leopardi's father and uncle became increasingly worried at his contacts with liberals in Florence.

2 Teresa Malvezzi; see previous letter.

118

To Paolina Leopardi • Recanati

Florence, 7th July 1827[1]

My dear Paolina. I've received your letter of the 27th of June, and here I am giving you a very full account of my doings. I saw Stella in Bologna, he stopped for five days, he stayed in the same lodgings as me, in the room next to mine; we dined together, and led a shared existence; I accompanied him, I introduced him where he wished. He's arranging for my usual stipend to be paid from May on; but as for arrears, not a bean.[2] He did tell me that from now on he'd see I was paid more than normal per month; but he didn't say how much.[3] Here they're really courting me to take on other commitments; but as I can't and don't want to wear myself out, no arrangement can suit me as Stella's does; in consequence I must hold on to it as tightly as I can. Besides, the displays of friendship and of extraordinary esteem that Stella made towards me, and what he's said about me to other people, couldn't have been more flattering.

Here I'm lodged at the Fontana Inn. It's expensive and you don't get much to eat; but the linen is changed almost every day. It's difficult to find full board by the month in private houses, and it costs a third as much again as in Bologna. I'm treated with great consideration by Florentine men of letters, or those settled in Florence. All the leading ones have come to see me. I've been to see Cavaliere Reinhold, now Minister for Holland in Tuscany. He and his wife send their kind regards to Papa and Mama. Their daughter, who has become a fine young lady, asked after you and the Mazzagalli girls. It's thought that Reinhold will soon be appointed Minister for Foreign Affairs in Brussels.[4]

As for my health, I'm well, thank God; apart from a few complaints of no consequence. My Bolognese ailment hasn't recurred, not even on the journey. The problems I have are with my eyes and teeth; there's nothing for it but to have the teeth pulled. The dejection this foolish thing has caused me this last month is not to be believed.

It's quite true about the enthusiasm aroused by Persiani.[5] I've heard several connoisseurs or amateurs say that Persiani is a remarkable talent. Everyone speaks very well of him, as regards his character and his absolute honesty as well. There's a story that last winter, not having any money, and not wanting to defraud the landlord who was putting him up, he spent several nights *à la belle étoile*. I'd been told that after the success of this opera he'd been signed up to compose in Naples: but the other evening the Spada girl from Macerata, married

1 In Moroncini [M1086] this letter is dated July 6th.

2 Stella had stopped paying Leopardi when he returned to Recanati; Leopardi had hoped he might be persuaded to make good the missing months, as he had continued to work on the prose anthology throughout the winter; see [110], n. 2.

3 And in fact Stella failed to increase the allowance as promised.

4 Belgium was not to become independent of Holland until 1830; Leopardi had met Reinhold in Rome in 1822; see [63], n. 5.

5 Giuseppe Persiani, a musician, was a Recanati contemporary of Leopardi.

here to Colonel Palagi, assured me that he's contracted here to write two more Operas within a year, for eight hundred *scudi.* The joke is that when he took on the commitment to write the *Danao,* the agreement was that if the public didn't like the opera, the impresario wouldn't pay. I haven't been to hear it, because my eyes hurt too much at the theatre.

I'm so sorry to hear what you write about Mama. I can well imagine how distressing it must have been for her, not being able to move. Write and tell me how the swelling of her leg and foot is, and if it's still stopping her from walking. Thank her very, very much for her concern on my account, and give her a heartfelt kiss on the hand from me.

Giordani has told me several times, and very insistently, to give you his very kind regards. And to give his regards to Papa, Mama and Carlo as well; each one separately. What's Carluccio doing? how fond is he of me? give him my regards; give my regards to Luigi, Pietruccio and Don Vincenzo. I wrote to Papa by the first post after my arrival in Florence; kiss his hand, and ask for his blessing in my name. Thank you for the news you give me about Bunsen: I was pleased to hear it. I'll do as you ask about the perfumes. Be fond of me, because (in case you don't know it) I'm as fond of you as it's possible to be, and I think of you all always, all the time. Adieu, my dear Paolina.

119

To Francesco Puccinotti • Macerata

Florence, 16th August 1827

Dear Puccinotti. I've been here for about two months, and your letter of the 29th of July has just reached me here from Bologna. You must forgive my long silence, because I can write very little, as I'm suffering from an extreme weakness (or whatever I'm to call it) of the nerves of my eyes and head, which forces on me an inactivity much gloomier than death. Certainly a dead man spends his day better than I do. Would you believe I still haven't received the copies of my *Operette* sent to me from Milan? that's how well they look after me. The little Pletone translation was also printed in the *Raccoglitore,* which ought to be available there in Macerata.[1] You tell me nothing about your studies. Are you thinking about your physiological work on temperaments? I exhort you and urge you to think about it, because I'm sure that it will be a work worthy of Italy, useful for the world. Dear Puccinotti, I am fond of you; I'd like to see you here with me. I'm tired of life, tired of philosophical indifference, which is the only remedy for misfortunes and for boredom, but in the end is itself boring. I have no other plans, no other hopes than to die. In truth it wasn't worth making such an effort to end up like this. I'll be here until the middle of October: then I'm not sure whether I'll go to Pisa or to Rome. But if I feel very ill, I'll come to Recanati, as I want to die with my family around me. Be fond of me, and don't forget me. Yours,

Leopardi.

[1] Leopardi's translation of an oration by Giorgio Gemisto Pletone, a Greek rhetorician of the fourteenth-fifteenth century, is in *Poesie e Prose* II, pp. 186-198.

120

The difficulty of actually getting the monthly payments promised by Stella became an increasing cause for anxiety.

To Antonio Fortunato Stella • Milan

Florence, 23rd August 1827

Dearest Sir and Friend. I apologize a thousand times over for my tardiness in replying to your letters of the 1st and the 6th of this month. The reason was that I cannot go much to the post, which in this most civilised of cities is only open in the hottest hours of the day.[1] I do not trust sending someone else. Mr Molini, without my presenting your note (which I burned), doled out 23 Florentine *scudi* and 27 *crazie*, equal to 130.70 Italian *lire* and 24 and a half Roman *scudi*. I presented your note to Mr Piatti. He said he would call on me the next day, and he would bring me the money; but I have not seen him since. I earnestly entreat you to ensure that what you promise is carried out, that is to arrange a reliable means of getting the money to me each month; since unfortunately, if I do not have what is still owing from August (15 and a half Roman *scudi*) to hand by the 20th of September, I shall find myself sorely embarrassed.

As for Manzoni's novel[2] (of which I have only heard a few pages read aloud) I'll tell you in confidence that here persons of taste find it falls far short of their expectations. Other people generally praise it.

Regarding the judgment on the *Operette morali* you report to me, what can I say?[3] I'll only say it is not unexpected. I am not aware that my principles are all negative; but it would not greatly surprise me, because I remember that remark of Bayle's, that in metaphysics and morals, *reason* cannot build, but only destroy. As for my opinions not being *based on reason but on a few partial observations*, I hope it is true.

I am very glad that meeting my good friend Papadopoli gave you such pleasure. It will be difficult for me to undertake a journey as long as the one to Venice this year. I am still working on the Encyclopaedia, and I am doing my best to make it as popular a work as possible, in style as well. I have heard a few foreigners here praising the *Operette morali* to the skies. I think if you send copies abroad, they perhaps will not be wasted. I know that in Rome your Petrarch is used by private individuals who give lessons in Italian language and literature to all those English people, etc. who pass the winter there. That should result in good sales of the work to foreigners in Rome, if there were someone there who could follow it up. I very much hope you and your family have a pleasant stay in the country. A thousand best wishes to you all; and please be fond of me; I remain your most cordial friend and servant,

Giacomo Leopardi.

[1] From midday to 4 p.m.

[2] The first edition of *I promessi sposi* had been published in June.

[3] Stella had passed on Tommaseo's opinion that the *Operette morali*, though the 'best written book of our age', was nevertheless, because of the negative principles which informed it, marked by 'a chilling coldness, a dispiriting bitterness' [*una freddezza che fa ribrezzo, una desolante amarezza*].

121

He told Paolina of his plans for avoiding the cold in winter.

To Paolina Leopardi • Recanati

Florence, 30th October 1827

My dear Paolina. It's been a while since I've had your news, and I'm sorry. I'm writing to give you mine. Here, thank God, we've had a splendid October, a real autumn, better than September and the end of August. I made the most of it to go for walks, and my eyes have been better, and my teeth much better. I've had some indigestion, because I was hardly eating anything any more for fear of its disagreeing with me; but now I hope I'll get better, because I've mended my ways, and I'm beginning to get my appetite back. As for next winter, I've now decided to go and spend it in Massa di Carrara, which is 70 miles from here; a very convenient journey. The climate there is excellent, similar to the climate in Nice, and perhaps better than in Rome: it never snows there, people go out and walk without a cape, orange trees grow in the middle of the public square, planted in the ground. Apart from that, the city is very small (although it's the capital of the Duchy of Massa and Carrara), there are no men of distinction, and living there is very gloomy: so you see that I'm certainly not making the decision to go there for pleasure, but because of the absolute need I have to spend the winter so as to manage without a fire, and to go out a lot and get a lot of exercise; in order not to catch an ailment in winter which then lasts until the following winter. I shan't leave Florence until the severe cold weather drives me away, because staying in Massa doesn't appeal to me at all. Before leaving I'll write one more time. And what are you doing? and what are Papa and Mama and Carlo and Luigi and Pietruccio doing? Give them all my regards: Giordani sends his regards very warmly to you and Carlo. Write me all the news you can. I'll tell you an old thing: that I'm fonder of you, and of all of you, than of my own life. Adieu, adieu.

122

Newly arrived in Pisa where he had now decided to pass the winter, Leopardi wrote enthusiastically to his sister describing his first impressions.

To Paolina Leopardi • Recanati

Pisa, 12th November 1827

My dear Paolina. I received your letter of the 2nd in Florence, and you can imagine how much I appreciated it: I'd written to you just before, being very impatient to have news from home. I told you I'd be going to Massa, but my friends in Florence made me decide for Pisa, a much better city and with a reliable climate. I left Florence on the morning of the 9th in the mail-coach, and I arrived in Pisa in the evening, a journey of 50 miles. Last night, for the first time in more than six and a half months, I slept not in a boarding house but in a private house where I have a place as a paying guest, on very reasonable terms. I'm delighted by Pisa on account of its climate: if it carries on like this, it will be a blessing. In Florence I left behind a cold one degree above zero; here I've found it so warm that I've had to throw aside my cape and wear lighter clothes. I like the look of Pisa much better than that of Florence. This Lungarno[1] is a spectacle so fine, so spacious, so grand, so lively, so cheerful, that it's captivating: I've not seen anything like it in Florence, or Milan, or Rome; and truly I don't know if in the whole of Europe many views of this sort are to be found. Then in winter people walk about there with great pleasure, because there's almost always an air of spring: so that at certain times of day the street is full of people, full of carriages and pedestrians: you hear ten or twenty languages spoken, a splendid sun shines on the gildings of the cafés, the shops full of pretty wares, and onto the windows of the buildings and the houses, all of fine architecture. Apart from that, Pisa is a mixture of big city and small city, of urban and rustic, a mixture so romantic that I've never seen its like. In addition to all its other attractions there is its attractive language. And then to that is to be added that I, thank God, am well; that I eat heartily; that I have a room facing West, overlooking a big kitchen garden, which opens right out so that you can see all the way to the horizon, a thing you have to forget about in Florence. The people of the house are good-natured, the prices not high, an excellent thing for my purse, which wasn't too happy with the Florentines: and I wouldn't want you to think that I came here in the mail-coach, as I told you, to be grand: I came in one of these small Tuscan *diligences*, which charge less than the coaches.

Give my regards to everyone; give me news of everyone: kiss Papa's and Mama's hands for me: and write to me, write to me soon, and give me all the news you know, first of home, then of Recanati, then the Marches. Ask Carlo if he's still fond of me. I'm waiting for some news from Bunsen when he comes through Bologna again this December. That's what we arranged. He'll pass through Recanati too. Adieu.

[1] The Lungarno is the road which runs alongside the river Arno through the centre of the city.

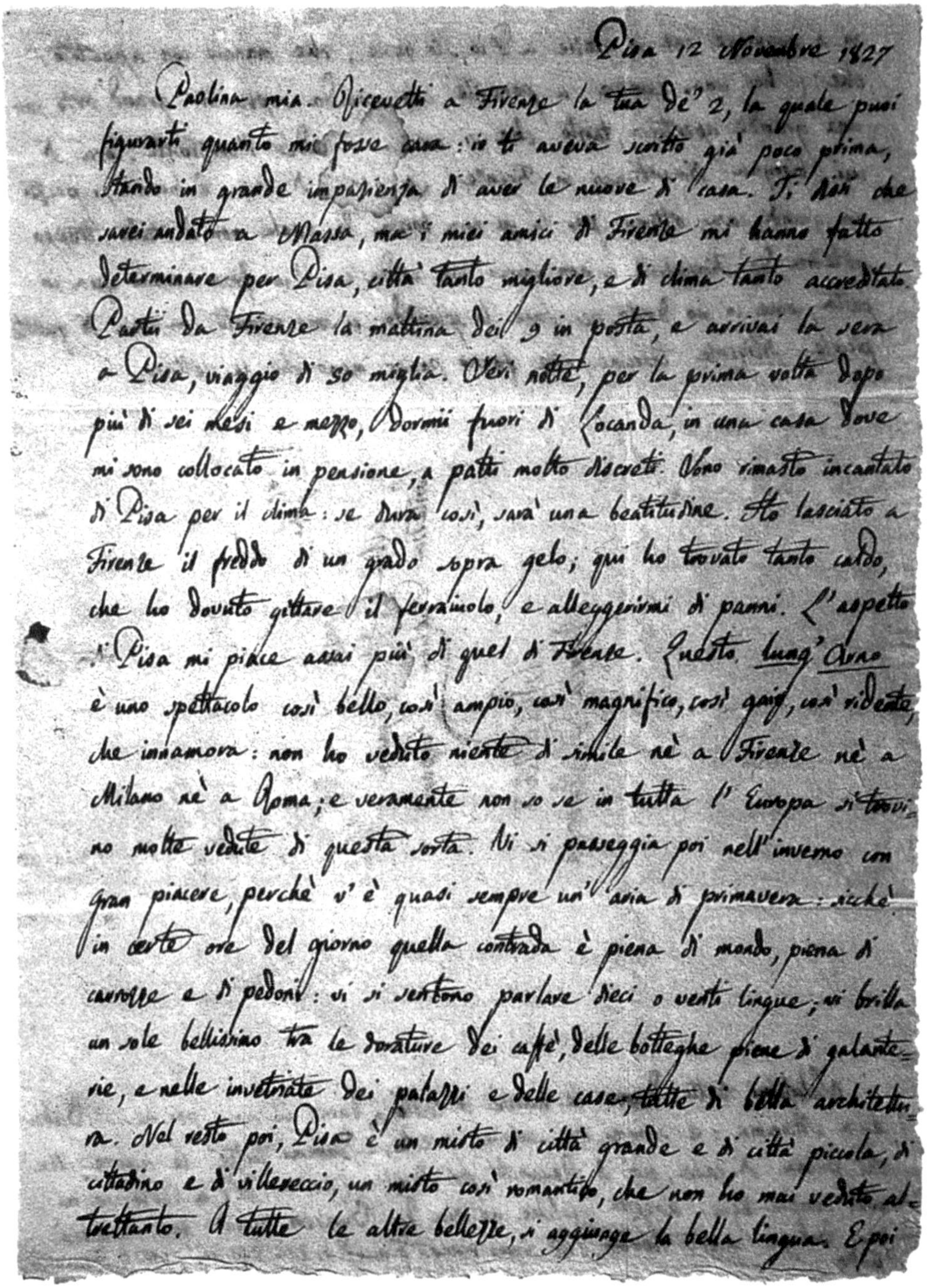

Pisa 12 Novembre 1827

Paolina mia. Ricevetti a Firenze la tua de' 2, la quale puoi figurarti quanto mi fosse cara: io ti aveva scritto già poco prima, stando in grande impazienza di aver le nuove di casa. Ti dirò che sarei andato a Massa, ma i miei amici di Firenze mi hanno fatto determinare per Pisa, città tanto migliore, e di clima tanto accreditato. Partii da Firenze la mattina dei 9 in posta, e arrivai la sera a Pisa, viaggio di 50 miglia. Ieri notte, per la prima volta dopo più di sei mesi e mezzo, dormii fuori di locanda, in una casa dove mi sono collocato in pensione, a patti molto discreti. Sono rimasto incantato di Pisa per il clima: se dura così, sarà una beatitudine. Ho lasciato a Firenze il freddo di un grado sopra gelo; qui ho trovato tanto caldo, che ho dovuto gittare il ferraiuolo, e alleggerirmi di panni. L'aspetto di Pisa mi piace assai più di quel di Firenze. Questo lung'Arno è uno spettacolo così bello, così ampio, così magnifico, così gaio, così ridente, che innamora: non ho veduto niente di simile nè a Firenze nè a Milano nè a Roma; e veramente non so se in tutta l'Europa si trovino molte vedute di questa sorta. Vi si passeggia poi nell'inverno con gran piacere, perchè v'è quasi sempre un'aria di primavera: sicchè in certe ore del giorno quella contrada è piena di mondo, piena di carrozze e di pedoni: vi si sentono parlare dieci o venti lingue; vi brilla un sole bellissimo tra le dorature dei caffè, delle botteghe piene di galanterie, e nelle invetriate dei palazzi e delle case, tutte di bella architettura. Nel resto poi, Pisa è un misto di città grande e di città piccola, di cittadino e di villereccio, un misto così romantico, che non ho mai veduto altrettanto. A tutte le altre bellezze, si aggiunge la bella lingua. E poi

Fig. 5 Letter to his sister Paolina from Pisa, 12th November 1827
Courtesy of Casa Leopardi

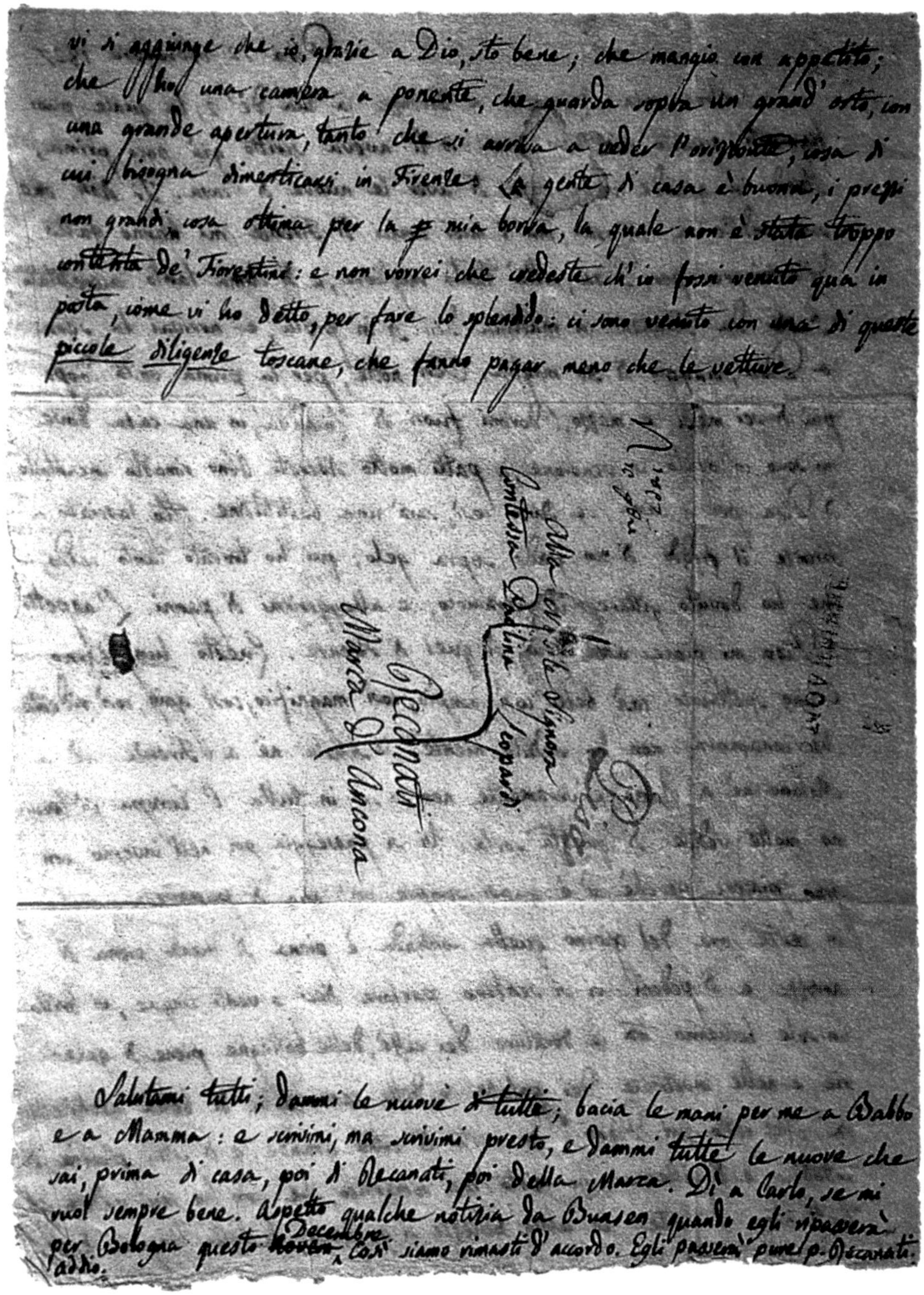

vi si aggiunge che io, grazie a Dio, sto bene; che mangio con appetito; che ho una camera a ponente, che guarda sopra un grand' orto, con una grande apertura, tanto che si arriva a veder l'orizzonte, cosa di cui bisogna dimenticarsi in Firenze. La gente di casa è buona, i prezzi non grandi, cosa ottima per la mia borsa, la quale non è stata troppo contenta de' Fiorentini: e non vorrei che credeste ch'io fossi venuto qua in posta, come vi ho detto, per fare lo splendido: ci sono venuto con una di queste piccole diligenze toscane, che fanno pagar meno che le vetture.

Alla Sig.ra Contessa
Contessa Paolina Leopardi
Recanati
Marca d'Ancona

Salutami tutti; dammi le nuove di tutte; bacia le mani per me a Babbo e a Mamma: e scrivimi, ma scrivimi presto, e dammi tutte le nuove che sai, prima di casa, poi di Recanati, poi della Marca. Di' a Carlo, se mi vuol sempre bene. Aspetto qualche notizia da Bunsen, quando egli ripasserà per Bologna questo Decembre. Così siamo rimasti d'accordo. Egli passerà pure p. Recanati. addio.

123

He gave an equally enthusiastic account to Vieusseux.

To Giampietro Vieusseux • Florence

Pisa, 12th November 1827

My dear Vieusseux. Here is my news, just as I promised you. My health is good, after a slight indisposition caused by the journey, and caused by what I'd least have expected: the sun and the heat. I'm more than pleased, I'm really enchanted by this sky. I left winter behind in Florence, and here I've found autumn, so that I've had to toss aside my heavy overcoat and wear lighter clothes. I very much like the look of Pisa as well. The Lungarno, on a fine day, is a captivating spectacle: I've never seen anything like it: you who have travelled half the world will perhaps have seen something of this sort in Holland or elsewhere; but this sun, this sky, are ornaments you won't have found outside Italy, and yet they are a large part of this scene. Apart from that, I find here a mixture of big city and small city, of urban and rustic, in things as well as in people: a mixture that is really romantic. Dr Cioni, who has done me a thousand favours, has found me a house here in Via Fagiuoli (the house belongs to Dr Comandoli, and is occupied by a Mr Soderini, who is employed in some tribunal or other), where I've taken board and lodging. The people in the house are good-natured; and in short I find I'm content in Pisa, except in the evenings, which I don't know how to fill. A thousand regards to Giordani, Montani, Colletta, if you see him, and all our friends. Go on being fond of me. Adieu, adieu. Yours,

Leopardi.

If you write to me, give me your news, and news of friends, and news of literature, if there is any of interest.

124

He discussed the project for a poetry anthology with Stella.

To Antonio Fortunato Stella • Milan

Pisa, 23rd November 1827

Dearest Sir and Friend. I am replying to your letter of the 12th of this month, first of all confirming mine of the same date, written immediately after my arrival in Pisa. I am very grateful to you for the news you give me about Monti: I thought it appropriate to write and thank him directly for the regards you kindly passed on to me.

The Encyclopaedia, being a thing dependent on imagination, inspiration and mood, which cannot always be at our beck and call, proceeds more slowly than I would wish; and for this reason I had already decided to ask you to suggest some other project to your satisfaction, which might be less dependent on imagination, and which I could work on in between times, and finish sooner. Now that you suggest the poetry Anthology, I find you have anticipated me, and I have no reason or difficulty that prevents me from embarking on this venture. However I must point out first of all that this project requires more work and more tranquillity than the prose Anthology: we are talking about poetic beauties, which cannot be appreciated reading hastily or skimming the pages, as is possible with prose. They must be savoured slowly, and this takes a great deal of time: besides which Italian literature is as rich in versifiers as it is poor in prose-writers, from each and every one of whom it would be possible to.extract some good passage suitable for an Anthology: so that the work is vast by its very nature. In the second place, the prose Anthology had no other Italian work in competition with it; but a poetry Anthology will have to compete with Brancia's, which is very tolerable: it will have to compete with several hundred or thousand Parnassuses, Collections, poetry Selections of every kind, among which there are many which are at least middling in quality. To produce a work whose perfection makes it stand out from all the countless works of the same sort (and it is pointless to embark on it if it does not) requires sustained and steady effort. Finally my poor eyes, which already suffered a great deal and still have not recovered from the strain of all that reading and all that copying I had to do for the other Anthology, will not allow me to work too hurriedly on this second one. For all these reasons I reckon that I cannot promise you the poetry Anthology before the beginning of next autumn. You will be able to tell me if this timing suits you or not. If it suits you, I will devote myself at once to the work with all the diligence my health will allow: if not, we will need to think of some other project. I embrace you, as usual, with all my soul. Your most cordial friend and servant,

Giacomo Leopardi.

125

To Giampietro Vieusseux • Florence

[Pisa] 3rd December [1827]

My dear friend. I owe you a reply to your two affectionate letters, for which I thank you warmly. I was very saddened by the death of our good friend Valeri, for your sake too.[1] I'll write to Puccinotti, and I'll let him know, as you wish, your reasons for not accepting those articles. I'm not very well informed about the San Silvestro business,[2] any more than I am about any other new development, because I don't go out at all except to walk, and I don't see anyone at home. You'll already know about the wonder-working Mother Superior, who miraculously replenished the oil in a lamp, by pouring some in again secretly every night: you'll know of the flattery, the threats, the tricks, the harsh treatment used on young

[1] Giovanni Valeri (1775-1827) was a contributor to the *Antologia*.

[2] A decree had been issued by the Grand Duke of Tuscany against the nuns in question.

convent-school boarders to induce them to take a vow of virginity before they knew the meaning of the word, and then to become nuns in that convent: you'll know of the apparitions that were used to achieve this: apparitions of angels, and apparitions of demons; the demons were rats, on which they put small black capes and a pair of horns (they had their own tails), and dressed up like that they let them loose in the dormitory at night.

My eyes are better, but that doesn't mean I'm good for doing anything, because the cold is killing me. From morning to evening all I do is shiver violently, without finding a remedy for this complaint, especially when it rains and walking is impossible: you can imagine, with that continual shaking, what desire or indeed possibility I have of working.

When shall I see you again? what's become of Colletta? is he still in Florence, or in Livorno? All best wishes to Giordani, to Montani, to all our friends. Don't stop loving me, and believe me all yours,

Leopardi.

126

Even in Pisa the cold continued to be a problem.

To Monaldo Leopardi • Recanati

Pisa, 3rd December 1827

Dear Father. I am writing to you from a desire to get a letter from you once in a while; I have not had one for a very long time, and you are well aware that I would like to get one not once in a while, but often, if that were possible without it causing you any inconvenience or nuisance. After being undecided for a very long time about where to spend this winter, I have finally made up my mind to spend it here, in order to have the possibility of going for long walks, given the mildness of the climate, there not being much wind, the city streets being good, and with enough shade to be able to walk during the day out of the sun. I came here prepared to put up with a great deal, in order not to suffer ill-health, which for me is inevitable when I am forced to spend whole months without getting any fresh air and without taking any exercise: in spring I begin to be prey to a thousand complaints, which last all summer, as happened to me this year. In the autumn I began to take a lot of exercise, and so far I have not missed doing so even one day. I have felt and feel much better than in recent months, though I still suffer a great deal from the cold, as I had foreseen; because at home all I do is shiver, as I cannot have a fire, and I do not have those priceless and matchless comforts I would have at home. All the same I am not afraid, I face up to the cold, and thank God, I am pretty well. The climate here is much less harsh than in Florence and Recanati, and there is no comparison with Bologna: but even here its gets really quite cold, and even here we have had snow, though later than in Recanati, and not for three days, as Paolina writes me, but for just one day, and it did not settle. I have several friends here, and I would have more, if I wished to call on people; because I am welcomed everywhere very warmly: but the cold takes away my courage and my desire to go out and about, except to go for walks very well wrapped up; and all the rest of the day and the evening I stay at home in my usual way. Please, please do write two lines telling me your news and everybody's, and assuring me that you are fond of me. My very loving regards to Mama and my brothers and sister. I kiss your hand, asking for your blessing, and reminding you that I love you with all possible intensity and tenderness of affection and gratitude. Yours,

Giacomo.

127

Responding to his father's complaint of a lack of intimacy in his letters, Leopardi tried to account for his reserve, attributing it to habits contracted in infancy; he explained once more why living in Recanati was impossible for him.

To Monaldo Leopardi • Recanati

Pisa, 24th December 1827

Dear Father. Your last letter has not stopped making me feel distinctly sad with the reproaches it contains, loving though they were. You reproach me for the dryness of my letters; it derives from a lack of subject matter, and it is common to all my letters because my life is monotonous and lacking in anything new. You would like me to see your heart for just one moment; and on this subject allow me to make a protest and a declaration, which from now on may always serve to shed light on the way I feel towards you. I tell you, then, and protest with all possible truthfulness, before God, that I love you as tenderly as it is or ever was possible for any son to love his father; that I recognize very clearly the love you feel for me, and that I feel a gratitude as heartfelt and as deep as human gratitude can ever be for what you have done for me and for your tenderness; that I would willingly give you all my blood, not just from a sense of duty, but from love, or to put it another way, not just from thinking but from very powerful feeling. If then you sometimes desire in me more closeness and more displays of intimacy towards you, the lack of these things comes simply from the habit contracted in infancy, a habit that brooks no disobedience and cannot be conquered, because it goes back too far and began too early. If I did not openly state my intentions about the coming winter, and if in some way I led you to believe that I would spend it at home, that was because I myself knew nothing more about it; and I was always undecided on this point right up to the moment I left Florence for Pisa. I did not write to you directly about this decision of mine, but to Paolina, imagining that the letter would be shared with all the family, but presented principally to you: and besides I supposed, from expressions in your earlier letters as well, that where the decision was concerned you were leaving me the freedom to take the course of action which best suited my health. The journey from Florence to Recanati could not have taken place without causing me serious financial difficulties, and even more serious damage to my health, being a matter of five days, through the mountains, in the state I was in at that time. Then staying in Recanati in winter would without a shadow of doubt have been as deadly for my health as it would have been welcome to me for the presence and the company of you and the family (which I prefer to any pleasure). You can be quite certain that for me having a fire is absolutely and utterly impossible; since even the brazier, which I use extremely sparingly, causes me many problems, and the colour of my urine is constantly reddish in hue, though I drink only water. But leaving aside the fire, in Recanati I would not have been able to live except in the house, because there is never a day there without wind or fog or rain: and if by a miracle there is a fine day, I cannot go for a walk on account of the sun, because there is no shade in the city or outside it. A winter spent in the house and (as is natural) entirely given over to studying would have ruined the nerves of my eyes, and my digestion, and along with my digestion my whole state of health, so that I would then pass a very unhappy summer, as I passed this last one, as happened to me before I left for Milan, as has always been my experience since I left childhood behind me. Here there is never any wind, never any fog; there is always shade, as there is in all big cities, and if there are rainy days, since I keep the hours I choose and I am free to dine in the evening (as I always do), it is very unlikely that I won't find an interval of time in which it is possible to go for a walk. In fact, since I have been in Pisa, no day has passed in which I have not walked for between two and three hours: a thing absolutely necessary to me, and the lack of which is death to me; because the continual exercising of the nerves and muscles of the head, without corresponding exercise of the nerves and muscles of the other parts of the body, produces that total imbalance in the machine,[1] which is infallibly the ruin of scholars, as I have seen in myself from such long experience. As for the climate, after three or four days of exceptional cold in November (much less severe though than what it was elsewhere), here through the whole of December we have had and are still having a temperature such that I must protect myself from the heat more than from the cold. As well as my daytime walk, I go out in the evening too, often without a cloak; I read and write with the windows open: and in a room which has very thin walls, and which never has a fire, I have to take great care not to have too many bedclothes. These things can show you the real difference there is between the climate of Pisa and the climate of Recanati: and add that this month (and the same thing happens in all the other months) we have so far had two storms with lightning, and as big and long as they might be in summer. Finally I protest and swear that I have no greater desire than to live in your company, and in the bosom of my family; and that when I can live in Recanati in reasonable health, and with a reasonable possibility of occupying myself with work to pass the time, I shan't delay racing home for even a moment; and renouncing glory, renouncing the pleasure and the benefit of living in a place where I am appreciated, sought out, almost courted, instead of being scorned and shunned, as I necessarily was in Recanati (a thing which by the way has jeopardised my character forever), I shall settle there, to live by your side, and never go away again. [...]

With all my heart I wish you, Mama and my brothers and sister a merry Christmas and a happy New Year. I am, thank God, tolerably well. I ask for your blessing, and tenderly kissing your hand, straight from the heart, I remain your very affectionate son.

[1] Leopardi uses the word 'machine' [*macchina*], here as elsewhere, for his physical organism and its functioning or malfunctioning.

128

The 'Antologia' had been banned in Turin: Leopardi wrote to Vieusseux to commiserate.

To Giampietro Vieusseux • Florence

Pisa, 31st December 1827

My very dear friend. I must thank you so very, very much for your many acts of kindness and your many displays of affection, made to me through Cioni, and contained in your letters. It pains me very greatly to hear that you are feeling troubled, and I would like to be able to raise your spirits. The Turin business in particular I'm immensely sorry about. I saw your last *Antologia.* I assure you that it's a fine issue, and that it does honour to the Journal. Many people may not be pursuaded by the article on Manzoni, but they certainly can't reasonably be dismissive of it. The only thing I disliked is the way it treats Manzoni as a god, because it smacks of adulation, and excesses are never commendable. But who on earth is this Caroline of Giordani's? neither Cioni nor I have been able even to guess. I've never asked you for books, because now that my eyes allow me to do something, and the cold has let up a little, I am very busy with things for Stella, for whom I've done nothing for more than six months now. So I have no choice but to spend all my time now for him: and that is why I still haven't even read Marchetti's book. Pomba should thank Heaven that so far no philologist has spoken about his Classics. I assure you that the project would have gained nothing by it. Give Carmignani's regards to Giordani; the fair Mrs Vaccà's to Giordani and to Montani, and mine as well. Make my apologies to Forti, that when he came to call and didn't find me, I did not return the visit: the reason was that in winter I don't call on people, in order not to shiver with cold. You've been misinformed about my salons. If we're talking about the ones where I've been introduced (by force), there are more than two: if about the ones I attend regularly, fewer; because I don't go regularly to any of them, in fact I never go out in the evening. Please pay my respects to Reynhold, Capponi, and Father Mauro. I enclose the articles sent by Puccinotti; please have them posted from Florence: because, for various reasons, I don't want Puccinotti (who has written to me about them as well) to know I've seen them.

Adieu, my very dear Vieusseux. I am really impatient to embrace you again. Meanwhile love me as I love you. Yours,

Leopardi.

129

He was again worried by lack of news from home.

To Paolina Leopardi • Recanati

Pisa, 21st January 1828

My dear Paolina. I'm very troubled at not having had news of all of you for such a long time. I wrote to Carlo, then I wrote to Papa: but it's already more than a month since I had any letters from Recanati. The Brancia Anthology went to Bologna, but I've had no further news of the French one. Please, please write to me, either you or Carlo: and never let so much time go by without a few lines from you. How are you both? how's winter treating you? Here this year we aren't aware of it: December was like March, January is like April: even the air has a smell of spring about it some days. I hope you'll all have a similarly mild winter too, because I hear that it's mild everywhere for the time of year. I'm pretty well, and I go for endless walks in the daytime: but in the evening I don't go out; I get a great many reproaches for this from the gentlemen and ladies of Pisa and abroad: I've protested to all of them that they're not to expect to see me at a salon until March. They laugh at my timorousness, but I let them laugh, and I chose not to go even to the splendid parties given here (as usual) for the Grand Duke by one of the leading families in Pisa. Adieu, my dear Paolina: kiss Papa's and Mama's hands for me, and all best wishes to our brothers. Write to me *at once.*

130

Leopardi had become friendly during his stay in Bologna with two generations of the same family, Antonietta and Giacomo Tommasini and their daughter Adelaide and her husband Ferdinando Maestri. On leaving Bologna he corresponded regularly with the two women. Later Professor Maestri would try to secure a university chair for him in Parma.[1]

To Antonietta Tommasini • Bologna

Pisa, 31st January 1828

My dear Antonietta. I owe you a thousand thanks for your very affectionate letter of the 21st. My memory of you is no less vivid, it never fades; and if I let some time go by without writing to you, I do it in order not to bore you, as I have nothing to write about. Here winter has not just been mild, but so mild as not to deserve the name winter. I haven't noticed it, and to tell you the truth I'll never stop being grateful for this most blessed climate of Pisa, which seems a real paradise to me more with every passing day. I wouldn't know what to tell you about my work, except that I'm not working at all: I only read a little as a pastime, that is as

[1] See [151].

much as my eyes permit; they are better than they were last summer, but still not good, and they are showing signs of going back to being very bad in spring. These nerves of mine leave me no hope any more; not eating much doesn't help, nor does eating a lot, nor does wine, or water, or walking for half a day at a time, or taking no exercise at all: in short no diet and no routine benefits me. I can't fix my mind on a serious thought for a single moment without feeling a convulsion inside me, and without having an upset stomach, a bitter taste in my mouth, and things of this kind.

This ought to mean that I should never think of you. I do think of you all the same and will do so despite my stomach and my nerves. Remember me to Professor Tommasini and ask him to spare me a thought: I don't know if he's more lovable or more admirable. If you see Orioli, be so kind as to give him my very best regards. If I should see the Pazzini family, I shan't fail to do as you ask. Until now I've really only seen the lawyer, who was kind enough to come and call on me. And I've talked often and at length with him and a lot of other people about your dear family – there's no other like it. Lots of kisses for little Emilio. Be fond of me always. Adieu, adieu.

131

He explained his living arrangements in Pisa to Vieusseux, who was looking for something similar for him in Florence.

To Giampietro Vieusseux • Florence

Pisa, 25th February 1828

My dearest Vieusseux. I got your fond regards from Torri and Cioni; I got the packet of books you were kind enough to send, and then the *Bracciolini* from Cioni: I got your letter of the 10th, and now I've just got your other one of the 23rd. Thank you no end for all these things; and I'm also very grateful to you for making the acquaintance of Mayer, as I'm expecting to do thanks to you. As for the lodgings, I'll tell you that here in Pisa I have: 1. a room, with light, bed linen and table linen, and service; 2. a meal in my room, at a time of my own choosing; consisting of soup, three courses, bread and water (no fruit and no wine); 3. breakfast, consisting of coffee-with-chocolate, and two good biscuits; 4. cleaning of boots and shoes; 5. laundry and ironing; 6. a fire in the brazier all day, and a bed-warmer in the evening: and all of this costs me eleven *monete* a month. The owners are pleased; and they made this arrangement after having tried it out, and seen what I eat, etc. And if I don't eat much in winter, in summer I eat almost nothing; besides which in summer there is no need for heating. All the same I'm quite happy to spend more in Florence: I leave it to your discretion how much: but I wouldn't want it to be more than 14 or 15 *monete* at most. Believe me, I cost whoever supports me very little. Eating with the owners is quite out of the question for me.

For now I couldn't tell you the exact time of my return. As far as I'm concerned, I'd like to be back there already; but it will have to depend on the weather: and it is also worth noting for my finances that I had to undertake to pay the rent on the room (i.e. three *monete* a month) until the end of May, the usual end date for student rentals.

I think there is no point in my telling you again that I continue to love you with all my heart; in fact I love you more every day, if that is possibile. My very warm regards to Giordani and Montani; my respects to Gino and to Reinhold. Carmignani (whom I see often) sends his warm regards to Giordani. If in your own good time you can let me have Foscolo's *Poems* and Varano's *Visioni*, you will be doing me a great favour. I'm still busy with the confounded poetry Anthology, which is taking a terrible toll on my eyes. Adieu, adieu. Yours,

Leopardi.

132

To Antonio Papadopoli • Venice

Pisa, 25th February 1828

My dear friend. I was very pleased to get your letter of the 10th, and would have been even more pleased if it had contained any news of your health and your present occupations. I've seen Manzoni's novel, which in spite of its many faults I like very much, and it is certainly the work of a great mind; which is what I found Manzoni to be in several conversations I had with him in Florence.[1] He is a truly amiable and estimable man. I've seen Countess Malvezzi's poem as well. Poor woman![2] I'd already seen the manuscript. I haven't seen the Strabo and the Synesius.

I'm pretty well on the whole; and I'm very pleased with the climate here. Studying and working are things I've forgotten, and they become more alien to me every day. Given the sort of judgment and criticism to be found today in Italy, anyone who puts a lot of effort into thinking and writing is a bloody fool. Writing without making any effort and without thinking is fine, and I commend it highly, but it won't do for me, and I can't manage it. A proposal has been made to me by a publisher from the Marches for a collection of my translations from the Greek. I don't know whether I'll want to bother with it. Adieu: go on being fond of me, and believe me entirely yours.

1 Manzoni had been a guest at the Gabinetto Vieusseux when he visited Florence. In fact Giordani had monopolized him in conversation and shocked other members by the intemperance with which he expressed his anticlerical views.

2 See [112, 114, 116, 117].

133

He reported to Paolina that he was feeling more his old self.

To Paolina Leopardi • Recanati

Pisa, 25th February 1828

My dear Paolina. Thank you so much for your letters of January 16th and February 15th, and for the news you give me of home and of Recanati. Believe me, I'm really very eager to have this news, even the tiniest items; it doesn't bore me at all, indeed I'm sorry you write so briefly and put in those 'etceteras'. I was very pleased about the canonry, but the Council business put me in a very bad humour.[1] I understand that it will be of no consequence to Papa, and that's fine; but that Recanati riff-raff fills me with rage. We've had two weeks of cold weather here as well, but no snow. Now the warm weather has come back, and it's spring. Would you believe that I still haven't managed to see a copy of the Anthology? Stella is already thinking of a second edition, and in Tuscany the first still isn't available: that's how slow communications are between Tuscany and Lombardy. I don't have any copies of the *Spettatore* here with me. Do ask Papa on my behalf to write me a few lines, when he has time; because I'm really upset at not seeing his handwriting for such a long time: kiss his hand for me. Thank Mama very, very much for what she had you write me in your last letter but one. What's Carluccio up to? and why doesn't he ever write to me? and Luigetto and Pietruccio? I'm always dreaming about you all, asleep or awake: here in Pisa I have a delightful street, which I call *Via delle rimembranze*:[2] that is where I go to walk when I want to day-dream. I assure you that where imagination is concerned, I seem to be back to my good old times. Adieu, my dear Paolina. Give my regards to Don Vincenzo and the Curate.

1 His brother Pierfrancesco had taken possession of the canonry, but his father had not been reappointed to his position on the town Council.

2 i.e. Memory Road

134

To Pierfrancesco Leopardi • Recanati

Pisa, 31st March 1828

Dear Canon. Now I really can call you canon with conviction, because you are not a canon without a canonry any more, but a canon in reality. I assure you that the news of your taking possession of it cheered me up no end. Have someone tell Montaccini, if he wants to have peace of mind, not to make the housekeeper or servant or cat fast, but to fast himself after Easter for eighty days, and he'll see that it will do him good. On the subject of Easter, be sure that this year you don't mistreat those poor hard-boiled eggs: eat them without making them suffer, and not too many of them. I shan't eat hard-boiled eggs or anything else; because I can't eat anything, although I'm well, and I get through 48 hours on a bowl of soup: I regret it desperately, but never mind. If you tasted the *schiacciate*[1] they have here for Easter, I'm sure you'd like them more than the Easter tart: I'd send one through the post to Paolina (because it's very sweet stuff), but they have to be eaten hot, and I can't send the oven through the post too.

I've already written to Paolina that I've got a book ready for you; it has engravings too. I'll bring it for you myself, unless I find some opportunity sooner. Tell Paolina that the French Anthology still hasn't arrived.

Who is this Monsignor Scerra you talk about? And what is the San Sebastian benefice? perhaps the one the archdeacon is contesting? Write to me about it or have someone else write. Thank Papa for the lines he writes in your letter, and wish him a happy Easter from me. The same goes for Mama, and everybody, including the Curate and Don Vincenzo. Today you're busy at the Cathedral, and I don't want to hold you up any longer. So, kissing both your hands, I have the honour etc. Your brother and servant,

Giacomo.

[1] A kind of flat loaf.

135

Leopardi learnt with some concern that the family had not been well.

To Paolina Leopardi • Recanati

Pisa, 2nd May 1828

My dear Paolina. You complain about my long silence. But after replying to Pietruccio I wrote to you a short while ago, and I made the same complaint to you; now I see you didn't get that letter. I was very sorry to hear the news you give me about the ailments suffered by Papa and Mama and all of you, although thank God they weren't serious; indeed I'm still concerned about them; and please, please, as soon as you receive this, write to me at once and tell me that you've all made a full recovery and are well. Also tell me if tomorrow you go on your usual outing to the country.[1] Also get Pietruccio to give you the letter I wrote him, and answer a question you'll find in it. Thank God, I've never had a fever, like all of you; spring has caused and is still causing me many ailments, but it's never made me really ill, and the ailments clear up quickly. But really the weather has been bad for the time of year here too, not so much because of the cold as the changeableness, and the unseasonal heat. Here and in Florence the earthquake was not felt, except by a few people who said so after they saw it reported in the newspaper. Tell me if it was strong enough there to be frightening. Tell Carlo that in exchange for copies of the Anthology I've acquired here (among other books)

[1] The family usually went to their country property at San Leopardo on the 3rd of May to celebrate a local festival.

Ginguené's history, the French edition, which I remember he used to enjoy reading. Kiss Papa's and Mama's hands: give my regards to everybody: take care of yourself, and don't stay in the sun. I've now finished the poetry Anthology: and after two years I've written poems this April; but poems just like the ones I used to write, and with the heart I once had.[2] Adieu, adieu.

[2] Famously, this is the first mention of *A Silvia* and *Il risorgimento*, which signal the renewed flowering of Leopardi's lyric gift in the great poems known as the *grandi idilli*.

136

Despite, or perhaps because of his renewed creative activity, Leopardi was as depressed as ever. As so often before, he made his despondency the theme of a letter to Giordani.

To Pietro Giordani • Florence

Pisa, 5th May [1828]

My dear friend. I hear that a few days ago you asked after me of Vieusseux, expressing amazement at my long silence. I've been silent because I know nothing about anyone else's affairs, and couldn't know anything in Pisa that was of any importance and that you didn't know: as for my own affairs, I'd have liked to tell you something new, as for example that life was tolerable for me: but I've never had anything to tell you except old things, which I didn't want to bore you with. My life is tedium and suffering: I can work very little, and that very little is likewise tedious; and if in my work I could still follow my own inclinations, seeing the quality of the judgments of this age, I wouldn't have the heart to wear myself out doing things that satisfied me. My health is still such as to make any enjoyment impossible for me; any tiny pleasure would kill me: if I don't want to die, I must not live.

But leaving aside these imprecations, and coming to more important things, I'd be doing a great wrong to you and to myself if I were to repeat that I still love you as a friend without equal, that I adore you as a man worthy of the best age of the human race. But I don't think I'm doing any wrong in asking you to carry on loving me. This last year you were able to get to know me better than before; you were able to see that I am nothing: this I'd already told you more than once; it's what I tell everybody who wants to have news of my existence. But you must not on this account be less fond of me, for that is based on the qualities of my heart, and on the long-standing and tender love I swore to you in the first flower of my poor youth, and which I've always kept for you since and will keep until I die. And I want you to know (or remember) that apart from my family you are the only man whose love I've ever considered of a kind I could use as an altar of refuge, a pillar *dove la stanca mia vita s'appoggia.*[1]

I'll come back to Florence soon, but I still don't know on which day. Give my regards to Montani, Vieusseux, Colletta, Capponi. Adieu adieu.

[1] Petrarch, *Rime*, CXXVII, 61: *whereon my weary life leans.*

137

Leopardi's younger brother Luigi died suddenly on the 4th of May at the age of 24. On learning of his death Leopardi immediately wrote to his father.

To Monaldo Leopardi • Recanati

Pisa, 18th May 1828

Dearest Father. I will not speak to you of my grief, which is so great that I cannot encompass the whole of it. I am too conscious of the fact that you need comforting rather than anything else; and the thought of your state, and Mama's, and my brothers' and sister's, is one of the chief ones that are causing me to weep so much.

From the moment I received your letter of the 2nd,[1] the distance between us began to seem very cruel to me. Now it has become almost unbearable; and if the whole journey from here to Recanati could be done by night, as one can count on doing from here to Florence, I assure you with no exaggeration that by now I would already be heading towards you, or on the point of leaving. But because I know that having to travel by day, at this time of year when the season is already well advanced for me, I could not tolerate the heat, which even here I have to be exceptionally careful about, I am forced to my dismay to wait until a cooler season; at which time, if God grants me life, and health good enough just to be able to get into a coach, nothing in the world will prevent me from setting out to come back to you. Meanwhile, for these few months, I entreat you to make sure I get news of you all as often as possible: I could not have any peace of mind at all any more, if for any length of time I were to be without accurate news of your state. I for my part shall not fail to inform you of mine equally often. Now, thank God, I am well, and resigned to the will of heaven.

I got your letter the day before yesterday; but that day I did not have the strength to write. I have not seen Rossi, and I am not surprised, because you cannot have known his Christian name (Antonio), and as there are a great many Rossis here, it is unlikely that the letter reached the person it was meant for. My fond regards to all of you. Take care of yourself, and bless me. Yours,

Giacomo.

[1] Count Monaldo's letter (dated the 2nd, but in fact written on the 6th, two days after Luigi's death) spoke of Luigi's failure to respond to treatment, as a way of preparing Giacomo for the bad news.

138

He felt an urgent need to hear from Carlo.

To Carlo Leopardi • Recanati

Pisa, 21st May 1828

My dear Carluccio. It seems almost impossible to me that you should doubt that I'm thinking of you every day, or rather all day. Yet I feel a kind of ungovernable need to write to you to assure you of it, and to swear it to you as though I thought it possible you might doubt it. I have an incredible longing to see you again and be with you, a longing that gives me no peace. In this state of impatience, until I'm able to satisfy it, I see no other possible relief than that of getting a few lines from you. Write to me as you wish; write me just two words, as I am doing too; because the things we are feeling cannot be expressed, and it is very natural that our letters should be like great passions, that is mute. It will be enough for you to send me a kiss. I send you one too, as heartfelt as if we were together, and clinging to one another in an embrace; which we shall do, God willing, shortly. Let this kiss say everything. Adieu, adieu. Give my regards to everybody.

139

In this letter, for the first time, Leopardi addressed his father as 'Papa' instead of 'Signor Padre', although he still used the formal third-person 'Ella' form of address.

To Monaldo Leopardi • Recanati

Pisa, 26th May 1828

My dear Papa. Among the many causes for grief which your letter of the 16th brings me, one thing (apart from the religious reasons) gave me some comfort; and that was receiving the outpouring of your grief, and persuading myself that this outpouring may have mitigated it, at least for a moment. I cannot undertake to console you, all the more so as I am inconsolable too. But among the reflections that I make all day long on your state, it dismays me to think that up until now you certainly will not have made any effort to distance your mind a little from the thought that dominates and torments it. Dear Papa, I am well aware that sensitive souls, in cases of this kind, would almost be ashamed of themselves if they tried to escape from their grief, and if they accepted some comfort: it seems like a sacred duty to give ourselves up entirely and with no concern for ourselves to the thought that distresses us. But I cannot fail to entreat you to seek a little distraction: and your mind will find less difficulty in doing as I ask, if you think I am asking for a reason as sacred and tender as the one that is causing your grief; I am asking not for your sake, but for our sakes who live in you and through you, and who would feel our lives diminished and mutilated if your health were to suffer. For my part I can swear to you that, humanly speaking, I live only for you and for my dear family: I have never enjoyed life except in relation to all of you; and now life means nothing to me except in view of the grief I would cause you if I were to lose it. So try to do as I ask, and make the same entreaty to Mama on my behalf; I cannot tell you how my present anguish is increased by the doubt and fear that your health and hers may suffer in these circumstances. In recent days I too have taken the holy sacraments, with the intention you are aware of.[1] My health, thank God, is good. I am sustaining myself with the thought of being with you all soon, all other relief is to no effect. In a few weeks time, God willing, I reckon to be in Florence; perhaps I shall not stay there long, but I shall move on to Siena, and from there to Perugia, and so slowly, in accordance with what is possible for me, draw nearer to home. Papa, embrace my brothers and sister for me, and, if it is not superfluous to say so, think that you will always find me one of the most loving sons there ever has been or could be in the world. Yours,

Giacomo.

1 His father had urged him to take the sacraments [M1232]: 'I have no doubt that you too will give this sign of love to your dear brother'; it seems unlikely that he actually did so.

140

He begged his father to allow himself some distractions.

To Monaldo Leopardi • Recanati

Florence, 17th June 1828

My dear Papa. I have just got your letter of the 1st which has been forwarded from Pisa. Your letters are absolutely the only consolation I have; but from this last one I feel all the comfort that the love of one's dear ones can give amidst great tribulations. You express your love so tenderly that it manages to cheer me up; all the more so because I really do feel that I am entirely deserving of it, if love is deserved by loving.

I enter with all my soul into every particular of your grief. It would be impossible for me to decide if in the sorrow I have felt and am feeling a greater part is played by my own personal sense of our common misfortune, or by the reflection in my mind of the family's grief. But how could I decide, if the misfortune is so great that I can say I have never completely understood it, and still do not? I have wept mechanically, almost without knowing why, without any clearly defined thought that moved me.

Meanwhile you will forgive me if once again I beg you to accept some distraction. For as long as God wants us to live, you are necessary to us, and we to you: we must take care of our health, not for our own sakes any more, but each for the sake of the others. For my own sake I urge you with all my heart to consent to treat your mind in such a way that your health does not suffer. And I am certain that my dear Mama and my dear brothers and sister, each and every one of them, make the same prayer for their own sakes.

It is likely that the letter to Cavaliere Rossi was not collected by anyone and is still at the Post Office. I am pleased that you have seen and enjoyed Manzoni's Christian novel. It is a truly fine work; and Manzoni is a very fine mind, and a dear man. A sort of continuation of the novel will be published here shortly, all of which passes through my hands. It will be a thing of no great value; and I am sorry to say so, because the author is a friend of mine, and confided this secret in me alone, and compels me to look over his work, page by page: but I do not know what on earth to do about it. But please you too keep the matter completely secret. I kiss Mama's hand, and embrace my brothers and sister fondly. Bless me: and, straight from the heart, I remain your very loving son,

Giacomo.

I am well, thank God.

141

He wrote to Antonietta Tommasini assuring her that, though grieving, he had no thought of suicide.

To Antonietta Tommasini • Bologna

Florence, 5th July 1828

My dearest Antonietta. From your last very affectionate letter I see that it really was foolish of me to write Adelaide those few lines which upset you so much.[1] Rage dictated them, and I let them run: then I immediately regretted it, and now I regret it even more. But I assured Adelaide then, and I swear to you now, that the boundless love I feel for my friends and relatives will always keep me in this world until destiny decrees; and let us never speak of this matter again.[2] In the meantime I can't tell you how touched I am by the affection demonstrated by your fond words. I have no need of esteem, or glory, or other things of this kind; but I do need love: you can imagine how much it means to me, and how greatly I value it, finding it so deep and so sincere in you and your family, whom I would love with all my heart, even if I were not loved by you in return, because that is what your merits would deserve in and for themselves. I am not very well, and I regret it, because I cannot do anything and I cannot travel; but my ills so far are not of a kind to deserve the honour of sounding an *allarme*. Therefore, although my desire to see you again is very great, I'll tell you honestly that I would not like you to undertake the journey to Florence just on my account. As for my news, I shan't fail to give it to you from time to time, as you wish. Believe me, and have no misgivings on my account, for I am not misleading you. As for my coming to Bologna, you already know the reason for my not coming. This autumn (since now it seems

1 His letter [M1264] had spoken of a desire to 'make myself a little more perfectly immobile' [*rendermi immobile un po' più perfettamente*].

2 The reason hinted at here for not committing suicide (that is, to avoid causing distress to one's friends and relatives) represents Leopardi's definitive thinking on the subject; compare the discussion of suicide in the *Dialogo di Plotino e Porfirio* (Dialogue between Plotinus and Porphyry, 1827 [187]), and the passages written in 1821 in the *Zibaldone* (I, p. 555 and p. 1240f.) which emphasize the rationality of suicide as a choice in the modern world. Two canzoni, *Bruto minore* and *Ultimo canto di Saffo*, had explored the theme imaginatively and very powerfully through the words of a historical figure on the point of taking his or her own life.

that the cold disagrees with me less than the heat) we shall see what I can manage. Please don't delay in giving me news of Adelaide, for in spite of what you tell me to reassure me, I am still very worried about her.[3] Give her my regards a thousand times over, and the same to our illustrious Professor: I thank him no end for the kindness and concern he expresses towards me. Give me news of the excellent Lawyer as well, and give him my fond regards.[4] Take care of your health, and believe that I love you with all possible friendship; and that what is more, just as one can love two countries as one's own at the same time, so I love two families as my own at the same time: mine and the Tommasini family; which from now on, if you like, I shall call mine too. Adieu, my dear Antonietta.

[3] Adelaide was in bed ill.

[4] The Professor and the Lawyer are respectively Antonietta's husband and son-in-law; see [130].

142

He reflected on the necessary principles of imperfection in human society.

To Pietro Giordani

Florence, 24th July 1828[1]

My dear friend. I'm handing this letter to Antonietta Tommasini, asking her to give it to you in Bologna, if she finds you there when she gets back, or to send it to you in Parma if you have already left. Antonietta and Adelaide tried hard to persuade me to come with them to Bologna. Now that I don't have your company, if it had not been for my poor state of health, which prevents my travelling in this heat, I would have left Florence very willingly, because I confess I find this city very gloomy when you're not here. These alleyways they call streets suffocate me; this universal filth sickens me; these foolish, ignorant, arrogant women make me angry; I don't see anyone except Vieusseux and his circle; and when I don't have their company, as often happens, it is as though I'm in a desert. In the end I begin to feel nauseated by the arrogant disdain professed here for all literature and everything beautiful: especially as I cannot get it into my head that the pinnacle of human knowledge is knowing about politics and statistics. Indeed, reflecting philosophically on the almost perfect uselessness of the studies made from the age of Solon on to attain the perfection of civil states and the happiness of nations, I am inclined to laugh at this frenzy of political and legislative calculation and quibbling; and I humbly ask if the happiness of nations can exist without the happiness of individuals. Individuals are condemned to unhappiness by nature, not by men and not by chance: and as a consolation for this inevitable unhappiness I think that the study of beauty, of feelings, imagination, illusions, is more effective than anything else. So it is that the delightful seems to me more useful than everything useful, and literature more truly and certainly useful than all these very arid disciplines; which even when they achieve their objectives, would be of very little benefit to the true happiness of men, who are individuals

[1] In Moroncini's edition this letter is dated 29th July.

and not nations; but when *do* they achieve these objectives of theirs? I shall be pleased to have instruction on this point from one of our professors of the *historical sciences.*

I hold (and not fortuitously) that human society has inherent and necessary principles of imperfection, and that its states are more or less bad, but none can be good. In any case, depriving men of what is delightful in their studies seems to me to be a true crime against the human race. When you can do so in your own good time, you are to write to me with your news as fully as you can; in Guastalla you're to give my regards to Counsellor Dodici (don't forget); and everywhere and always you're to be very fond of me, because I adore you. Adieu, adieu.

143

Once again he was forced to raise the question of money with Stella.

To Antonio Fortunato Stella • Milan

Florence, 19th August 1828

My very dear Sir and Friend. In response to your most recent letter of the 9th of this month. I would already have drafted the preface to the poetry Anthology had I not been prevented by a bad attack of my usual complaint, intestinal inflammation, which has made any serious concentration impossible until now. I shall apply myself to drafting it as soon as my poor head can function again without danger: I hope it will be soon. In the meantime see if you are happy with the title I enclose.

Since a good deal of the work on the Encyclopaedia of Useless Information and Things That Are Not Known still remains to be done (not as regards the material but the style),[1] I see quite clearly that I shall not be able to complete it without devoting all of next winter to the task, since winter is the only time of year in which my health allows me to work fairly steadily. It would be indelicate to ask that your monthly payments should continue to be made to me until that time, and far be it from me to do so. However necessity compels me to ask you to give instructions that they be continued until the end of this year, or at least until the end of November, by which time I shall be able to undertake the long journey required to return home from here. Given the continual danger of congestion and inflammation to which I am prone, a danger greatly exacerbated by travel, I could not undertake the journey at the present time (as I would do at once if I could), and I shall have to wait for the cold weather. From that time on your monthly payments, and our financial relations, will cease; yet without my giving up the right to continue to be of service to you always in the future, both in literary matters and in any other way, in accordance with my limited abilities. Meanwhile accept my renewed protestations of gratitude for the favours I have received from you until now: my respects to your amiable family, and consider me without fail your most grateful and most cordial friend and servant,

Giacomo Leopardi.

[1] The Encyclopaedia was to have been compiled using material drawn from the *Zibaldone.*

144

Less than four months after his brother's death, the family faced a new crisis when they discovered that Carlo was infatuated with his cousin Paolina Mazzagalli, a quite unsuitable match in his parents' eyes. Leopardi wrote assuring his father that Carlo would not behave rashly.

To Monaldo Leopardi • Recanati

Florence, 28th August 1828

My dear Papa. The day before yesterday I got your letter of the 11th, delayed by the disgraceful negligence of the post, together with your other letter of the 19th. The news you give me has come as a great shock to me; and in the midst of my anguish, I cannot refrain from grumbling affectionately about you as well, for having kept this thing hidden from me until now, as though I were not deeply involved in the matter by my concern for all family affairs, which is beyond words. At this distance from you, which I am finding increasingly painful, I cannot say anything in detail on the subject: I can only reassure you that, knowing Carlo very, very well and better than anyone else in the world, from having shared my life with him for 26 whole years, I think, or rather I know for certain, that his heart and his character are so good that without some supernatural force, it is impossible for them to become bad. And therefore I am quite sure that it is impossible for Carlo on reflection, and on a serious matter, to lower himself to failing in his duty towards you and Mama, and to causing you a terrible displeasure. I will surely be yours for as long as I live;[1] and I will die for you, if necessary: but believe me, my dear Papa, that without a doubt you will not lose Carlo either, however things appear now and whatever plans he may be mulling over. I was very doubtful whether my writing to him would serve any purpose: my heart has forced me to do so, not to tackle the matter head on, but to be in contact with him over this business, about which he has never written to me or had anyone write or say a single word.

My dear Papa, God sees how much I feel for you and Mama in this new tribulation. Oh, if only I could be with you already! Thank you very much for your thoughtfulness about the room; but I think it will be better to make arrangements when I am there, and I also think that I will be able to adopt a less inconvenient routine than the other time. Meanwhile take care of your health, and do not be too anxious about this matter; I am sure it will not end badly. I wrote to you about my health by the last post: now a slight eye infection prevents my writing at greater length, as I would like; but it is a small thing. Embrace me, dear Papa, wait for me, and remember that in me you have a very fond son. Please keep me informed of any new development.

[1] i.e. he will never start a family of his own.

145

He asked Carlo why he had not written.

To Carlo Leopardi • Recanati

Florence, 28th August 1828

My dear Carluccio. It really shocks me that you haven't written anything to me about your present situation. How can it be that you don't think any more about someone who loves you with a dream love, and often weeps from tenderness thinking of you? If you think I can have peace of mind in the face of your forgetfulness, and live serenely, you are much mistaken; and if you don't write to me, I really will become ill, as I already feel ill from the agitation caused in me by your silence in these circumstances. I need you to unburden yourself, and take me into your confidence as I'd take you into mine in any passion of mine, because you would certainly be the first, and perhaps the only person, I would tell about it. God knows how much I feel for you, and you know I love you more than my life; you surely know that better than anything else in the world. I'd like to write you many more things, but my eyes won't let me. I'll come as soon as I can: but in the meantime I can't be out of contact with you: even if it were possible for you to forget me, you'd forever be the pinnacle of all my love. The more I think about it, the more impossible it seems that you haven't written.

146

Again he assured his father that Carlo would not act rashly.

To Monaldo Leopardi • Recanati

Florence, 11th September 1828

My dear Papa. I have received your letter of August 31st. Certainly the way they have behaved and are behaving towards you and Mama, trying to snatch Carlo away from you by brute force, is a way no one will find excusable, and I would always have been hard put to believe could be used by such people. Carlo still has not answered me: perhaps he did not get my letter, or it has been held up in the post; I am waiting impatiently for his reply. In any case I am still quite sure he will never take the final step without your consent: nothing in the world could persuade me otherwise, except seeing it with my own eyes. Only a notion passes through my mind which at this distance won't stop troubling me: and it is that Carlo, seeing himself bound by his promise on the one hand, and by his duty towards you and Mama on the other, might be swept along by his enthusiasm and his desperation to form some fatal resolve against his own person. Carlo's determined character, which I know very well, gives rise to this misgiving, which I cannot refrain from communicating to you, so that being there on the spot you may observe Carlo's behaviour bearing this in mind. I cannot convey to you how much this notion, which has just come to me (and which will perhaps be a dream), torments me and brings me out in a sweat; especially in view of Carlo's absolute silence towards me.

As for the rooms, I think it is difficult for me to make a decision without being on the spot, and therefore I would not want you to make any change for the moment. In the meantime, thank you with all my heart for your kindness. My health is tolerable. I kiss your hand from my soul. Yours,

Giacomo.

147

He again begged Carlo to write.

To Carlo Leopardi • Recanati

Florence, 18th September 1828

My dear Carluccio. As long as you stay just as you are, and so does that heart of yours (which, like that of all men born great, is always child-like), I ask nothing more of you; and if communicating with me by letter is painful to you, I'm very far from expecting it. Perhaps in your state I'd feel reluctance at putting my feelings on paper too. Meanwhile be fond of me, and think of me as the one who's loved you and who loves you more than any person who was ever born or could be born. I'll come as soon as I can, and I'd come now; but I'm forced to wait for the cold weather, because you know that when travelling the thing I fear and am above all obliged to avoid is getting over-heated, which I'm very prone to: and because of the risk of this I must also refrain from making short trips of a few miles here around Florence, which I'd do in the pleasant company of people who invite me. You know that of my own accord I've renounced the pleasure of living in a big city, and of being among many good friends, in order to go back and be with you, who are for me a synonym of life itself. Adieu.

148

Leopardi returned to Recanati in November 1828. It was to be his last sojourn in his birthplace: he stayed there for 16 months, making repeated attempts to leave, and sinking ever deeper into depression.

To Giampietro Vieusseux • Florence

Recanati, 15th December [1828]

My dearest Vieusseux. I received your affectionate letter of the 4th, and shortly afterwards the latest number of the Antologia. Thank you no end for both of them. I frankly envy you the company of the estimable foreigners you mention (is Saint-Aignan the one who translated the Iliad?), and Cooper's.[1] Is it true that you're expecting Walter Scott there as well?[2] The Antologia number is full of important things, as usual. As for Tommaseo's article, I can assure you that I liked it very much.[3] Without sharing all the author's opinions, I admire the richness and variety of his thoughts, and I genuinely believe that an article of equal merit on that subject won't be seen in Italy. Congratulate Tommaseo on my behalf, and give him my regards. – Something will certainly be done on the *Greek subject* and the *Roman* one,[4] if my state of health does not prevent it: so far I have no grounds for praising this climate: my poor eyes began to ache the very day I arrived; that is what always happens; and they are getting worse all the time. Nonetheless this dreadful climate is what fate has allotted me. I'm taking advantage of your friendship to ask you to hold the enclosed letter to Colletta, as I don't know where he is at present. Give my regards to Giordani, and all our friends. Don't weary of loving me: the thought of your friendship, and the memory of the time I spent with you, are a consolation for my solitude, and will still be a comfort for my old age. I haven't seen the *Arcadico*,[5] because literary journals don't reach here. Please let me know if the books I left have been sent to Bologna or somewhere else. Adieu adieu: I embrace you with all my heart. Yours,

Leopardi.

[1] James Fenimore Cooper, the American novelist, was in Florence.

[2] Scott only came to Italy in December 1830.

[3] Tommaseo had written an obituary for Monti in the *Antologia*.

[4] Leopardi had agreed to write on Niebuhr's *Roman History* (which he knew in the English translation), and on Homer.

[5] A Roman periodical; see [22], n. 2.

149

In Florence Leopardi had met and become friendly with Pietro Colletta, a Neapolitan general who had now retired from active military involvement and settled in Tuscany, where he was writing a history of Naples. Colletta was to prove another staunch supporter. Here Leopardi explained his financial predicament.

To Pietro Colletta • Livorno

Recanati, 16th January 1829

My dear General. Thank you no end for your letter of December 25th. I can't tell you how much it cheers me to hear that your health is much improved: and I'm delighted too to hear that you've already completed the sixth book of the History; all the more delighted for its being unexpected, or rather the opposite of what I expected. Your other friends who have read it admire the intrinsic merits of your work: I admire how you have managed to carry on with such an exhausting work in the midst of all the many bodily aches and pains you have had to put up with almost continually; and I'm disconcerted to think that when I am indisposed I'm no good for anything at all, and I don't mean for writing, but even just for talking. Another thing would have cheered me greatly if I'd been in Tuscany; and it is what Vieusseux tells me, that you've decided to leave that blessed villa of yours and spend the summer from now on with your friends in Florence. You're as affectionate and as good-hearted as you are clever. Since you want me to tell you about my state, to show I am grateful and do as you ask I don't balk at the risk of boring you. If I want to live away from home, I must provide for myself; I mean, not live off my father; because my father does not want to support me away from home, and perhaps he cannot, given the great shortage of ready cash we suffer from in this province, where owning property produces no income, and gentlemen live on what their land produces, not being able to convert it into money; and bearing in mind as well that my family's estate, though one of the largest in these parts, is sunk in debts. Now, I cannot provide for myself except by working hard; and with this health of mine I won't be able to work hard again in my life. That is why I had to release myself from the obligations I had contracted with Stella, and lose the allowance I had from him, which was enough for me to live on tolerably: it was, as I think you know, twenty Roman *scudi* (nineteen Florentine) a month. If I found a position that was not too onerous, I mean a public and honourable position (and public positions do not usually require a great deal of work) I would willingly accept it: but I cannot find one here in the papal state, where everything is for priests and friars; and away from here what chance can an outsider have of finding a position? The less able I am to carry out my literary plans, the more of them I have; because, not being able to do anything, I spend my time making plans. The titles alone of the works I would like to write take up several pages; and for everything I have a wealth of materials, partly in my head, partly jotted down roughly on paper. I can give you details of some of these titles, if you wish, and as many as you wish, in another letter; this one is already too long. Be fond of me and write to me, as you promise. If you see Prof Doveri, be kind enough to give him my regards. I embrace you fondly.

150

He continued to explore possibilites for paid employment with his friends from Bologna.[1]

To Giacomo Tommasini • Parma

Recanati, 30th January 1829

Dearest Sir and Friend. The great warmth of feeling you show towards me in your letter of the 16th is not new to me, and does not surprise me; all the same I am touched by it as though it were unexpected. Seeing such great affection for me in anyone at all, I could not fail to feel very pleased; so just imagine seeing it in someone like you. When I wrote those few lines to Adelaide about a position, I knew very well that you would be able to do a great deal on my behalf, even in the situation you were then in: I see that you will be able to do much more now in your new state;[2] my heartfelt congratulations on it, because I consider it to be very suited to and advantageous for your peace of mind and your dignity; but I'm still saddened for this State and for poor Bologna; losing you, one can say it loses the University. The offer you make me to come and live with you is so sweet and so tempting that I accept it, without further thought, as of now, with the greatest gratitude in the world; on the understanding though that this acceptance of mine puts you under no obligation, except insofar as the thing is compatible with your circumstances and your convenience at the time when it can be acted on. Since, as regards the timing, I could not decide that for now. Taking you into my confidence as you take me into yours, I shall tell you that I cannot give my family this burden of supporting me away from home any longer.[3] On the other hand I cannot live in this dreadful town, a tomb for the living, either. So I would willingly accept a position. It is futile to hope to find one here in the State; because, in spite of repeated and solemn promises made by the two most recent secretaries of State, and to foreign ministers as well who had very persuasively pressed my claims, nothing ever came of it. I'd therefore accept a position outside the State; and if it were possible to obtain one in Parma, I'd very willingly come to live in Parma. I'd come anyway if there were some not-too-remote prospect of a position. But without some such basis I could not easily decide to come in autumn, with the necessity of spending the whole winter (and a very severe one) in Parma, employed or not; because once the cold weather had started, my health would not allow me to make the journey again until spring. There, I've explained my situation. Apart from that I have an intense desire to embrace you again as soon as possible: and I ask and I trust you, when the time comes, to use your power on my behalf in Parma, in the way that best suits you and that you judge appropriate. Because truly I would owe my life to you, if by your doing I were to leave this prison, to come and live by your side.

1 See [130].

2 Tommasini, a professor at the University of Bologna, had been promoted to a position at the court and university in Parma, where he might be able to use his influence even more effectively to secure employment for Leopardi.

3 In fact, of course, they had not been supporting him, but this is a tactful way of insisting on his need for independence.

I hope that Antonietta's headache cleared up quickly, and that at present she is in good health: and I am not going to put a sinister interpretation on your silence about Adelaide's health and Ferdinando's. Give them all my fondest regards. Love me, and if there is anything I can do for you, do ask.

151

In his desperate desire to get away from Recanati, Leopardi was prepared to consider improbable solutions, even that of a University chair in a subject (Natural History) of which he disarmingly confessed he knew very little.

To Ferdinando Maestri • Parma

Recanati, 6th February 1829

My very dear friend. I'll begin by thanking you for having banished that confounded Spanish third-person formality, to treat me with the intimacy that befits our friendship.[1] I don't want to begin thanking you for the supreme, boundless warm-heartedness that you and Antonietta and Adelaide show towards me, because that on its own would take up more than the whole sheet of paper; and then I'll assume you understand it without my talking about it: because people capable of such affection as you are must know the strength of the gratitude my mind feels, much better than I could express it.

So I come to the matter in hand:[2] here I see two very serious difficulties. The first is that on that subject I am, strictly speaking, a dunce: and God knows when it will be possible for me to set about studying it in depth, in order to learn as much as is needed to teach it to other people, given my state of health which, as far as being able to study is concerned, is growing worse every day. Will-power together with good health can achieve a great deal, but will-power without health can do little or nothing. The other difficulty is the stipend. I'll tell you frankly that four *luigi* a month (in fact not even that much) is too much for my deserts, but too little for my needs: I've never been able to live anywhere on less than five. And after all Parma is a capital city, it has a Court, there is no shortage of money there; in consequence prices there can't be too low. My frail health requires certain comforts in life that other people would not need, and in particular I'd have to spend more than another person to protect myself from the cold, which in Parma goes on for a long time, and for me would feel severe as I'm used to milder climates. And even in them winter is for me a continual and present danger of serious illness.

I don't know if it will be possible to get around these difficulties. But so that you can see that my frame of mind is positive, I'm putting some questions to you; please answer them in detail.

If I were to accept the chair, when would I have to come to Parma? Note that, if I want to learn something of the discipline, it would be necessary for me to come and live in Parma or

[1] Maestri had in his letter for the first time addressed Leopardi as *voi*. The more formal third-person form of address, introduced into Italian in the sixteenth century, was a heritage of Spanish domination in the peninsular.

[2] i.e. the offer of the chair of Natural History at the University of Parma.

Bologna some time before beginning to lecture; because here there is no way of doing so.

Is it necessary, or is it definitely advisable (which amounts to the same thing) to base one's lectures on one's own material; or can one take and explicate a course or other scientific book that has already been published?

Is the course in this subject completed in just one year, i.e. (as you say) about sixty lectures; or in several years?

To lecture in the University is it necessary to have a degree? because I am not a graduate of any Faculty.

Now I add that the desire I have, not just to escape from here, but to escape soon, is truly genuine and heartfelt. And even more heartfelt and deep is the desire I have to come and be in your company, my rare and precious friends. If you thought it appropriate to thank as of now the person who was kind enough to think of putting my name forward for the chair, do so, and very, very warmly. I'd particularly like to write to Antonietta and Adelaide: but my eyes and digestion have no regard for affection and obligation, and do not allow me to satisfy either one. You speak to them for me; indeed do the same for yourself as well, because I say again that I have no words to express the gratitude I feel to you. All of you continue to be fond of me. If Prof Tommasini is still there, wish him all the best in the world from me. When you write to me, don't fail to tell me about your own state of health and that of all the family. I embrace you fondly. Your very affectionate and very devoted friend,

Giacomo Leopardi.

152

Carlo's infatuation with his cousin Paolina Mazzagalli continued. The granting of a dispensation for their marriage had aroused Count Monaldo's alarm. Leopardi, seeking to reassure his father, who was temporarily away in Rome, reported on the state of affairs.

To Monaldo Leopardi • Rome

[Recanati] 10th February [1829]

My dear Papa. I wrote you nothing about that foolish confounded business with this mad Vicar,[1] because it was not a matter of any consequence, and because I could not imagine the misgivings that to my regret I see you have been experiencing. I know that Carlo has written to you about it, I do not know in what terms, but certainly in a way that means you will now (I hope) be calmer. The arrival of the dispensation was not a new development. Paolina's Mother arranged it and perhaps Peppe. But Paolina said that, if it arrived, what she wanted to do with it was keep it in a drawer with Carlo's letters:[2] when it arrived, she said they could tear it up. The Vicar, either of his own accord or pushed by her Mother, went to tell Paolina that the dispensation had arrived, and to urge her to get married at once. Paolina replied

[1] The vicar is Paolina Mazzagalli's uncle, who approved of the union.

[2] i.e. not actually use it to get married.

irritably that she would get married when it suited her, not him; that there had been no untoward behaviour of a kind to make getting married necessary or advisable, soon or ever. The Vicar began preaching about the perils of the flesh if they continued seeing each other without getting married. Paolina turned her back on him. Then the Vicar sent the first canonical reprimand to Paolina and Carlo. Her Mother, who likewise had made a complete break with Paolina over her refusal to marry, does not want them to see each other in the house any more: she is only allowing them to write to each other. They see each other at the theatre, they talk to one another, not from one box to another any more, but in the Mazzagalli's box. The Vicar is lying low, and seems not to want to make a move.

As for the state of affairs apart from that, I assure you and swear to you that Paolina and Carlo are not only averse to marrying, but eager not to do so, now or ever. They are equally determined, however, to remain friends. Carlo is in love, not madly, as he would once have been, but all the more deeply and from the heart. Paolina is certainly in love, although she hates marriage. Desperation alone could lead them to marry, that is if they were prevented from seeing each other any more and from having contact with one another; if they can continue to do so as they did before, which is all they want, they will never get married. Meanwhile Mama continually serves our enemies' ends by scheming in every possible way to prevent Carlo from having any contact with Paolina: it seems she can have no peace of mind as long as Carlo can say or write a word to Paolina. Carlo assures me that Mama does not tell you everything, or the truth: and I believe it. The effect of this scheming could only be the exact opposite of what we want. Time and interfering as little as possible are (you are well aware) the best medicine for passions of this sort. They would like to observe the proprieties as they have done up till now, never having been alone together: gossip, if it is not stirred up and no attention is paid to it, would have no effect. Another thing I swear (and Carlo has promised this to Mama): not even desperation could induce Carlo and Paolina to take a decisive step while you are away.[3] I would also like you to believe me that her Mother and the Vicar, and perhaps other people, have had and have hostile intentions towards you; but Paolina does not; she has acted and acts youthfully, out of passion of heart, and not calculation. If ambition came into it, it was an ambition for gallant attentions, not for anything else. That is why she has made an enemy of her own Mother, more than of other people.

I ask you of necessity, and from the heart, not to make any direct use of any of the things I have told you in confidence here about Paolina's and Carlo's intentions. You are well aware that these are secrets, and that they do not belong to me. Likewise from the heart I ask you not to worry about this unfortunate business, which is no more on the verge of producing consequences now than previously. As for me, I would very willingly do what Mama wishes, persuading Carlo to give Paolina up entirely, if I could persuade him; but you tell me if you have ever known, if you think there has ever in the world existed, a person who has abandoned a passion because of speeches and exhortations. I would write at greater length, but God sees if my eyes and my digestion allow me to carry on. I kiss your hand, and ask for your blessing from my soul. Yours,

Giacomo.

[3] Leopardi's confidence on this point was misplaced: Carlo and his cousin married a month later while his father was still in Rome.

153

Leopardi sent Colletta a list of projects ('castles in the air') he was planning but was now unlikely ever to write.

To Pietro Colletta • Florence

Recanati ... March 1829

My dear General. Certainly, if I come back to Florence, and you are living in the city, we shall be together a great deal, and we'll almost be living together. Oh, you do give me a fine hope. But for now (forgive me) I don't want to hope for anything, so as not to risk falling from too great a height; and then I'm accustomed to not having great hopes, and rarely finding I'm wrong. As for your History, I don't see what services I could perform for you, other than ones of a pedantic kind. In this respect I would willingly be of service; and to shorten the labour for you and lessen the boredom, I'd do everything you wanted. I want nothing but for you to be in good health and well-disposed; for you are in time not only to bring your work to completion, even working on it at your leisure, but to see and hear and enjoy its fame for a long time. As for civilisation, I agree with you: and if I say that there is still much to recover from the civilisation of the ancients, I do not by that mean to deny, or even call in doubt, that modern civilisation has a great many very fine aspects that the ancient world did not have.

The treatise on the nature of men and things would include questions on abstract subjects, on the origins of reason, on the destinies of man, on happiness and suchlike; but.perhaps it would not be obscure, or repeat things said by other people, or be lacking in practical usefulness. Here follows news of my castles in the air.

The story of a soul, a Novel which would have little external action, and that very commonplace: but it would relate the inner experiences of a mind born noble and sensitive, from the time of its earliest memories until death.

Moral characters.

Paradoxes. Not Cicero's, or Zanotti's, or that sort: further from common opinion and no less true.

Lectures on, or a Course on, or the Science of common sense. That is, of the most natural, most sensible and most correct way of thinking about the commonest subjects in life, matters of politics, morals, and such like.

A parallel between the five languages of which our family of languages of culture is composed, that is Greek, Latin, Italian, French and Spanish. Romanian is not a language of culture, nevertheless it would be touched on in passing too; Portuguese goes with Spanish. I already have almost all the material for this; and it would make a big book. The material still has to be organised, and the style as well.

Conversations between the old me and the new me; that is between the man I was and the man I now am; between the man before he had experience of life, and the experienced man.

The Life and Collected Bulls of Peter the Second, pope, joyfully awaited.[1]

[1] The title is ironical: there has been and can be no Pope Peter II. The phrase 'joyfully awaited' [*della felice espettazione*] mirrors and inverts the expected phrase 'of blessed memory' [*di beata memoria*].

You'll laugh at such an abundance of titles; and I laugh at it too, and I see that two lives wouldn't be enough to carry out so many plans. And these are not even a fifth part of the ones I'm leaving out so as not to bore you any further, and because I couldn't explain my thinking about them in a few words. But if my health were good enough for me to be able to write, I'd choose the ones that appealed to me most at the time; and the material intended for the plans that weren't carried out would in large measure go into the works I was writing. After all, this is only chatter, and in all likelihood I'll do nothing with all these plans; you, with just one, not plan, but book, will go down to posterity. I say I'll do nothing, not from not wanting to but from not being able to; for there is no lack of will on my part; and as for glory, I agree with you about that too. Anyhow, instead of glory I'll have your friendship and that of your peers. And I tell you truthfully that reflecting: I saw this or that amiable and admirable man, and I lived with him for a time, and I'm certain that he loved me or he loves me, will be a great comfort to me at all times, however fate chooses to dispose of the life that is left me. Adieu, adieu.

154

He reported to Vieusseux on his increasing gloominess.

To Giampietro Vieusseux • Florence

Recanati, 12th April 1829

My dearest Vieusseux. What excuse can I offer you for my very long silence? what except the state I am in, and the fact that it is almost impossible for me to write? I shan't tell you about my life, and the despondency in which I pass my days, oppressed by a melancholy that by now is not far short of madness: I do not want to bore you and myself with gloomy talk. Your letters are always full of love: tears come to my eyes when I remember you, and the time when I enjoyed your company.

The January-February Antologia, to the extent that I've been able to read it, seemed to me excellent as usual. But you don't know how to restrain yourself, or stick to your good resolutions; and your issues always run to more than ten sheets. Tell Montani that among the many friends his Antologia articles have made for him he is also to count my sister, who gets the Antologia here, and is very happy whenever she sees that *M.*

At this point I get your last letter *with no date.* I'm glad the Niebuhr arrived. Bringing it with me wasn't a waste of time, because before sending it back I took endless notes.[1]

Thank you for the news you give me about our friends, and about the *Monaca di Monza*: I assure you that I'm hugely grateful for it. But you don't tell me anything about your own health any more. I hope that the warmer time of year has completely freed you from the aches and pains the cold caused you.

As for the poetry Anthology, I did everything I could; but whether it was my own

[1] Leopardi had been unable to review Niebuhr's *History* as he had hoped, because of his ill-health.

inadequacy, or the quality of the materials, the work turned out very badly, and I'm extremely dissatisfied with it. That is what I've always told everybody; and that is what I'd like you to say too to Giordani, to Montani, to anyone who might happen to talk to you about it.

From a phrase in Poggi's last article in the *Antologia* (an article which was certainly looked over by Zannoni) I deduce that the Accademia della Crusca, in order not to give the prize to the *Operette morali*, is intending rather to break the rules by awarding the prize *spontaneously* to the *Promessi sposi* by Manzoni, who was certainly not in competition.[2] But please for now don't talk about this suspicion of mine, so that talking about it does not have the effect (should my suspicion be unfounded) of suggesting this course of action to the Academicians: rather, store it away in your memory, as a prediction, and tell me about it in due course.

I've had no further news of Gioberti for a while, and I know he's not getting my letters. My regards to all our good friends, and especially to Montani, Forti, Capei, Tommaseo. Please don't fail to remember me to each of them *individually*. Be fond of me; and if there are Saints who plead for the death of those who desire it, put in a word with them for me. Adieu adieu. I embrace you. I wrote to Giordani a short while ago. Yours,

Leopardi.

Would you be able to give me up-to date news of Brighenti? he never sent me the packet containing my books.

[2] The *Promessi sposi* and the *Operette morali* had both come out in June 1827. Leopardi's guarded approval of Manzoni's novel (see [120, 132, 140]) contrasted with Count Monaldo's huge enthusiasm for it (see Damiani, p. 377), which in turn contrasted with his attitude to his son's book (see [171]).

155

Leopardi had met Vicenzo Gioberti in Florence, where for a few weeks they had been constantly in each other's company, and had travelled with him in the same coach when he returned to Recanati.

To Vincenzo Gioberti • Turin

Recanati, [17th April] 1829

To my great regret I've had no news of you for a long time now. I replied at once to your first and last letter of January 12th, with a long letter in which I thanked you for the literary news you gave me, assuring you that I greatly appreciated it, especially living as I do so far from the civilised world, and that your letters couldn't be so long that I wouldn't wish them to be even longer. I congratulated you on your way of writing, which seems to me very clear and very natural, and I urged you not to put off any longer sharing with the public some of the fruits of your intellect and your learning, both of them very rare. I said many other things, which I do not now recall. Above all I urged you to look after your health, which I really am worried about; although I'm convinced that my letter never reached you, and that this is the reason for your silence, and not indisposition. If this letter reaches you, write to me as soon and as fully as you can, and tell me about your studies and how you are. Vieusseux from Florence asks after you, sends his regards, wants some articles of yours for the *Antologia*, and would like you to find subscribers for him in Turin if you can. My father, who is just back from Rome, sends his warm regards, and so do the rest of my family. Giordani, to whom I've written about you several times, thinks highly of you on account of the great good he has heard about you from those who know you. Adieu, dear Gioberti, give my regards to the illustrious M. and D. Love me as much as I love you, and it won't be little; because I love you as much as you deserve.

156

Leopardi responded negatively to a suggestion from Colletta that he come and live as his guest in Florence, and pay his way if and when he earned money from writing.[1]

To Pietro Colletta • Florence

Recanati, 26th April 1829

My dear General. As I am not confident that I can thank you enough for your letter of the 18th, I am writing to Giordani asking him to thank you as well in my name. The remedy you propose – to imitate Botta[2] – has a great many advantages; but I confess that I cannot bring myself to advertise my destitution in that way. Botta had to do it in order to eat: for the moment I am not under that necessity; and if I were, I'm not sure whether I'd choose begging first or starvation. And don't think that this reluctance of mine comes from pride; but in the first place the thing would make me base in my own eyes, and would thus deprive me of all my mental faculties; then it would not achieve my objective, because living in a big city I wouldn't dare to appear in company, I wouldn't enjoy anything, stared at and pointed out by everybody with pity. I am very, very eager to live near you or with you, but to be self-supporting, not some other way. I'm not refusing to be indebted to you; indeed I declare that, for your many past favours, and for this most warm-hearted and generous offer, I am and will be indebted and have an obligation forever. If I do not accept this course of action, I hope you will not take it amiss; because I have no friend or relative so close that I could accept similar conditions from him; I would not accept them even from my father, if what I get from my father were not rightfully mine. – On top of what is needed for board and lodging, a small additional sum (three or four *monete* a month) could suffice; because for clothing I'd be provided for sufficiently from home. And all told, with two hundred *scudi* a year

1 M1426.

2 Carlo Botta (1766-1837) was the author of a *History of Italy from 1789 to 1814*, which won the Accademia della Crusca prize when the *Operette morali* were in competition; see [154] and [158].

or a little more, I could manage to live. But I wouldn't want you to take too much thought and too much trouble over this matter: because in the end (I understand this very well) if it is difficult to find a livelihood for someone who is capable of doing something, what will it be to find it for someone who, for reasons of health or for other reasons, is not capable of doing anything?

You say nothing about your own health. I take the silence to be a good sign: yet I'd like to know for certain that you are well. And how is the History coming along? Reading your letter again I'm touched to see such great concern and such great affection on your part. Be certain that what you are doing for me is no small thing, since you love me.

157

He was still in touch with his Bolognese friends.

To Adelaide Maestri • Parma

Recanati, 22nd July 1829

My dear Adelaide. I received your gift and Ferdinando's, with your letter of the 6th. But your reply to my letter of the 22nd of May never arrived. I thank you for the snuff, and for all your many affectionate acts of kindness, as best I can, in my mind more than in words: I'd never have enough of them for that, even if I were able write at length. Tell Ferdinand that his Oration seemed to me very fine in its style, and full of true feeling; and that I will write to him about it as soon as I can. My health is not very good; but don't be anxious on this account: my complaint is not fatal, nor of the sort that gives any hope of becoming so shortly. The secondary complaints of inflammation (which I'd never suffered from in Recanati) have stopped, it can be said; but the main one, which consists in an exhaustion and a *slackening* of the nerves (and which began here), with this climate, this inordinate gloominess, this lack of any variety and any exercise, has increased to the point where I not only cannot do anything, digest anything, but I no longer have any respite day or night. My mind, however, remains always very calm, not from philosophy, but because I no longer have anything to lose or to hope for. How many things I'd like to tell you! but in two days I haven't managed to get beyond these few lines. Do please take care of your health, and be cheerful.

158

He congratulated Vieusseux on the latest number of the 'Antologia,' and enquired again about the Accademia della Crusca prize.

To Giampietro Vieusseux • Florence

[Recanati] 28th August [1829]

To remind you of me I am making an attempt to write, my dear Vieusseux; in three or four days (!!) perhaps I'll manage to complete a short letter. I saw the one hundredth issue of the *Antologia*, I was delighted with it, and I offer you my sincere compliments on the noble and generous candour, frankness, philanthropy and rightness of the views which shine forth in your *Address to contributors.* I assure you that when I receive an issue of the *Antologia*, I think I'm receiving not a number of a journal, but a book. And to my mind your Journal is already in a position no longer just to *help* but to *bring honour* to Italy.

When you write to me, please be so kind as to tell me in which month in 1830 the judging of the quinquennial Crusca prize is to take place.[1]

I got your letter of the 21st of May; thank you so much for the news you gave me of literature and friends. Please do the same thing every time you write. Meanwhile remember me to and give my best wishes to Montani, Forti, Colletta, Gino, Cioni, Capei, Valeriani, Jesi, Pieri, Tommaseo, and Count Gommi. As I write to Florence so seldom, I'm not wrong to name them here one by one, to show that I remember each one of them, and that each one of them is close to my heart.

I'd also greatly appreciate it if through your Turin correspondents you were able to get some news of Gioberti, who has not been answering my letters; and knowing that he spat blood and had other serious ailments in Milan, I am unfortunately very fearful that he may be ill or dead.

Please be kind enough to tell Giordani that I answered the last letter I had from him, dated June 15th, on the 3rd of July; and that his prolonged silence is making me feel anxious and downcast.

My dearest Vieusseux, carry on doing good for Italy and for humanity, and being fond of me, who love you, as you know, with all my heart. Adieu: I embrace you fondly. It goes without saying that, when you write to me, before anything else you are to give me news of yourself. Adieu adieu. Yours,

Leopardi.

1 The Crusca prize was both prestigious and valuable, worth 5000 *scudi*; Leopardi did not win it (see [156], n. 2).

159

He reported gloomily on his health to Bunsen.

To Carlo Bunsen • Rome

Recanati, 5th September 1829

Dear Sir and Friend. My father who loves to imagine that I am better off under the paternal roof than anywhere else, has given you an idea of my state very different from the reality. Not only my eyes but my whole physique are in a worse state than ever. I cannot write or read or dictate or think. Until I have completed it this letter will be my only occupation, and even so I shan't be able to finish it in under three or four days. Condemned by want of means to this horrible and detested abode, and already dead to any enjoyment and any hope, I do not live except to suffer, and I ask for nothing but the repose of the grave.

I have had to go into these tedious details to excuse the lateness of my reply to your letter of August 7th, and also to justify my not responding to your kind invitation to write for the new archeological Journal. Meanwhile I will say in all sincerity that the project, in my humble opinion, could not have been better conceived, thought out and planned, nor carried out with greater distinction. The articles in the *Bollettino* (thank you kindly for the copy), and especially yours and those of Mr Gerhard, are, as far as I have been able to see, exactly what they ought to be to achieve your objective in the most desirable way. I confess too that I am not a little amazed at seeing so successfully overcome the great difficulties you must have encountered in Rome in obtaining a clean print and correct and intelligible Italian.

Towards the end of last winter I was finally able to read Niebuhr's History of Rome in the English translation. Few other books have I ever read in my life with such great and continuous pleasure, and perhaps no modern book has inspired in me such great admiration and respect for its author as this work has. I cannot write at greater length, but I assure you that I count among the very few blessings of my life (which I hope or certainly wish is almost over) that of having been personally acquainted with the author of this history, which will mark a new era in the annals of philosophy applied to philology and knowledge of the ancient world.

Please be so good as to give my regards to Dr Nott, and pay my respects to Councillor Kestner and Mr Gerhard, both of whom I had the honour of meeting in Florence. Look after yourself so that literature may flourish, and be fond of your most devoted and loyal friend and servant,

Giacomo Leopardi.

Please accept my father's good wishes.

160

He congratulated Colletta on the progress of his History of Naples.

To Pietro Colletta • Livorno

Recanati, 22nd November 1829

My dear General. Your letter of the 31st of October was a great comfort to me, as further evidence of your compassion for me, and still more because it has eased my mind a little about your health, which was causing me great anxiety. Now I am very hopeful about it, because I think I have managed to work out that the cold time of year in the end suits you better than the hot. You truly do need monuments, as you say, for staying in the shade. The edifice and monument, *aere perennius*,[1] will be your History: I'm delighted that it has grown by two volumes: and God knows how much I would enjoy hearing it read aloud. But I swear to you that I see no possibility or hope of leaving this detested place; although at this point horror and despair at my state would lead me, in order to escape from this Hell, to put aside my old pride, and embrace any course of action, accept any offer: but, except for dying, I see no possible recompense, as I am not fit for anything. Meanwhile for the loving invitation you extend to me I thank you fondly, and almost tearfully, over and over again; and equally often I urge you to take care of your health, which is precious to Italy and dearer to me than my own life, which I hope you will long outlive. Write to me as much as you can; give my regards to Gino and Giordani, who does not answer my letters any more, or perhaps his letters go astray. Adieu, adieu with all my heart. Your loving and grateful

Leopardi.

[1] *more lasting than bronze.*

161

After sixteen very unhappy months in Recanati – during which time, however, he wrote four of the great masterpieces of Italian lyric poetry[1]*– in desperation Leopardi again tried to find a way of supporting himself away from home, not ruling out even the most undignified occupations. By this time he was a writer and scholar of international standing.*

To Giampietro Vieusseux • Florence

Recanati, 21st March 1830

My very dear friend. I am resolved, with the little money that remains from when I was able to work, to set out on a journey to seek health or to die, and never to return to Recanati again. I will not be particular about what I do; any situation compatible with my health will suit: I shall not mind humiliations; because there does not exist a humiliation or abasement greater than what I suffer living in this centre of European boorishness and ignorance. I no longer have anything to lose, and even putting my life at risk, all I risk is gaining something. Tell me *in all sincerity* if you think that in Florence I could manage to survive by giving lessons or talks on literature *at home*; and if I would find something quickly; because the money I have to live on won't last long. I mean literary lessons of any kind at all, even the most elementary: of language, grammar, and suchlike. And I would like you to reply as soon as you can, because I shall leave soon, and in the light of your reply I shall decide if I am to head for Florence, or search out other glimmerings of hope in other places. Adieu, dear and precious man. You will already have my letter of the 3rd. Give my regards to Giordani, Colletta, Montani and all our friends. A fond embrace and kiss. Yours,

Leopardi.

I'm asking you this question about giving lessons, because I cannot compose, write, read. I could give lessons, that is teach, having someone else do the reading.

[1] *Le ricordanze* (Memories) [August 1829], *La quiete dopo la tempesta* (The Calm after the Storm) and *Il sabato del villaggio* (Saturday in the Village) [September 1829], and *Canto notturno di un pastore errante dell'Asia* (Night Song of a Wandering Shepherd in Asia) [October 1829, completed the following spring].

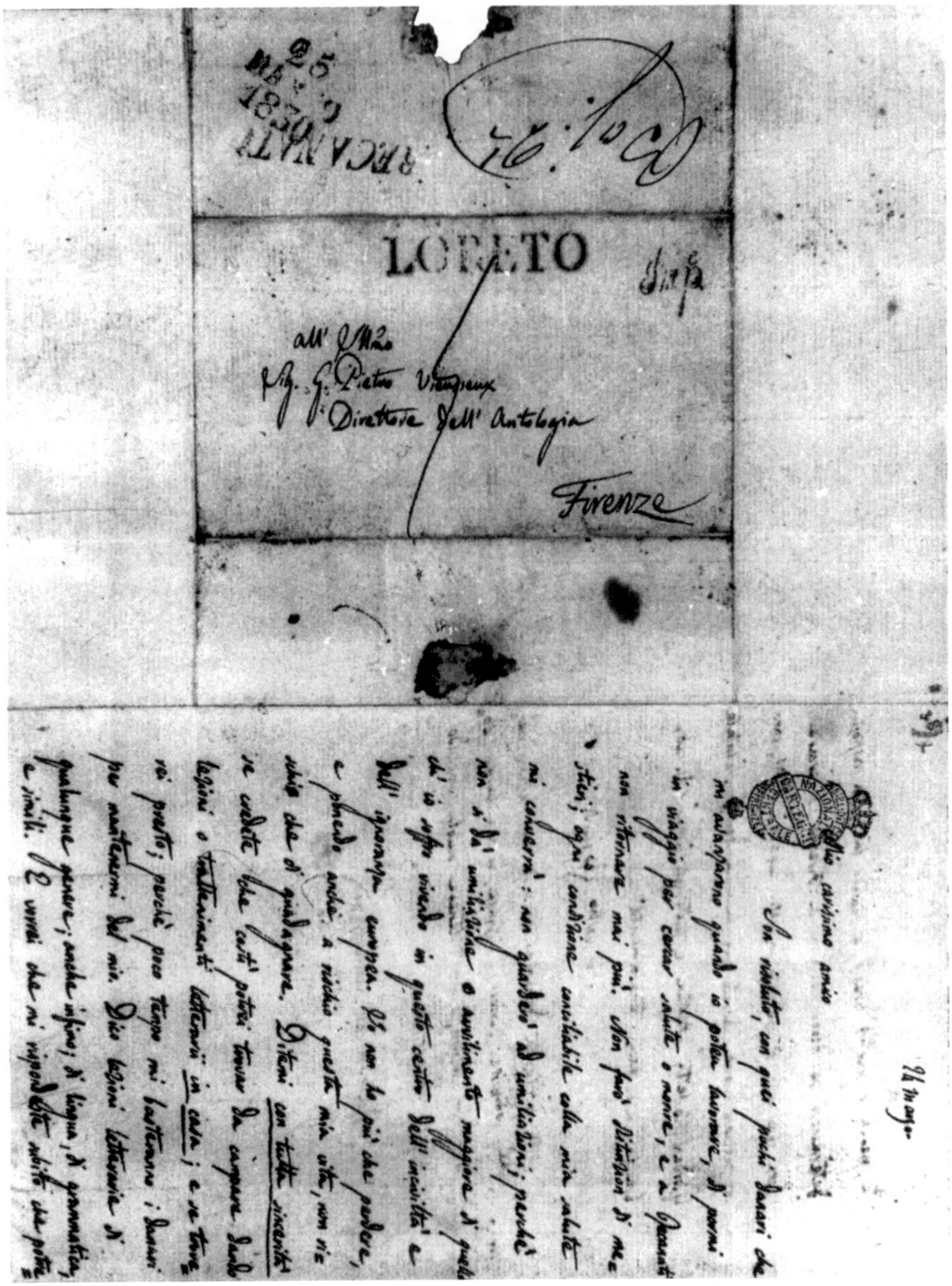

Fig. 6 Letter to Giampietro Vieusseux from Recanati, 21st March 1830
Courtesy of the Biblioteca Nazionale Centrale, Firenze

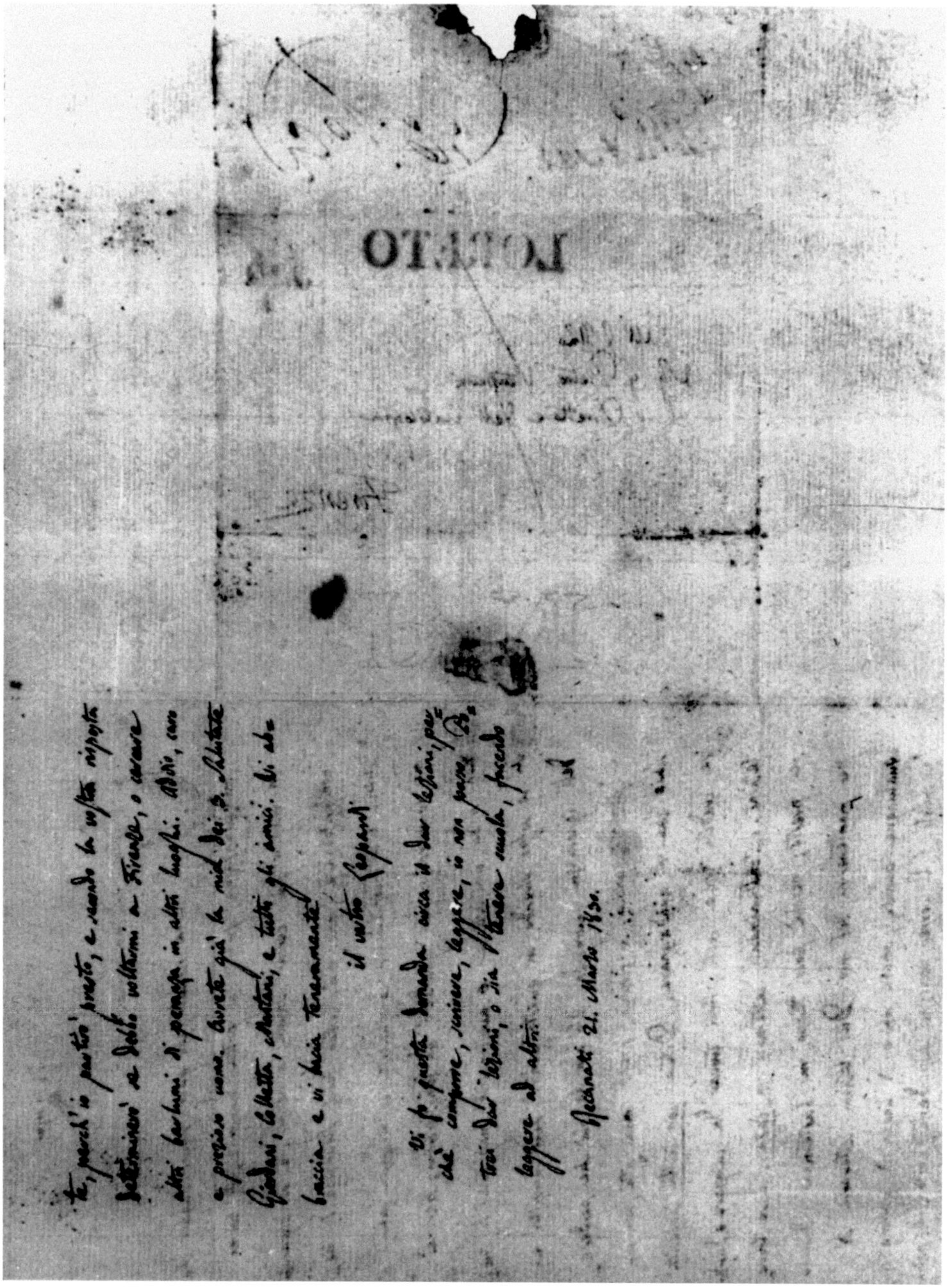

te, perch'io partirò presto, e secondo la vostra risposta determinerò se debbo voltarmi a Firenze, o cercare altri barlumi di speranza in altri luoghi. Addio, caro e prezioso uomo. Avrete già la mia dei 3. Salutate Giordani, Colletta, Montani, e tutti gli amici. Vi abbraccio e vi bacio teneramente

il vostro Leopardi

Vi fo questa domanda circa il dar lezioni, perchè comporre, scrivere, leggere, io non posso. Potrei dar lezioni, o dir meglio tenere scuola, facendo leggere ad altri.

Recanati 21. Marzo 1830.

162

Colletta had written reporting that 18 francesconi a month, the sum on which Leopardi had said he could live, were now available for him for a period of one year.[1]

To Pietro Colletta • Florence

Recanati, 2nd April 1830

My dear General. My circumstances would not allow me to refuse your kind offer, from wherever and however it came, and you and your friends know how to offer help in such a manner that the most reluctant man would consent to be the recipient of help from people such as you. I therefore accept what you are offering me, and I accept it so confidently, that not being able (as you know) to write, and barely able to dictate, I put off thanking you to when I can do so in person, which will be soon, because I shall leave in a few days. For now I will only say that your letter, after sixteen months of dreadful night, after a way of life from which God preserve my worst enemies, was like a ray of light to me, more blessed than the first glimmer of dawn in the polar regions.

I lived in Florence for three months in Via del Fosso (which is mostly confused with Via Fiesolana), at number 401, first floor, with the Busdraghi sisters, good-hearted and sensible people. If you will be so kind as to send someone to ask them if they have a room free *for me*, and should they have one, to let me know in *Bologna*, you'll be doing me a service I'd much appreciate, because I'll go straight to their lodgings and get off the coach there. Should they not have one, it would be enough, without writing again, if you were so kind as to ask the people at the Fontana to see if they can keep the room I used to live in free for me.

Adieu, my dear General. I won't ask about your health or the History, because I hope to talk to you about them soon, and we'll talk about them at length. Yours,

Leopardi.

If you write to me in Bologna, please write poste restante, otherwise they would forward the letter to Recanati.[2]

1 M1487. The tact and delicacy with which the anonymous offer was made are worth noting: 'You will have 18 *francesconi* a month for a year, beginning, if you like, next April. I shall hand that sum over to you in advance each month; but I shall have no other duty and role than passing it on: nothing shall come from my purse: those who give do not know to whom they are giving; and you who receive it do not know from whom it comes. It will be a loan, should you choose to give back the sums you receive; it will be less than a loan, should there be no opportunity to reimburse it: no one would know who to ask for it; you would not know who to reimburse. There are no conditions attached to it. May Italy's good fortune decree that you, regaining your health, are able to write works worthy of your intellect; but this hope of mine does not constitute an obligation for you.'

2 The signature and final sentence are missing in Moroncini's edition.

163

Having accepted Colletta's offer, Leopardi returned to Florence, where he arrived on the 10th of May. He sent Paolina a copy of an etching based on a pencil portrait of himself which had been done by Luigi Lolli in Bologna in 1825.

To Paolina Leopardi • Recanati

Florence, 18th May 1830

Dear Pilla. The portrait is very ugly: nevertheless show it around in Recanati, so the townsfolk can see with their own eyes (the eyes of the body being the only ones they have) that *the Leopardi hunchback* is reckoned to be something in the world, whereas Recanati isn't even known by name. The enclosed will help you retrieve the package, when you have occasion to go to Ancona. Antonietta Tommasini still hasn't received my letter, after all the trouble we took over sending it. A few months ago word spread in Italy that I had died, and the news gave rise here to a grief so universal, so genuine, that everybody still talks to me about it with feeling, and they describe those days to me as full of agitation and mourning. You be the judge of how much I ought to value the friendship of such people. I'm in my usual state as far as my head is concerned, apart from that pretty well. Regards, it goes without saying, to Don Vincenzo too. I'll write to Mama soon. Tell Carlo to write to me.

164

In this letter to his mother Leopardi countered what seem to have been explicit charges of hypochondria.[1]

To Adelaide Leopardi • Recanati

[Florence] 28th May [1830]

Dear Mama. I have been ill with the rheumatism I brought with me, neither more nor less than I was in Recanati in those bad attacks I suffered. Now I am better, and yesterday I lunched at his villa with the Minister, Corsini, who sends every day to enquire after my health.

I have just received the letter from the family dated the 18th. I am delighted that Papa's feverish spells have stopped. Would to God that my complaints were only in my mind because I look well. It seems impossible that anyone should dismiss as imaginary the dreadful unfitness of my eyes and mind for any slightest use, the utterly wretched way of life that mine is. I hope that death, which I constantly invoke, will do me this blessing too along with the countless other blessings I expect from it – that it will convince other people of the reality of my suffering. Commend me to the Madonna, and I kiss your hand with all my soul.

[1] The letter to which he is replying does not survive.

165

He reported on his health to his friends in Bologna.

To Antonietta Tommasini • Parma

[Florence] 19th June [1830]

My dear Antonietta, my dear Adelaide. Here is a brief report on my health. *All* my organs, the doctors say, are healthy; but *not one* of them can be used without great suffering, on account of an extreme, unheard of *sensitivity*, which in the last three years has very stubbornly increased *every day*: almost every action, and almost every sensation, causes me pain. I am delighted that your health is tolerable. I came here (where I do have many friends) for reasons it would take too long to explain: I shall stay for as long as the small amount of money I have lasts; then the dreadful night of Recanati awaits me. I can't write any more. My fondest regards to all of you.

166

He reported to Paolina that all his philological manuscripts had been handed to De Sinner, a foreign scholar who would see to their publication.

To Paolina Leopardi • Recanati

[Florence] 15th November [1830]

Dear Pilla. The foreigner who wanted the *Eusebius* is a German philologist[1] to whom, after many sessions together, I've formally handed over all my philological manuscripts, notes, comments etc., beginning with the *Porphyry*. God willing, he'll write them up and complete them, and have them published in Germany; and he promises me money from them and a great name. You can't think how cheered I am by this development; for a few days it has taken me back to the ideas of my early youth; and God willing, it will give life and usefulness to vast labours, which for many years now I'd regarded as utterly wasted, because of the impossibility of perfecting works of this kind in Italy, because of the contempt in which studies of this kind are held by us, and worst of all because of my physical state. That foreigner has trumpeted my praises in Florence as a hidden treasure, as a better philologist than all the French philologists (Italian ones don't rate a mention, and he lives in Paris); and he says he wants to trumpet my praises like this throughout Europe. I think I won't go to Pisa, because I'm very fed up with moving. If someone from Recanati is writing to Melchiorri, tell him to send me the signatures or names of the subscribers he's got, unless he wants them to be useless to me, as I'm on the point of using them. I've heard nothing from him. Adieu adieu. Hugs to everyone.

[1] Luigi De Sinner (in fact a Swiss), who would become an important correspondent; see [176, 185, 187, 205, 211, 218]. Leopardi's achievement as a philologist is assessed by Sebastiano Timpanaro in *La filologia di Giacomo Leopardi* (Florence, Le Monnier, 1955), which includes a list of studies devoted to the question of De Sinner's role in this context.

167

With the spread of revolutionary uprisings to Romagna and the Marches, a provisional governing committee had been set up in Recanati; on 19th March 1831 Leopardi was officially chosen to represent his birthplace as deputy to the National Assembly in Bologna. (Count Monaldo, with typical deviousness, signed the official invitation but wrote privately to his son urging him to decline the post.) By the time he received the news and wrote his answer ten days later, both the Recanati Committee and the National Assembly had been overturned by the arrival of the Austrians.

To Monaldo Leopardi • Recanati

Florence, 29th March [1831]

My dear Papa. I hope you will be happy with the enclosed, which you are to seal. However I very much want the city and the province to forget me and my family completely now: be quite certain that they can do nothing that is more in our interest. I am pretty well. The Austrians are in Rimini. I already wrote to you a few days ago. Yours,

Giacomo.

Having written my answer, I see from more recent news that perhaps the Austrians will get to Recanati before this letter does. I therefore think it is enough for you to make this answer in my name, adding whatever you think appropriate. I would like you to let Morici know that I received his letter of the 16th, and I send him my regards; that I did not reply because I can write very little, as usual, and because events themselves are a sufficient answer.

168

His official response to the Governing Committee expressed his sense of honour at the appointment.

To the Provisional Governing Committee • Recanati

Florence, 29th March 1831

Dear Sirs. I am infinitely sensible of the honour done me by your Excellencies and by the City Council, in electing me as your Representative to the national Assembly which was to take place in Bologna, as I am informed by your honoured dispatch of the 21st of this month. I imagine that Your Excellencies are now aware of the occupation of Bologna effected by the Austrian troops many days ago, and of the departure of the Provisional Government from that city to set up its headquarters in a safer place. It is not easy here to get accurate information about this place, which in any case seems to change from one day to the next, and it would be impossible as well to get passports for there. At least for the moment, therefore, the changed circumstances make it impossible to act on the decisions taken by your Excellencies in relation to me, but they destroy neither the very deep gratitude I feel at the trust shown in me by your good selves, nor my passionate desire to serve this country of mine, whatever the cost to myself and whatever the effort, whenever the times allow it and my activity does not seem doomed, as in this case, to be completely out of place.

With profound respect I remain your Excellencies' most humble, most devoted, most obliged servant,

Giacomo Leopardi.

169

Antonio Ranieri, a dashing young Neapolitan living in exile in Florence, had become a good friend. Letters to him would have a new conspiratorial tone.

To Antonio Ranieri • Florence

[Florence, before October 1831]

Make it quite clear to the travellers' guide that it's a question of women and not something else: mightn't he be a spy? Think hard about it. I'd like to see you before you go to call on Fanny Targioni.[1]

[1] i.e. Fanny Targioni Tozzetti; see [170, 175, 189].

170

Leopardi had asked Paolina to send some of his letters from well-known people, to give to Fanny Targioni Tozzetti, a prominent figure in Florentine social life who had become a new friend. She collected autographs.

To Paolina Leopardi • Recanati

[Florence] 2nd July [1831]

Dear Pilla. I received the package in perfect condition, and I thank all of you for it from the heart.[1] The portrait must certainly be sent with a wrapper, as printed matter. If I said *wrapped*, I meant to say open at each end, that is with a broad strip of wrapping paper. I'd like a cilindrical tube, or something rigid, so that the portrait didn't get crushed: if the post office won't have it, take it out: but I don't think that's the problem; all that's needed is for the etching to pass as printed matter and not as a parcel, which is achieved by leaving it visible.

*Charlotte Bonaparte is a charming person; not beautiful, but with much wit and taste

[1] The package contained autographs for Fanny.

and very cultivated. She draws well, she has fine eyes. I went to see her yesterday evening for the third time; she'd been ill for several days. She asked me to write my name in her Album: that means that I must pay her a compliment in writing. As I don't like improvising, I asked for time. She made me promise I'd go back this evening, whether I was ready or not.

Adieu, my dear Pilla.* I'm well, thank God, though still weak, still incapable of enjoying myself, not able to read or write or walk much, and all entertainment is a strain for me. A hug for Carlo and Pietruccio (why don't you say anything about him?) and a kiss on the hand for Papa and Mama. Adieu, ma chère Pillule.

* The text between the asterisks is in French, as are the last four words of the letter.

171

His father had offered unsolicited advice about emending passages in the 'Operette morali' which were not to his liking. Leopardi tried to explain his approach.[1]

To Monaldo Leopardi • Recanati

[Florence] 8th July [1831?]

God knows how grateful I am to you for your advice about my book. I swear to you that my intention was to write *poetry in prose*, as the custom is nowadays; and so to follow this or that mythology as I chose; as one does in poetry, without in consequence being thought a pagan, Moslem, Buddhist etc. And I assure you that that is how the book has generally been taken, and so with the approval of very strict theological censors it has circulated freely in the whole of the Roman state, and from Rome, from Turin etc. I have had praise for it from very learned priests. As for correcting the passages you indicate, and which at the moment I cannot call to mind, I promise I will think seriously about it; but God knows now whether it would be *physically* possible for me, I don't say to correct the book, but to reread it. You must trust the experience I have in these matters by now, that any declaration or protest I were to publish would only create a scandal, and whatever there might be in the book that was dangerous would only be more sought out, more remarked on, and more harmful. I am delighted, and many people will be delighted, at the publication of the *Memoriale*.[2] I would not like the portrait to go outside the family, among people who do not know me: it is too ugly. If it is sent to Rome, no matter what the agreement is, the printer will make copies for himself, as always happens. I am pretty well, thank God; but my eyes and my head do not get even a tiny bit better. Yours,

Giacomo.

1 Count Monaldo's letter does not survive.

2 Count Monaldo, competing with his son who had done the same thing (see [99], n. 1), had composed a fake fourteenth-century text, which was now to be republished.

172

Leopardi had gone unexpectedly to Rome (probably to keep an eye on Ranieri, who was pursuing an actress, Maria Maddalena Pelzet) and aroused Carlo's curiosity.

To Carlo Leopardi • Recanati

Rome, 15th October 1831

My dear Carluccio. Thank you so very, very much for the affectionate curiosity that dictated your letter. It's natural that you can't guess the reason for my trip to Rome, when even my Florentine friends, who have a great deal of information that you don't have, are making conjectures that are way off the mark. Please exempt me from relating a long story, much grief and many tears. If one day we see each other again, perhaps I'll have the strength to tell you everything. For now, I want you to know that my stay in Rome is like a very bitter exile, and that as soon as possible I'll go back to Florence, perhaps in March, perhaps in February, perhaps even earlier. I sent the books back to Recanati because they are no use to me. Take care, I entreat you, not to let it transpire that there's any mystery about my move. Talk about the cold, about makeshift plans, and suchlike. Forgive me if I'm so laconic: my heart doesn't let me say any more; then I have ten or so letters to write, and my eyes are bad. Give my regards to our Paolina and your Gigia;[1] and keep me fully informed of the gossip that N. N., and the rest of Recanati, who surround me and persecute me with visits, will surely invent when they talk and write about me. Not the least of the trials I suffer in Rome is seeing myself practically back at home; so much Recanati riff-raff, unknown in all the rest of the world, is here in this city. I congratulate you warmly on your savings, and urge you to keep it up. Adieu, my dear Carluccio.

[1] i.e. their sister Paolina and Carlo's daughter Gigia (whose mother was also called Paolina).

173

Leopardi's unexplained absence from Florence had inspired rumours about ecclesiastical preferment which incensed him.

To Giampietro Vieusseux • Florence

Rome, 27th October 1831

My dearest Vieusseux. I've received your letters of the 8th and the 18th of this month from our excellent friend Capobianchi, and the July *Antologia*, which (unless you tell me otherwise) I'll give back to you in Florence with the others you choose to send me. I still can't tell you anything about articles or literary pursuits, because I'm swamped with visits, formalities, and tiresome things of every sort, which, in this capital city of diplomacy, must then be punctiliously returned: things that make me despair. In general I saw that your latest issue is even stronger than usual in good articles. I've spoken to Odescalchi and Betti: but for now there's no talk of stopping the *Giornale Arcadico*; on the contrary I think they are prouder of it than ever, as a European work, an instrument for the *civilising* and perfecting of man. Thank you for the news you give me about Colletta, sad though it is: please remember me to him often, and say a thousand fond things to him in my name.

Before I left I told anyone there who wanted to know, and I'm telling everyone here, that I'll go back to Florence when the cold weather is over; and so it shall be, if I don't die first. I'd like you to repeat this to anyone who talks about holy orders or cardinals' hats, things I'd consider insults if they were said seriously. But they can't be said seriously except as a deliberate lie, as my way of thinking is very well known, and it is known that I've never betrayed my thoughts and principles by my actions.

Give my very warmest regards to the admirable Gino, to Montani, to Capei and to Forti; and then to everybody who might appreciate your passing them on. I wrote to Giordani a short while ago. Ranieri sends his fond regards and thanks you for remembering him. Adieu, dearest Vieusseux: I give you a heartfelt embrace; please be fond of me. Yours,

Leopardi.

174

Carlotta Lenzoni was a marchioness whose salon he had attended in Florence.

To Carlotta Lenzoni • Florence

Rome, 29th October 1831

Dear Lady and Friend. Thank you no end for your letter of the 14th, which I am late answering because I have been and still am really overwhelmed by visits and formalities that leave me no peace. Among my other regrets on leaving Florence was that of not having been able to greet you on your return from Paris, nor talk to you at length about your trip, nor enjoy your salon this winter. I say this winter, because in truth it never entered my head to settle in Rome, as they told you in Florence; and it is not my fault they said so, because before leaving I left word for anyone who wanted to know, that when the cold weather was over I would come back to Florence. And now I say again to you that unless I die first (a thing highly desirable, but not probable), I shall most certainly go back to Florence in February or March. And if I were to pay heed to the aversion I feel at these antiquated customs, and at seeing priests treated deferentially, and at hearing talk of his eminence this and his holiness that, I'd be capable of turning my back on all these fine columns and fine palaces and fine walks, and returning to Florence without even waiting for the cold weather, which this year seems to be in no hurry.

I saw decent, amiable Tenerani,[1] and talked to him a great deal about you, and we shall do

[1] The sculptor Pietro Tenerani (1789-1869), a pupil of Canova's and friend of Giordani.

so again, if I see him often, as I mean to. I don't know if you are familiar with another Psyche he is working on, which I thought very fine, as I did also his bas-relief for the tomb of a young woman, full of grief and sublime steadfastness.

Giordani wrote to me not long ago: I replied at once enclosing the letter in one to Adelaide Maestri for safer delivery.[2] Ranieri thanks you warmly for remembering him, and pays his respects; and I ask you please, please to remember me often to Buonarroti, Forti, Jesi and in general to your whole clever, kind salon. Be fond of me, and continue to give me news of your health, which I very much hope may remain as good as it is at present.

And if there is anything I can do for you in Rome, do make use of my services.

[2] Giordani was under police surveillance.

175

Fanny Targioni Tozzetti had now become an important figure in his emotional life.

To Fanny Targioni Tozzetti • Florence

Rome, 5th December [1831]

Dear Fanny. I haven't written to you until now in order not to bother you, knowing how busy you are. But in the end I wouldn't like you to take silence for forgetfulness, although perhaps you know that forgetting you is not easy. I think you once said to me that often you did not reply to your best friends, but you did to other people, because you were sure that your best friends would not take offence at your silence, as others would. Do me the great honour of treating me as one of your best friends; and if you are very busy, and if writing tires you, don't reply. I long to have news of you, but I'll be content to get it from Ranieri or from Gozzani, whom I ask for it.

I don't think you are expecting any news from me. You know that I detest politics, because I believe, or rather I see, that individuals are unhappy under any form of government; the fault is nature's, which made men for unhappiness; and I laugh at the happiness of the *masses*, because my small brain can't conceive of a happy *mass* made up of individuals who are not happy. Much less could I talk to you about literary news, because I confess that I'm in great fear of failing to recognise the letters of the alphabet, from lack of practice in reading and writing. My friends are shocked; and they are right to seek glory and to do good for mankind; but I who do not presume to do good, and do not aspire to glory, am not wrong to spend my day lying on a sofa, without batting an eyelid. And I find very sensible the custom of the Turks and other Orientals, who are content to sit cross-legged all day long in a daze staring this ridiculous existence in the face.

But it is quite wrong of me to write these things to you, who are beautiful, and privileged by nature to shine in life, and to triumph over human destiny. I know that you too are inclined to melancholy, as all kind and gifted souls always have been and forever will be. But

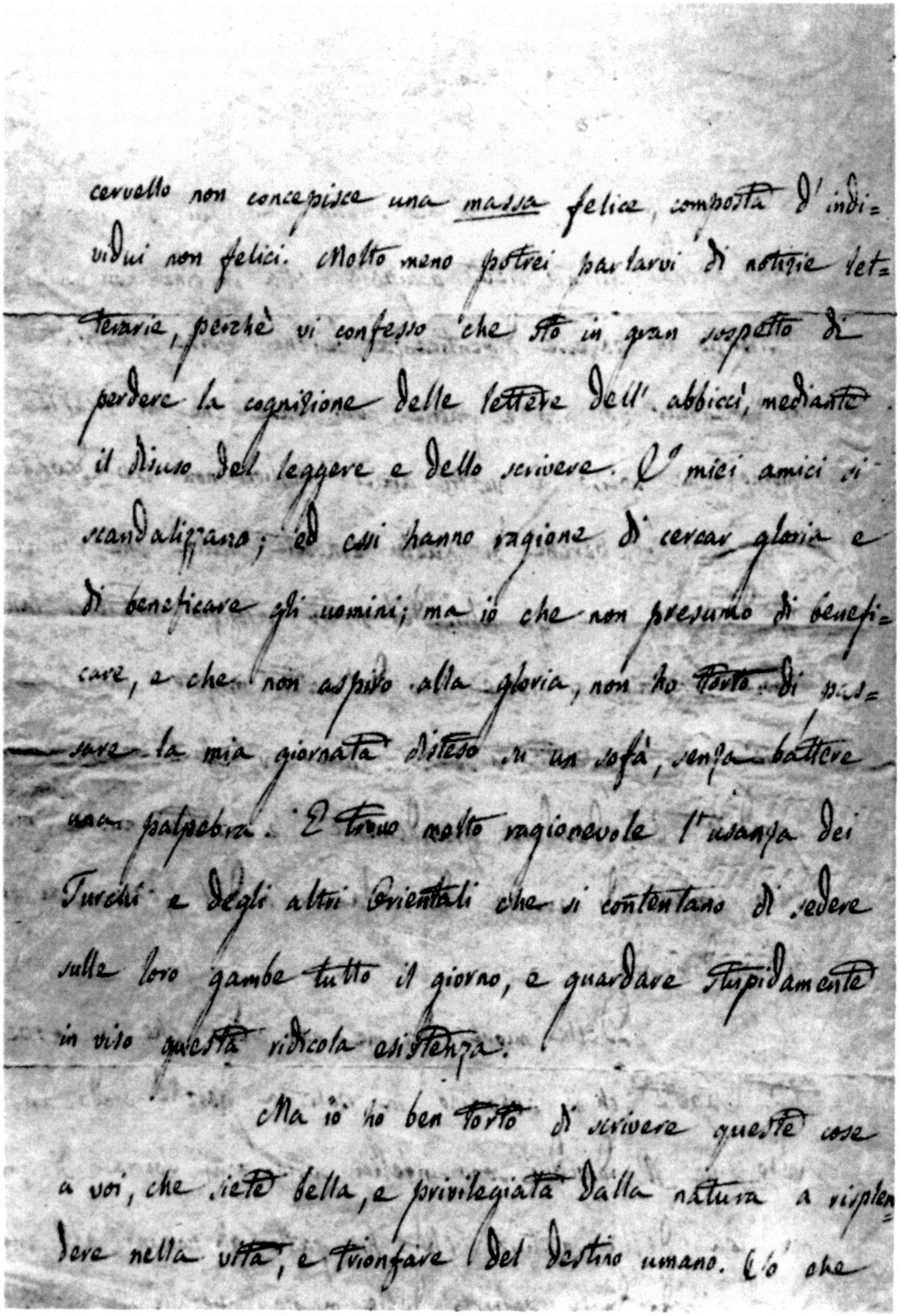
cervello non concepisce una massa felice, composta d'indi=
vidui non felici. Molto meno potrei parlarvi di notizie let=
terarie, perchè vi confesso che sto in gran sospetto di
perdere la cognizione delle lettere dell'abbicci, mediante
il disuso del leggere e dello scrivere. I miei amici si
scandalizzano; ed essi hanno ragione di cercar gloria e
di beneficare gli uomini; ma io che non presumo di benefi=
care, e che non aspiro alla gloria, non ho torto di pas=
sare la mia giornata disteso su un sofà, senza battere
una palpebra. E trovo molto ragionevole l'usanza dei
Turchi e degli altri Orientali che si contentano di sedere
sulle loro gambe tutto il giorno, e guardare stupidamente
in viso questa ridicola esistenza.

Ma io ho ben torto di scrivere queste cose
a voi, che siete bella, e privilegiata dalla natura a risplen=
dere nella vita, e trionfare del destino umano. Ciò che

Fig. 7 From the letter to Fanny Targioni Tozzetti from Rome, 5th December 1831
Courtesy of the Archivio di stato, Firenze

in all sincerity, and notwithstanding my black and desperate philosophy, I think that melancholy does not suit you, that is to say that although it is natural, it is not entirely reasonable. At least I'd like that to be so.

I've several times met Countess Mosti, who has also given me news of you. Adieu, dear Fanny: say hello to your little girls from me. If you deign to give me your instructions, I want you to know that for me, as for the other people who know you, to be of service to you is a joy and a glory. Yours,

Leopardi.

176

Luigi De Sinner, now a close friend and trusted confident, had gone to Paris.

To Luigi De Sinner • Paris

Rome, Via de' Condotti 81, 3rd floor
24th December 1831

My dear, distinguished friend. It has been a matter of great regret to me that I have been so slow in replying to your letter of the 24th of October. But apart from the fact that I received it very late, because by the beginning of October I'd already left Florence, I was then ill for a very long time with rheumatism in the chest, from which I'm still recovering, and it has not been possible for me to write until now. I'd already heard about your trip to Germany from Madame Lenzoni. I assure you that I'm very downcast to hear that your labours on the *Thesaurus* won't go beyond the letter A. All flattery aside, the few specimens I've seen of your work made me hope that Europe would have from you a Lexicon as close to perfection as possible. I know you have published the first instalment, and a few copies of it came to Florence, which it was not possible for me to see. Here I've looked for it, but I haven't managed to find a single copy. It is true that I still haven't seen Monsignor Mai, who could perhaps give me information about it. It would be a great solace for me to have you in Florence, and to be able to live for an extended period with you, for you are one of the most precious and dear acquaintances I have, from whom I could learn so many things. I shall certainly go back to Florence at the end of the winter, and stay there as long as my modest means (already on the point of running out) allow: when they are gone, loathed and uninhabitable Recanati awaits me, unless I have the courage (which I hope I have) of taking the only rational and manly course of action left me.

Madame Lenzoni wrote to me and had people tell me more than once that she was endlessly grateful for the attentions you were kind enough to bestow on her, and that she greatly regretted your trip to Germany, which prevented her from profiting from your kindness for longer and from enjoying your company. So thank you for the honourable treatment accorded the person I commended to you. Mme Lenzoni is now in Florence, well enough in health, and very complimentary about you. I have not seen Rosini this year; he came to Florence after I had gone. He'd had a play of his, *Torquato Tasso*, performed in Pisa, very well received, by his own account. Apart from that, he is still working on his new novel *Luisa Strozzi*. It is a long time since I've seen Mr Mourawieff. He left Florence with his family to go sea bathing at Viareggio, and I don't think he was back when I left.

I'll never be able to thank you enough, my dearest, excellent friend, for the endless trouble you've taken to make my poor things known in these unhappy times. It would be impossible to find someone as zealous for my reputation as your kindness makes you. You are right about Piatti's indolence: it is so extreme that he still has not sent a copy of my *Canti* not just to Paris, but to Siena, thirteen leagues from Florence – a city where there are more than 60 subscribers. I think what you say about the will you intend making should the *Cholera* spread to France is a joke;[1] anyway my manuscripts would be no use to me, since I can't concentrate any more than in the past; and you, if you chose to die, should make a legacy of them to some learned and intelligent friend of yours, to dispose of as he thought best.

You are perhaps expecting me to tell you something about Roman philology. But my health here has been so bad until now that I cannot give you any satisfying news in this connection, as I'm obliged almost always to stay at home. It is true that I am often honoured by literary visits, but they are not at all philological, and in general it can be said that if here people know a little more Latin than they do in northern Italy, Greek is almost unknown, and philology almost entirely abandoned in favour of archeology. How successfully archeology can be cultivated without a thorough knowledge of the classical languages, I leave to your imagination. There are no well-known foreign philologists to be found in Rome this year. I very often see the worthy minister for Prussia, Cavaliere Bunsen, who was a friend of poor Niebuhr's.[2] He has a gathering for scholars in his house every week; so far I haven't been able to take advantage of it, because of my health, as he lives a long way away from me. As you know, he is publishing the *Annals* and the *Archeological Bullettin*, along with Gerhard (a decent, able young man) and other Italian and foreign scholars. I've talked to him a lot about you: he knows you by reputation, but still has not seen any of your work.

Please carry on giving me your news, and keeping me informed about your plans and your hopes. You, my very dear friend, knowing my limitations, never do me the honour of asking me to do anything for you, while on the other hand you never stop doing your utmost on my behalf. But if you think that good will can in some way compensate for my limited ability, please do not spare me. When you write to me, don't put the address of my lodgings on the letter, because in Italy this causes the letters to go astray, given the carelessness of the postmen. Adieu, my excellent friend. Take care of yourself and love me. Yours,

Leopardi.

[1] The cholera was already raging in Germany, and subsequently spread throughout Europe, reaching Naples (where Leopardi was by then living) in 1836-7.

[2] Niebuhr had died in Bonn earlier in the year.

177

The friendship with Antonio Ranieri had now become central to Leopardi's existence. He tried to effect a reconciliation between Ranieri and Ranieri's father, from whom he was estranged, by appealing to common friends, hoping that he and Ranieri might settle in Naples, as in fact they eventually did. (The full story of Ranieri's predicament is told in [181].) Filippo is a code-name for Ranieri, used to avoid his identification by the authorities.

To Carlo Troya • Naples

Rome, 29th December 1831

Dear Sir and Revered Friend. Lady Margherita Altemps has drawn your attention to poor Filippo's hardship, and explained to you the dire straits in which he finds himself. My writing to you as well is not because I presume to have much influence over you, nor because I think many entreaties are needed to move you, but to acknowledge my indebtedness for what you may be able to do for the young man's benefit. I don't know what your view is of the reasons Filippo thinks he has for not going back: I can only assure you that in my opinion, were those reasons explained to you in full, you would consider them valid and fair, unless it were possible (which it is not) for Filippo to go back for a short time. But leaving this aside, because it is not a subject that can profitably be discussed, poor Filippo, because of the debts contracted in order to live in these last six months, and because of his very pressing needs from day to day, finds himself in truly dreadful straits. I am in them too along with him, I can say quite accurately, because we two are so much one thing that I can scarcely imagine any longer how I could live without him. I shall say no more about this joining forces of ours, which is as close as it could be, in order not to go on endlessly. Poor Filippo will try to find some kind of employment so as not to need assistance from his father; but something to help meet his present needs, and the expenses incurred in six months of being left entirely on his own, some allowance, however small, for however short a time, but for just as long as it takes him to manage to find a way of not dying of hardship: any father who is not a beast ought to grant this, and I am very confident that the intervention of a man who has the authority and commands the respect that you do, must induce Filippo's father, even if reluctantly, not to refuse it any longer. Knowing your high-mindedness, I am certain that you will not take offence at the liberty I am taking in drawing your attention to this matter on my own initiative and as something that concerns me, notwithstanding the small disagreements that have arisen between you and Filippo. I am brief, because my eyes, as you perhaps know, cannot stand any strain, and even were I to write at length, I could never commend myself to you enough to match my concern. I say commend myself to you, because the affection which has bound me to Filippo for some time now is such that our destinies are no longer separable, and commending him, I commend myself, for I live in great anxiety on his account. Thank you for the very affectionate and kind things you were good enough to write to Lady Margherita for me, and I assure you that my mind distinctly reciprocates your warmth of feeling. May I have the honour of being given your instructions, and find myself able to be of service to you. Your most obliged servant and friend,

Giacomo Leopardi.

178

Leopardi sent Carlo a copy of the edition of the 'Canti' which had just been published, with instructions that his parents must not see it.

To Carlo Leopardi • Recanati

Rome, New Year's Eve [1831]

My dear Carluccio. I've sent you a copy of my *Canti* with Mandolino,[1] who came to see me as he was on the point of leaving, so I couldn't write to you then, or rather write to you again, because I'd already written you a letter (which I then burned) to send with Corradi. I don't want that copy to be seen by anyone except you, Paolina and Pietruccio; then I want it to be jealously kept safe, to be placed when the time comes in the complete collection of my *works*: since I don't have any other copy. Bear with me, and don't get angry that I still haven't talked about the things you asked about in your last letter. I'd have to write at too great length to give you an adequate account of the state I'm in: besides, I want you to know that coming and living in Rome was and is a huge sacrifice for me, and no gain, but the ruin of my finances. You'll know that poor Colletta died on the 11th of November. If you can, let them know at home that I collected the 40 *scudi* from the diligence;[2] it arrived when it should have, but wasn't handed over earlier because of the doltishness of the Post Office here. I'm well; a bit fed up with the care I have to take because of the time of year and my past illness; I'd got so out of the habit in the last ten months. Don't give a thought to that Carlotta, who's got nothing to do with my circumstances. Adieu, Carluccio: a thousand kisses for Gigia: I'll go back to Florence probably this March.

1 Apparently a coach-driver who operated between Recanati and Rome.

2 The money was a Christmas gift from his father.

179

He continued to plead Ranieri's case.

To Carlo Troya • Naples

Rome, 9th January 1832

Revered Sir and Friend. I have nothing to add to what the excellent Lady Margherita will write to you à propos of Filippo, except just to thank you on my own behalf for the promptness and the effectiveness with which you took up my friend's cause, and to confirm in every detail the account that will be given you by Lady Margherita, assuring you on my word that there is no exaggeration in it, nor anything feigned or concealed. And in particular I think I ought to confirm that having seen from your letter that Filippo's father's mind either is not, or will easily cease to be, as hostile towards his son as was thought, all my efforts have been directed towards inducing Filippo to agree, as he was already inclining to do, to satisfy his whole family by returning to Naples. Indeed to save both him and me the pain of separation – a further cause of his reluctance in the past to return – I have suggested that I should accompany him to Naples, not without very great inconvenience to myself, and hand him over myself into his father's hands. He has decided to make this journey, and I along with him, and we would do so at once, were there not very powerful reasons, which Lady Margherita will be kind enough to explain to you, that oblige us to put it off for two months, that is until the beginning of spring. It remains for you to complete the work begun, by seeking to get the entreaties being made through the illustrious Lady Margherita acted on there in Naples; without this, it will be readily apparent to you that Filippo's situation will be pitiful, and I too (if talking about me matters or means anything) will find myself in great and for me unprecedented difficulties. With deep gratitude and respect, I remain your most obliged servant and friend,

Giacomo Leopardi.

180

In January 1832 Leopardi's father anonymously published a book, 'Dialoghetti sulle materie correnti nell'anno 1831', which seems to have been conceived as a reply or counter-statement to the 'Operette morali', and which immediately became very popular with reactionaries. Here, and in [182], Leopardi merely refers to its success (three editions in the space of twenty-seven days). Later, when it was mistakenly attributed to him, it became a source of great chagrin, and he was forced to issue public denials of authorship; see [183, 184].

To Paolina Leopardi • Recanati

Rome, 2nd February 1832

The *Dialoghetti*, dear Pilla, have been a raging success here: everybody is talking about them. They are in great demand, and I still haven't been able to see them. If you can send me copies by post, I'd be very obliged to you; but do it at once and send as many as you can. I've several times seen and see worthy, decent Matteo, who wishes to be remembered to Papa. I'm spending a fortune here, but it's the fault of the person who found me these rooms in Piazza di Spagna, where all the foreigners are, everything costs four times as much, the service is abysmal, and you're robbed all day long. Anyway, apart from that, Rome is the Italian city (not excluding Milan) where you spend most to get least in the way of amenities and goods. Lodgings especially are outrageously expensive in winter. Summer is a different matter; but then Rome is uninhabitable. Give my best regards to Carlo, and give me news of him. Giordani sends his regards to both of you. Mandolino had no trouble at all finding me, as nobody does who wants to find me. Via Condotti is the busiest place in Rome. The other packet I mentioned is the one I sent to Carlo. Mazzagalli lives not far away from me. Even my landlord comes and asks for a copy of the *Dialoghetti*, although he doesn't know who the author is. Adieu adieu.

181

Leopardi told Bunsen of Ranieri's predicament.

To Carlo Bunsen • Rome

Rome, 16th March 1832

Revered friend and sir. Having never left the house, and seldom left my bed, before my departure, which will be tomorrow, I have not been able to come in person, as I should have done and would have wished, to take my leave of yourself and your good wife, and to ask if there is anything I can do for you in Florence. I want this letter to bear witness to the sorrow I feel, as I leave, that my poor health has prevented me from enjoying your learned and very agreeable company as much as I would have wished, and to remind you also of the intense gratitude that I profess towards you and will profess for as long as I live. Believe me, most worthy and excellent friend, that leaving Rome I feel no other regret as deeply as that of leaving you behind.

The story of young Ranieri, which I would have liked him to tell you, in substance is this. Through no fault of his own, but because of his many close links with an Italian man of letters you know (Mr Carlo Troya), with whom he was at that time travelling around Italy, Ranieri was exiled from his birthplace, the states of Naples, and suffered the distress of receiving the first news of that fact at the moment of asking for his passport in Florence in order to rush to see his dying mother, who subsequently died. Summoned back in January 1831, he would have gone back to Naples, if he had had the certainty, or at least the probability, of being able to leave again. But being left in no doubt, by the example of all the others who had been summoned back, that the opposite was the case, and seeing himself obliged, if he returned, to abandon forever the way of life he had embarked on in the five years he had spent away from his birthplace – that is, to abandon his studies, and all his dearest and most useful contacts – he obtained his father's consent, after some initial reluctance, to his remaining away. However when a few months had passed, his father, a man of weak and completely passive character, now surrounded and dominated by very hostile enemies of the young man, who with his mother's death has lost all his supporters, stubbornly insisted that his son return, revoking the consent given and the promises made, and he suspended his allowance, which the young man has been entirely without for nine whole months. In this state of affairs, I asked your permission to introduce him to you, with the intention that he, confiding his circumstances to you, might ask if you would agree to put in a good word for him with the Prussian delegate, were he to go back to Naples, so that a word from him (and that is all it would have taken) might enable him to get his passport, if he wished to leave again. But I myself then dissuaded him from speaking to you about it, fearing that, notwithstanding his political innocence and your personal kindness, simply because of the position you occupy, you might think it (and it might be) out of place to ask you for a favour on behalf of a person who had once come under suspicion from his government. Now he is going back with me to Florence, resolved to perish rather than bury himself in a place where you know and the whole world knows how one lives.

Adieu, my most revered and precious and incomparable friend. Continue to wish me well; please pay my respects to your good wife, and believe me entirely and forever yours,

Giacomo Leopardi.

182

The popularity of the 'Dialoghetti' was unabated; by now the book had run to six editions (and it would quickly be translated into German, Dutch and French).

To Monaldo Leopardi • Recanati

[Florence] 5th April [1832]

Dear Papa. I received everything from Giambene, except for the letter you told me to expect; which does not surprise me, given the habits of the appalling postal service in that wretched region,[1] where receiving a letter 20, 30, 40 days after the date of arrival *post-marked on it* happens continually and *to everyone*; and this not for political reasons, but from a strange and inexplicable incapacity on their part, which makes them unable to find names; an incapacity found nowhere else in the world, and comparable only to all the other failings of that poor and hopeless government. Here too I have found the *Dialoghetti* very well known, and although the principles and the general spirit (which here are different from that of Rome and Modena) do not allow them to become as popular here as there, nonetheless everybody acknowledges the author's intelligence and merit, Tuscans being very reasonable and impartial in their judgments. Thank you for the new copy of it you sent, especially as I had none left, since a Lady failed to return the last one that I had been keeping for myself. If there was something important in your last letter to Rome, I hope you will be kind enough to repeat it to me. I have had the great misfortune to find my usual rooms, my usual lodgings, occupied, and then on top of that to find the new rooms I had taken damp, so I am obliged to move out immediately, leaving me out of pocket and seriously inconvenienced. Give my fond regards to everybody, and, with all my heart, please bless me. Yours,

Giacomo.

[1] i.e. the papal State; the letter had been sent to Rome.

183

Although the 'Dialoghetti' had been published anonymously, the publisher had let slip the information that the book was by Count Leopardi. By May it was clear that it was being widely attributed to Leopardi himself, and he was forced to issue public denials of authorship.

To Giampietro Vieusseux • Florence

Florence, 12th May 1832

My dearest Vieusseux. I declare that I am not the author of the book entitled *Dialoghetti sulle materie correnti nell'anno 1831*, which some people are attributing to me. Please publish this declaration in your worthy Journal the *Antologia*. I embrace you with all my heart; with best wishes,

Giacomo Leopardi.

Please also arrange, if it is possible (as I hope it will be), for this declaration, *with my name*, to be included in the list of contents on the cover of the issue, and, if possible, on a separate line (a new paragraph), so that it cannot be missed.

184

Leopardi was particularly offended by the rumour that he was a convert to reactionary views.

To Giuseppe Melchiorri • Rome

Florence, 15th May 1832

Dear Peppino. You must do me the favour of putting the attached letter into the *Diario di Roma* immediately. If there is a charge, let me know, and you'll be reimbursed at once. But for God's sake don't fail to do me this favour no matter what. Nobody is compromised by it: it is always permissible to state the truth in this kind of thing. My father himself will find it quite right that I shouldn't usurp the honour owing to him. Besides I can't take any more of this, I really can't. I don't want to show my face any more with this blot on it, of having produced that dreadful, truly dreadful, evil book. Here they all think it's by me: because the author is Leopardi, my father is quite unknown, I'm known, therefore I'm the author. Even the government is looking askance at me because of those filthy, fanatical, awful dialogues. In Rome I couldn't mention my name any more or have it mentioned anywhere, without hearing someone say: *ah, the author of the Dialoghetti.* It's impossible for me to tell you all the ridicule I've had to suffer because of that book. In Milan they are saying in public that I'm the author, that I'm a convert like Monti. In Lucca the book circulates under my name. I'm printing my declaration in all the Italian Journals: it is coming out any time now in the

Tuscan ones. I'm sending a much more strongly-worded one to France. But Rome matters a great deal to me, and although it is a very simple thing I'm asking you to do, that doesn't stop me asking with great feeling. There can't be any difficulty, as I've said, it being always permissible to state that a book is not by you, be it the best and most holy book in the world. [...]

Dearest Peppino, do excuse me all the endless trouble I cause you, without ever being satisfied. Please do forgive me, and carry on being fond of me. Give my regards to Tuta, Nanda and Giacomino; let me know if there is anything I can do for you, and believe me, yours ever,

Giacomo.

185

In this letter to his Swiss friend De Sinner Leopardi tackled head-on, and with great dignity, the charge that his pessimism was entirely explicable in terms of his deformity and ill-health; he invited those who dismissed it in this way to answer his arguments.

To Luigi De Sinner • Paris

Florence, 24th May 1832

I could never tell you how much your charming letter of the 26th of April cheered me, my dear, distinguished friend, and how grateful I felt on seeing the account you give me in it of the endless trouble, beyond price, that you have taken to build your friend's reputation. I'm very sorry, though, that you are so laconic about yourself, especially as you say you are not happy with your situation. Can we hope to see you again in Italy? Can I in particular nurture the sweet expectation of once more seeing at my side a friend so learned, so affectionate and warm-hearted, so indefatigable, with whom I would spend long hours learning, and sharing feelings that few people understand? [...]

I received the pages of the *Hesperus*;[1] for which I thank you very fondly. You are quite right to say that it is absurd to attribute a religious tendency to my writings. *Whatever my misfortunes may be, which they have seen fit to expose and which have perhaps been exaggerated a little in this Journal, I have had enough courage not to seek to diminish their weight either by frivolous hopes of a supposed future, unknown happiness, or by cowardly resignation. My feelings towards fate were and still are those I expressed in *Bruto minore*.[2] It was as a consequence of that same courage that, being led by my researches to a philosophy of despair, I did not hesitate to embrace it whole; whilst on the other hand it has only been

1 A Stuttgart newspaper which in April 1832 had published an article on Leopardi and translations of a poem and of one of the *Operette morali*.

* From this point on the letter is in French.

2 The canzone written in 1821 which purports to record Brutus's last words before he took his own life; see also [23, 77].

because of the cowardice of men, who need to be persuaded of the value of existence, that people have wished to consider my philosophical opinions as the result of my personal suffering, and persist in attributing to my material circumstances what is due solely to my understanding. Before I die, I'm going to protest against this invention of weakness and vulgarity, and ask my readers to apply themselves to destroying my observations and my arguments rather than blaming my illnesses. [...]

186

To his father he accounted for his disclaimer of authorship of the 'Dialoghetti' in terms very different from those he had used to his friends.

To Monaldo Leopardi • Recanati

[Florence] 28th May [1832]

My dear Papa. Paolina tells me that I let months go by without writing. This proves to me that my letters get lost in the post, as I see that among others one has gone missing in which I told you about the books I received from Nobili,[1] and answered some of your questions. The article on the *Evangelical History*, which you will see in the latest number of the *Antologia*, is by Montanari di Savignano, one of the contributors.

In the same number, and in the *Diario di Roma*, and perhaps in other Journals, you will see or will have seen a declaration of mine to the effect that I am not the author of the *Dialoghetti*. You must be aware that, bearing in mind the identity of name and family, and bearing in mind that I am personally acquainted with many people, the knowledge that the book is by *Leopardi* has caused it to be very widely attributed to me. In Rome, where you are better known, two thirds of the public thought it was by me: and I had barely to mention my name or be mentioned by name anywhere and I was hailed as the author of the *Dialoghetti*. Then in Tuscany *everybody* who thought it was by Leopardi (and not by Canosa or other people to whom it has been attributed) thought it was by me. In Lucca the book was circulating under my name. They are saying it has brought about great conversions because of this belief: at least that is what many people have told me: and the Duke of Modena, who probably knows the truth of the matter, nonetheless says publicly that I am the author, that I have changed my views, that I am a convert, that the same thing happened to Monti, that that is what decent men do. And everywhere people are talking about what some are calling this conversion of mine, and others apostasy etc. etc. I have hesitated for four months, and finally I have made up my mind to speak out, for two reasons.

The first is that I thought it unworthy to usurp in a way what was rightly owing to someone else, and above all to you. I am not the man to tolerate taking the credit for another's merits. If Manzoni's novel had been attributed to me, I would have set about denying the

[1] The publisher Nobili had sent Leopardi copies of two of his father's books, the *Dialoghetti* and the *Evangelical History*.

rumour in all the Journals the day I heard it, not four months later. The second reason is that I will not, and ought not, to allow it to be said of me that I am a convert, or that I am like Monti etc. etc. I have never been irreligious or revolutionary in my behaviour or my principles. If my principles are not precisely those which are professed in the *Dialoghetti*, and which I respect in you and in anyone who professes them in good faith, they have still never been such that I had to, or ought to, or wish to, censure them. My honour demanded that I declare that I have not changed my views at all, and that is what I meant to do and did (insofar as it is possible today) in a few Journals. In others I was not allowed to do so.

I believe you will approve of my decision. I would tell you other things and relate them to you in this connection, but my eyes are too strained, and the post is leaving. Perhaps in another letter I will return to this subject. I kiss your hand, and ask for your blessing with all my heart. Yours,

Giacomo.

187

He told De Sinner that the lwo latest 'Operette' could not easily be published in Italy.

To Luigi De Sinner • Paris

Florence, 21st June 1832

My incomparable friend. I replied to your letter of the 26th of April. Now I must thank you for the other one of June 1st, which is all the more appreciated as it gives me your news a little more fully than the earlier one. Mr Pestalozzi had told me that you were bored with the *Thesaurus.* I quite understand that your intelligence and your learning can shine more brightly in works less vast and more truly your own. A position in Germany will perhaps suit you better than anything else. As for me, I sincerely deplore that Italy is so backward in philology, and so poor in resources of every kind, as to leave me with almost no hope of seeing you settled near me. Your presence would be a delight for me, truly a delight, just as your friendship, and your kindness towards me, are a gift from heaven. Souls like yours are so rare that, once known, not only would forgetting them be impossible, but so would not making every effort to retain their affection. You say our friendship must last beyond life. I can't tell you how much comfort these words give me. Yes certainly, my precious friend, we'll love one another for as long as the capacity to love lasts in us. My love will be full of gratitude, yours will have that noble satisfaction that comes from the awareness of having done good.

I've finally got the first installment of the *Thesaurus.* The work lives up to the very great expectations I had for it. I'll say no more, except that I would hope both for myself and for learning that the work might be continued and completed wholly along these lines. Furthermore my friends here are urging me to write a considered article about it for the *Antologia* (which is now the best literary Journal in Italy): and if my health allows it for once, you can imagine with what great pleasure I'll devote myself to this subject. But I don't know how much I can hope for it.

Please do remember me to Mr Bothe, and thank him for being so good as to employ his fine style to make my poor writings known in Germany. You are right about the biography of Ottonieri, an invented name. I'll be grateful for the copy you promise me of Mr Bothe's pages. [...]

The poem that Poerio spoke to you about, and that I was composing at just the time I had the good fortune to make your acquaintance, was never finished, and I don't think it will be. Other unpublished poems, destined to see the light of day, I do not have. I do have two dialogues to be added to the *Operette*, one between *Plotinus and Porphyry* on suicide, the other one, *Copernicus*, on the worthlessness of the human race. You are at liberty to do with these two works what you will: all I need is time to have them copied, and to check the copy. They could not easily be published in Italy. From Rome I have so far only had vacuous replies to the questions you put to me: but I'll go on persisting until I get something precise. It is quite true that it is difficult to do anything in the Vatican Library in the holidays, which last from June to November. The libraries in Rome are closed throughout this whole period.

Adieu, dearest, best and incomparable friend. Heaven grant you a propitious journey. Don't forget the promise you made to write to me at least about Germany, and carry on loving your very devoted friend,

Leopardi.

188

Leopardi was finally reduced to asking his father outright for money to live on, painting a desolate picture of the prospects for literature in Europe.

To Monaldo Leopardi • Recanati

Florence, 3rd July 1832

My dearest Papa. God forbid that I should be upset by the things you say with paternal kindliness in your very affectionate letter of June the 12th. On the contrary, I thank you for them with all my heart, and with my usual sincerity: and God willing, I shall not stop profiting by your advice in the way that seems most appropriate and useful. As for the dry manner in which my declaration was worded, that was exactly what was required, because no censor would have let pass a word for or against the book, or its precepts, or any part of it, or have allowed the slightest hint of discussion on the subject. Besides which my relationship to the author of the book was of such a nature as to rule out any expression of opinion about it on my part, favourable or otherwise.

I am now going to speak to you on an unusual subject: if it upsets me a great deal to talk about it, it will not upset me at all if my talking is to no effect. I think you are convinced of the desperate efforts I have made for seven years to find a way of being self-supporting. You know that the final ruination of my health came from the work I took on four years ago, for Stella, to that end. Reduced to the point where I could no longer read or write or think (and for more than a year not even speak), I did not lose heart, and although I could no longer do anything, yet just with what I had already done, with the help of friends, I tried to continue to find some means. And perhaps I would have found it, partly in Italy, partly abroad, if the extraordinary inauspiciousness of the times had not come to conspire with the other difficulties and make them victorious in the end. Literature is destroyed in Europe: publishers bankrupt, or on the point of it, or reduced to a single printing press, or forced to abandon projects on which a promising start had been made. In Italy it would be ridiculous now to presume to sell anything with honour where literature is concerned, and to propose new projects to publishers: from France, Germany, Holland where I had sent a great quantity of philological manuscripts with very well-founded hopes of earning some money, instead of money I only get Journal articles, biographies and translations. I thus find myself, as you can well imagine, without the means to carry on.

If anyone ever desired death as sincerely and as earnestly as I for a long time have desired it, certainly no one ever desired it more. I call on God as witness to the truth of these words. He knows how many fervent prayers I have said (to the point of reciting triduos or novenas),[1] to obtain this blessing; and how at every slight hope of danger near or far off, my heart lifts with cheerfulness. If death were in my own hands, again I call on God as witness that I would never have talked to you like this: because life *anywhere* is abhorrent to me and a torment. But since it still does not please God to grant my prayer, I would go back to Recanati to end my days, if living there, especially given my present inability to occupy myself, did not exceed my huge powers of endurance. This truth (of which I think you too are persuaded by the last bitter experience),[2] is so fixed in my mind, that in spite of the great sorrow I feel at being far away from you, from Mama, and from my brothers and sister, I am unshakably resolved not to go back to Recanati to live except when I am dead. I have an intense desire to embrace you again, and only the lack of a means of travelling has been able and will be able to prevent me from doing so when the time of year is favourable: but as for going back to Recanati without the material certainty of having a way of leaving again after a month or two, my mind is made up on this point, and I hope you will forgive me if my strength and my courage do not extend to bearing a life that is not to be borne.

I do not know if family circumstances will allow you to pay me a small allowance of twelve *scudi* a month. On twelve *scudi* you cannot live decently even in Florence, which is the Italian city where living is least expensive. But I am not seeking to live decently: I shall make sacrifices, so that all told twelve *scudi* will be enough. Death would be better, but death one must await from God. Should you be able or wish to do this, all you would have to do would be to place the sum of 24 *scudi* at my disposal every two months care of some agent of yours in Rome, informing me who the person is; against it I would draw the same sum here by promissory note. I would appreciate it if your order were for 24 *francesconi*, which would not increase the cost for you by very much, and would make a big difference to me, as one loses a great deal now changing Roman *scudi* or *colonnati* into *francesconi*. And you know that here one spends *francesconi* the way one spends *colonnati* in Recanati.

If circumstances, my dear Papa, will not allow you to grant this request of mine, I urge you

[1] i.e. prayers lasting three and nine days respectively.

[2] i.e. his stay in Recanati from autumn 1828 to spring 1830.

with all possible sincerity and warmth not to have any scruples about rejecting it. I will take some other course of action; and perhaps I should have done so without bothering you at all with this talk: but since the course of action I speak of is such that, my health being what it is, it is likely that in a short time I would succumb, I was afraid you might have cause to reproach my memory, for having adopted it without first taking you into my confidence about the things I have explained. Besides, on the one hand I feel such pain at bothering you, and on the other I am so far from any capricious aim and any cheerful hope in wanting to live away from Recanati, that I have even wished, and would still wish, that I had no possibility of any recourse to my family, so that not being able to support myself, and much less being able to beg, I might find myself in the very real and unavoidable necessity of starving to death.

My dear Papa, forgive this melancholy talk which I have had to have with you for the first and last time in my life. Be assured of my supreme indifference towards my future on this earth, and if my request strikes you as excessive, or importunate, or unseemly, pay no mind to it.

In any case, if God decrees I should go on living, I will not stop striving, as I have in the past, with all my strength, to find a way of living without being a burden on the family, and to put a stop to the allowance that I am asking you for now.

Bless me, my dear Papa, and pray to God for me; I kiss your hand with all my heart. A thousand best wishes to Uncle Carlo and the cousins. Again I apologize for the melancholy with which from necessity, and contrary to my every inclination and habit, I have come this time to pester you. Your very affectionate son,

Giacomo.

189

To Fanny Targioni Tozzetti • Livorno

Florence, 16th August [1832]

Dear Fanny. I am writing to you, then, although you will be back soon; not to ask for your news any more, but to thank you for your kind letter on Monday. That you were pleased at my wishing to hear about your health is a consequence of your kindness. You have cheered me up a great deal telling me that you are well, and that the bathing is doing you good, and the children too; I was a little worried about it because sea bathing seems to me not entirely free of risk.

Ranieri is still in Bologna, and still busy with that love of his, which is making him unhappy on various counts.[1] And yet certainly love and death are the only two fine things the world offers, and absolutely the only ones worthy of being desired. Just think, if love makes man unhappy, what will other things do that are neither fine nor worthy of man. From Bologna Ranieri had asked me several times for news of you: I sent him your little letter at once the day before yesterday.

[1] Ranieri was still infatuated with the actress Maria Maddalena Pelzet.

Adieu, fair and charming Fanny. I scarcely dare ask you to let me know what I can do for you, knowing that I can do nothing. But if, as they say, desire and will give strength, you can consider me very well able to do your bidding. Remember me to your little girls, and believe me always yours,

Leopardi.

190

He reported to Paolina that he had seen Stendhal, a favourite author of hers.

To Paolina Leopardi • Recanati

Florence, 31st August 1832

Dear Pilla. In these two months of silence you talk of, I've written at least twice: if you haven't got the letters, I don't know what to say: I was beginning to think that your silence had gone on rather a long time too: your last letter, undated, had reached me on the 10th of July. It's been hot here as well, 29 degrees to be precise, except perhaps for a few days in July which I think went over 30. I've felt very weak and unwell on account of it, as all my health and energy depends on moderate temperatures, and without that I'm always unwell. My eyes especially have suffered more than usual. I've no news to give you, except that I've seen your Stendhal again here; he's the French consul at Civitavecchia, as you know, and the other evening I spoke with the medical commission sent from Rome to pay its compliments to the cholera in Paris; they are assuring us that the disease will come to Italy: a prediction the doctors here are laughing at, because they don't believe it: and I laugh with those who believe it and with those who don't. Adieu, my Pilla. A kiss on the hand for Papa and Mama, and a hug for Carlo and Pietruccio.

191

He told Giordani that he might be going to Naples.

To Pietro Giordani • Parma

[Florence] 6th September [1832]

Thank you a hundred times over for your letter of the 21st of August. Carlo and Paolina are always talking about you, and ask you to spare them a thought. Poor Enrico, as some people say, or, as I say, very lucky Enrico, ended his short life on the 26th of last month.[1] Studying, drinking, smoking and womanizing quickly wore him out, and reduced him to expiring after two months of not very painful illness. Very wise in his ways, and most fortunate among a thousand young people! I'll never speak of his fate without boundless envy:

[1] Enrico was the son of Carlotta Lenzoni; see [174].

although I'm quite sure that, when he realized death was near, he'd willingly have exchanged his state for mine: such being the merciful dispensation of Providence, that true and great blessings only befall those who think them misfortunes and loathe them. It is not impossible that in a few days time I may leave here for Naples. But please keep this secret, especially if you write to Florence. My doings are of very little interest to anyone, but not so little that my pleasure in sharing them with other people isn't even less. Give my fondest regards to the Tommasinis and the Maestris and remember me to Toschi as well. You know very well that if you were to write me a long letter you would give me enormous pleasure, and you wouldn't *bore* me, as you are pleased to put it: but reasonably you have nothing to write to me about. Love me, as you must, if loving those who love them is what well-born souls do. I think of you always, and adore you as the greatest spirit I know, and the dearest I have. Adieu adieu.

192

Count Monaldo had reacted to his son's request for financial assistance by telling him to ask his mother. He now wrote to her, repeating the request.

To Adelaide Leopardi • Recanati

[Florence] 17th November [1832]

My dear Mama. I never write to you, and now I am doing so to bother you with a request. I very much regret it, but you know the reasons for my ordinary silence, and necessity is the cause of my exceptional request. It is already some time since I wrote to Papa informing him of my circumstances: I explained to him all the efforts I have made up to now to find a means of supporting myself without being a burden on the family; I showed him how and why that has become impossible for me; and I ended by asking him to agree to grant me a monthly allowance of 12 *francesconi*, on which I would meagrely endeavour to make do. Papa replied that I should write to you directly. I have been ill, and my convalescence has left my eyes so weak that until now, for all that the need was pressing, I have absolutely not been able to write. Today at last, not being able to delay any longer either, I am reduced to this step, which costs me a great deal, and I make the same request to you as I did to Papa.

Believe me, my dear Mama, that being a nuisance like this is a thousand times more painful for me than it is for you. But on the other hand, if I were to return to Recanati to live, I would consume a great deal at home, and I would be a huge and continuous burden with my strange ways, and my melancholy. And in addition I would not be on hand to grasp the opportunities that might turn up for supporting myself, and for freeing the family of this burden, as I still hope I might yet manage to do at some point, if I live in places where such opportunities may arise. You can see that all I am asking for in order to live here is the allowance granted to Carlo in Recanati.[1] I will not remind you that I have always tried not to cause you any displeasure, because I do not think that constitutes any merit on my part: I

[1] Carlo, now married, was no longer living at home, and was in receipt of a modest allowance.

merely point out that I would not want to give you this first bother now, if necessity in the full sense of the word did not compel me to do so.

If, as I hope, I obtain a favourable response from you, I shall at the end of the month draw 24 *francesconi* from a banker here, and I shall give him in exchange a promissory note payable by Papa at the end of December. I assure you that from when I wrote to Papa, which was at the beginning of July, I could have used at least the first bi-monthly payment for August and September; and I have not got this far, except by using my very last reserves, which I had put aside to meet exceptional needs, which every month never fail to arise. I said 24 *francesconi*, that is a first bi-monthly payment for October and November.

Mama, forgive me, and when Papa has let you read my July letter, as I hope he will, you decide with him as you think best; but still love me and bless me, for I am and will forever be your very loving son,

Giacomo.

193

Ranieri had gone to Naples in autumn 1832, and remained there until April 1833. During his absence Leopardi wrote to him every few days, the letters becoming shorter and shorter because of the state of his eyes.[1]

To Antonio Ranieri • Naples

[Florence] 25th December [1832]

My dear Ranieri. Will you believe that your letters of the 15th, 18th and 20th all arrived together today? so that after the news of your illness given me by your compassionate sister, I was a week without any news of you? I say no more, I don't even say *just imagine*. Who in the world can imagine what this week of death has been like? Oh Ranieri, Ranieri, the price of too great a blessing, like your friendship, must be exceptional suffering. And now I'm fearful that you are not taking enough care of yourself, and are in too much of a rush to leave, in this cold weather. Try, Ranieri, since we must be reunited forever (for I want to follow you to any part of this world or the next), try not to prevent this great blessing by recklessness. Thank your compassionate sister no end for the angelic kindness that moved her to write to me with news of you: I urge her not to let you leave unless you are quite recovered. Adieu, my only and irreplaceable treasure whose loss could never be made good, adieu without end. I've not seen Miss Pelzet and I shan't see her, I think; it not being likely that she'll come to call on me.

[1] In M1798 he calls them 'my microscopic letters.'

194

To Antonio Ranieri • Naples

[Florence] 5th January [1833]

My dear Ranieri. How very distressing I find your letter of the 1st. Oh my God! But never fear on my acount: I'm not in any danger, and even if I were to fall ill, nothing would come of it, because there's not enough life in me for it to have the strength to kill me. Caramelli[1] laughs at this jest of mine but agrees that it is very true. My poor Ranieri! if men mock you because of me, at least it consoles me that they certainly mock me too because of you, because where you're concerned I've always shown and will show myself to be more than a child.[2] The world always laughs at those things it would be forced to admire if it did not laugh; and it always criticises the things it envies, like the fox. Oh Ranieri! when will I have you back? until I've obtained this huge blessing, I'll be fearful that it can't be true. Adieu, my soul, with all the strength of my spirit. Adieu countless times. Do not weary of loving me.

1 Leopardi's doctor.

2 The mockery was probably occasioned by the triangular relationship with Fanny.

195

To Antonio Ranieri • Naples

[Florence] 15th January [1833]

My wretched letters that are so short are not much comfort to you. Oh Ranieri, how I wish I was suffering instead of you! If all you have is me, yet you have me wholly and forever: you can be more sure of that than of the existence of solid bodies. As for joining you, I'm still at your disposal. Take care of your health, which I always worry about. Did you get Fanny's letter? Adieu, my dear and only hope.

196

To Antonio Ranieri • Naples

[Florence] 29th January [1833]

My dear Ranieri. Just think, you say, that soon we must be reunited forever. You know very well that this thought is my daily bread. *E questo solo ancor qui mi mantene.*[1] Fanny is more than ever yours, and always asks me to pass on her regards to you. Do you know that Carlino left for New York? She's begun to ingratiate herself with me, so that I can serve her purposes with you: for which *sum paratus.*[2] Adieu, my dear soul, a thousand times.

1 Petrarch, *Rime*, CCLXVIII, 33: *and this alone sustains me here still.*

2 *I am ready.* Leopardi had no illusions about who Fanny was really interested in.

197

To Antonio Ranieri • Naples

[Florence] 5th February [1833]

My dear Ranieri. You don't need me to tell you that wherever and however you want, I'll be with you. Think carefully and coolly about what suits you, but without getting carried away: I mean without getting too carried away: and then make up your mind. Mine was made up a long time ago: I decided not to be separated from you ever again. Adieu.

198

To Antonio Ranieri • Naples

[Florence] 14th February [1833]

My dear Ranieri. I still haven't got your letter by today's post. I'm writing very briefly because my eyes are in a deplorable state. Every day I become more unhappy at your being far away, because all the time I pass without you seems and is truly lost, as all my pleasure is in your company. Adieu no end.

199

To Antonio Ranieri • Naples

[Florence] 16th February [1833]

Dear soul. My eyes only allow me to say hello. I've got your letters of the 9th and the 12th which comfort me for all misfortune. Adieu.

200

To Antonio Ranieri • Naples

[Florence] 9th March [1833]

Believe me, my dear Ranieri, that this nothing I'm writing is more than the *maximum* of which I'm capable. My father and brothers and sister write weeping because they've had no reply or news of me for 3 months, and I don't finish reading their letters. I call for you all day.

201

To Antonio Ranieri • Rome

[Florence] 13th April [1833]

My dear Ranieri. I'm sending this letter as well to Rome without knowing if I'm doing the right thing, because I still don't have today's letter from you. God grant that I see you again before I die; which I now think hardly likely, certainly through no fault of yours. Adieu, *ὦ πολὺ ἐπικαλούμενε*,[1] adieu with all my heart.

[1] *o much invoked one.*

202

Ranieri's over-reaction to the previous letter precipitated a crisis. The news reached the family in Recanati, and Paolina wrote to Vieusseux: 'A terrible rumour has reached us from Rome reporting that our dear Giacomo is very seriously ill.' Leopardi wrote at once to reassure her.

To Paolina Leopardi • Recanati

[Florence] 6th May [1833]

My dear Pilla. A letter of mine of two lines – unfortunately ambiguous – to a close friend of mine in Rome, who raced here with the courier, has caused all of you what you know, and me the unspeakable distress of hearing your letter to Vieusseux. My dear souls, God knows that I cannot, I cannot write: but be quite calm: I cannot die: my machine[1] (my excellent doctor says so as well) does not have enough life in it to conceive a fatal disease. I leave you perforce, embracing all of you with immense fondness.

Give me news straight away about everybody for my own peace of mind. And be *absolutely certain* that were anything serious to happen you will never lack information from friends *from here.*

[1] Leopardi again uses the word 'machine' [*macchina*] to refer to his body and its malfunctioning.

203

Leopardi broke the news to his father of his intended move to Naples.

To Monaldo Leopardi • Recanati

Florence, 1st September 1833

My dear Papa. Since the doctors have advised the climate of Naples as the very best remedy for my health, which has never been as ruined as it is now, a close friend of mine who is leaving for there was so insistent on taking me with him in his coach that I could not resist, and I leave with him tomorrow. I feel a very great sorrow at going even further away from you; and my intention was to come and spend this winter in Recanati. But I am all too well aware that the climate there, which has always been harmful for me, would now be very harmful; and besides my eye complaint is too serious to be entrusted to the doctors and apothecaries there. I would have liked at least to make a detour and pass through Recanati. But that was not reconcilable with my taking advantage of the splendid opportunity that presented itself to me. When I have spent a few months in Naples, if I derive the benefit from it that I am hoping for, I shall at last have the incredible pleasure of embracing you once more. I shall give you my news again from Rome, where I will be on Sunday evening. I am obliged to have someone write this letter for me, because those few hours in the morning when by making an enormous effort I could write a line or two, I spend of necessity treating my eyes.

Bless me, my dear Papa; I kiss your hand with all my soul.

204

He reported on his safe arrival.

To Monaldo Leopardi • Recanati

Naples, 5th October 1833

Dear Papa. I arrived here happily, that is to say without injury and without misadventure. My health otherwise is not up to much and my eyes are still in the same state. Yet I find the mildness of the climate, the beauty of the city, and the amiable and good-natured temperament of the inhabitants very agreeable. Your letter of the 10th of September was waiting for me here. The false news given in the French newspapers came from their having confused me with somebody else with the same surname.[1] As for my principles I shall say nothing except that if present times had any power to influence them, they could only confirm them. God grant that I can assure you of this face to face. Yours,

Giacomo.

[1] The false news was that he had been arrested for political reasons.

205

Already dissatisfied with Naples, he raised the possibility with De Sinner of going to Paris.

To Luigi De Sinner • Paris

Naples, 20th March 1834

My dear, excellent friend. [...] For many reasons, and very strong ones, I'm eager to come and end my days in Paris. My health no longer frightens me. In Naples I have become convinced that north and south are at best indifferent for my ills. The difficulties are in the means; and more in the means of getting to Paris than living there: because, once there, I hope it would not be difficult to find a way of living there as frugally as you know I live in Italy. Do you think that in Paris I could usefully occupy myself with a new collection of Italian Classics, to be supervised, illustrated, etc by me? I assure you that none of the projects of this kind produced so far in France has been entrusted to Italians capable of overseeing them properly. Could you speak about it to some publisher? Or would you know of some other project there that might suit me better and be more useful? Either way, could you in your reply to this letter give me an answer on this point with a statement I can show people, in which you give me certain hope that, having got to Paris, I would find employment immediately, giving *in detail* the names of the project, the publisher, etc.? With a letter of that kind in my possession I think it would be possible for me to find enough money here to get me to Paris and to live there the first few months. A separate note attached to your letter would tell me the true state of affairs with complete frankness. In any work I took on I would have the efficient help of my close friend *Ranieri*, to whom I'm dictating this letter, and who has joined his destiny with mine. He sends his sincere good wishes. [...]

Adieu, my excellent friend. You understand that the desire to embrace you again is not one of the least powerful of the motives that make me want to come to Paris. In the meantime I hope that when you reply you will give me your own news in detail. Adieu with all my heart. Yours,

Leopardi.

P.S. Please address your reply to *Mr Antonio Ranieri Tenti, Naples.* You can be sure that if I make use of your letter I'll be very careful not to compromise you in any way.

206

He complained of receiving no news from home.

To Monaldo Leopardi • Recanati

Naples, 5th April 1834

My dear Papa. After your letter of the 23rd of December, which I answered at once, I have had no further news from home. This silence confirms the disagreeable suspicion aroused in me, as I told you, by a turn of phrase in your last letter, that my letters from here are not reaching you.

The benefit produced in me by this climate is barely perceptible – even after moving to where I enjoy the best air in Naples, living high up with a view of the whole gulf of Portici and Vesuvius, whose smoke I contemplate every day, and every night its burning lava. My eyes are being treated with corrosive sublimate. My eagerness to see you again grows all the time, and I shall leave Naples as soon as I can, even though the doctors say that the benefit of this climate can only be experienced in the warmer months.

If God allows this letter to reach you, cheer me up at once with your news. A kiss on your hand with all my soul, and a thousand fondest regards to Mama and my brothers and sister.

Yours,

Giacomo.

207

He hoped he might pass through Parma and see old friends when he left Naples.

To Adelaide Maestri • Parma

Naples, 5th April 1834

My dear Adelaide. For several days here rumours had been spreading about what had happened to Giordani, but it was only your letter that confirmed it for a fact.[1] Imagine my distress, and at the same time my gratitude to you for having clarified a matter where you are well aware that being in doubt and not knowing the circumstances were causing me great anxiety. If you have some way of conveying to Giordani how sorry I am and of passing on my regards, do so, for it will be a great comfort to me.

I've recovered from the eye complaint I had when Ferdinando saw me. But my eyes are still very weak, and that is the only reason for my not writing to you earlier, and now I am having someone else write this for me. I've always wanted to see you and your family again; and I still do. But I don't know when I'll be granted that pleasure. The Naples climate is of some benefit to me; but in other respects living here doesn't suit me very well...I hope we'll leave here soon, my friend and I. I still don't know where we'll go. If I happen to have a chance of passing through Parma, just think how pleased I'll be! Fond regards to Mama, Papa, Ferdinando and Clelietta, whom I no longer dare kiss. My friend sends his fond regards again to clever Ferdinando; and for you a kiss on the hand. Yours,

Leopardi.

Adieu, my dear Adelaide, adieu with all my heart.

[1] Giordani had been seized and imprisoned. He was released after three months.

208

The unreliability of the post continued to cause anxiety.

To Monaldo Leopardi • Recanati

Naples, 3rd February 1835

My dear Papa. For two whole months I have been painfully in the dark about news of you, having had no reply to the letter I wrote at the end of November, and not knowing what to make of your silence, until finally today the post sent me your letter of the 4th of December *which reached here on the 11th of December.*[1] More than other circumstances, intense and exceptional cold weather, which began here on the 10th of December and continued steadily

[1] i.e. the letter had reached Naples on December 11th, but had only been delivered on February 3rd.

for a month, prevented me from setting out before the new year, as I was hoping to do. Now my chief concern is to arrange things so that I can uproot myself from here as soon as possible; be quite sure that as soon as it is humanly possible I shall leave for Recanati, being from the bottom of my heart very eager to see you again, as well as needing to get away from these scoundrels and buffoons, high class and low, all thieves and rogues, b.....s[2] who fully deserve the Spaniards and the gallows. My health, thank God, continues to improve notably; an effect, I think, of the season rather than the climate. Bless me once more, and accept boundless good wishes for every imaginable prosperity from your very loving son,

Giacomo.

2 Speaking with uncharacteristic though euphemistic directness to his father, Leopardi here uses the initials b.f. [b.f. = *baron fottuto, baron con l'effe*, literally 'buggered rogue'].

209

Leopardi had never forgotten Bunsen's generosity at a time of financial difficulty [92]. Hardship now forced him to take desperate measures.

To Carlo Bunsen • Rome

Naples, 20th June 1835

Revered Sir and friend. Ten years ago you were generous enough to put at my disposal in Bologna, where I then was, a sum of money with which I could make the journey to Rome, which you thought useful to my interests. I now find myself in serious and unforeseen difficulties, in which, for a number of reasons, it is not possible for me to turn to my father. I have taken a liberty with you that I never have and never would have taken with any other person in the world: that is of drawing against your address a promissory note for twelve *luigi*, which I shall repay to you as soon as I can, and I hope to be able to do so shortly. I do not add any excuses: forgive my temerity, and consider it one of the greatest proofs I could ever give you of the almost unequalled esteem and respect in which I hold you. I would have preferred to avoid putting your address on the promissory note, and drawn it indirectly; but not for the moment being able to think of any way of being able to do this, and not knowing the name of your banker in Rome, I must ask you to forgive me this sort of incivility as well. Your most devoted, most obliged servant and friend,

Giacomo Leopardi.

210

Bunsen responded with characteristic graciousness.

To Carlo Bunsen • Roma

Naples, 26th September 1835

Dear sir and friend. I had your letter of the 5th of July from Dr Schultz: for the kindness of your letter, and for the generosity with which you were good enough to honour my promissory note, I thank you without being surprised at it, as one who has long been acquainted with the excellence of your character and your worth. I continue to be mindful of my debt, and hopeful of repaying it shortly.

I have delayed replying to your very friendly letter until now, waiting until I was able to make you a gift of the volume which accompanies this letter, which was not published until this week.[1] You are right that in my prose pieces the melancholy is perhaps excessive and perhaps even sometimes clouds my judgment. Blame my character in part, and in part the age at which they were written, because I wrote them when I was 26 years old, and since then, although they have been reprinted with a few corrections by me, I have never been able to reread them right through until today. My own experience teaches me that growing older, among the many changes it produces in man, also perceptibly alters his way of thinking. If you had the patience to glance through the volume that comes with this letter, you would perhaps find some melancholy excesses in it as well, and you would reproach me for it and you would not be wrong.

In my last letter I neglected to congratulate you on your new position as Plenipotentiary Minister. Today, though tardily, I perform this agreeable duty: but at the same time I confess that I am enough of an egoist to have difficulty in making up my mind and wishing your promotion to be so rapid that Italy (as I hear is more than possible) must shortly lose you. I assure you, putting aside any trace of formalities, that the thought of not seeing you again would cause me great sorrow. On the other hand I trust that wherever your noble destiny calls you, you will not fail to carry with you some memory of me, just as certainly no distance will be able to destroy my memory of you.

Dr Schultz is now travelling in the province busy with his historical research. Please pay my respects to your good wife, and my best wishes to your distinguished and amiable children. Continue to wish me well; I remain your very devoted and affectionate friend and servant,

Giacomo Leopardi.

[1] The Starita edition of the *Canti*, published in Naples in 1835, with additional poems written since the Florentine edition of 1831.

211

Leopardi wrote to De Sinner after a lengthy interval, reporting that his health had improved in the Naples climate.

To Luigi De Sinner • Paris

Naples, 3rd October 1835

My excellent, dear friend. This time our, or rather my, silence has really gone beyond every limit. After your very charming letter of July 1834, for many months I was very unsure of the place where I would spend the next week, and I would not have known where to ask you to send your reply. Then, finding myself still settled for a further period in Naples, sometimes the weak state of my eyes, sometimes some small piece of work, and finally my desire to accompany my letter with the little volume which I am posting to you today,[1] and which was only published last week, made me delay the pleasure of talking to you by letter.

I was hoping to receive your news and some of your recent publications from Alessandro Poerio, who came back here in spring this year. But he, engrossed in the profound wisdom of an Italian or rather Dalmatian dunce called Niccolò Tommaseo,[2] whose sublime lectures kept him busy in the last days of his stay in Paris, had no time to see his friends again, and brought me no news of you other than that you were definitively and honourably settled there in Paris: if this is true, as I hope and believe, I'm truly happy about it. You yourself then be kind enough to give me your news in detail, talk to me about your studies, your plans, at last bring me up to date about what has happened to you, eliminating the gap created by the extended silence not in our friendship, but in our being in touch with one another.

After almost a year of living in Naples, I finally began to feel the beneficial effects of this climate which really is good for one's health: and it can't be denied that I've recovered here more than perhaps I'd have dared hope. Last winter I was able to read, compose and write a few things; in the summer I was able to attend to (although not very successfully as regards the proof-reading) the printing of the little volume I am sending you; and now I hope to resume my studies again in some measure, and to keep on working on something during the winter.

The difficulties of execution, which I soon discovered, made me give up the idea I'd mentioned to you, and which you spoke about in such a friendly fashion in your last letter, of writing for French Reviews. I'm still in a precarious way in Naples, as I was in Florence, but still with no prospect or definite plan for change. Ranieri, with whom I'm living, and whom only Jove's thunderbolt could separate from me, sends you his respects a thousand times through me, and is very eager to meet in person a man he hears me speak about often and with greater interest than I customarily easily show in anyone. Who knows if and when we three shall be able to see each other? In the meantime, no matter how great the distance between us, don't forget me. I'll be happy if you keep a memory of me like the one I have of you. Write me a long letter, if you want to please me. Give me as much literary news as you

[1] The new edition of the *Canti*, see [210], n. 1.

[2] Leopardi's dislike of Tommaseo is attested elsewhere; see [218] and [80], n. 2.

can, and especially philological. Not reading newspapers, I am in the dark about everything. I know very well that you are not expecting news of philology from me, because what philology is there in Italy? It is true that Mai is about to become a cardinal, and Mezzofanti will be close behind him; but they owe that to Jesuitism, not to philology.

Adieu, my very rare friend. Do you have any news of Gioberti? Adieu: love me, and believe me your very affectionate friend for life,

Leopardi.

212

To Paolina Leopardi • Recanati

[Naples, 4th December 1835]

Dear Pilla. I knew that Recanati had paved streets, and had restored the Monaci and Palazzo Luciani facades, but Bath paper[1] and stamped sealing wafers as well? Clearly civilisation is making great strides everywhere. You say there are a million things you'd like to write to me about, yet in the meantime you've been more than a year without telling me anything. It's true that I don't write much, but you all know the reason for that: and you who can write a lot mustn't take it into your head to give tit for tat, but you should write to me often without counting my letters, without thinking of the *carlino* your letter will cost me, because no *carlino* will seem to me so well spent. Kiss Mama's hand for me, and say hello to Carlo and to Pietruccio, who reads a lot, I know, and could remember his big brother from time to time too, and give him his news. As for me, dear Pilla, I die of melancholy whenever I think of the long time I've passed without seeing all of you; when you see me again, you'll stop making accusations. If it were necessary I'd tell you that I haven't changed one iota towards all of you, but between us these things aren't said except in jest, and I say them to you with a laugh. Adieu, then: give my regards to Don Vincenzo, the Curate, the Marchioness; I know you continue to call on her on Sundays. This time, when we see each other again, I shan't be short of stories and tales to keep you happy in the evenings for many weeks. Adieu adieu. Send another kiss from me to Gigina.

[1] Fine quality writing paper from Bath.

213

Monaldo had founded a periodical called 'La voce della ragione' (The Voice of Reason), which had now been closed down by the authorities.

To Monaldo Leopardi • Recanati

Naples, 19th February 1836

My dearest Papa. With the usual inexplicable delay, your letter of the 19th of December, though not (as far as one can tell) opened, was only handed over to me by the post office at the beginning of this month. I thank you and Mama fondly for the gift of ten *scudi*, which I have already put to good use in the usual way. I was very saddened to hear that the authorities are showing themselves so ungrateful to your pen for all its battling in their cause. I say saddened, but not surprised: because this is the way men of all parties behave, and because the authorities (allow me to say it) are not too keen for their cause to be defended with words, given that merely acknowledging that there is someone on the terrestrial globe who calls in question the plenitude of their rights is a thing that goes far beyond the freedom granted to the pens of mortals: besides which they very wisely have a preference (over reasons, which for better or worse can always be answered), for the arguments of the cannon and imprisonment, to which for the moment their opponents have no answer.

I would very much appreciate receiving the copy of the *Voce della Ragione* you describe as being complete; and if, as you say, I wanted to dispose of it I could give pleasure to many people, as your name is much respected here too. But I cannot ask you to act on your good intention, because receiving foreign books in Naples is a desperate business, not only on account of the terrible customs charges (3 *carlini* for every tiny volume, and 6 if the volume is big) which are extremely difficult to avoid, but because of the endless health regulations (all printed matter from outside the kingdom, if it has a sewn binding, remains in quarantine for 50 days) and censorship regulations, which dismay even the most resolute soul. On more than one occasion I have been asked for your Evangelical History, which I was obliged to leave behind in Florence, and your book on usury: by writing to you I could easily have obtained the volumes, and it would have given me a great deal of pleasure to satisfy the people who were asking for them: but I had to give them a rough indication of what they had to do to get them, without taking on the burden of the charges, as something beyond the ordinary strength of men. And the same goes for some of my own books which I really could have used, and which are not available here: I did not even think of having them sent from Recanati or anywhere else, as I considered getting them a thing close to impossible.

My health, in spite of the unfavourable time of year, continues, thank God, to be quite satisfactory. I want to know that the same has been true for all of you in this year which has been exceptional everywhere for diseases. I hope I shall have the immense blessing of seeing you again, and Mama, and my brothers and sister, towards the middle of May, as I reckon to set out from here at the beginning of May or the end of April. Ranieri sends his respects, and at the first opportunity will send you the other four installments so far printed of his

History.[1] Regards and a hug to my brothers and sister; I kiss Mama's hand and yours, asking both of you to commend me warmly to the Lord. My joy in seeing you again will be equal to my love for you, which is certainly increased (if it could increase) rather than diminished by distance. Bless me; I remain your very affectionate son,

Giacomo.

[1] Ranieri was writing a history of Italy from the fifth to the ninth century. It would appear as a volume in 1841.

214

Leopardi was still in touch with his Bolognese friends.

To Adelaide Maestri • Parma

Naples, 5th March 1836

My dear Adelaide. Although I always hope that you keep me in your memory, it still means a great deal to me to have some sign of it like your letters of the 9th of September and the 20th of February, which I have just received together. The last letter I had from Parma was from your Mama and Papa, who promised me a copy of the third edition of Mama's *Pensieri*. But please tell them that I never received either this copy or the copy of the second edition, which was likewise promised to me, or rather sent, I don't know whether to Florence or to Rome. In the same way from a few words in your last letter I learn that Giordani has not mentioned to you, and (as I think) has not received, a book I sent him by post at the beginning of last October. I'd see about sending him another copy, but how to do it, if the post is no good?

Thank you very much for the news you give me about your own and your family's health. I hope that Mama's and Papa's has picked up, with the help of the mild weather, and your convalescence turned into sound health. For the last year and a half I haven't been able to complain about my health, but especially so since coming, about a year ago, to live in a spot in this city that is almost the country, very high up, with very dry air, and really healthy. I'm scribbling away, not as much as I would like to pass the time; because I have to help with a collection of my trifles that is being prepared here: the first volume of which (in large part unpublished, like the others) is the book I sent Giordani. I already asked your Mama to thank Ferdinando for me and tell him the pleasure it gave me to read his fine Eulogy. I hope your Mama won't have forgotten to do that for me. Give him my fondest regards, and also regards from Ranieri, who says thank you for remembering him. It is pointless, or rather impossible, for me to tell you how many things I want you to say for me to your Papa, your Mama, and to Giordani; please ask all of them to remember me affectionately. Give a hug from me to Clelietta and Emilio too. All of you be certain that time, distance and even silence haven't changed and won't change my feelings towards you by one jot from how it was when we were living, so to speak, together. Adieu, my dear Adelaide; be fond of me. Adieu with all my heart.

215*

A young French friend of De Sinner's had written to Leopardi, who replied with his usual courtesy.

To Carlo Lebreton • Paris

[Naples, end of June 1836]

No, Monsieur, if I were seeking approbation, yours would certainly not be a matter of indifference to me; it is for spirits like yours, for tender and sensitive hearts like the one which dictated your charming letter, that poets write, and that I would have written if I had been a poet.

My excellent friend, M. de Sinner, has painted me for your eyes in colours that are too favourable, he has lent me many embellishments; mind that you do not take him at his word; his friendship for me will lead you too far from the truth. Please tell him that in spite of the grandiose title *works* that my publisher saw fit to give to his collection, I have never produced works, I have only made attempts, reckoning always that they were a starting-point, but my career went no further. Although I do not deserve the other feelings you are kind enough to express towards me, I accept your friendship with gratitude, and if I am still alive when you come to Italy, it will be a real joy for me to embrace you, and a real pleasure to question your young and lively imagination about the impressions which this land of memories will have caused it to feel.

G. Leopardi.

Be sure, Monsieur, that there is no other etiquette to be observed with me than saying what one feels.

* The letter is in French.

216

Leopardi gave an account of the outbreak of cholera to his father, assuring him that having moved to the countryside he was out of danger, although financially his situation was precarious.

To Monaldo Leopardi • Recanati

In the country, 30th October 1836

My dear Papa. I did not reply to your March letter, because as I was feeling shame-faced myself (though God knows how innocent) at my long delays, I had made up my mind not to write to you until I had already left or was on the point of leaving for Recanati. But gloomy necessities, which I shall never be able to give you an account of without writing a whole volume, have held me back from one day to the next until the gloomiest of all, which is the cholera, which first broke out, as you will know, in the provinces of the Kingdom, and then in the capital. As I do not read the newspapers, my friends had taken care to keep it from me that there was cholera in Ancona. Had I known of it, I think no force could have prevented me from coming, even on foot, to share your danger. Now from the news I have been able to gather, I think the region around Recanati is free of it, although I am not easy in my mind even about that; but here nobody is thinking any more about anywhere outside Naples, given the confusion that cholera produces in a city as huge and populous as this. Fortunately before the outbreak I had been able to retreat into the countryside, where I live in an excellent climate, and in good company, almost 12 miles distant from Naples. So have no worries on my account, because I take such precautions of every kind that, by any human reckoning, everybody else will have to die before I do. But since in such circumstances everything has to be done with money, and the prices of everything have increased out of all proportion, everybody is holding on to their money, and a predicament seems imminent in which it may not even be possible to obtain money drawn on an outside account, I was forced on the 25th of this month, contrary to all my previous expectations and arrangements, to make use of Uncle Carlo exceptionally as guarantor for the sum of 41 *colonnati*, with a bill of exchange which I was only able to negotiate by a singular favour. I kneel before you and Mama to ask you, in the plight in which along with me half a million people find themselves, to condone this inconvenience which with the utmost reluctance I am causing you. My health, thank God, apart from my eyes, is excellent in all respects. If God grants me life, and if the plague does not keep us cut off for a long time still, I shall certainly kiss your hand again perhaps sooner than you will be expecting, after all the hopes of doing so that I have nurtured in vain. Bless me, and you and Mama both commend me to the Lord, and if you can put my mind at rest concerning conditions in your part of the country give me that comfort. I embrace my brothers and sister, and assuring you again that my position here is practically out of danger, straight from the heart, I remain your most affectionate son,

Giacomo.

217

The unsympathetic response from his uncle to the forced move described in the previous letter led Leopardi to spell out his financial hardship to his father.

To Monaldo Leopardi • Recanati

[Naples] In the country, 11th December 1836

My dear Papa. I did not know what to make of the complete lack of any response from Recanati, which I have lived with until today, when the post brings me 7 letters (among them yours of October 22nd and November 10th) and when with my very wretched eyes I am *starting* this letter. The confusion caused by the cholera, and the death of three post office employees, may *perhaps* explain this delay. Thank you and Mama no end for your kind gift to me of the 41 *colonnati*. The somewhat dry tone of your letters is quite justified in someone who of necessity cannot know my true state, because my eyes have never been up to writing a letter that cannot be dictated, and that cannot fail to be interminable; and because certain things should not be written down but only said face to face. You certainly think the last seven years have been a bed of roses for me, whereas they have been a bed of reeds. When Mama realizes that my requesting an exceptional subsidy *cannot* happen and has not happened except when I lack money even for *bread*; when she learns that none of you has ever in his life been, nor ever will be, thank God, in straits of the terrible kind I have found myself in *many times* through *no* fault of my own; when she sees the state of my clothes when I stand before her once again, and realizes as well that the refusing of a promissory note means its dishonouring, and the dishonouring of a promissory note of mine, since I cannot repay the equivalent sum, means my instant arrest; perhaps she will feel some regret at the hostile refusal uncle Antici announces to me in a letter of November 6th, which I have just got together with your two.

It was a great comfort to me to see that the plague, which our age calls cholera out of politeness, has made little impression in your part of the country. Here, leaving aside the rest of the sorry story, which my eyes do not allow me to relate, after more than 50 days (I mean in Naples) the disease seemed almost to have run its course; but in recent days the death toll has risen again. My health has suffered notably from the dampness of this house in the winter months; and I cannot go back to Naples, because anyone who goes there after a long absence unfailingly falls victim to the plague; which in any case has spread to the countryside too, and around here several people have died from it.

My dear Papa, if God grants that I see you again, you and Mama and my brothers and sister will realize that in these seven years I have not been unworthy of the tiniest particle of your earlier fondness for me, unless unhappy circumstances diminish the love of parents and siblings, as they destroy it in all other men. If I die first, my justification will be entrusted to Providence.

May God grant all of you in the coming festivities the cheerfulness that I am unlikely to feel. From my heart I ask you to bless your most affectionate son,

Giacomo.

The latest news on the cholera in Naples and the surrounding district is, today the 15th, good.

218

He reported to De Sinner that the planned edition of his complete works, including three volumes of hitherto unpublished material, was suspended, perhaps even abandoned.

To Luigi De Sinner • Paris

In the country, 22nd December 1836

My dear, excellent friend. This letter will be very dry and lacking in substance, and will merely serve to show you that I'm still alive, but won't be able to satisfy any of your questions, because I'm in the country, not so much from fear of the cholera as because, finding myself here when the disease broke out in Naples, which was on the 18th of October, I did what other people did in my situation – that is to say, stayed put. The cholera is now dying down in Naples, but certainly has not stopped. When that happens, and I am back in Naples, I'll be able to answer your philological questions, one of which (that is the one about Eunapius's *History*) I think I can answer in the negative straight away. I can't speak to you about your books either, which I thank you for no end, and which I'm most eager to see: because all I was able to find out about the packet you sent in May before I left for the country on the 20th of August was that it was at Marseilles in a safe place. The quarantine precautions now make it very difficult in Naples to get things from abroad, but they will end soon, so do not stop sending me everything you were intending to send, for as soon as I'm in Naples I'll take all necessary steps to collect every last one of the things you've sent. You've published a great deal, and I congratulate you on it. You don't say whether the edition of *Chrysostom* is going ahead, as I think it is; nor how far you've got with it; nor whether after *Chrysostom* you will bring out some other *church Father*, as you wrote me on another occasion. I'm very grateful that you intend sending me some of your publications: this will be further proof to me of your affection, and will give me cause not just to be pleased but to be proud.

Do you have any news of Gioberti? Did he ever get a letter of mine written several months back? Borelli from Parma, whom I saw in Naples last June, told me that for a long time he'd had a letter of Gioberti's for me, which I never managed to get from him. If you write to Gioberti, please tell him all this, giving him my very warm regards. Give my regards also to your good, clever pupil Mr Lebreton, and thank him for his letter. Please also pay my respects to Mr Bothe, whose *Homer* I shall look at with great interest.

The edition of my *Works* is suspended, and more likely abandoned, from the second volume on, which it still hasn't been possible to sell publicly in Naples, since permission to publish has not been obtained. The priests didn't like my philosophy: here and in the whole world, under one name or under another, they are still in control of everything and always will be. If you want me to post you another copy of the second volume to make up the fifth number, all you have to do is write to me.

Adieu, my excellent friend. I feel a deep and very strong desire to embrace you, but how and where will it be satisfied? I'm very much afraid that it will only be *κατ' ἀσφοδελὸν* λειμῶνα.[1] Ranieri pays his respects and sends his regards as warmly as possible. Talk to me about your studies, and go on loving me. Adieu with all my heart. Your true friend,

G. Leopardi.

Do you think that if I were to send a copy of my poems or my prose works to Paris, with a lot of unpublished corrections and additions, or else a book that has never been published, it would be possible to find a publisher (like Baudry or someone else) who *without my paying anything* would bring out an edition at his own expense? I think not; and that crazy fool Tommaseo, who is despised in Italy and makes people think he's a great man in Paris, and who is a personal enemy of mine, would take the trouble to dissuade any publisher from such a project.

Excuse the appalling paper: it is what can be got on the slopes of Vesuvius, where I have been living for four months. [...]

1 *in the fields of asphodel*, i.e. in the after-life.

219

He told his father about the health precautions in force because of the cholera.

To Monaldo Leopardi • Recanati

Naples, 9th March 1837

My dear Papa. I never had any response to a long letter of mine last December, and I do not know who to complain to about it, because our post is still in such a state that a letter of yours to me could well have been there for some months, and never been given to me. I am safe from the cholera, thank God, but at a high price. After having spent several months in the country amidst incredible suffering, facing a good half dozen times a day dangers that were life-threatening, imminent, and might happen from one hour to the next; and after having suffered from cold the like of which I had never experienced any other winter except that one in Bologna; my poor organism,[1] ten years older than in Bologna, was unable to resist, and from the beginning of December, when the plague was starting to die down, my knee and right leg swelled to twice the size of the other one and turned a frightening colour. Nor was it possible to consult doctors, because a doctor's visit to that remote countryside could not cost less than 15 ducats. So I bore this infirmity until the middle of February, at which point, because of the excessive harshness of the weather, although I did not once leave the house, I fell ill with a chest infection accompanied by a fever, still without being able to consult anyone. When the fever went away of its own accord, I came back to the city, where I immediately took to my bed as a convalescent, which is what I am still, one can say, as from that day on I have not ever been able to leave the house to build up my strength with fresh

1 Leopardi again uses the word *macchina*, 'machine'.

air and exercise, because of the dreadful weather. Nonetheless the wholesomeness and the warmth of my lodgings are making me feel better all the time; and the swelling in my knee and leg has gone down as a result of this, and of staying in bed, and of the humour's having discharged itself by another outlet, so that I am almost recovered from it.

Meanwhile communications with our State have not been reopened; and until these last few days I was told by the Nuncio's office that it was very unlikely that they would be opened again for now. And it is a natural thing: because the cholera, besides being virulent at present in several other parts of the Kingdom, never died out in Naples either, there being cases every day, or almost every day, which the government tries to hide. In fact in recent days such cases seem to have increased, and more and more doctors are predicting the return of the contagion in spring or summer, a return that seems very natural to me as well, because the disease has not run its usual course, perhaps because of the cold weather. This very inconvenient obstacle prevents my making any decision, and in addition places me under the harsh (but very necessary) necessity of taking lodgings here *for a year*: a necessity of which someone who has not lived in Naples will not easily be persuaded. Here furnished rooms *by the month* are not available, as they are everywhere else, because that is not the way it is done, except at huge prices, and in families for the most part of thieves. The first month after I arrived I paid 15 ducats, and the second 22, and because of my strong-box I was attacked at night in my room by people who were certainly a part of the household. Unfurnished rooms are not available for renting except by the year. The year always begins and ends on the 4th of May, but notice of quitting is given on the 4th of January; and in the 4 months between these two dates the search for houses goes on and contracts are drawn up. But houses here are a commodity so extremely in demand, that mostly after January not a single inhabitable set of rooms is to be found which is not already rented out. It follows that a wretched foreigner must know and make a firm decision in January about what he will be doing in May; and if, having not renewed the contract for his lodgings and having made up his mind to leave, he lets the months pass without making provision; then if some external impediment crops up, like this one of interrupted communications, or an unexpected illness, a thing always very possible for someone with health like mine, or any other obstacle to his leaving, he can be sure that come the 4th of May he will either have to set up camp with his bed and his furniture in the middle of the street, or go to a boarding house, where the foulest room, with no light and no air, costs at the very least twelve ducats a month, without service, which is provided by the most dreadful riff-raff in the world. I am only telling you these things so that you may sympathize with me a little for having landed in a place which, because it is truly barbarous, is full of difficulties and real and continuing dangers, much more so than can ever be believed by someone who has not been there, or by someone who has spent a fortnight or a month there looking at the rare sights.

If this letter reaches you, please do not leave me without news of yourself, of Mama and of my brothers and sister, whom I embrace with all my soul, wishing them every possible consolation in the coming Easter. Ranieri (whose sister has had the cholera) pays his sincere respects. Bless me; I remain your unhappy but always very affectionate son,

Giacomo.

220

The last letter Leopardi wrote was to his father.

To Monaldo Leopardi • Recanati

Naples, 27th May 1837

My dearest Papa. You will perhaps find this hard to believe, but your letter of the 21st of March, post-marked here with the date April 1st, was sent me by the post on the 11th of May together with two other letters post-marked April 3rd. After I received it, for the first time in my life I suffered a real and genuine asthma attack, which prevents me from walking, lying down and sleeping, and I find myself obliged to have someone write this reply for me because of my right eye which is threatened with amaurosis,[1] or cataract. I really do not know where Fucili's friend could have got the good news he brought of me; having come back from the country ill on the 16th of February, I never left my room until the 15th of March, and from that day to this I have not managed to go out more than a dozen or so times on my own to take a walk without seeing anyone.

Do not think that it is easy here to sublet rooms after the 4th of May, because the very rush everybody is in to arrange something before that date means that, once it has passed, everyone has made arrangements, and houses are left worthless. Foreigners who come for a few months do not move out of their boarding-houses, as they cannot go buying and selling furniture. Without subletting the rooms, it would be more than ever difficult, without paying the whole year's rent in advance, to leave and above all to remove the furniture and the bed, which are not mine, because the landlords have the right not only to hold on to the furniture but to block one's passport, being protected by the law in every way and very distrustful because of the size of the city and the universal skulduggery. Perhaps in the end it would be possible to get around all these difficulties. But the main difficulty is the cholera, which began again here on the 13th of April, as had been predicted, and since then has gone on spreading, although the government is trying hard to keep it hidden. People here are afraid that as happened in Marseilles the second wave of cholera may be more virulent than the first; in Marseilles too it began in October and having wreaked havoc on a small scale returned in April. Here the second wave of cholera would have to be twice as bad as the first, for the disease to take a toll in Naples in proportion to the population. Communications were opened for two or three days around the 20th of April; but when it was known that the contagion had returned, the stringent measures were redoubled. The quarantine does not take place on the road to Rome, but in Rieti, on the Abruzzi road which is full of thieves, and anyone who wanted to reach Rome or is heading in that direction must turn back at Rieti. The outlay for the twenty days would be very heavy because of the taxes, which must be paid in full and which always amount to a large sum, as happens to poor travellers, and also there would be no small danger of having to live for twenty days with dubious people in the room the inn-keepers saw fit to allocate to you. Finally all the experts advise against setting out

[1] Loss of sight arising from disease of the optic nerve.

when the cholera is well established, it being known from experience in all countries that the change of air brings on the disease in individuals, and there being many examples of people setting out in good health from an infected place who died of cholera on arriving in the arms of their relatives in a healthy place. If I survive the cholera and as soon as my health allows I shall do everything possible to see you again whatever the time of year, because I too feel a sense of urgency, convinced as I now am by events of what I have always foreseen, that the end prescribed by God for my life is not far off. My daily and incurable physical sufferings have with age reached a point where they cannot increase: I hope that when at last the small resistance my dying body opposes to them is overcome, they will lead me to the eternal repose which I invoke passionately every day not out of heroism, but because of the severity of the pain I feel.

I thank you and Mama fondly for the gift of the ten *scudi*, I kiss you both on the hand, I embrace my brothers and sister, and I beg all of you to commend me to God so that after I have seen you all again a good and speedy death may put an end to the physical sufferings for which there is no other cure. Your very loving son,

Giacomo.

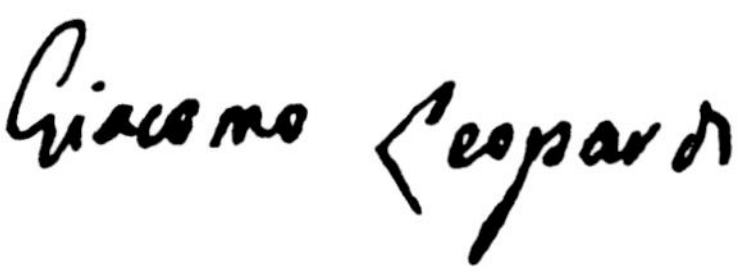

TABLE I *Leopardi's correspondents*

[Numbers in square brackets indicate the letters in this volume addressed to the person in question.]

Immediate family

Leopardi, Count Monaldo (father), 1776–1847
[30, 60, 63, 81, 84, 87, 96, 97, 108, 126, 127, 137, 139, 140, 144, 146, 152, 167, 171, 182, 186, 188, 203, 204, 206, 208, 213, 216, 217, 219, 220]

Leopardi, Adelaide Antici (mother), 1778–1857 [58, 164, 192]

Leopardi, Carlo (brother), 1799–1878
[29, 59, 62, 64, 65, 68, 69, 70, 82, 86, 88, 90, 99, 103, 104, 107, 138, 145, 147, 172, 178]

Leopardi, Paolina (sister), 1800–1869
[61, 66, 85, 89, 93, 95, 100, 102, 118, 121, 122, 129, 133, 135, 163, 166, 170, 180, 190, 202, 212]

Leopardi, Pierfrancesco (brother), 1813–1851 [94, 134]

Relatives and family friends

Antici, Marquess Carlo, 1772–1849 [83]
Leopardi's uncle, a native of Recanati and his father's closest childhood friend, who moved to Rome in 1802 when he married; his career is summarised in [21].

Broglio D'Ajano, Count Saverio, 1749–1834 [28, 31]
A native of Macerata and a good friend of the Leopardi family in spite of his more liberal views; Leopardi's unwitting accomplice in helping him to obtain a passport when he tried to escape from home in 1819.

Melchiorri, Giuseppe (Peppe), 1796–1856 [73, 76, 184]
Leopardi's cousin, the son of his aunt Ferdinanda, who lived in Rome, where he pursued literary and historical interests.

Friends and literary acquaintances

Brighenti, Pietro, 1775–1848 [38, 41, 42, 44, 45, 47, 55, 77]
A man with a complicated history who after 1815 settled in Bologna, where his interests were entrepreneurial and literary. He supervised the printing of various works for Leopardi, who became friendly with his family when he stayed in the city. He was, unbeknownst to his friends, an informer for the Austrian police.

Colletta, Pietro, 1775–1831 [149, 153, 156, 160, 162]
The Neapolitan general and historian, who lived from 1823 in Florence, where he dedicated himself to writing his History of the Kingdom of Naples, and where he and Leopardi became friends. He generously organised money for Leopardi to live on for a year away from home. The relationship seems to have cooled because Leopardi was unable (because of the state of his eyes) to help him revise his History, as he had hoped.

Gioberti, Vincenzo, 1801–1852 [155]
Met Leopardi in Florence in 1828, where for a brief period they were in daily contact. One of the earliest admirers of the *Canti.*

Giordani, Pietro, 1774–1848
[1, 2, 3, 4, 5, 6, 7, 8, 9, 10, 11, 12, 13, 14, 15, 16, 17, 18, 19, 20, 21, 22, 23, 25, 26, 27, 32, 34, 35, 37, 39, 40, 43, 46, 48, 49, 50, 54, 56, 57, 67, 72, 79, 136, 142, 191]
Writer and intellectual from Piacenza, liberal and anti-clerical in his views; Leopardi's first important contact outside Recanati, who recognised his promise and encouraged him in his literary interests and ambitions.

Lenzoni, Carlotta [174]
A marchioness who ran a literary salon in Florence, where Giordani, Colletta and other writers, intellectuals and artists met.

Maestri, Adelaide [157, 207, 214] and **Ferdinando** [151]
Daughter and son-in-law of the Tommasinis; he was a lawyer.

Mai, Angelo, 1782–1854 [36, 52]
Classical scholar and ecclesiastic who became Librarian in the Vatican, where he discovered Cicero's lost *De re publica.* Leopardi celebrated the discovery with the canzone *Ad Angelo Mai,* but his initial enthusiasm for Mai's work subsequently cooled.

Malvezzi, Teresa Carniani, 1785–1859 [112, 114]
Florentine by birth, married to Count Francesco Malvezzi de' Medici in Bologna, where she pursued her literary ambitions and had a prominent role in the social life of the city.

Montani, Giuseppe, 1786–1833 [24]
Critic and intellectual, a friend of Giordani's, whose liberal sympathies he shared. In Florence he was part of Vieusseux's circle and collaborated on the *Antologia.*

Papadopoli, Antonio, 1802–1844 [116, 117, 132]
Venetian intellectual with extensive contacts in the literary world, he met Leopardi in Bologna, probably through Giordani.

Pepoli, Carlo, 1796–1881 [111]
Patriot and writer, a friend of Leopardi's in Bologna, where L. recited the poem he had written in his honour (*Al conte Carlo Pepoli*) at the Accademia dei Felsinei; later he wrote the libretto to Bellini's *I puritani,* and became a member of parliament in 1861.

Perticari, Giulio, 1779–1822 [51, 53]
Writer, son-in-law of the poet Vincenzo Monti, a co-founder of the *Giornale Arcadico* in Rome.

Puccinotti, Francesco, 1794–1872 [105, 115, 119]
A native of Urbino, he practised medicine in Recanati, where he became a friend of Leopardi's, subsequently moving to take up a chair at the university in Macerata.

Ranieri, Antonio, 1806–1888 [169, 193, 194, 195, 196, 197, 198, 199, 200, 201]
Friend and companion in Leopardi's last seven years, first in Florence and then in Naples, where the two set up house together. Neapolitan by birth, a writer and historian, he travelled widely as a young man, and in later life became an academic and a politician.

Stella, Antonio Fortunato, 1757–1833 [78, 80, 106, 109, 110, 113, 120, 124, 143]
A publisher and printer in Milan, who had contacts early on with the Leopardi family. Leopardi later worked on various literary projects for him for very modest remuneration; he printed some of L.'s works.

Targioni Tozzetti, Fanny, 1805–1889 [175, 189]
Society hostess in Florence, a married woman with many male admirers, among them Leopardi.

Tommasini, Antonietta [130, 141, 165] and **Giacomo** [150]
She was an intellectual and writer, he was a professor and a friend of Giordani and Papadopoli. The whole family (including their daughter, Adelaide Maestri and her husband Ferdinando) became very friendly with L. in Bologna and remained his friends for life.

Trissino, Leonardo, 1780–1841 [33]
A native of Vicenza, liberal in his outlook; introduced by Giordani to Leopardi, whose canzone *Ad Angelo Mai* had a dedicatory letter to him.

Troya, Carlo, 1784–1858 [177, 179]
Neapolitan historian, a friend of Ranieri's, on whose behalf he intervened in order to effect a reconciliation with Ranieri's father which enabled him to return to Naples, accompanied by Leopardi.

Vieusseux, Giampietro, 1779–1863
[74, 75, 101, 123, 125, 128, 131, 148, 154, 158, 161, 173, 183]
Swiss by birth, a protestant, from 1819 he lived in Florence, where he founded a *Gabinetto di lettura scientifico-letterario*; its members, intellectuals and scholars, were liberal in outlook, and included Capponi, Colletta and Montani. Founder and director of the *Antologia*, a periodical which set out to be national and cosmopolitan in outlook, and which was published from 1821 to 1832.

Foreign scholars

Jacopssen, A. M. [71]
A young Belgian man of letters who met Leopardi in Rome.

Bunsen, Carlo [Christian Karl Josias von Bunsen], 1791–1860 [91, 92, 98, 159, 181, 209, 210]
A German diplomat, historian and archeologist, who served as secretary to the Prussian embassy in Rome when Niebuhr was Minister, and subsequently himself became Minister.

De Sinner, Luigi [Georg Rudolf Ludwig von Sinner], 1801–1860 [176, 185, 187, 205, 211, 218]
A Swiss scholar who settled in Paris where he pursued his interest in Greek philology, he met Leopardi through Vieusseux on a visit to Florence. Leopardi entrusted his philological manuscripts to him when there was no longer any possibility that he could continue to work on the material himself.

Lebreton, Carlo [215]
A pupil of De Sinner's in Paris, where he was studying rhetoric.

TABLE II *List of Letters*

Letters in this volume with the corresponding numbers in the editions of Moroncini and Flora.

Year	Letter	Moroncini	Flora
1817	1	M27	F25
	2	M36	F26
	3	M48	F32
	4	M54	F35
	5	M61	F39
	6	M64	F40
	7	M68	F42
	8	M71	F44
	9	M78	F47
	10	M88	F55
	11	M91	F56
	12	M95	F59
1818	13	M99	F61
	14	M102	F62
	15	M115	F69
	16	M122	F72
	17	M127	F74
	18	M132	F77
	19	M137	F79
	20	M141	F81
1819	21	M149	F86
	22	M178	F104
	23	M192	F109
	24	M200	F113
	25	M206	F116
	26	M207	F117
	27	M210	F118
	28	M212	F119
	29	M214	F120
	30	M215	F121
	31	M218	F123
	32	M221	F126
	33	M232	F131
	34	M235	F133
	35	M240	F135
1820	36	M244	F136
	37	M245	F137
	38	M249	F138
	39	M259	F143
	40	M262	F146
	41	M264	F147
	42	M268	F148
	43	M270	F149
	44	M271	F150
	45	M275	F152
	46	M282	F156
	47	M300	F164
	48	M303	F166
	49	M329	F179
1821	50	M341	F185
	51	M362	F192
	52	M363	F193
	53	M367	F194
	54	M377	F199
	55	M378	F200
	56	M380	F201
	57	M390	F204
1822	58	M427	F218
	59	M429	F219
	60	M433	F220
	61	M435	F221
	62	M437	F222
	63	M439	F223
	64	M444	F225
1823	65	M474	F241
	66	M478	F243
	67	M482	F247
	68	M484	F248
	69	M490	F252
	70	M507	F260
	71	M537	F275
	72	M546	F280
	73	M569	F290
1824	74	M575	F293
	75	M581	F296
	76	M586	F297
	77	M590	F299
1825	78	M645	F327
	79	M656	F331
	80	M659	F333
	81	M671	F340
	82	M676	F344
	83	M678	F345
	84	M691	F351
	85	M699	F355
	86	M700	F356
	87	M707	F359
	88	M716	F364
	89	M717	F365
	90	M734	F374
	91	M735	F375
	92	M746	F379
	93	M766	F389
	94	M776	F395
	95	M777	F396
1826	96	M792	F403
	97	M799	F407
	98	M805	F409
	99	M824	F418
	100	M829	F420
	101	M833	F422
	102	M846	F427
	103	M871	F439
	104	M906	F452
	105	M909	F454

	106	M915	F457
	107	M920	F458
	108	M929	F462
	109	M971	F478
	110	M984	F484
	111	M988	F486
	112	M1068	F488
	113	M1004	F494
1827	114	M1040	F507
	115	M1044	F510
	116	M1062	F519
	117	M1082	F527
	118	M1086	F530
	119	M1103	F538
	120	M1107	F541
	121	M1135	F554
	122	M1138	F555
	123	M1139	F556
	124	M1155	F563
	125	M1163	F567
	126	M1164	F568
	127	M1177	F575
	128	M1180	F576
1828	129	M1188	F578
	130	M1193	F580
	131	M1201	F581
	132	M1202	F582
	133	M1203	F583
	134	M1216	F590
	135	M1223	F593
	136	M1225	F595
	137	M1233	F598
	138	M1235	F599
	139	M1237	F600
	140	M1256	F606
	141	M1275	F613
	142	M1293	F621
	143	M1312	F629
	144	M1321	F631
	145	M1322	F632
	146	M1329	F637
	147	M1332	F638
	148	M1366	F658
1829	149	M1383	F664
	150	M1391	F666
	151	M1394	F667
	152	M1395	F668
	153	M1406	F670
	154	M1423	F676
	155	M1425	F677
	156	M1429	F679
	157	M1449	F688
	158	M1456	F690
	159	M1459	F691
	160	M1473	F695
1830	161	M1486	F700
	162	M1489	F701
	163	M1498	F706
	164	M1502	F707
	165	[—]	F710
	166	M1554	F734
1831	167	M1574	F744
	168	M1575	F745
	169	M1594	F756
	170	M1604	F760
	171	M1606	F762
	172	M1624	F772
	173	M1633	F777
	174	M1635	F778
	175	M1651	F782
	176	M1658	F788
	177	M1662	F789
	178	M1663	F790
1832	179	M1666	F792
	180	M1672	F795
	181	M1691	F806
	182	M1698	F810
	183	M1706	F812
	184	M1707	F813
	185	M1712	F816
	186	M1716	F818
	187	M1725	F822
	188	M1729	F824
	189	M1738	F831
	190	M1743	F832
	191	M1745	F833
	192	M1757	F841
	193	M1772	F852
1833	194	M1777	F856
	195	M1782	F860
	196	M1787	F864
	197	M1789	F866
	198	M1792	F869
	199	M1793	F870
	200	M1800	F876
	201	M1811	F887
	202	M1814	F889
	203	M1821	F895
	204	M1823	F897
1834	205	M1828	F898
	206	M1829	F899
	207	M1830	F900
1835	208	M1840	F905
	209	M1855	F908
	210	M1863	F910
	211	M1864	F911
	212	M1868	F913
1836	213	M1872	F915
	214	M1879	F916
	215	M1885	F918
	216	M1896	F922
	217	M1901	F923
	218	M1903	F924
1837	219	M1909	F926
	220	M1919	F931